Letters of
HARTLEY COLERIDGE

AMS PRESS
NEW YORK

HARTLEY COLERIDGE

Aet. 10

Letters of
HARTLEY COLERIDGE

Edited by
GRACE EVELYN GRIGGS
and
EARL LESLIE GRIGGS

London
OXFORD UNIVERSITY PRESS
HUMPHREY MILFORD
1936

Library of Congress Cataloging in Publication Data

Coleridge, Hartley, 1796-1849.
    Letters of Hartley Coleridge.

    Reprint of the 1936 ed. published by Oxford University Press, London.
    Bibliography: p.
    Includes index.
    1. Coleridge, Hartley, 1796-1849—Correspondence.
2. Poets, English—19th century—Correspondence.
PR4468.A4   1976   821'.7   75-41063
ISBN 0-404-14524-8

Reprinted from the edition of 1936, London
First AMS edition published in 1976
Manufactured in the United States of America

AMS PRESS INC.
NEW YORK, N.Y.

To Professor
LOUIS A. STRAUSS
this work is affectionately
dedicated

PREFACE

SAVE for a few letters included in two or three biographies and obscure sources, the correspondence of Hartley Coleridge has never been published. Ernest Hartley Coleridge, whose editions of his grandfather's works and of Byron's poems give him an important place as a scholar, seems to have planned an edition of his uncle Hartley's correspondence; and although many of the original letters were transcribed and annotated, unfortunately his work never reached completion. The last few years have been characterized by a marked revival of interest in the elder Coleridge; and these letters of his son, it is hoped, will be welcome for their intrinsic value no less than for the light they throw on the whole Coleridge–Wordsworth circle.

Letter-writing to Hartley Coleridge was a means of disburdening himself, and he seems to have written to his family much as he wrote in his diary. Both Hartley and his father understood themselves with remarkable lucidity, and both men were wont to analyse themselves. In Hartley's analyses of himself there are the same self-condemnations, the same sense of retribution, and the same promises of amendment, as one finds in the letters of his father. Coleridge's self-portraiture is more penetrating, but Hartley's more pleasant, because there is always a vein of good humour and more acceptance of the dispensations of Providence. Coleridge was well equipped to meet the world; society had a place for him, as it were. Hartley, on the other hand, was a misfit, a dreamer set in a world of reality. Conventions were utterly abhorrent to him. In reading Hartley Coleridge's letters, therefore, one must expect the quaint, the bizarre, and the strange. The personality is delightful, as it emerges from this chronicle of comedy and tragedy which gradually dethroned Hartley from a position of honour and security to one of wandering and dependence.

Hartley Coleridge possessed a keen wit and a brilliant intellect. He was widely read in English and Classical literature, and his critical remarks as revealed in his letters are always acute. When, after Coleridge's death, De Quincey and Ferrier published statements accusing Coleridge of plagiarism in the *Biographia Literaria*, Hartley, with an amazing impartiality, strove to find a plausible explanation of his father's use of German sources.

Wordsworth, Hartley loved and admired; but his almost filial reverence did not blunt his critical faculties, and he recognized and deplored Wordsworth's weaknesses.

It is not so much, however, *what* Hartley Coleridge wrote of himself, of his contemporaries, or of literature, as *how* he expressed himself, that makes these letters so attractive. Did he not catch something of the manner of his friend, Charles Lamb? His style, indeed, has a flavour of its own; but there is something Lamb-like in the mixture of humour and pathos, the never-failing good nature, and the wholesome delight in digression. Lamb's style is more controlled, showing perhaps the strength of character that made him master of his destiny; but if Hartley's style is less the result of will, it makes up the deficiency in grace and ease.

Most of the letters in this edition are to members of Hartley's family, particularly to his mother, father, sister, and brother. We have not striven to include all the letters which exist but have attempted to select those letters which best reveal Hartley Coleridge's mind and personality.

The text of most of the letters is taken from the originals in the possession of the Rev. G. H. B. Coleridge. In a few instances where the original letters have not been forthcoming the text is taken from transcripts made by members of the Coleridge family. Several letters are reprinted from the *Memoir* prefixed to Derwent Coleridge's edition of the *Poems by Hartley Coleridge*. The original of the letter to Miss Barker is in the Harvard College Library, and the originals of the letters to Thomas Poole are in the British Museum. We have endeavoured to reproduce the text exactly, but inaccuracies in spelling and confusing punctuation have been corrected, and initial capital letters have been printed in lower-case, unless there seemed to be a reason for their capitalization. Hartley's spelling is often erratic and it hardly seems wise to reproduce mere careless blunders. 'Cheif' is, therefore, corrected to 'chief'; 'Gillman' is consistently spelled with two 'l's, and the slip of 'New Colledge' is rectified. The punctuation in the letters, as one would expect, is haphazard; the dash is used for the comma, semicolon, full stop, &c; quotation marks and italics rarely appear. For the convenience of the reader, the punctuation has been supplied or revised, but never unless the omission or error seems obviously due to mere epistolary haste.

Because the life of Hartley Coleridge is little known to the average reader, short biographical and explanatory commentaries have been added. It might be well to add that the complete story of the sad wreck of Hartley's career at Oriel is here told for the first time; and for this reason all of Hartley's letters relating to the affair have been included, and an Appendix added, containing the series of letters to and from the College authorities.

Unless otherwise specified, all references to Hartley Coleridge's published poems are to *The Complete Poetical Works of Hartley Coleridge*, edited by Ramsay Colles, in 'The Muses' Library'.

To the Rev. G. H. B. Coleridge we owe a debt of lasting gratitude. The whole of his collection of manuscripts has been placed at our disposal, and he and Mrs. Coleridge have extended to us the utmost courtesy and hospitality.

To the Administrators of the Faculty Research Fund of the University of Michigan we are indebted for grants made to assist in the expensive work of collecting materials and preparing this work for publication.

We are deeply indebted to Mr. C. J. Connolly of the Manuscript Room of the British Museum for painstaking assistance in the reading of difficult passages in the manuscripts; to Mr. A. I. Ellis of the British Museum Reading Room, and to Prof. Warren E. Blake of the University of Michigan for assistance in connexion with the Greek and Latin passages; and to Mr. Geoffrey Grigson and Mrs. Margaret Deeter for a careful reading of the work in manuscript.

GRACE EVELYN GRIGGS
EARL LESLIE GRIGGS

TABLE OF CONTENTS

TABLE OF CONTENTS

TABLE OF CONTENTS

TABLE OF CONTENTS

PRINCIPAL REFERENCES

1. *Poems by Hartley Coleridge, with a memoir of his life by his brother (Derwent Coleridge)*, 1851.

2. *Hartley Coleridge: His Life and Work.* Earl Leslie Griggs, 1929.

3. *Letters of Samuel Taylor Coleridge.* Edited by Ernest Hartley Coleridge, 1895.

4. *Unpublished Letters of Samuel Taylor Coleridge.* Edited by Earl Leslie Griggs, 1932.

5. *Letters of the Wordsworth Family.* Edited by W. A. Knight, 1907.

6. *The Complete Poetical Works of Hartley Coleridge.* Edited by Ramsay Colles (for 'The Muses' Library'), 1908.

7. *Biographia Borealis; or, Lives of Distinguished Northerns.* Hartley Coleridge, 1833.

8. *Lives of Northern Worthies. By Hartley Coleridge.* Edited by Derwent Coleridge, 1852.

9. *The Dramatic Works of Massinger and Ford, with an introduction by Hartley Coleridge*, 1840.

10. *Essays and Marginalia. By Hartley Coleridge.* Edited by Derwent Coleridge, 1851.

LETTERS

THE story of Hartley Coleridge up to the time of his entrance at Oxford is an amazing narrative of 'the oddest of God's creatures'. Born on September 19, 1796, at a time when his father, Samuel Taylor Coleridge, was embarking on a career including philosophy, theology, and poetry, Hartley soon became the centre of attraction in the Coleridge household at Nether Stowey. Coleridge watched his little son with the solicitude and curiosity of parent and philosopher; and at the very time the *Lyrical Ballads* were being conceived, Coleridge wrote to Thelwall 'you would smile to see my eye rolling up to the ceiling in a lyric fury, and on my knee a diaper pinned to warm'. Nor did Coleridge's interest stop here. Imbued with the doctrines of Wordsworth and remembering his own unhappy childhood, he determined to give his son the freedom of a natural education; and in two poems he tells us of his plans. In *Frost at Midnight* he says:

> For I was reared
> In the great city, pent 'mid cloisters dim,
> And saw nought lovely but the sky and stars.
> But *thou*, my babe! shalt wander like a breeze
> By lakes and sandy shores, beneath the crags
> Of ancient mountain, and beneath the clouds,
> Which image in their bulk both lakes and shores
> And mountain crags;

and in *The Nightingale*:

> And I deem it wise
> To make him Nature's play-mate . . .
> .   .   .   .   .   .
> But if that Heaven
> Should give me life, his childhood shall grow up
> Familiar with these songs, that with the night
> He may associate joy.

Hartley grew up in a house divided against itself. Although in the early years of marriage his parents seem to have been happy enough, by the time Hartley was four or five, Coleridge had begun to talk and write of his domestic infelicity. From 1802 on he was more often travelling than at home, and little Hartley, 'the darling of the breeze', could not enjoy in full measure the companionship and direction of his father.

In July 1800 the Coleridges moved to the north, settling in Greta Hall, in the environs of Keswick. Greta Hall, a double house lying in an open field with Skiddaw and several other

I

'broad-breasted brethren' rising behind, and the long stretch of Derwentwater in the foreground, is too well known to need description here. Mr. Jackson, who lived with his housekeeper, Mrs. Wilson, in half the house, leased the other half to Coleridge; and there Hartley was to spend most of his time until he went to Oxford in 1817. Mrs. Wilson ('Wilsy' as she was affectionately called), a kindly, middle-aged, motherly woman, soon became Hartley's nurse, and the other children's, too, for on September 14, 1800, Derwent was born and two years later (December 24, 1802) Sara.

In 1803 the Southeys, bereaved of their own child and seeking comfort from the Coleridges, came to Greta Hall on a visit that lasted the remainder of their lives. Coleridge at this time was in miserable health, his domestic affairs seemed unbearable, and a deep dejection was settling over him. In the autumn of 1803 he set off for London and a few months later for Malta, in a desperate effort to regain health and peace of mind. Afterwards, too, he was at home less and less, and the presence of Southey among his children was a comfort to him. Thus he came gradually to delegate to Southey the responsibility (at first moral but later financial) of his family. With the Southeys had come Mrs. Mary Lovell (another of the Frickers) and her son Tom. A strange *ménage* it was, of Coleridges, Lovells, and Southeys.

Hartley was a constant source of wonderment to those about him. 'Hartley', said his father, 'is considered a genius by Wordsworth and Southey; indeed by every one who has seen much of him.' At the age of three he 'sported of his own accord a theologico-astronomical hypothesis', saying, 'Stars are dead lamps, they be'nt naughty, they are put up in the sky.' When some one remarked, 'It is not now, but is to be,' he replied, 'But if it *is* to be, it is.' Southey, who called him Moses, said 'Moses grows up as miraculous a boy as ever Pharaoh's daughter found his namesake to be'; and in 1802, Wordsworth, in a flash of presentiment, composed his prophetic lines

To H.C. Six Years Old

O thou! whose fancies from afar are brought;
Who of thy words dost make a mock apparel,
And fittest to unutterable thought
The breeze-like motion and the self-born carol;
Thou faery voyager! that dost float
In such clear water, that thy boat
May rather seem
To brood on air than on an earthly stream;
Suspended in a stream as clear as sky,
Where earth and heaven do make one imagery;

2

O blessed vision! happy child!
Thou art so exquisitely wild,
I think of thee with many fears
For what may be thy lot in future years.

I thought of times when Pain might be thy guest,
Lord of thy house and hospitality;
And Grief, uneasy lover! never rest
But when she sate within the touch of thee.
O too industrious folly!
O vain and causeless melancholy!
Nature will either end thee quite;
Or, lengthening out thy season of delight,
Preserve for thee, by individual right,
A young lamb's heart among the full-grown flocks.
What hast thou to do with sorrow,
Or the injuries of to-morrow?
Thou art a dew-drop, which the morn brings forth,
Ill fitted to sustain unkindly shocks,
Or to be trailed along the soiling earth;
A gem that glitters while it lives,
And no forewarning gives;
But, at the touch of wrong, without a strife
Slips in a moment out of life.

In 1806–7 Hartley went travelling with his father—first to
Coleorton and then to London. The change of environment
afforded him a new range of experiences, and throughout his
life he was wont to refer to this *annus mirabilis* of his childhood.
Coleridge, after two unhappy years at Malta, had returned home,
only to follow the Wordsworths to Coleorton, near Leicester; and
with him he took Hartley. The Wordsworths were temporarily
settled in a farm-house on the estate of Sir George Beaumont,
the patron of Wordsworth and Coleridge, whose art collection
formed the nucleus of what has now become the National Gallery.
At Coleorton, Hartley was to hear his father expatiate on Euro-
pean politics and the new discoveries of Humphry Davy, and
to have his portrait painted by Sir David Wilkie. From Coleorton,
Hartley was taken to London, where the theatres, the busy
thoroughfares, and especially the Tower of London, opened new
realms for his imagination.

The following letter was written to Robert Southey from
Coleorton, when Hartley was ten years and six months of age.
It contains Hartley's earliest attempt at verse; and those
acquainted with Coleridge's own poem, *To a Young Ass*, will be
amused to find Hartley's humorous remarks on the animal. It
may be of interest to point out that Southey wrote a delightful
answer (included in the *Memoir*, xliii–xlvi) to Hartley's letter.

LETTER I

To ROBERT SOUTHEY, *Greta Hall, Keswick, Cumberland.*

Coleorton. March 4, 1807.

My dear Uncle

Pray, excuse any Blunders in this, my first Attempt at
Poetry, and also my long Neglect of writing to you: the
Reason of which was, that I wished to send you my Poem,
which was not finished sooner on Account of my Idleness.
First I must tell you that my Father in some Places smoothed
the Metre, which was before as rough as a Road that would
have made you ill to travel over; and he also helped me to
the Moral.

Poetry on an Ass.

This Ass, which I am wont to ride,
And whom the World for Obstinacy chide,
   And blame, as stupid beyond Measure,
Yet in him I've no small Pleasure.
   Excuse me, good People! but always I hate
To prattle a Falsehood at any Rate.
And to tell the simple Truth,
I trust, in Manner not uncouth,
    I hate all Prosing,
As my Tale does not shew Sin.
   And now my good Friends! we proceed to the Tale,
As I do not intend my Performance for Sale.
   An Ass as it played in an African Wild
At a Time when the Air was balsamic and mild
   Heard the fierce Lion's loud Roar,
But thought he should never hear more:
   The Roar was so loud,
   That all the great Crowd
Which in London's vast Streets do parade,
Could not make this poor Ass more afraid
   Than This single fierce Lion, it did—
   More dreadful, because he was hid
At Length in a Transport of Fear the Ass set up a Bray
So horribly harsh, that his Foe fled away.
He leapt and he leapt, plunged, and then plunged again
Till he reached at his Cave and slunk into his den.

And now to say a Word by Way of Moral
As I would gladly win the Laurel
My Tale shews that Cowards fear not more the brave Man's Eye
Than brave Men loath the Cowards Cry.

And now my dear Uncle to my Mother Brother and Sister to my two dear Friends to my Aunts and to Edith and Herbert give my Love. Remember me to be your affectionate Nephew—

HARTLEY COLERIDGE.

Like all children, Hartley attempted to reproduce in an imaginary way all that he heard and saw; and by far the most interesting of his creations was his invention of Ejuxria. That politics and religion were in large measure a part of his dreamworld was only to be expected; for no one living with Coleridge, Southey, and Wordsworth could escape such topics. Little Hartley heard and wondered. He pretended that at a future time a small cataract would break forth in the fields near Greta Hall, and he named the stream Jug-Force. Soon he founded a people to live along the banks; then he extended the region, until it became a separate world, an island-continent, where he reproduced all that he knew of the real world, and to which he gave the name Ejuxria. He was familiar with the political difficulties of his imaginary country, and he loved to weave his fancies into a story. 'Stamping about the room,' Hartley dictated to his mother, 'with all the importance of an unfledged authorling,' a *History of St. Malo, an enthusiastic Reformer and Hierophant*, the scene of which is laid in Ejuxria, but beyond the fragment in the following letter, the manuscript does not seem to be extant. The letter, which is addressed to Miss Barker, is in the handwriting of Hartley's mother, who has added a postscript.

LETTER 2

To MISS BARKER

Keswick, April 10, 1808.

My dear Miss Barker
I have a wild story, the history of an Ejuxrian, which I am sure is not worth sending, yet as you wished to have it, nonsense and all, I send it, but dear Miss Barker, pray do not shew it to any body till I can do something better.

The history of Saint Malo—

Augurias Malo was born in a village near Nolo, in the Southern part of the kingdom of Maza. From childhood he

5

was wild and enthusiastic, and from the beautiful forms of
Nature, conceived that there *must* exist powers greater than
man. One morning his father perceived him more grave and
solemn than usual; he enquired the reason. I have dreamed
a dream, said the Son, and behold I was reclining on a bank,
as I am wont, and there appeared unto me a Spirit, shining
as fire. It cried aloud Malo! Malo! and I answered, 'here am
I,' and it said 'There are powers greater than man! I will
instruct thee in dreams! awake! arise! go to thy Father—inform him of this thy vision.' His Father wondered much,
but believed him. To describe every dream of Malo would
be tedious and useless—we shall now only relate the essence
of his dreams. The principal Gods of which he spake were
Fanaticon, who presided over man, his actions, and his fate
—*Ordanicus*, Lord over the brute creation—*Pomonia* the
Goddess of the vegetable world, and *Cordianto*, God of minerals—the presider over Tempests, the Elements, etc., etc., etc.
There were also inferior Deities, having Attributes peculiar
to themselves, and subject to the greater, such as *Dandanus*,
God of war—*Crusion*, of music, and poetry and *Harsean*, over
philosophy and prose compositions of every description.

Saint Malo's Theory of the earth, will appear strange and
romantic to civilised ears. The station of the above mentioned
Deities, he supposed to be the Sun, but determined to create
beings, like, but inferior to themselves, and partaking of their
spirits—Cordianto struck from the body of the Sun large shat-
ters of which he created the Earth—Seas—Air—Stars—and
Sky—Pomonia clothed the Earth with vegetation. Ordanicus
created the Brutes—and Fanaticon the human race.

Malo now thought to instruct all around him in his ideas
of revealed religion, and he began in his own family. His
code of Laws will appear as we proceed. Being much
respected in his own neighbourhood, and making many converts, he was encouraged to go to Nolo, where he also was
much followed and respected; Saint Marcus, St. Petrinus,
St. Francis, they great with many others were natives of this
Town.

As he was walking in company with these men, they
adjourned to the Tribunal, and Moravius Antonius, Governor of the City, whose tyranny was now carried to such a
pitch of despotism that he made it a capital crime to look
through the gates of his numerous and superb Gardens.
Now there was a poor boy in the Tribunal whose eyes were

to be put out, for having dared to walk within the bounds of one of these Gardens, for the advantage of holding by a rail, while a band of Soldiers were rushing impetuously by at night, and in a storm, being frightened by the flashes of lightning against their Armour. Malo, as soon as he understood the affair, branded the Tyrant with all the opprobrious epithets of Despotism—Is not this boy, human, like thyself? Is he to be trampled under the feet of thy Soldiers? and for what? Are thy Gardens the sacred haunts of the Gods? Antonius was astonished. What Gods meanest thou? Malo answered 'The same that were revealed to me in Dreams'—Antonius said to the Guards, Why admitted ye this madman? One answered, 'He forced himself through with the crowd.' The Governor turning towards Malo demanded of him that he would give an account concerning the Gods of which he had spoken. Malo now calmly related the substance of his dreams. Antonius answered, 'granting this to be true, what is there in it to prevent my punishing the boy?' Malo replied 'The boy did no wrong: was one plant injured by his only holding the rail'—'Be that as it may, I made the Law and will enforce it.' This horrid piece of cruelty was about to be committed when the Mob, many of whom were St. Malo's converts, and enraged at the frequency of these detestable butcheries, his own guards not excepted, fell with one accord upon the Tyrant dragged him from the Tribunal, and cast him headlong into a deep well—Petrinus said unto Malo 'these men have committed murder'! he answered 'How many murders has Antonius committed? The people must not be slaves that Villains may live'!

And there was great rejoicing at the destruction of the Tyrant throughout the City. The next day St. Malo set out on his journey to Loco, the capital of Flornetia, teaching with great success by the way. At Loco too, he made several converts, in particular, Andrian, Count of Locia—till the unfortunate news arrived of Petrinus having been teaching at his native Village a different religion from St. Malo's, instructing his hearers that they were to worship the Images of the Gods, to offer Sacrifices, and he also allowed persecution for Religion's Sake, which St. Malo did not permit. Another mortification occurred to the zealous Malo. One Harmonicas, as he was walking by the Sea-side, found a book —it was the Bible!—

To be continued—

7

Now I know my dear Miss Barker that this ῥιγμαρωλ does not deserve an answer, yet I must be so bold as to hope for one. My Uncle and his brother are expected Wednesday the 4th of April. We shall all be very glad to see them, and I hope we shall see my father in May. My Mother and Aunts are very sorry that the Colonel and Mrs. Peachey do not come to Keswick this Summer. Little darling Emma Southey is a sweet Angel, and his little Shorship [?] Herbert runs about and calls Mama and Anty. Sarah and Edith are a sweet pair. Mrs. Wilson is a darling friend. Derwent is a teasing little dog, yet very good natured, and I am dear Miss Barker a most horrible writer and terrific speller and yet, (if you will permit it) very affectionately yours

HARTLEY COLERIDGE.

P.S. Dear Miss B. I think it scarcely possible for you to wade through this amazing scroll! My Sisters beg to join me in kind regards. We all wish to know how you are—it is long since we laughed at your most entertaining account of the introduction—S.C.

In the autumn of 1808 Hartley and his brother were sent to school. Hitherto Hartley's training had been most desultory. Coleridge had taught him Greek, and he had learned (from his mother probably) to read and write. He had felt no restrictions; nor did his elders see fit to repress his wild fantasies. His mother, indeed, saw him developing a fateful resemblance to his father; but Coleridge, and Southey, too, seemed to have been so amazed by the gradual unfolding of his intellect that they were little concerned with any consistent attempt to direct him. The little fellow enjoyed a fuller measure of freedom and indulgence than is the lot of most children; and his mental and moral outlook was broadened not by study but rather 'by the living voice of Coleridge, Southey, and Wordsworth, Lloyd, Wilson, and De Quincey'.

The school Coleridge chose for his sons was under the mastership of the Rev. John Dawes, a kindly and liberal-minded pedagogue. Dawes, like every one who met Coleridge, had fallen under the influence of the poet's magnetic personality, and from the first he was honoured to have Hartley and Derwent under his tutelage. Hartley, too, won the admiration of Mr. Dawes, who was so impressed by evidences of genius in the boy, that he refused to accept any remuneration.

'I have a little favour to ask of you,' he wrote to Coleridge, 'and, as I know to give pain is foreign to your nature, I hope you will not deny it me, for believe me, if you do, it will pain me most severely. It is, that, while I have the honour of having

Hartley under my care, you will permit me to do the best, that my humble abilities will allow me, to promote his instruction, without receiving any other remuneration than what arises from the pleasure of the performance. In full confidence that you will acquiesce in what will afford me a real happiness —I have ventured to return half the Sum—in a Bill inclosed.'

The interest of Mr. Dawes in Hartley was apparently noticed by the other schoolchildren; for Derwent said to his father:

'that Mr. Dawes does not *love* him [Derwent] because he can't help crying when he is scolded, and because he ain't such a genius as Hartley—and that though Hartley should have done the same thing, yet all the others are punished, and Mr. Dawes only *looks* at Hartley and never scolds *him*, and *all* the boys think it very unfair—he *is* a genius.'

Mr. Dawes's school was not like the schools of the day. Had Hartley been subjected to the persecution Cowper suffered, his sensitive nature might have been permanently marred. He and Derwent lived away from the school, under the hospitable roof of Mrs. Longmire; and after school hours they were as free as they had been at home. Then, too, the school being at Ambleside, the boys were occasionally taken home to Keswick and they regularly spent their week-ends with the Wordsworths at Grasmere.

Although Hartley left Mr. Dawes's school in 1814, he was not yet quite ready for college; and, mainly under the guidance of Robert Southey, he spent the following year in independent study. Brilliant in the classics, he was deficient in academic learning and needed further study. Coleridge, who was now settled at Bristol under the friendly roof of Josiah Wade, remained strangely silent to the entreaties of Southey, Mrs. Coleridge, and others concerning plans for Hartley's college education, neither commending nor disapproving their efforts. Much has been made of Coleridge's neglect, but passages from his letters, such as the following, show that he suffered the pangs of remorse and that even in the period of darkest despair and hopeless slavery to opium, the realization of his duty to his family remained. Writing to Morgan in the spring of 1814, he says:

'By the long long Habit of the accursed Poison my Volition— . . . was compleatly deranged, . . . so that I was perpetually in the state, in which you may have seen paralytic Persons, who attempting to push a step forward in one direction are violently forced round to the opposite. . . . The worst was, that in *exact proportion* to the *importance* and *urgency* of any Duty was it, as of a fatal necessity, sure to be neglected. . . .'

Southey, therefore, with his characteristic generosity and solicitude, took matters in his own hands and set about making provision for Hartley to be sent to Oxford. He wrote to Coleridge's

9

brothers at Ottery St. Mary; he sought the co-operation of Wordsworth; he and Wordsworth procured promises of small contributions from Thomas Poole, Sir George and Lady Beaumont, Cottle, and Basil Montagu; and so it was that plans were made for Hartley's entrance at Merton College, a scholarship (a Postmastership) obtained, and funds enough added for college expenses.

What Southey thought of Hartley at this time can best be exemplified by the inclusion of a letter he wrote to Hartley's cousin, John Taylor Coleridge, on March 14, 1815:

'Let me tell you, as well as I can what kind of youth this cousin of yours and nephew of mine is. Without being an ugly fellow, he is a marvellously odd one—he is very short, with remarkably strong features, some of the thickest and blackest eyebrows you ever saw, and a beard which a Turk might envy. His manners are almost as peculiar as his appearance, and having discovered that he is awkward by nature, he has formed an unhappy conclusion that art will never make him otherwise, and so resigns himself to his fate. My endeavours have not been wanting to remedy or rather palliate this; but it is bred in the bone—and you know the remainder of the proverb. I have even habitually quizzed him for the purpose of teaching him to bear such things with good humour, knowing how much he will be exposed to it.

'Thus much for the outward man. Hartley's intellect will soon overcome all disadvantages that his exterior may incur, if he do but *keep the course*. And here, indeed, I feel how fortunate it is that he has a kinsman on the spot so willing and able to direct him, and whom he is so well prepared to respect. The great lesson which Wordsworth and myself have endeavoured to impress upon him is that he goes to Oxford to devote himself to the studies of the place, and that no degree of general ability or general knowledge can, or ought to atone for any deficiency in the attainments which the University requires; that to these he must apply himself *totis viribus* while he is there, and when he has attained by these that establishment for which we look, life will be before him to cultivate his intellect in whatever manner he may then please.

'His disposition is excellent, his principles thoroughly good, and he has instinctively a devotional feeling which I hope will keep them so. An overweening confidence in his own talents, and a perilous habit of finding out reasons for whatever he likes to do, are the dangerous points of his character. To extravagance he has not the slightest propensity—but he knows as little of frugality, and it is well that he has a friend at hand who may question him concerning his ways and means, for in these things he is, I believe always will be, a child—I ought to say that Hartley has Greek enough for a whole college.'

ERRATUM

Page 11, Letter No. 3, addressed to Charles Lamb. The references to Mr. and Miss Lamb and to Mrs. Wordsworth would make it appear that the letter is to Wordsworth, but it is unmistakably addressed to Lamb.

The following letter to Charles Lamb (which is the only one extant from Hartley to Lamb) was written ten days after Hartley matriculated. Lamb and the Wordsworths had apparently gone up to Oxford with Hartley, to help him get established. Lamb, whose friendship with Coleridge was life-long, had from the first taken an interest in Hartley. On a visit to the Lakes in 1802 he had given Hartley several children's books; and in the years following, Hartley saw a good deal of him. Lamb, it is certain, remained an idol for Hartley; and one sees the mark of 'Carolo-Lambian' humour in Hartley Coleridge's literary work.

LETTER 3

To CHARLES LAMB, *Temple, London.*

Merton College, May 16, 1815.

My dear Sir

Being now tolerably established a Collegian, feeling my gown rather less burthensome, and myself less strange, I hasten to perform my promise of scribblelation, and to become my own historian. On the same day that you left Oxford, I called on my Tutor (a very pleasing, gentlemanly man) was by him examined in Homer, Xenophon, Aeschylus, Virgil, Horace, and Tully, and appearing to have learning enough to admit me member of the university, I was equipped in my academicals, and conducted to the Vice chancellor where I was matriculated. On Sunday morning I first appeared in chapel, and took possession, pro tempore, of the rooms I have at present, which belong to a Gentleman commoner, who is absent on account of his health. In the course of this week I shall enter on my own that are to be, and my postmastership together, as the present occupier of both will take his degree, and quit College. The thirds are low and the rooms though dark, sufficiently large and pleasant. I have regularly attended lecture in hall, which has been constantly in the Greek Testament or Grotius, and have had one private Lecture in Aeschylus. I have heard nothing of the lost parcel: if I can do any thing to procure the value of it, or give a chance of its being found, inform me of it by letter and I will do my best, though of my own talents for business I must speak humbly. I hope you have procured commodious lodgings, and that you had no difficulty in getting them. Is London much the same as it was when I used to run up and down the court-yard in Thornhaugh street? or should I see much alteration in place or people? If none, the metropolis has suffered less change than other places. Since my last visit there, I find every goodly and familiar form strangely altered, and myself most altered of all, but whether for better or worse I cannot tell. I have now in some measure, to support the part of a man: and, to tell the truth, I feel not unlike an actor who has come upon the stage to speak, with his character but half-learned. Luckily I have in my cousin,[1] a ready prompter: and now I begin to know more faces and to receive more good-mornings. College-business is perfectly easy, and we are not outdone in quantity of labour. The only thing in which I have found myself glaringly deficient is Prosody, not so much from ignorance of its rules as from habitual negligence in applying them. In order to correct this the Tutor has advised me to practice Latin verses, and accordingly I have knock'd a few together. The mere mechanical part I shall easily learn; but I have no ear, and without counting cannot tell, with all attention paid, if a verse have a foot too many or too few. Therefore, whatever other honours or advantages rigid application may gain for me, I fear I shall never write a prize poem. *Poeta nascitur non fit.* Yet I shall not neglect this exercise. We have every week a prose Latin Theme to compose; but as all are given to a particular postmaster, called the steward, who carries them to the Tutor, we have not the advantage of his corrections. That for last week was, *Prima sapientia est stultitiâ caruisse*, which I found rather barren. On Sunday I walked with my Cousin to Cowley of which he is minister, and dined with him at the parsonage, a pretty place clothed with creepers in front, and opening on the backside into a green paddock, with a true village garden crammed with herbs and flowers, particularly Tulips and Lilies; a pleasant repast for the eyes, and probably for the smell, but a cold has suspended that sense in me from all its functions. The church was crowded both morning and after-noon, the people apparently neat and respectable though my cousin complains of their ignorance, and gave me one instance of it which deserves to be repeated. He was con-versing with a very old woman, of some little property, on the subject of religion, and asked her, where she expected to go after this life. She replied she hoped to go to Heaven. 'What are your grounds for hoping so'? 'Why,' said she, 'I

---

[1] The Rev. William Hart Coleridge (1789–1849), student of Christ Church, afterwards Bishop of Barbados.

can't tell, I wish to go there.' 'Well, but why do you wish to go there?' 'Why, Sir,' said she, 'I'll just tell you my mind truly; I'm almost fourscore, and I'm very weak and full of pain, and I've heard that heaven is a place where there's no pain at all, and therefore I wish to go there.' Now though my Cousin produced this as a proof of the old lady's ignorance, yet *I* seriously doubt whether three fourths of mankind, educated and uneducated, have any higher idea, and I'm certain, none would more prevail with the generality of old women to make themselves fit partakers of the blessed habitation. It was a very pleasing sight to see the children of the Sunday school gathered together in the parsonage kitchen, and to observe the respect paid by them, and by all the parishioners to my cousin, whose performance of his sacred office seems to be a pattern for all who are about to assume the same function. It is now, 'a sunshine holyday'. The morice dancers, [a] relict of ancient times [which I] was very glad to see, are playing their antics in all the villages about and in Oxford itself. I know not why less respect should be paid to an innocent vestige of old manners, which serves to bring times of yore to mind, than to a fragment of ancient sculpture. The Whitsunales are I believe, often alluded to by our early writers.

Give my kindest remembrances to Mrs. Wordsworth whose health has not, I hope, suffered by the fatigues of Travelling. To Sir George and Lady Beaumont I beg to be remembered with assurance that no neglect or ill conduct of mine shall make their bounty ineffectual [and] unprofitable. My best regard to Mr. and Miss Lamb, Mr. Montagu[1] and Basil, if you see him; and when you meet my Cousin John,[2] give him the grateful love of his yet unseen, but not altogether unknown kinsman:

I remain, dear Sir

Yours affectionately,

H. COLERIDGE.

N.B. I think I may venture to send my Cousin's remembrances to you, though when I called to ask him what he had

---

[1] Hartley refers to Basil Montagu (1770–1851), the editor of Bacon's *Works*, who, though partly responsible for the Coleridge–Wordsworth quarrel, remained one of Coleridge's warmest friends. On Hartley's first visit to London in 1807 he had charmed the Montagus by his quaint, childish ways; and after leaving Oxford he was their guest for a considerable time.

[2] John Taylor Coleridge (1790–1876), son of Coleridge's brother, Colonel James Coleridge, later a famous lawyer and Justice of the King's Bench.

to say, he was not in his rooms. William Jackson [will] be shortly going into the north. I breakfasted with him last Thursday. I am very sorry to say that your friend Cookson has been pluck'd.

Hartley's first vacation was spent with his father at Calne (1815) at the very time Coleridge was writing the *Biographia Literaria* and when he was continually talking of his great philosophical work, his *magnum opus* on the Logos, which was never published and only partially completed. The references in the last part of the following letter to his father probably refer to the latter work.

By 1817 Coleridge had won, if not a complete, at least a satisfactory victory over his opium habit. He was settled at the Grove, Highgate, with James and Ann Gillman, in a home where he was to live the remaining eighteen years of his life, and there Hartley spent several of his college vacations.

LETTER 4

To SAMUEL TAYLOR COLERIDGE, *Highgate, London.*

Merton Col. March 18, 1817.

My dear Father

After waiting with great anxiety for nearly a month, (not without apprehension, that your silence has been occasion'd by ill health) for an answer to my last, which I think could not miscarry, I cannot but feel it my duty again to address you, though I cannot tell you that I have proceeded on the work you proposed to me, being unable to procure a copy of Nemesius at Oxford, although it was published there in 8vo., 1671. As the Easter vacation is now at hand I should have had leisure to have translated it; and will still set about it, if you will put me in the way of procuring the original. Tho' I must say, I should be alarm'd at seeing my name in a printed Title-page; but will certainly follow your advice.

I have employ'd the last term chiefly in making myself master of Pindar, and of the Νικομάχεια 'Ηθικά of Aristotle. I have not found the former very difficult, any further than as deep thinking and conceal'd connection in a writer always demand deep thinking and close attention in the reader: his numerous historical and mythological allusions certainly require considerable collateral knowledge, but I think he is rarely liable to the charge of obscurity. I am obliged to you for more correct notions of his style and peculiar excellence than I could have gathered from the ordinary cant; certainly at least I could discover very little of that fire and precipitation so much talk'd of in him; nor does it seem a very reasonable supposition that frequent digressions are a sign of hurry and ardour. Pindar may not unaptly be compared to a boy going to school, who picks every flower by the road side, merely because his journey's end is unpleasant. Conscious that his subjects were deficient in permanent interest, he seeks to generalize them by introducing all the moral and political observations that can be deduced from them. These precepts are seldom such as would naturally proceed from a heated imagination: his morality is founded on prudence and circumspection. With regard to the Ethics, I cannot but think it is treating Aristotle unfairly to take a single treatise, evidently design'd to be taken in concert with his other works, contemplating virtue merely as far as it is a mean of political welfare, and to palm this part upon young men as a whole. One thing I cannot but admire in this Philosopher; that tho' he lived under a despotism, in a court, and in habits of intimacy with great men, he never pays any compliments to his patrons; much less lays down any slavish principles, in which he has a great superiority over Lord Bacon.

There are many things I stand in need of your instruction in, both in classics and other matters, particularly Logic, in which a Parrot might pass an examination at Oxford. I earnestly expect your work on the Λόγος, which I hope will restore that art to something like just esteem.

I hope you persevere in the course you described to me in your last, and that health and easy circumstances will enable you to embody and make permanently useful the knowledge you have acquired with so much labour and patience. I trust soon to see you: then you may judge whether my progress has been what it ought to be or not. We are, to tell the truth, very ill off for Tutors in Merton, and a private Tutor would draw on my finances inconveniently.

> I remain, Dear Father
> your truly affectionate Son
> H. COLERIDGE.

In 1796, when Hartley was only a baby in arms, Coleridge had settled at Nether Stowey in order to be near his newly found

friend, Thomas Poole, an opulent tanner and farmer living there.
Poole continued to be interested in the Coleridges even after they
moved to the north, and to him Mrs. Coleridge wrote a long
series of letters, at intervals of about a year. It was natural,
therefore, that Wordsworth should have applied successfully to
Poole for financial assistance towards Hartley's education, and
that Hartley should have been a welcome guest at Stowey.

LETTER 5

To THOMAS POOLE, Esqre., *Nether Stowey, Somerset.*

Merton Coll. Nov. 16, 1817.

Dear Sir

At present I am divided between two apprehensions,
either I have been negligent in not writing sooner, or I transgress on your time by writing now. Yet your kindness en-
courages me to hope that you will forgive the offence,
whether it be of idleness or impertinence. It is a great delight
to me to call to mind the pleasant hours I spent under your
roof, and all the kindness and hospitality I experienced in
Stowey and its vicinity. And here I must take an opportunity of expressing my gratitude for the reception I met from
Captain and Mrs. King—had I been known to them from
my infancy, it could [not] have been warmer. Several of
my father's Bristol friends enquired particularly after you,
among the rest the poet Cottle. During my stay at Mrs. K's
I saw Miss O'Neil in Mrs. Oakley and in Belvidera—she is
certainly wonderful in both; but her tragedy is much
superior to her comedy. There is a depth in her voice, a
chastity in her action, and a pensiveness in her air, that,
while they give a peculiar charm to her serious characters,
and 'beget a temperance' in the 'whirlwind of her passion'
comparatively unfit her for light and humourous scenes. Her
chief excellence in Mrs. Oakley, I think to be, that she pre-
serves the Lady in situations where an ordinary actress would
have [been] vulgar. Nothing can be more affecting than her
representation of Belvidera—it is almost reality. There is but
an indifferent company at Bristol—some of the conspirators
looked as if they had been reprieved from hanging 'for that
night only.' I was very much delighted also with Mr. Acra-
man's collection of pictures—the Madonna by Carlo Dolci
is the loveliest face I ever saw. He has just got a Domin-
chino of our Saviour glorified—a beautiful painting, amaz-

ingly fine in the colouring, but I found something wanting in the expression—in such a subject perhaps one naturally demands too much.

I have been about three weeks in Oxford, but nothing remarkable has there occurred. We are of course all in mourning for the princess, and I believe the day of her funeral will be solemnly kept here, with prayers and fasting. Her loss is indeed a severe national calamity, and a most remarkable circumstance, that the direct line of the royal family is likely to be soon extinct, tho' its members are more than was ever known since the conquest. I hope Mrs. R. Poole's recovery will not be delayed by the approach of winter. If she and Elizabeth are still with you, as I presume is the case, give my kindest remembrances to them both. Remember me also to Mr. and Mrs. Ward, and ask Susan and *Ann Oddity* if they have forgotten me. Has the Baby any more teeth? Mr. W's nephew Dan is now in Oxford studying with Mr. Stephens of Wadham—he is a fine, honest, good-natured fellow, and I like him very much. Are Mr. and Mrs. Acland now at Fairfield? If they be, give my respects to them when you see them, and to Captain and Mrs. Crofton, and tell Mrs. C. that I have abjured my heretical opinions with respect to the ladies. I desire my best respects to Mrs. Buller, Mrs. Francis Poole, Miss Harriot and all their respective families. After my rational friends, I may venture to mention Jack, Edward, and the Parrot. I hope the school is going on well, and that your musical meetings are more regularly attended.

Pardon me for trespassing thus long on your time,
and believe me most gratefully and affectionately
Yours

H. COLERIDGE.

N.B. Give my love to Daddy and Mammy Rich.

As an undergraduate Hartley won the admiration of his fellow students by his conversational powers and brilliance of mind; but his academic knowledge was spectacular rather than general. Three times he tried for the Newdigate prize for English verse; and his failures, particularly the first, left an indelible mark on his sensitive nature and reinforced a belief in his own insufficiency. Hartley began with too much hope that his *Horses of Lysippus* would win the prize in his first attempt—he bet everything on his winning, as it were; the tidings of some one else's success at first fired his enthusiasm.

'The truth is,' he records in one of his note-books, 'I was *fey*. I sang, I danced, I whistled, I leapt, I ran from room to room announcing the great tidings, and tried to persuade even myself that I cared nothing at all for my own case.' 'But,' he adds significantly, 'it would not do. It was bare sands with me the next day. It was not the mere loss of the prize, but the feeling or phantasy of an adverse destiny. I was as one who discovered that his familiar, to whom he has sold himself, is a deceiver. I foresaw that all my aims and hopes would prove frustrative and abortive; and from that time I date my downward declension, my impotence of will, and melancholy recklessness. It was the first time I sought relief from wine, which, as usual in such cases, produced not so much intoxication as downright madness.'

Hartley's examination at the conclusion of his college course was uneven; and his examiners, recognizing both his natural genius and his academic shortcomings, compromised by giving him a second class *in literis humanioribus*, in the Michaelmas term of 1818.

The following letter is addressed to George Coleridge, who twenty-six years previously had watched over Samuel Taylor Coleridge's own college years with a father's rather than a brother's interest. He was probably the most active of the Ottery Coleridges in assisting Hartley at Oxford.

LETTER 6

To the REV. GEORGE COLERIDGE, *Ottery St. Mary, Devon.*

Mert. Col. December 6, 1818.

My dear Uncle

You are probably already apprized, through George or Edward, that I have past my examination. With regard to the place I shall occupy on the list, I can give you no additional information, as the class-paper is not yet publish'd; nor indeed, likely to be so for a week to come, but of course you know that my chance of high honours is extremely precarious. I am as sorry for this as the case deserves, and perhaps more so, but if I know myself at all—the loss of distinction is what least afflicts me. The disappointment of my friends to whom I owe an additional obligation besides my natural duty, the uncertainty whether or not I shall fall under their censure, (which I am not, however, conscious of deserving, in any great degree) and the still greater efforts needful to procure myself an independance here or elsewhere, are considerations that would be insupportable, if self-reproach were added to them. But I can say for myself—and those who best can judge—and support me in the plea—that unfortunate circumstances weigh'd heavier against me than any fault of my own. In my Logic, Latin composition, Aristotle, and most part of my history, I was respectable; in Divinity and Ethics perhaps rather above par; in my Sophocles I fail'd, chiefly from being put on in a misprinted passage—for the play was one I had studied with more than common attention. In Virgil I stumbled from mere confusion; the passage I had read, and that too carefully—fifty times at least. In Pindar I was not very far amiss; in the O-dyssee alone I have real cause for shame, for to tell the truth, I took it up for a make-weight, in the expectation of not being put on in it at all. My Iliad, Euripides, Aeschylus, and Horace, were given me on paper. I heard nothing how these were done, but I hope, respectably. Here I must take an opportunity of expressing the high sense I entertain of Mr. Ellison's kindness, whose mild and gentlemanly system of examination, enabled me to acquit myself in many particulars, better than I should otherwise have done. Mr. Keble[1] volunteer'd his assistance in examining me previous to my appearance in the schools—a good office I gratefully remember.

By the last intelligence I received from the north my mother, sister and other relatives are well. Mr. Southey is engaged in a life of John Wesley, which promises to be one of the most useful and interesting of his works. The third volume of the history of Brazil is nearly printed, and the account of the peninsular war will speedily be put to press.[2] Derwent is well and goes on with his tutorial duties to the satisfaction of his patrons. Sara is as diligent as such a little soul can be.

A few days ago I received a letter from my father apparently in good health and spirits—I believe, engaged in a course of lectures.[3] I shall see him this Christmas, and at the same time shall have an opportunity of advising with William upon my future prospects. As I was prevented by illness from keeping last Easter-term, I am afraid I shall derive no benefit from my exhibition, and if so my battels (tho' the lowest in College) will run away with all the money I have

---

[1] John Keble (1792–1866), whose sermon in 1833 initiated the Oxford Movement, was at this time a Fellow of Oriel College.

[2] Southey's *Life of Wesley* was published in 1820; the *History of Brazil*, vol. iii, in 1819; and the *History of the Peninsular War*, vol. i, in 1822.

[3] Hartley refers to Coleridge's last courses of lectures, which were delivered at the Crown and Anchor Tavern between December 14, 1818 and March 25, 1819.

left. The time I trust is not far distant, when I shall be able
not only to subsist myself without assistance, but even to
assist such of my friends as are in need; but of this be assured,
that I will rather enter into any line of life that is honorable,
tho' never so irksome and laborious, than remain a burden to
you an hour longer than is necessary.

My best respects to all my Uncles and Aunts—Aunt
George in particular. Love to my yet unknown Cousins
and be assured that I remain

Your obliged and truly affectionate Nephew

HARTLEY COLERIDGE.

P.S. I ought to have thank'd my Uncles, Edward and the
Colonel for their kind remittance, but trust they will excuse
the neglect, when they consider how hard I was reading
when it arrived.

LETTER 7

To THOMAS POOLE, *Nether-Stowey, Somerset.*

Merton College, Feb. 26, 1819.

My dear Sir

Since I last addrest you, I have gone through a series of
Academical labours, with the result of which you are perhaps already acquainted. Though my success was not so
decided as might have been wished, the place I occupied in
the class-list was respectable, and as good as I expected—my
friends are in general well satisfied with it. I cannot plead
guilty to a sweeping charge of idleness, though the want of
regular instruction, before and after my entering the University, not without some fault on my own part, which I do not
avow without the resolution, with the assistance of heaven,
to amend, prevented my studies bearing constantly on the
great point in view. What I most failed in was the critical
knowledge of the Greek and Latin Languages. I have now
taken my degree, and have five pupils, who occupy me from
10 till 3. After which I keep up my own reading, and
intend, if nothing occurs to alter my purpose, to become a
Candidate at Oriel college on the ensuing election, which
will take place in Easter-week. I must labour hard meantime to supply what is deficient in my knowledge, as far as
possible. I am by no means sanguine in my hopes of present
success; but a respectable examination, though it should fail
of securing my election this year, will pave my way for happier efforts on the next opportunity; and at all events, the

trial will be attended with little or no expense, will be rather honourable than the contrary, and the having an object to aim at will lighten my toil. I shall endeavour likewise to find time for a try at the essay-prizes (verses I am precluded from attempting, being superannuated) but this must give way if needful to more important considerations. I have had a promise from the Tutor of Merton, and from one of the fellows, of a good word as to my conduct and regularity. I should not have been thus diffuse upon my plans, if I did not think it proper to lay them open to you, as your liberality has in part, placed me in the situation to form them. I spent the Xmas vacation with my father at Highgate. He was, on the whole, pretty well, and gave his Lectures with spirit. Those on Shakespeare were well attended, the Philosophical course but so, so—he did not, however, make it too metaphysical. Mr. and Mrs. Gillman are inestimable friends.

I have not been in the north since the long vacation. We were all pretty well then, excepting our habitual invalids. Derwent is well satisfied with his situation, and what is perhaps still better, gives satisfaction in it. There are some dawnings of hope of his getting *to* College. He is indifferent as to Oxford or Cambridge. If I should obtain a fellowship here I might possibly be of use to him. I hope my Stowey friends are all well. I beg particularly to be remember'd to them, especially Mr. and Mrs. Ward, and my little favourite Susan, (pray ask her whether she has forgotten me). The Bullars, or whatever other name any part of the family may bear—Miss Harriot Poole and her little nieces—Mr. and Mrs. F. Poole, etc.

I was glad to see young Bullar's name in the list of Cambridge honours. I suppose Mrs. R. Poole and Miss Lizzy are now at Wells. I desire my best respects when you see or write to them, and also to the Fairfield family and Mr. Brice. I hope Miss Brice is better—I don't forget Mammy Rich, nor Nurse or Betty. I was extremely sorry to hear of poor Bill's death, which must have happen'd very unexpectedly. May he find the change a happy one.

I remain, dear Sir, With all respect and gratitude
Very affectionately yours

HARTLEY COLERIDGE.

P.S. I find my poetic ability utterly incompetent to the production of an epitaph on Jack, but I do not, therefore, the less lament his death.

Shortly after taking his degree, Hartley stood successfully for a Fellowship at Oriel College. Oriel was headed by Dr. Edward Copleston, and among its Fellows were John Keble, Richard Whately, Edward Hawkins, and Thomas Arnold. The election of Hartley was in recognition of his unusual gifts.

'You probably stared,' wrote John Keble to John Taylor Coleridge, 'I'm sure I did, when you found that we had really elected your illustrious cousin, but his examination was so superior that one could hardly make up his mind to reject him "odditatis causâ." I trust he is not yet too old to unlearn some of his manifold tricks, and he seems to have the first requisite for learning, a sense of his Imperfection.'

Hartley was not alone in his elation over his success. His father was overjoyed, and his friends in the Lake Country—the Wordsworths, Mr. Dawes, and Southey—not to mention his mother, were delighted; an account is given by Mrs. Coleridge in a letter to Poole:

'He [Hartley] therefore, went to bed on Thursday night with a full determination to sleep out the *ringing of the Bells* which would peal to the happiness of his rivals next day; when sitting and yawning over a late breakfast, the welcome annunciation was brought in, which he thought must be only a deceitful dream, so much was he stunned by the tidings, until the succession of fees with their "imperative faces" stamped the real thing.

'Little William Wordsworth, on his return in the evening from School told his Mother that he never saw *master* [Mr. Dawes] in such good humour in his life; "As soon as he got the letter about Hartley, he rose up, gave a shout, and proclaimed a holiday: the boys all huzza'd and there was *such an uproar*, Mother!" '

LETTER 8

To THOMAS POOLE, *Nether Stowey, Somerset.*

Oxford, April 19, 1819.

My dear Sir

Success has at length crown'd my literary labours, and I am fellow elect of Oriel. After five days strict examination, on Friday last the joyful tidings were announced that I was chosen. Nothing could have been more contrary to my expectation, for I was doubtful whether or not I should stand, and at last determined on it rather with the view of opening the way for a second trial, than of coming in immediately. I had two rivals for the fellowship I stood for, which was a close one—i.e. confined to Worcestershire and

Gloucestershire men. Both had taken higher honours than myself, which certainly made the odds against me.

I have been busily employed in tutoring for the last term—a business of more profit than pleasure—and am going with a pupil to the isle of Wight next Tuesday.[1]

I heard from my father the other day; he was well, and had just concluded his Lectures. I believe my mother had written to you lately, so I need [not] trouble you with any northern news. Pray give my best remembrances to all the numerous members of your family at Stowey, particularly the Bullars, Miss Harriot Poole, Mr. and Mrs. Francis, Daddy and Mammy, Sam King, etc. Not forgetting Nurse and Betty.

I suppose Mrs. R. P. and her daughter are at Wells, but I desire my respects to them when you write.

My compliments to the Fairfield family. I should like a few lines, if it be not too great a favour to ask to tell me how all my Stowey acquaintance are, whose kindness to me I shall long remember. Does my friend little Suckey grow up pretty? I hope Mr. and Mrs. Ward are well. Remember me to them.

The weather must be very favourable to your farm, if it be as good in Somersetshire as it is here.

With a due sense of the kindness I, and all my family are indebted for to you

    I remain dear Sir

        Your very grateful and sincere little friend

                H. COLERIDGE.

N.B. My direction for the next three weeks will be Post-office, Ryde, Isle of Wight.

During the Christmas holidays of 1819–20 Hartley went on a visit to his relatives at Ottery St. Mary. While Samuel Taylor Coleridge had emigrated to London, his brothers remained in Devonshire; and at Ottery, James Coleridge (the Colonel and the head of the family), the Rev. George Coleridge, and Edward Coleridge, were living with their families. George May Coleridge, to whom the following letter is addressed, was the son of the Rev. George Coleridge. The next two letters are of interest for Hartley's unique record of the impressions made on him by his numerous relatives.

---

[1] The pupil whom Hartley endeavoured to tutor was St. Aubyn. St. Aubyn was apparently unable to meet the requirements for his examination—at least Hartley's efforts ended in failure.

LETTER 9

To GEORGE MAY COLERIDGE, *Christ Church, Oxford.*

Ottery, St. Mary, Jan. 3, 1820.

Dear George

All the world are wishing for you (I mean all the Ottery world) and I'm sure, if loves and compliments were half as ponderous as the lightest gas, my letter would be enough to break the Coach down. We have had several parties—vain attempts at merriment—but alas—it's all body without spirit —Nitrogen without Oxygen—the tragedy of Hamlet with the character of Hamlet left out. A young man in the neighbourhood, who has pick'd up a smattering of Astronomy from Guths grammar, has publish'd a woeful new ballad call'd the aberration of Georgium Sidus—with the tears of Venus—the malice of Saturn etc., very pithy and profitable. Babes cry for you—fair maids sigh for you—you are as the Apple of their eye to the young—and teeth to the old. I have been intending to write to you for a week at least, but it is the plague of epistolatory correspondence, that ever and anon it brings to mind the sad recollection of your absence. Ottery is very pleasant, very pretty. Summer and yourself alone are wanting to its perfection. For my own part, I have [been] treated with as much humanity as I had any right to expect—and have not been once horse-whipp'd, kick'd down stairs, or even pull'd by the nose. I am much obliged to you for the deep insight you gave me into the state of the human animal in these parts—only you were rather too diffuse on the grotesque—not a word of the beauty and fashion of the place—which however forgets not you so—for you are, in truth, the adored of the adorable. By the way I most sincerely beg your pardon for forgetting your letter, but I never am above half-witted when on the eve of a journey—and such a journey as I had too—never take your advice in that matter again—forced to wait at Whitchurch for almost 17 hours. No room inside—could not for the soul of me keep my eyes open on the top—off went my hat—gone—Coachman would not stop—rain—damn'd cold—so I thought the wisest way all things consider'd, to stay all night at Hindon—and next morning—(Sunday)—I contrived to purchase a cover for my skull, which, may by courtesy, be call'd a hat. Roads confoundedly heavy—sleet—did not arrive till 7, found a good fire and a hearty welcome. How do you get on with Aristotle,

24

Livy and Co.? Take care what you're about, for I've
pledged myself to your getting a first. Classes ran low last
time—this is not fair. I suppose you are not absolutely an
anchorite, or compelled to act dialogue with Dammy. If
you are, I will give my old Friend Scratchy a letter of introduction. You will find him a very agreeable and useful
acquaintance, and very expert at interpreting Aristotle; as in
fact that Philosopher was very little more than his Amanuensis. He's a great Dab too at Divinity—and particularly at
home upon Praedestination.

Is Burton[1] in Oxford at present? But I believe you're not
very intimate with him. If you were, I should drop him a
line to keep a sharp look out on you, for your thoughts are
only to do evil continually. Sam Archer—curse his jaw—has
told the folks here of the Tortoise-shell Cat, and I was forced
to ring it the other night at Aunt Luke's before the Newcomes
—who by the way, seem to be good sort of Cattle. Mr. N. is a
merry old gentleman and his daughters are not above speaking to the like of me. No beauties tho' but play delightfully
and afford Ned an opportunity of displaying his taste and
galantry. I love to see the Dog in his regimentals—who
would not be loyal for a red coat and a long sword? You
know of course that he's gone into the Yeomanry. We must
contrive a rumpus in the west, if it be but to prove his bottom.
Frank is a lad after my own heart and spouts divinely, and all
folks I've seen here may pass among the million—and with
only tolerable luck escape hanging. Poor Fanny has been
call'd away to attend her Aunt Brown. She is almost as
great a loss as you—a sweet creature, and not ashamed of her
poor relations. She absolutely condescended to speak to me
at the ball, which raised me 15 degrees at once in female
estimation. Even the fair Miss Smith recollected that she had
seen me a night or two before. She is a fine girl and admires
you woundedly. Fanny tried hard to make me dance, but
it wouldn't do. She had herself the satisfaction of dancing
with Mr. Lowe. 'Love has eyes' it is certain—but they're
devilish queer ones. Edwin figured away famous [ly] with Miss
Risk, Mrs. Hodge etc. He is a noisy, goodn[atured] Dog—
loves his dinner better than his book. We dine with the
Colonel today. I hope the dinner and my appetite will be
good. The company I'm sure will be agreeable. Your Papa
and Mama desire their love to you. So does Aunt and Uncle

---

[1] Robert Burton, one of Hartley's college friends.

Edward and little Bessy, and half a score more would, I dare
say, but I've no time to ask 'em. Pray be so good as to call
at my lodgings and you'll find a letter with the Postmark—
Milnthrop—I believe on my Toilet. It is from Derwent
—pray forward it—and ask when I must be at Oxford, for
I've forgotten. Remember me to all my friends, and ask
Miss Green at my lodgings how my Kitten is
       And believe me, Dear Geordie
                      Your truly affectionate Coz.
                           H. COLERIDGE.

N.B. Aunt Edward tells me to tell you that she has post-
pon'd her ball till you can be there. Your Daddy and
Mammy are going to cram their Carcases with us next
Wednesday—we shall drink your health in small beer. We
gluttonised on Thursday at Warden House.

LETTER 10

To DERWENT COLERIDGE, *Keswick, Cumberland.*

[January, 1820.]

Dear Derwent

Worn and hacknied as I am in the apologetic strain, long
as I have been accustom'd to write about not writing, I am
positively at a loss how to begin to address you, after so un-
conscionable an interval, and tho' I could easily explain my
silence, I must confess myself utterly unable to excuse it. The
fact is, however, that your last letter came to me but one day
before my setting off for Ottery. I was in company at the
time, busy all day after, knew that the perusal of your *pot-
hooks* and *hangers* (for in very truth, my dear Brother, your
hand out-villains villainy) would be no ordinary job, so put
it aside till I could sit down and enjoy it, and alas, in the confusion of packing, yours took flight, and has never since
return'd. I am as sorry as ashamed for this, tho' I doubt not
some four years hence to find it in some corner or other.
Shame for this circumstance, with long *desuetude* (a word after
your own heart) have kept me thus long intending to write
to you. Forgive me. 'Tis all I have to say for myself. Now
I have an infinite deal to tell thee, and much more to observe
thereon, not falling short in the interrogative department—
much of Oxford, much of Ottery, much of love, and more of
folly. As *imprimis*, that I returned from Woolmer's with St.

Aubyn, read with him, hours, days, and weeks—there was no
deficiency of pains on either side—whatever want there
might be of method I take entirely on myself, but we both
did our best—you probably heard that it was in vain. I think
he was hardly used, but that can't be help'd now. He is a
man for whom I shall always feel kindly, for with many
faults, (the consequence of imperfect education, or perhaps
more strictly, of imperfect superintendence over his youth,
and of too early contact with the world) he possesses strong
sense, much humanity, great gratitude and warm affections.
His faults are the result of his situation—his virtues are his
own. He is now gone abroad, and his father has very politely
written to me upon the subject of his making a third attempt.
I *disvised* it with all the delicacy in my power, and shall
return a similar answer to a letter I have just received from
one of his brothers, now at Cambridge. St. Aubyn's failure
has been no great comfort or advantage to me, you may be
sure, for a part of the disgrace is naturally reflected on me,
and I am afraid I did not help the matter much by my apparent impatience under his lot; but 'tis over, and must be
borne.[1] You are impatient, I dare say, to hear about Ottery,
and I am glad to conclude a painful subject—So to Ottery we'll
go. With my reception there, I must say, I was agreeably
surprized—every branch of the family gave me hearty good-
old-family-welcome, and even by other old folks I was not
used like a stranger. *Entre nous*, however, Fanny, Aunt Luke,
and Frank were the only people that came up to my notions
of perfection. Uncle Edward is good-natured, the Colonel
generous, and George benevolent. Aunt George is kind-
heartedness itself, Mrs. Colonel is as good, motherly, a personage as need be, and remembers that she was young once,
and goes to Balls, and does not make her daughter come
away with her just when the fun's beginning, as I've seen
some Mamas do; and Aunt Edward is a sensible, conversable,
good-tempered, good-natured, good-company-loving, good-
appearance-making, good-order-keeping, bad-English-hating
dame, that talks rather too much about gentility and prudence, but will go to heaven for all that. Then for the
juniors, Edwin is a great boy, with good principles and fair
abilities, well enough for 16, but I shall like him full as well

---

[1] This letter contains the first intimation that all was not going well with
Hartley as a Fellow of Oriel College, and shows that the failure of the authorities
to renew his fellowship a few months later may not have been wholly unexpected.

four years hence. Little deaf Bessy is a darling, affectionate, sweet-tempered and feeling, quick and sensible to a wonderful degree considering her defect, and with a great deal of natural good taste, which she shews particularly in drawing. Her extreme readiness of eye is a striking instance of the liberality of nature in supplying her own deficiencies. She is as happy as any human being can be—so little do, what we think inflictions weigh in the scale against the divine bounty that flows through the universe, filling it with joy and beauty and perfecting every seed of goodness to its own glory. This, my dear Derwent, is a strange transition, but I hope my scrawls will never be published, and with you at least I like to pursue the course of my thoughts, wherever they flow. You see that some of my earlier feelings are alter'd, that my religion, whereby I mean the whole body of my inward convictions, all faith in things unseen, all insight into the mystery of beings, (Deuce take that bell) is become cheerful, and therefore more thankful. We will converse if not face to face, yet by letter, heavens knows, not only darkly, but blackly—more in future and by laying open our thought to each other, may perhaps be saved from some errors and gain some truths. I must dress—more after.

I believe I was talking about the good people at Ottery—you are quite [tired] of them, I'm afraid, and paper is scant, or I would tell you about Fanny, how she is a dear and a love, with fine dark hair and eyes, plays angelically, and is according to the vulgar phrase, too good for this world, which said phrase is a little uncharitable, for were it not for such sweet souls on earth, the manufacture of hell would have no originality about it—a mere duplicate, the old thing over again. If I'd time, I could draw a parallel, or contrast, which you like, between her and our dear little one—they ain't a bit alike, God bless 'em both nevertheless. For the rest of the Otters, I can't discuss 'em at present, only I must mention that there were two remarkable pretty damsels there, of quite distinct characters of beauty—if you've any curiosity—I'll tell you more about 'em in my next. N.B. I fell in love with neither of them. Shame on me for having talk'd so long of myself and my kin, and not a word of your beauty. Your account of her was charming. I think I can imagine her, tho' any thing like love in you or I, is the height of fatuity. I can't either condemn it or get rid of it in myself, so I'll not be intolerant towards you. Let me know

all about it for goodness sake, but, my dear fellow, be your
own affection's counsellor, as far from sounding and discovery—you know the rest—but beware of making confi-
dants, especially of female ones. You laugh at my idea of a
maid incapable of love, but I am pretty confident I have
seen more than one such. Not among the cold, supercilious
and self-enamoured only, but among the most devoted, the
purest hearted, the fondest, but this is a point it would take
more room to discuss than I have now to bestow on it. M. is
lovely and beloved as ever, tho' I am better reconciled to
hopelessness than I was formerly. I know, at least I think,
she does not care for me. I almost believe that she has no
conception that I more than like her, and perhaps it is as
well it should be so[1]—But enough. I have no pupils at present but Cousin Ned,[2] a good hearted, rattle-pated fellow,
with a vast deal of cleverness about him. But I have plenty
to do, for besides my theological studies, to which I purpose to
devote the main part of my time, I am engaged about the
Prize-essay, and am going to publish a translation of Aeschylus into prose, in the notes to which I shall contrive to introduce some new ideas, on the ancient dramas and on Grecian
literature in general, that may excite a livelier interest therein
than is felt at present among our young men of best promise. I shall begin with the Prometheus, which will serve as
a sort of text, for some observations on the sacerdotal religion
of Greece, and on the sources and spirit of mythology.[3] In
my next I will send you a specimen. If you've any curiosity
to see it. I scarce know how to direct to you, but Keswick is
safest. Pray answer this as soon as you are in the mood, for

---

[1] The facts of this love affair are very meagre. John Taylor Coleridge,
writing to Gillman in June 1820, says: 'I am informed. . . . that he [Hartley]
has contracted an attachment for a young person, the daughter I think of an
architect; I hear her well spoken of individually, but any such engagement at
his time of life and under the circumstances is to be deplored.'

[2] Edward Coleridge (1800–83) was at this time an undergraduate at Corpus
Christi College. Hartley is supposed to have 'put him on the right path' for the
Aristotelian Scholarship. Edward Coleridge later became a confidant of his
uncle, Samuel Taylor Coleridge.

[3] The *Prometheus* of Aeschylus was of absorbing interest to Hartley and his
father, and for the next few years references to the tragedy are frequent in the
letters of them both. Coleridge, writing to Derwent on May 16, 1821, says: 'H.
has the noblest subject that perhaps a Poet ever worked on—the Prometheus . . .
and I have written a small volume almost to him . . . on the full import of the
most pregnant and sublime Mythos and Philosophene.'
In May 1825 Coleridge read a paper, *On the Prometheus of Aeschylus*, which was
the result of his interest. Hartley's efforts culminated in a brilliant poetical
fragment, *Prometheus*, published posthumously.

it's an age since I heard from Mama or Sara—afraid letters have miscarried. I wish that little dear spright was stronger —don't like experiments to be tried on her shape etc., but hope will be for the best. I begin to be alarmed at asking for Wilsy: it has been such a cruel winter, and our good old King's death [Geo. III] will make the veterans look to themselves. But God's will be done. She need not fear death at any rate. Why the devil can't they let folks go off quietly, without tolling bells and black bombazine to make the world look gloomy—hate to see the girls all dresst alike, and the men looking like buck parsons. I shall write to Mama soon, but you must give love to Aunts, Uncles and Cousins, if you're in the way. Brougham I see is going to trouble your peace again. No chance, I suppose. Don't like him, yet can't [help] thinking he ought to come in, or at least the Lowthers be thrown out. My father in his last letter promised to tell me his arrangements about you at Cambridge: shortly you will go, I trust, with good and comfortable prospect. Cousin Harry[1] stood for the University scholarship— we are ignorant as yet of the result.

[No conclusion or signature.]

The next series of letters deals with Hartley's loss of his Oriel Fellowship, which took place after he had held it only a year; and the effects of the failure form, perhaps, the saddest chapter of his life, for he fell from a position of honour and independence to one of frantic dread of consequences and utter loss of self-assertion. Yet if we would understand his subsequent career we must look rather carefully at the unhappy occasion.

But we must first retrace our steps. Hartley came to Merton College from the Lake Country, a youth wholly untutored in the ways of the world, and although he had entered Merton with fearful apprehensions, he seems by virtue of his conversational powers and brilliance of mind to have won the approbation not merely of his fellow undergraduates but of the college authorities as well. The atmosphere of Oriel, however, was as distinct from that of Merton as black from white. Thus Hartley was taken from a college where gaiety and easy conversation were at least condoned, and placed among a group of men noted for austerity, sobriety, and decorum. The Oriel authorities had elected Hartley probationary Fellow, not without misgivings, simply because his intellectual gifts were so unmistakable, hoping that his avowed sense of his shortcomings and his youth would aid him in adapting

---

[1] In his first year at King's College, Cambridge, Henry Nelson Coleridge (1798–1843) stood second for the University Scholarship.

himself to their ideals. 'His examination was so superior,' Keble had written after Hartley's election, 'that one could not make up one's mind to reject him "odditatis causâ" '; but Keble went on to add: 'One thing especially I could wish him taught, i.e., to refrain from *abstract* questions in conversation. He sits silent and contented enough as long as indifferent matters and points of view are being debated, but a Proposition in A, as Arnold says, rouses him immediately.' Hartley, too, entered on his probationary year with a conscious conviction of his deficiencies.

Some time ago we received a letter from Dr. L. R. Phelps, who until recently was Provost of Oriel. Dr. Phelps's information is based on his personal contact with Edward Hawkins (who was a Fellow of Oriel during Hartley's probationary year and later Provost); and his letter throws so much light on the story that we have included it in the Appendix (A).

Dr. Phelps notes that Hartley was set down among men least likely to prove congenial to him or to overlook his aberrations. To this society Hartley was elected probationary Fellow, and with him he brought several handicaps—the desire for congenial companions, who like himself could forget the ultimate purpose of life; an ever-growing tendency under the stimulation of conversation to voice opinions in a manner highly objectionable to men of conscious restraint; and an inability to resist the temptations of an extra glass of wine when in company.

The story of Hartley's loss of his Fellowship can now be fully told for the first time. Recently an old desk once belonging to Hartley was opened, and in it was found a complete series of letters dealing with this incident. These letters are included in the Appendix (B–K) and by means of them the story can be unravelled.

At Oriel a Fellow had to serve a probationary year before his election was confirmed. This procedure was in keeping with the statutes, and was originally planned as a means of insuring the appointment of the highest type of men for election. So careful were the authorities in the selection of probationary Fellows, however, that their refusal to confirm Hartley's election was unprecedented. Hartley knew from the first that he was on probation. He was, indeed, told that he was expected to withdraw from the society of undergraduate friends at Merton, maintaining a certain aloofness as befitted his station in the University, and to court instead the society of the Oriel Fellows and Probationers; and he was especially cautioned about exemplary attention to discipline; constant attendance at chapel, particularly in the morning; and conformity in dress, manners, and mode of living to the habits of those with whom he was associated by his elevation. All this Hartley understood, but he was a born rebel and would not conform. He continued to associate with undergraduates; his attendance at chapel and other college functions was most irregular, and in the Common Room he frequently showed himself excitable and argumentative. He was, moreover, several times guilty of intoxication, and though the frequency of his intemperance cannot now be determined, certainly Hartley's occasional indulgence was unseemly for a university don. These irregularities were noticed by the Oriel authorities, but Hartley persisted in his independent and rebellious way even after being warned by the Provost and several of the Fellows.

Sometime during the latter part of May 1820 Hartley was called before the Provost, Dr. Copleston. 'I was informed', says Hartley, 'that my remaining Fellow was extremely precarious— "as my conduct had, of late, been not only irregular, but grossly immoral".'[1] Hartley seems to have treated this as another warning. Remembering that he had been at 'two passing wine parties' from neither of which he 'came scot-free', Hartley felt that in 'strict language' his conduct had been immoral; and he confessed to the charges, promised amendment, and said he relied on the mercy of the college. As Hartley's probationary year was now drawing to a close, the authorities determined to call a meeting of the resident Fellows to confer on his case; and in order to confirm their suspicions, as well as what they considered a confession from Hartley, an inquiry was instituted among the college servants and elsewhere. The results of this inquiry confirmed only too well the charges of intemperance, and at the meeting on May 30 it was determined by the Provost and the resident Fellows that Hartley was not a suitable person to be elected permanently into the Society. (Cf. Appendix B.) Though this decision was informal, it was presented to Hartley by the Dean, with the suggestion that he resign his Fellowship before October, when the formal meeting concerning Fellowships was held; thus Hartley would be spared the disgrace of being rejected, and they the painful necessity of making their action public. Three accusations were made against Hartley: the neglect of college duties, the habit of seeking undesirable companions (i.e. undergraduates and others beneath his station), and frequent cases of drunkenness.

It was now clear to Hartley that he should step forward in his own defence. Whatever conviction he had of his own shortcomings he rightly resented the accusation against his character, i.e. the charge of habitual drunkenness. He expostulated freely with

---

[1] 'I consider drunkenness', wrote Keble to John Taylor Coleridge, 'to be a flagrant immorality and to be proved against poor Hartley.' Immorality, therefore, did not mean to the authorities licentiousness. Indeed, Dr. Copleston later wrote to S. T. Coleridge: 'I declare most solemnly that I never heard the charge of licentious conduct with women laid against him [Hartley], nor the slightest suspicion of that kind expressed.'

the Provost, the Dean, and several of the Fellows. He continued
to promise amendment and he urged them to give him a second
trial. The authorities, however, remained adamant. (Cf. Appendix, D and E.) Finding every effort he made in his own behalf
thwarted, Hartley seems to have fled from Oxford, leaving no
record of his whereabouts.

Samuel Taylor Coleridge's first intimation of Hartley's misfortune at Oxford came, as far as can be discovered, not from
Hartley but from John Taylor Coleridge, who, after learning of
the whole proceeding from Keble (cf. Appendix, C), wrote a full
account on June 29, 1820, to James Gillman, Coleridge's host.
(Cf. Appendix, F.) The blow fell upon him, Coleridge wrote to
Allsop, 'with all the aggravations of surprise, sudden as a peal of
thunder from a cloudless sky'. Derwent, in speaking about the
affair, records the effect of the news on his father: 'I was with
him at the time, and have never seen any human being, before or
since, so deeply afflicted: not as he said, by the temporal consequences of his son's misfortune, heavy as those were, but for the
moral offense which it involved.' Nor was Coleridge's suffering
merely temporary. Two years later he spoke of Hartley's loss
of the Oriel Fellowship as one of the four major sorrows of his life,
and many times in the years that followed he referred to the action
of the Oriel authorities as both cruel and unjust.

Derwent was immediately sent to Oxford to look into matters,
but, either just before or soon after his arrival, his brother disappeared. Derwent at once reported Hartley's disappearance to
his father and communicated as many of the details of the Oriel
affair as he could gather. Coleridge's answer to Derwent, written
on July 3, 1820, shows his agony over his son:

' I were, methinks, to be pardoned, if even on my own account
I felt it an aggravation of my sore affliction that, your Brother
without writing or any other mode of communication should
have bent his course to the North as tho' I were not his Father
nor he himself bound to Mr. and Mrs. Gillman by his own
knowledge of the affectionate and scarcely less than parental
anxiety with which they follow him thro' luck and unluck, good
report and evil. . . . Ignorant of all the *detail* of the case, of the
Persons, and their relative Bearings both on Hartley's present
and his prior situation, I do not permit myself to form any
positive Judgement on certain parts of your letter. . . . But
deferring the whole question of your Brother's acquaintances
and connections, I can only gather from your letter the ascer-
tainment of which I had before supposed—that Hartley had
converted difference of manners, views and opinions into positive dislike, and, I sadly fear, into settled enmity by his ungracious style of repelling the requests and admonitions of the
fellows of Oriel—that then instead of fortifying himself against

the hostility, so excited, by more than common guardedness of conduct he managed to put himself completely in their power by a succession of trifling (many of them perhaps, unconscious) indiscretions, irregularities and unpunctualities, which have been woven together into a Web, with that cruellest sophism of Calumny, which destroying the actual distances and inter-spaces gives a false context and interprets fault by fault— . . . You have not said, whether Dr. Coplestone is at Oxford or not! and if not, where he is? The names and present addresses of the Fellows of Oriel you should likewise procure. And then if your Brother have left Birmingham or . . . perseveres in going to Keswick, I expect you here with as little delay as possible. . . . O surely if Hartley knew or believed that I love him and [hunger] after him as I do and ever have done, he would have come to me. . . . If Hartley be at Birmingham, and you think, that your presence would enable you to persuade him to return hither with you, of course you will go there.

'I am vexed to find that the Post is gone—Tuesday morning 4 July. I have this moment received your heart-wringing intelligence. I wish that I dared believe that Hartley is bonâ fide on his road to Keswick—but the same Dread struck at once on Mr. G's mind and mine—that he is wandering on some wild scheme, in no dissimilar mood or chaos of feelings to that which possessed his unhappy father at an earlier age during the month that ended in the Army-freak, and that [he may] even be scheming to take passage from Liverpool to America. . . . If there were tolerable assurance of a Letter reaching him, I would by hook or crook get and send him a sum of money sufficient to prevent any additional bewilderment from immediate pecuniary distress—

'What he [Hartley] should do now, is as evident as the hope, that he will do it, is (I fear) vain—He should put in execution what he *says* he can do, and I doubt not, truly says. He should state the whole affair in succession as it really was in each point —distinguishing error from imprudence, and imprudence from admitted impropriety, . . . clearing up what had been mis-understood or misinterpreted, and admitting point by point whatever in his habits, conduct or demeanor appeared cul-pable, . . . and pledging himself to the requisite change. . . . Add to this a solemn contract of honor entered into by himself, and by his Father, that on a proved breach of his engagement in any of these respects and the desire expressed by the Provost and Fellows in consequence, he will instantly resign his fellow-ship—and then I might exert the influence of my friends with Dr. C. and with each of the Fellows singly, to bring things about. But all this he is precluding by gloomy resentment, or . . . from cowardice as to mental pain. Oh! if he knew how much

I feel *with* him as well as how much I suffer for him, he could not so forget that he has a most affectionate Friend as well as a Father in S. T. Coleridge.'

What transpired between July 3 and the formal meeting of the Oriel Fellows in October one can only conjecture. Nor is it possible to conjecture just when Hartley returned from his wanderings. Certain it is, that not many weeks after his disappearance we find him staying with the Montagus in London. At this time Hartley wrote two letters to his father (Letters 11 and 12) explanatory of his conduct and the determination of the Oriel authorities. Coleridge then wrote to Dr. Copleston. The original letter, which was posted to Oxford, has not come to light, but there are preserved by the Coleridge family several rough drafts of the letter in Coleridge's handwriting (cf. Appendix, I). These fragments show that Coleridge endeavoured to have the Oriel authorities change their decision before their formal meeting in October. He wrote at great length in defence of Hartley, pointing out his son's constitutional weaknesses but defending him against all charges of habitual drunkenness; and he referred Dr. Copleston to Southey, Wordsworth, and Mr. Mence (the minister at Highgate) whose estimation of Hartley's mind and character was, he insisted, the same as his own. Throughout his activities in Hartley's defence, Coleridge acted on the advice of Mr. Mence. Indeed, at the first intimation of the intention of the Oriel Fellows, Mence, who had been a Tutor at Trinity College, Oxford, had written to William James (a Fellow of Oriel); and he sent to Coleridge James's reply, which gives probably the most specific account of the charges against Hartley. (Cf. Appendix, G and H.)

Coleridge was not content to carry on his plea for Hartley merely by correspondence; and on October 15 he went to Oxford to make a personal call on Dr. Copleston and to lay before him the actual facts of Hartley's case. Nothing seems to have come of this meeting, save that Dr. Copleston reaffirmed his previous charges and furnished Coleridge with a memorandum containing a full account of the affair. (Cf. Appendix B, for this memorandum, and J, for Copleston's letter transmitting it.)

Returning to London, Coleridge felt that Hartley should prepare for the Provost a statement of the whole truth, both in the confession of guilt and in the denial of specific charges; and in order that there might be no delay and that a complete account might be rendered, Coleridge wrote out in the rough for Hartley an elaborate answer to the charges made by Copleston as well as a defence of Hartley's character. (Cf. Letter 13.) Urged by his father, Hartley then apparently wrote his own protest to the Provost with Coleridge's letter before him. (Cf. Letter 14.) On October 19, being himself in London, Dr. Copleston wrote to

Coleridge for a second conference (cf. Appendix, K); and Coleridge came, bringing with him Hartley's letter of protest to the Provost, mentioned above. This letter Dr. Copleston read and approved, but he continued to assert the validity of the charges and to affirm his determination not to renew Hartley's Fellowship; and a few days later at the formal meeting of the Oriel authorities Hartley was deprived of his Fellowship. Dr. Copleston had, indeed, asked for the interview, not to reconsider the contemplated action of the Fellows, but to offer to Hartley, through Coleridge, a sum of £300 from the College, that there might be no immediate suffering from the sudden loss of independence. From the first, the Oriel authorities had felt that their course of action was exceptionally severe; and as early as their meeting on May 30, they had apparently determined to give Hartley a liberal sum of money by way of recompense. Coleridge indignantly refused to accept the offer made by Dr. Copleston; such an acceptance, he insisted, would be tantamount to admission of guilt; and in his father's judgement Hartley concurred heartily. So the matter rested for over a year. John Taylor Coleridge had, however, kept in touch with Keble; and by January 30, 1822, we find Keble writing to him as follows:

'About poor Hartley's money Copleston desires me to say that some application should be made as it were officially—he said at first by Hartley himself, or his father, but afterwards he said if you applied in his name as expressly authorised by him it would be sufficient. I suppose he means we ought to have a letter which might be produced at an audit and kept among the College Papers, and as it need only be a request to have the money paid so and so without any kind of acknowledgement or allusion to past matters Hartley will probably have no objection to write or authorise you to write, tho' I confess I hardly see the necessity of it.'

The matter seems finally to have been settled by January 15, 1823, although even then Hartley did not accept the money, but he authorized John Taylor Coleridge to transmit to Mrs. Coleridge at Keswick, £216 16s., being what remained after his Oxford debts and £15 owed to Gillman had been paid.

This brings to a close the story of Hartley's unfortunate experience at Oriel. Severe, indeed, was the action of the Oriel authorities, especially for one of Hartley's sensitive temperament; but for the Oriel Fellows no other decision was possible. Yet the College bore no ill will. 'Suffice it that H.C.'s portrait is in the Common Room to-day. We have forgotten his shortcomings and remember only the brilliance of his gifts and the pathos of his life.' Thus concludes Dr. Phelps in his recent letter; and so may we too conclude this chapter in Hartley's life.

LETTER 11

To SAMUEL TAYLOR COLERIDGE.

[September, 1820.]

Dear Father

As you desire a full statement of all my transactions with
Oriel College, and of the relation in which I stand to the
Fellows, I will now give you all the particulars that my
memory supplies of their and my own conduct, from which
you may form a judgement, how far they have been justifi'd,
in the severity to which they had recourse, or in their own
language were driven; and of the provocation to terms like
those employ'd by Keble in his letter to John.[1] I believe you
will give me credit for concealing no part, even to spare
your feelings much less my own. If there be any inaccuracy,
due consideration should be had of the difficulty of recalling
minute circumstances, some of them taking place when my
attention was not directed to them, and others when confusion, grief for not being what I knew I ought in strict morals
to have been, and dim anticipations of future misery made
me less capable of noting down minutiae, had I even expected
any need thereof. You will also, understand, that this letter is
for you to form your opinion on. I do not disguise my own
feeling, that I have been wrong'd, illiberally, ungentlemanly
treated, but I am a prejudiced judge—speaking of men I
cannot pretend ever to have loved, though I highly esteemed
and revered them—who have certainly done me almost as
much harm as they could—do you judge whether that harm
was injury. You know I was placed, by no choice of my own,
in a College not famous for sobriety or regularity, without
acquaintance with the world, without introductions, and
after the first term, without any to guide or caution me. It is
true, William Hart [Coleridge] had introduced me to Keble
and Tyler, but it is also true, that neither of them thought
proper to look after me, or give me either advice or warning,
which, considering the friendship professed by the former for
my family, might to one unacquainted with Oxford, seem
rather extraordinary. At all events, I confess I felt it so;
nothing was more to my wish, than to have had some one
among the superiors of the University, interested for me,
whose eye might have kept me clear of folly—and the con-

---

[1] For the letter from Keble to John Taylor Coleridge see Appendix, C.

sciousness of this, contributed in no small degree to the freedom, with which I afterwards gave my society to Undergraduates, which has been emphatically call'd *'keeping low
company'*. It is needless to enter upon the History of what
past at Merton: suffice it to say, that, as any who knew me
will testify, I behaved as well as most would have done,
and form'd no acquaintances but such as I should be proud
to introduce to you. I don't deny that when at a party, I
drank as others did, and this was sometimes too much, but I
rather avoided than sought such company as induced drinking. In the latter part of my Undergraduateship, I kept
chiefly with three men—all temperate, and one of them, as
far as his choice carried him—a water-drinker. They all had
given me sincere proofs of attachment. I believe them all to
be open, noble-minded, and thoroughly principled, and one
of them in particular, a man of great talent, and taste. With
these men I continued to associate to the last, spending most
of my evenings with them—our pursuits in literature, the
general tone of our minds were like, with just so much of
difference as served to furnish matter of argument, and that
mutual forbearance, which more than the exactest agreement, tends to keep alive friendship.

Well, so things went on. I had establish'd a good character
in the College—I was highly respected by the Tutor—and I
believe really beloved by many of the young men. From
thence, I was elected, very contrary to my expectation, into
Oriel, and past through my probationary year. Just at the
end of this period, so that I had no time for recovering
myself, I was summoned before the Provost, and inform'd,
that my remaining Fellow, was extremely precarious—'as
my conduct had, of late, been not only irregular, but grossly
immoral'. I will confess, that I had, within a short period,
been at two passing parties—and I can't say I came absolutely scot-free from either of them; feeling, therefore, that
in strict language, my conduct had been immoral, I pleaded
guilty—said I relied on the mercy of the College—whereby I
meant, not the mercy which is contrary to justice, but that
which takes a liberal and hopeful view of errors, which may
be merely accidental, and at [any] rate cannot be considered in a very heinous light, as acts, tho' fearful in truth,
if taken as symptoms of a habit. Next day the whole was
decided—the evidence, who or what, I know not, were re-
examined—in form their depositions—some of which must

have been wilfully false taken down—my exclusion resolved on—and all this without any express communication to me. When I found, however, how things were going, I immediately called on Keble, and was inform'd of the result. He exprest great sorrow for the length he had been obliged to consent to; and spoke in terms very vague, and very severe, of my conduct—indeed his language might have [been] addressed more properly to one who was hardly ever sober, than to one who had been occasionally tipsy. I then formed a notion—that the charges against me must have been exaggerated—but consciousness of a recent fault, my habitual respect for his character, the amazement into which I was thrown by my misfortune, united to prevent my insisting, as I ought to have done, upon an explanation.

He advised me to resign my fellowship before the meeting of the College in October—which might prevent 'disclosures', and comforted me, upon the bad prospect of my affairs— saying—'When you can face your own conscience never fear but you may face fortune.' I had not any other feeling towards him than that of perfect gratitude—nay reverence, for I look'd on him and the rest as men performing a great, a painful and self-denying act of duty. I conceived of them, as friends in whom my character was most safely confided, and still hoped that when they came to consider the step they had taken, so deeply prejudicial to a young man against whom nothing dishonorable, nothing unfeeling, nothing premeditated, could be alleged, they might think his imprudences sufficiently punished by the alarm and warning I had already received. Under this impression I sought the advice of Rickards, my fellow-probationer. He appeared deeply interested in my behalf, promised his best aid, counsell'd my writing the letters, and shew'd so much apparent kindness, that I left him with tears of joy and affection. Next morning I set about the forementioned letters—which all amounted to this—a confession that I had been careless in respect to drinking, and deficient altogether in the gravity and circumspection beseeming my order in the University. Habitual intemperance I denied, but acknowledged that the suspicion required to be removed by a particular carefulness in that respect. Throughout the whole I was haunted with the fear of owning to less than the truth—of not representing myself in colours black enough. I measured my expression by the strictest standard, and as such I expected they would

have been taken. I had always understood that Oriel fellows
made Xtian perfection their rule and aim, and never suspected that they would employ the overflowings of my contrition as a witness against me. If a humble Christian, in his
prayers, calls himself a miserable sinner—shall this be made a
handle to accuse him of murder, or theft? The answers of
Whately and Hawkins you have seen.[1] I had little conversation with any of the fellows after that time. I saw Whately
twice; first, I exprest my hope, of getting into a school, which
he then highly approved of; but some time after—told me it
was but a precarious hope as 'I was a young man leaving
the University in bad Odour' and advised my going to
Canada—'on the ground that damaged goods do best for
the Colonies'. This, I thought a harsh phrase—and took no
liking at all to the scheme—but notwithstanding gave him
credit for good intentions. I also conversed with James—
who was very earnest, dwelling chiefly on my having taken
too much wine with a *Stranger*, and afterwards invited him
to dine with me. Now the fact was, that this Stranger was
a Master of Arts of the College—with whom I consented
(for I'm sure I should never have proposed it) to the introduction [of] another bottle. He certainly got drunk, and I,
from weak compliance, not sottishness, drank more than I
ought; but I was, at all events, sober enough to keep him out
of mischief.[2] This was the first offence. The two Parties
occurr'd a good while after; at one of them I drank but little,
coming in very late, but a few glasses, fast—and afterwards
some beer—which made me giddy as I was not well. Drunk
I was not, but probably appeared so on coming home. The
other time I was certainly knockt up, for I had undertaken to
pass the bottle about for a sick host, and was possess'd with
the freak of playing the generous landlord at another's table
—a very silly practical joke to be sure—and in my situation
highly improper—but surely not enough to justify so damning
a phrase as that whereby they have thought fit to designate
it. I had a short interview with Tyler, who advanced me
some money, and I believe the same day, I took leave of
Keble. Then and then only, I attempted a defense—but he
would not enter upon it. I told him the fellowship was out of
the question, but I had a character to vindicate—he said (if

---

[1] Cf. Appendix, D and E.
[2] See Appendix, G, for James's account of Hartley and this 'Stranger'.

I remember) it was only by amendment I could vindicate it.
I spoke of the charges being exaggerated; he said—He hoped
so, but added 'It's useless to deny the facts.' I stated that I
did not intend to deny the fact of having been intoxicated
more than once, but the habitual frequency of drunkenness.
He replied—'You are availing yourself of vague terms—
Frequency and Intoxication'; and then added—'I would not
mind the intemperance, so much, if I could separate it from
the praedilection for low company.' Whereby I understood
him to mean: 'The preference of the Society of men below
my own station in the University'—or at the utmost—the
carelessly contracting acquaintance and even engagements
as Tutor with men not famous for regularity of conduct—
'above all, men of Colleges not liked by Oriel.' As I saw he
was bent on not believing or hearing me, I bad him farewell.
This was my last transaction till I dined with Dr. Copleston
previously to my quitting Oxford. He spoke to me kindly—
as to a young man, who had shewn himself unfit for his situation—as to an incautious man who needed warning—but
still as to an unblemished character in the worldly accepta-
tion of the word, whom the College had rejected partly as
not being the sort of man they wanted—partly—as being
more likely to do honour to another station—Up to that
moment I had had but one . . .

[The remaining portion of this letter has not been preserved.]

LETTER 12

To SAMUEL TAYLOR COLERIDGE, *Highgate.*

Bedford Square [Basil Montagu's], October 2d [1820].

My dear Father

In obedience to the letter of your commands, I write
immediately, although I do not think my epistle will reach
you a moment sooner than if I had slept upon it. I cannot
speak for certain to the day when the fellows will meet for
confirmation, but think it may be about the 19th, but I will
write to ascertain. The account I have given you in that
immeasurable scrawl is the truth, and, as far as my recollections carry me, the whole truth; but I am tempted to say a
few more words to you on the subject, that you may not

form a wrong judgement, either of the Fellows of Oriel or of me. And first, allow me to express my conviction, that they could not, under their circumstances, have confirmed my Election, without injury to themselves. Of their system, of government, it does not behove me to speak: I could never reconcile myself to it, but I acknowledge that discipline of all kinds is not so much to my taste, as it ought to be. However you might be disposed to overlook the fact of intemperance, once or twice committed by an inattentive young man, under the excitement of company, yet you must reflect its effect and example did not pass away as fast as the fumes of wine from my brain. I might become sober and keep so, but I could not restore to the College its spotless character: the spell was broken—it was seen, and that too by the very persons, from whom it was most needful to conceal it, that Oriel men were but as others. Nay had I been suffered to remain among them, a very natural suspicion might have arisen, that they tolerated in their own body, what they punish'd in the young men committed to their care. For within my remembrance as many as six or more youths have been expelled for irregularities, most of them of high family and fortune, one the son of Judge Baily. Had my slips got to the ears of the parents of those young men, what a handle would it have afforded them? Consider this, as I know—you can—impartially—put me, and all your knowledge of me, out of the question, recollect that they could not know me as you do, and state the Question as a pure case to be mooted, thus:

A. a young man, only known for some talent, some weak good nature, and no little eccentricity, is removed from a society of lax manners, to another society distinguish'd for the reverse. He is inform'd on his entering this new society, what is expected of him, warn'd against such faults as have been supposed to attach to him, and in fine, instructed that his permanent settlement in the same society depends on his conduct during a year. Notwithstanding which, he neglects much of what he knows is expected of him, does not take pains to accommodate himself to their manners, is shy of their company, connects himself chiefly with his old comrades and others of like character, and is heard to speak of the strictness of those who have honour'd him by making him one of them, with ridicule: and after a time it is discover'd, that he has, at least more than once, fallen into an absolute moral misdemeanour, which accounts fully for a degree of indolence, irregularity, late hours, absence from stated meetings, and neglect and slovenly performance of stated duties, hitherto inexplicable. If to this be added, a hasty confession, and apparent dislike of entering into particulars, you will not be surprized, if this Society reject the young man A. as an unfit person for them, whom nothing but interest or vanity could have induced to come among them. Now this, my dear Father, is a plain statement of *facts*, which may prevent your committing yourself by defending me on untenable points. I must further tell you, what in the other letter I omitted, that of late I had been often seen with a man of no very genteel appearance, and whose looks certainly indicated drinking. The real truth was, this was a man of but moderate capacity, whom I had seen made a butt of by others not so much better in head as they were worse in heart. I knew that much was depending upon his getting thro' the University, and proffer'd my assistance, did my utmost, not without success, to make him read, and found much honesty and right feeling about him. I flattered myself I might be of service to him and certainly disregarded the impression my acquaintance with him might make on those who were but little inclined to impute any act of mine to the best motives. On the whole, you may easily perceive that I have been somewhat wilfully negligent of my own interest, and that, *entre nous*, I had a decided dispathy with the fellows. But yet all this, tho' it fully justifies their exclusion of me, is very far from even excusing the manner of it. Nothing I had done affected my character as a Gentleman; or made my credit worse than that of a Scout—nothing even palliated their undistinguishing avidity for reports against me. Above all, nothing that I can think of, can excuse their not making me we[ll] acquainted with the charges against me—their attempt to send me over the wide Ocean with a blasted character, to leave my name for a bie-word to my family—the one scabby sheep turn'd out of an immaculate flock—the sole jarring note in the concert of the Coleridges. Far enough short have I been of what I ought to be, short of what of I trust I shall be, but few Bishops on the Bench have not at some time been worse, if inexperience, and manifold temptations, subjective and objective, be considered. This is a boastful speech, but a persecuted man may be allowed to be vain. Enough of this for the present. I will

do what I can for Ebony¹—that is to say—A Romance in the
first person, setting forth the manifest disadvantages of
Ugliness, as an introduction to a series of Essays on divers
subjects, my signature Caliban. I am sorry for Mrs. Gillman's illness, and for the cause of it—but such things are.
Loves as a matter of course—can't expatiate for want of
room. Hang Wrangham!

I hope you are satisfied as to [my] *indignation,* for to tell the
truth, towards the end I got into a bit of a passion—But after
all I have not libelled them as they have libelled me.

Yours,
H.C.

LETTER 13

To the REVEREND THE PROVOST AND FELLOWS OF ORIEL
COLLEGE.

This letter, which is in Samuel Taylor Coleridge's handwriting,
was composed *for* Hartley, in answer to the charges contained in
Dr. Copleston's Memorandum. Cf. Appendix, B.

[Between October 15 and 19, 1820.]

Reverend Sirs

The regular time for the confirmation of the probationary
Fellowships having arrived, and it having been announced
both to myself and to my Father that it is the determination
of the Provost and Resident Fellows to negative the election
in my instance, and it being in the highest degree probable
that their suffrages together with the grounds and motives for
the same will determine the suffrages of the Fellows non-
resident; I take this means of laying before the Provost and
Fellows officially assembled the following declarations and
avowals. And first, I declare that I do not protest against
the measure itself, severe in itself and heavy in reference to
its certain and probable effects as it is, and the more so from
its being almost an unprecedented measure. On the contrary as far as the decision that during my probationary
year I have by sundry irregularities, omissions or careless
performance of the duties imposed on me by my situation
as probationary Fellow; or by social preferences incongruous
with the object which as a Competitor for a Fellowship of

---

¹ William Blackwood, of *Blackwood's Magazine,* had recently urged Coleridge
to contribute to that work; and apparently Coleridge wished his son to prepare
something for publication.

Oriel I had by my own act authorized the Provost and Fellows to expect that I should propose to myself, and therefore irreconcilable with my own virtual promise; and lastly, by single acts, if not of positive intoxication, yet of culpable intemperance; justified such doubts of my character as might conscientiously be deemed incompatible with an election implying in the minds of the electors a conviction of my fitness to become a member of their society and the belief that I should labor with them in the furtherance of the known ends and aims of the Society—as far as the determination and the grounds assigned for the same, are thus stated, I repeat a formal avowal, that I admit the justice of the measure, and throw myself wholly on the mercy of the Provost and Fellows. But I beg leave to add, that by mercy I do not mean a mercy that is opposite to justice, but such as consistently therewith might be suggested either by circumstances of palliation in reference to the facts, or by consideration of the severity of the punishment in reference to its certain and to its probable consequences on my present and future plans and prospects. But statements having been made to my Father by such a channel and in such form as permits no doubt of their authenticity, or of the full of the Belief of the Provost and resident Fellows in the truth and accuracy of all and each of the charges contained in the same, and as authorizes me in presuming that each had exerted an influence proportional to its moral importance in leading to the determination, of which they are, collectively, the assigned grounds and causes; and because by the ordinary course of things in similar cases I hold myself warranted in apprehending, that the effects of these statements, principally in consequence of sundry parts of the same not contained in the preceding declaration and avowal, will without and against the will of the Provost and Fellows extend far beyond their purpose and intention, not merely to the injury of my character at present, but by [it] to the endangerment of my future utility by depriving me of the means of retrieving it, inasmuch as the charges in question would tend to prevent my obtaining the situations of trust, which my acquirements and talents would otherwise entitle me to look forward to; for these reasons, and disclaiming all reference to any expressions used or communications made, by individuals in their individual character, by letter or in conversation, I here, secondly, protest against the charge of *frequent* acts of Intoxication, if by the word frequent more than two or at the utmost three single instances be meant; and declare that I am permitted by my conscience to admit the truth even of so many, only as far as by intoxication a culpable degree of Intemperance be understood, and not if by intoxication a temporary deprivation of my mental and bodily faculties, such as we commonly mean to express when we say that a man is thoroughly *drunk*, i.e. either does not know what he is doing or saying, or will be incapable of recollecting it on the return of sobriety; or (recollecting the same, or having had it brought to his recollection and knowledge) disclaims what he had said or done; as said or done in the suspension of his judgement and moral will; or finally, has lost or greatly impaired his powers of communicating his meaning, and effectuating his purposes, ex. gr. staggering, or stammering, or using one set of words when he meant another.

I solemnly, declare that but for the recollection of *one* incident, viz. that on my returning from a wine party given on the occasion of a degree passing, the Servant desired me to take care of my Candle, from which I inferred both at the time and again on the next morning (for the words were my first thought on awaking) that I must have had the appearance and marks of intoxication, and felt (not without self-reproach and sincere grief) that I must have drunk too much, and beyond what any occasion could justify, above all on a man whose duty, moral and prudential, it was with peculiar solicitude to eschew all scandal, and every approach to an evil example—but for the recollection of this one incident and the rightful inference from the same, I solemnly declare that I could not without offending against my own conscience have pleaded guilty to more than the negative (though still, and with unfeigned penitence, I admit, the serious) offence of not having been sufficiently anxious and careful in the performance of the positive duty, that of making myself an example of the opposite virtue—of behaviour decorous and circumspect and of Temperance beyond suspicion.

Thirdly, I solemnly protest against the inference that my non-attendance at Morning Chapel was occasioned by the intemperance and the late hours of the preceding day; and moreover I protest against, and emphatically deny the assertion that my late hours, when such did occur, were any way connected with Intemperance, as their cause, effect, or accompaniment. And that either the testimony, on which the contrary has been believed, is false and slanderous, or that the conclusions grounded thereon have been erroneous and not sustainable by facts—and were it required or permitted, I am prepared to bring evidence in disproof of the charge, by positive proof of the contrary—viz. that to those late hours, whether more or less frequent, either music and the blameless pleasures of mixed society in respectable families, or literary discussion, were the sole inducements and temptations.

Lastly, respecting the company kept by me I have already admitted the charge as far as, but only as far as, the negative is in question—namely, that I did not cultivate the society, or the academic rank of society, which I had by an implied and virtual promise bound myself to cultivate, and which it might have been reasonably expected and rightly required of me to seek and prefer. But in no *moral* sense of the word dare I admit that the society to which I did chiefly attach myself, can with truth be characterized by the words 'low company'—for it consisted of men with whom I had formed a friendship during my Undergraduateship, all men of good morals and sound religious principles. And I intreat permission to add, that in the one, for me most unfortunate, instance, of a private Pupil, my sole motive for prolonging my intimacy with him was the hope of rescuing him from the effects of former bad influences, the belief that there was a basis of good in him, and a consequent reluctance to abandon him increased by my sense of his unfortunate circumstances, the very circumstances which should, on prudential grounds, and perhaps as a duty owing to my own credit, have made me discontinue the connection.

Having made these declarations, I submit myself to whatever measures the Provost and Fellows may determine on, entering no protest against the refusal to elect me, in and for itself, or as grounded on the charges enumerated and admitted by me in the first ff. of this appeal; but on the contrary, confessing and gratefully acknowledging the several distinct warnings and admonitions given me with paternal kindness by the Reverend the Provost, and with friendly earnestness by the Reverend the Dean. If I protest at all against my exclusion from the Fellowship, I do so only as far as a belief in the truth of the Charges here solemnly denied by me, may have influenced you to a more severe proceeding than you would have adopted had no such charges existed or been credited by you—a point which none but yourselves can pretend to know, and concerning which no man has a right to question you—and therefore I do not protest against the measure at all—'I admit its Justice and throw myself on your Mercy.'

But as a pressing act of the duty towards my afflicted Parents and at the dictate of my own conscience I enter the above deliberate Protest, *independently* of the fact or question of my non-election as Fellow of Oriel, against charges calculated to injure me in addition to my non-election, and far more permanently, and to a far more aweful extent and degree; and if in the pursuit of this end I have in any word or sentence transgressed the limits of mere self-defence, I disclaim the same—and subscribe [myself]

[Yours respectfully]
[HARTLEY COLERIDGE.]

LETTER 14

To the REVEREND THE PROVOST AND FELLOWS OF ORIEL COLLEGE.

This letter, which was composed by Hartley with the preceding one before him, was presented by Coleridge to Dr. Copleston at their meeting in London.

[Between Oct. 15 and 19, 1820.]

Reverend Sirs

The time approaching for the confirmation of probationary fellows, when the reasons for my meditated rejection, will doubtless be taken into consideration, I hold it my duty to signify to you, how far I plead guilty to the charges alleged against me—and in what sense I acquiesce in the justice of my exclusion. In the first place then, I would not be understood to interfere, in the slightest degree, with your right of judgement, much less to retract any confessions heretofore made, while I was ignorant of the nature and extent of the evidence on which you were proceeding. So far, therefore, as you deem certain instances of intemperance committed casually—without previous prospect of being so overtaken, and never amounting to a loss of self-command or recollection, together with omission of College duties, and neglect to cultivate the acquaintance and friendship of those into whose society I had been admitted; so far as these facts are the ground of your decision, I have nothing to object to it: it lies in your own bosoms; but that the instances of intemperance were frequent: that they were more than two or three—all arising from peculiar circumstances: that they were the cause of my irregularities or late hours, that I ever chose, or even tolerated companions, because of their love of drinking—that I kept low company, in any sense in which that term is understood in the world, or that I selected for companions any but Gentlemen—men of good principles, and in general of intellectual pursuits, I deny; at least, if ever I mistook the characters of my associates, it was my inexperience and no prepossession for what was objectionable. Permit me then to protest against the charges of *habitual* intemperance, irregularity as a *consequence* of such intemperance, and love of improper society. At the same time, I must express my unfeign'd thanks for all past favours from the College, and particularly for the friendly advice and warnings of the Provost and Dean—which, I trust, will not be found utterly fruitless, tho' they fail'd of their immediate purpose.

I remain, Reverend Sirs,
With sincere respect and gratitude,
[HARTLEY COLERIDGE.]

LETTER 15

To an UNKNOWN CORRESPONDENT.

The text of this fragment of a letter of Hartley's is taken from a copy in the handwriting of Mrs. Derwent Coleridge.

Dec. 2, 1820.

... My father has been at Oxford, had an interview with Dr. Copleston, who talked in a very smooth strain, about my talents, acquirements, and dispositions, but continued to reiterate charges, which my father, and all my friends *believe*, and I *know* to be false, as to *frequent* intemperance etc., etc. The Dr. also defended the secret, inquisitorial manner of investigating the conduct of Probationers, which puts it in the power of any Scout or Shoe-black who may be dissatisfied with his perquisites, any inferior servant etc., etc., to ruin any man whose carelessness or occasional errors may dispose his superiors to receive ill impressions of him. As I hope for the love of all those whom I love best, I never, before I left Oxford, had any idea of the extent of the charges against me. I suspected, nay, I knew them to be exaggerated, but little thought to what degree! Little thought that my unfeigned contrition for the thoughtlessness which brought so heavy an affliction on my friends, would be taken as a confession of vices etc., etc.

In my former letters I told you the worst I know of myself and, as you say, it is bad enough, if compared with, *the rule of right and the fitness of things*—but I have had a pretty good warning to keep my contrition for my maker; and *above all*, not to be over free with it to the Fellows of Oriel.

But to continue. My father, having procured a *memorandum* from Dr. C. of the charges against me, much the same in import as those contained in Keble's letter, returned to Highgate, and in a few days, had another meeting with the Provost in town. He then presented my *protest* containing my acknowledgements of my *real* delinquency, and solemn disavowal of whatever else has been alledged beyond it. The Provost received this *protest*, praised it, continued his former affirmations against me, adding thereto, by way of descending from *generals* to *particulars*—that I had been 3 times picked up *dead drunk* in the Street, which, so help me God, *I never was in my life*! And, after all this, or rather along with it, repeated in the name of the College, an offer, which he made to my father in his own, while at Oxford, namely, that to prevent my feeling pecuniary embarrassment from my exclusion, I should accept from the College the Sum of £300. *and let the matters be hushed up.*

I cannot tell what may be their motive in this, certainly, liberal proposal—but among my friends, the Wordsworths, Mr. Frere, the Gillmans, etc., these have but one opinion with regard to the effect of accepting it, it would have tongue-tied me, it would have convinced the world that I was even such as they have named me. As to their promises of silence, of what use are they? The more mystery they make about the matter the worse will it be for me.

My father's answer to the proposal was in my name, and it expressed my feelings. 'If', said he, 'my Son be innocent of the heavier part of your charges, far be it from me to per-suade him to compromise his honour: if, after all his denials to me, he is guilty—he may do as he pleases but *I* will not be the channel of conveying the money to him.'

So here the business rests. I shall write to the Warden of Merton, to Sir G. B.[eaumont] and my Uncle Edward, a true account of the case and of the whole proceeding; I shall send them a copy of my protest, and of all the papers in our possession necessary to the elucidation of the affair.

[This letter breaks off thus.]

LETTER 16

To LADY BEAUMONT.

[December, 1820.]

Dear Madam

The generous kindness you have ever shown towards me, and the honorable place I have held in your estimation, add the sanctions of duty to my wish to prove myself as worthy of that kindness and that esteem as possible: and if, from past folly, I have laid myself open to imputations, that may cause you to regret your bounty, and recall your good opinion, it the more behoves me to step forward in my own defence, and confessing the imprudence of which I have been guilty, to deny the charges of which I was ever innocent. You have not, I suppose, to learn, that my election at Oriel has not been confirm'd: it is probable that you have heard reports, vast and vague, of the delinquencies that have occasion'd my rejection: and, you will very likely be told, that I have confessed them all. Trusting to that charity in your Ladyship's nature, which is the offspring of hope, I will fearlessly state how far I have been faulty; and confiding in your sense of justice, I will tell you how cruelly, though perhaps unintentionally I have been slander'd.

The Fellows of Oriel form a society, of closer union, and greater *esprit de corps*, than any other in Oxford. Electing their Members upon general good report, and approved literary competency, they set apart the first year for Probation; which they explain to mean, not an opportunity for their new associate to approve himself worthy, but an interval in which they are to discover whether he was so at the time of his election: in short, they do not want to find what he is likely to be, but what he is, and has been. And this Probation is, to the most regular men, a very severe trial. I have heard my fellow-probationers, whose conduct has past without reproach, complain of it, tho' they were acquainted with the severity of it, before they offer'd themselves as Candidates, which I was not.

Not only is strict conduct, regular compliance with

discipline, and conformity to the manners of the Society demanded: but a devotion to its wishes, a preference of it to all other company, a partaking of its spirit, and, with regard to certain matters (and those too none of the essentials of religion, morality, or even gentility) an adoption of its opinions. I do not say that all this is indispensable, but a deficiency in the least particular, will dispose them to believe alleged offences against the highest. In a word, they expect a young man, whom perhaps no one of them ever spoke to twice in their lives, before his election, to become one of them, all of a sudden, and are prepossessed against him who does not. And also, and perhaps reasonably, expect the person who is admitted among them shall no longer converse with his juniors on a footing of equality, and tho' they would not require a man to break off an old acquaintance, if not a disreputable one, still there must be a change, a coldness, a *chevaux de frise*; or he will at best be only tolerated. I will not say, that they are wrong in desiring this, for the purposes of Academic discipline may render it necessary, but surely the neglect of it ought not to be confounded with the love of low company in the ordinary sense; or an acquaintance, which had once been perfectly unobjectionable, spoken of in terms which are proper to connections disgraceful at any time and under any circumstances. But these demands do not comprize all the difficulties of a Probationary fellow. His situation is a very equivocal one, for while he is admitted in to the company of the Actuals as an equal, he is subject to a system of espionage, and liable to every misrepresentation which the officiousness or malice of servants, who always think they do a service when they can tell a bad tale, may give rise to. In fact he has the rank of a Fellow and more than the restrictions of an Undergraduate. At the same time, it is but fair to state, that nothing of this is conceal'd— unless it be, the fact that misconduct previous to Election, will if afterwards discover'd, subject the offender to ultimate exclusion. A young man is told in general terms, that his confirmation depends upon his good conduct, that he is subject to the Authority of the Dean, and that there is an eye upon his behaviour. I cannot say that *I* understood this to mean, that any Scout or Porter, or Shoeblack that might be dissatisfied with his perquisites, would have it in his power to recommend himself by secretly stabbing my reputation, but I suppose they meant that I should understand it so. Well, your Ladyship now may judge what my place required; the enclosed Protest, which was delivered through the Provost to the assembled Fellows at their last meeting, will inform you what I have been charged with, and how far my own confessions extend. That in one or two instances I drank too much; that my deportment was not that of a Fellow of Oriel, that I preferr'd other Society to that of my own common room, that I was more frequently seen with Undergraduates, than Masters of Arts or Doctors, that, being unused to a College of strict Discipline, and not expecting School-boy tasks, from which I supposed my age and station exempted me, and having had from my childhood an unfortunate habit of Procrastination, I neglected and transgressed the rules and exercises of the College—that I too frequently staid out late, and sat up at home still later—all this is but too true —to which I must add, that neither my attachment to the Fellows of Oriel, nor my compliance with its manners, were much increased by my knowledge, that I was exposed to a surveillance, almost inquisitorial; but [I deny] that I was at any time of my life pick'd up drunk in the street (which I am said to have been three times in the last year), that I came home intoxicated at least as often as sober, that ever (unless, indeed in the first year of my Undergraduateship, and in a manner by compulsion) I continued [drinking] after I felt myself disorder'd, that I chose for companions, Drunkards, or other than Gentlemen; that the indolence and procrastination which I have been guilty of too long—long enough before I well knew the taste of strong drink—were the result of habitual intemperance. It might be, that when men, not distinguish'd for Academic regularity applied to me for assistance, either literary or other, I only thought of them and their need; and neither of their character nor my own. I may even have attempted to rescue an individual of weak intellect but kindly nature from the ill consequences of his folly, or to put him on his guard against others, not so much better in head, as they were worse in heart—and this, considering the situation in which I stood, might be vastly imprudent—nay, seeing that others who ought to be dearer than myself to me, were depending on the judgement past by no very lenient judges on my character, it might be a criminal indulgence of over-good-nature. Still it does not make me a Sot, shews no preference for low company, and does not justify any man in giving me a name, which [if] I had [not] the power of shaking of [f], would entail disgrace and poverty on all the remainder of my days.

Do not think, dear Madam, I write in resentment—or lay the charge of slander on the Fellows. They invented no scandals—they heard some disagreeable facts, and being prepossessed by them, and my general eccentricity against me, believed all that was said by I know not whom. My own eagerness to condemn myself, and the contrition I exprest and felt, not so much for any thing I had done, tho' for that I felt sufficient sorrow, as for the agony to which the certainly not unforeseeable consequence of my imprudence exposed my father and mother, seemed to them sufficient proofs of my guilt—and tho' I always did deny the extent of their charges —yet I was fonder of confessing the truth, than denying the falsehood. I have, however, and thankful I am for it, convinced my father of my comparative innocence. He has been to Oxford, has had an interview with Dr. Copleston, has presented the enclosed Protest, which the Dr. commends, but evidently does not believe; an offer has been made to remove the pecuniary inconvenience of the measure, by making me a present of £300 from the College funds. To this offer my father return'd an answer which I cannot mend. 'If', said he, 'my son have told me the truth, he can accept nothing without compromise of character; if, thus deliberately, and after ample time for recollection, he have deceived me, he may do as he chooses; but I will not be the channel of conveying to him what he can have no title to.' Here then the matter rests. I have written to the Warden of Merton, a full account of the whole transaction.[1] As most of my evenings were spent with friends in that College—he can vouch for some of my statements, and I want not Witnesses for the rest.

My Father has acted throughout with the advice of Mr. Mence, the Minister of Highgate, formerly Tutor of Trinity, Oxford, who has proved himself a warm and intelligent friend. He, as well as my Father, strongly urges my returning to Oxford as the best mode of confuting the reflection thrown on my character, and thinks I may support myself by Private Pupils. I will be guided herein by good counsel, and

---

[1] Hartley's letter to the Warden of Merton College has not come to light. See, however, Appendix, L and M, for two rough drafts (one fragment in Samuel Taylor Coleridge's handwriting) of a letter to the Warden of Merton College. Coleridge apparently not only endeavoured to defend Hartley in the Oriel affair, but also wished to have him clear his reputation with the Merton authorities.

circumstances—my task will be difficult, but my success will therefore be the more consolatory.

Derwent[1] is hard at it at Cambridge. Heaven grant he may be wise from my imprudence, and know that it is needful in this World *videri* as well as *esse*.

I am at present staying with the Montagus in Bedford Square.

[This letter has no conclusion or signature.]

LETTER 17

To SAMUEL TAYLOR COLERIDGE.

[December, 1820.]

My dear Father

I know not what to say for myself for my long negligence and breach of promise: and am grieved to the heart to find you have been so uneasy. Were it not so late I should have set out tonight, and shew you, by my rosy face and black beard, that I have been labouring under no disease but that of idleness and abortive intentions. Tomorrow or the next day, tell Mrs. Gillman to get ready her well deserved scolding; and do you prepare your sharpest powers of Criticism for the immense load of Papers, which believe me—are positively in rerum naturâ, actual, and not potential—also the papers—and a Copy of the Warden's letter, which was a very difficult birth, costing a lot of paper in projections; at length it is deliver'd—and in truth—a thumper. To tell you the plain matter of fact, it has been the difficulty I had in satisfying myself in this composition, that has been the cause of your uneasiness, but it is done now, indeed.

I think John Coleridge's letter the unkindest stab of all. The bare, unmitigated credit, he has given to every tittle of my addition—Sot and all the rest—the unfeeling manner in which he alleges my acquaintance with the Harrises in proof of my love of low company; and his gratuitous assumption that I had enter[ed] into imprudent engagements—are instances of cold-heartednesses and prejudice I can sooner forgive than forget.[2] Whatever I may have felt for Mary—and from you I wish not to conceal aught—I never expressed to her a thought beyond the most unimpassioned esteem. Nor does this observation beseem one, whom I have heard

---

[1] Derwent was entered in May 1820 at St. John's College, Cambridge.
[2] For the charges made by John Taylor Coleridge see Appendix, F.

charged with marrying a linnet without one gold feather in
her wing. My best love to Mr. and Mrs. Gillman—from
whom I expect just castigation—but let the righteous reprove
me, and smite me friendly.

Your affectionate son
H.C.

After leaving Oxford, Hartley settled with the Montagus in
London, and under their parental solicitude seems to have
recovered himself. Cut off from a leisurely life at Oxford, and
having since boyhood thought of authorship as a profession, he
set about writing both prose and poetry. His most ambitious
work was a poem called *Prometheus*; although it was never completed, and was published after Hartley's death by Derwent, the
subject caught Hartley's fancy for several years and he makes
frequent references to his efforts. *Prometheus*, however, was not
Hartley's sole interest. To the *London Magazine* he contributed
a series of essays ('Parties in Poetry', 'Mythology', 'Black Cats',
'On Brevity', and 'Melancholy'), but his literary compositions
were the result of spasmodic attempts rather than of any continuous application. These efforts, moreover, were not enough to
pay his expenses, and he was dependent on his father and others
for his support.

While on the whole Hartley was happy in London, he often
fell into moods of despondency and self-condemnation. He could
not, he wrote to his father, obliterate the past; and a sense of
shame, combined with an unwillingness to face the reproaches of
his friends, sometimes led him to run away from his hosts, the
Montagus, and to conceal himself for several weeks at a time in
a public house or with indulgent friends. Derwent speaks of an
ever-growing habit of procrastination; indeed, from this time on-
ward, Hartley shows a volitional paralysis, an inability to hold
himself to any task, or to resist the temptation of alcohol.

Derwent Coleridge, to whom Hartley addressed most of the
letters written in London, had been entered in May 1820 at St.
John's College, Cambridge. Derwent, too, seems not to have
been wholly satisfied with his environment at college; but he was
less erratic than his brother and managed not to offend the college authorities.

LETTER 18

To DERWENT COLERIDGE, *St. John's Coll., Cambridge.*

Highgate, February 19, 1821.

My dear Snifterbreeches—

Truce awhile to the Muses—It behoves me to tie up
Pegasus, and turn humble pedestrian along the dusty and

hard-beaten track of worldly business. Thy bills arrived in all their multitudinous terrors: they are, all things considered, small—blame attaches not unto thee. What is better, they are paid: so Doctissimus Gillman bids me say; that is, to be more particular, that worthy diminisher of the poor's rate, hath drawn from the hands of Mr. George Frere (who, you will understand, is a lawyer, and not, like his brother, of Attic and Peninsular fame, a Genius) the sum of £80.0.0%, being the amount due to you by Mr. J. H. Frere's donation,[1] for the present year, and also, the said learned preventer of the pains of a protracted old-age, hath transferred all and several the said pounds, shillings, pence, and farthings, into the hands, or rather into the counter-drawer of Mr. Coutts the banker—(a gentleman of whose superfluous cash I should well like to partake) to be deliver'd when call'd for, to the great Swine-herd of Johnian hogs, Mr. Calvert.[2] Also, touching the said Mister, alias—Master, alias Professor Calvert, I am desired by Mrs. Gillman to acquaint you that the *books* (I know not what scriptures, sacred or profane, are thus emphatically denominated) were sent (but to use the short and expressive language of my brief) 'we cannot remember the time—it was a short time before he went to Coll.—I think— I know they were sent.' Mrs. G. is gone to town, or she might herself interpret these obscure notices, but you perhaps understand them—your brain may be as the stuff of the Spartan General, and in your knowledge as the optician's glassy Cylinder, the indistinguishable blots: and how is it? You remember the log in the *Remorse*—don't grieve if you don't, and are not *Remorseless*, look for it.

So much for your monied interests. I hope your mind is thriving on its dry food of Squares and Triangles. Do you take an occasional draft of the waters of Helicon to wash it down? Don't utterly neglect your Muse: for the poor thing will die broken-hearted if you desert her—we shall have a

---

[1] John Hookham Frere (1769–1846), the translator of Aristophanes, was a warm disciple of Coleridge's. In order to express his sense of obligation to Coleridge, Frere used these words to him: 'That you are above the run of Readers, and cannot be remunerated by the Press, increases not lessens the obligations of those who are conscious of having been especially benefited by you. It is not in my power to prove to you how much [I] feel this to have been my own case—but I can spare a certain sum which is at your service, and which I consider as your's.' The sum which Frere set aside apparently was £300 and was understood to be for Derwent's college expenses.

[2] Thomas Calvert (1775–1840), Fellow and Tutor at St. John's College, Cambridge.

woeful new ballad, setting forth the Seduction of Miss Erato
and her melancholy death:

> Come, listen to a woeful story,
>   Of an immortal maiden's death;
> She was admired by Whig and Tory
>   And by every Son of Seth.

> Her father was a blust'ring bully
>   A thunder-maker he by trade:
> And she did her white fame sully
>   And would no longer be a maid, etc.

Well, to be serious. I have paid much attention lately to
the flow and structure of Blank-verse, and upon comparing
my earlier with my more recent performances, I find a per-
ceptible improvement, tho' I know not whether I shall ever
attain to the swell and undulation, the varied correctness
which your best Essays promise. In rhime I have better
hopes. I certainly succeed better in intricate and difficult,
than in the plainer and simpler textures. The Sonnet is my
favourite.[1]

I had a letter yesterday from Snouderumpater; which
beside much kindness, and no bad news, contain'd £20,
being the amount of poor Wilsy's legacy,[2] from which the
Government-pickpockets infamously detract two, for stamp
duty, or Legacy tax, or some such invention of Satan. Never
grudged money so much in my life. If I had known in time,
it is not impossible but it might have been evaded, after the
example of the Duke of Northumberland and old George
Rose, which last contrived to transfer a large fortune, drawn
out of the pockets of the people, without refunding a
farthen. But he is dead, and so, let him rest—if the Devil
have any gratitude he will not be hard on his old friend.
The letter speaks very affectingly of you, dear Derry down
diddle, says that it is a great comfort to mother to see her
three children love each other. I hope we shall live to be
blessings to her after all. Not a word about Southey. Says
dear tiny one is pretty well—too much on the little mind—
and anxious to see Pappy—hope she will soon. Mr. Charles
Owen hath departed for Oxford, not having discharged his

---

[1] It is significant, perhaps, that the sonnet was so early Hartley's favourite,
since it is mainly for his sonnets that he is remembered.

[2] This refers to Mrs. Wilson, Hartley's much loved nurse, to whose memory
he continued to make affectionate references in his letters and note-books.

debt to me, which would have been as well. Prometheus prospers. Mrs. Gillman apologizes. Daddy sends love—so do half a dozen folk. Haven't time to ask him tho—

Remain, etc.

Write when you can
That's a good, little man,
Let me know all about you
Altho' the world flout you—
Be a good boy—
And read about Troy.

[No signature.]

LETTER 19

To DERWENT COLERIDGE, ESQRE., *St. John's College, Cambridge.*

[Postmark, May 2, 1821.]

Dear Derwent

I have now by me a close written letter of 3¾ sides intended for you, and replete with Criticism, Politics, and Sentiments. But as it so happen'd, that this same close written epistle (which begins by the way with an Eulogium on my own punctuality) was not sent off as soon as finish'd, being delay'd on account of some promised communication from Bob[1]—and as I have since seen your letter to Papa, which I consider in measure as to me also, I think it eligible to let the Criticism, Politics, and Sentiments rest for the present, and take into immediate consideration your wish to change your College. Nothing can be more highly creditable to you than the spirit of your letter. It states the plain truth without disguise and without exaggeration. I will comment upon it at some length, that you may have no want of my experience in forming your determination.

Your objections to St. John's seem to fall under two heads: your small chance of success there, and your dislike to the Society. With respect to the first, I have little to say. The Fellowship, or any Fellowship, is not worth the sacrifice of health or intellectual vigour, and I am sure that you will never scruple any other sacrifice, consistent with your duty. To assume a little of the Mentor, I certainly do not think that the mere laying aside of Classics for a time, in order to obtain a definite object, ought to weigh against the advantages of

---

[1] Robert Jameson, an Ambleside school friend.

an early competence, and a fixt home—goods, which I have learned to value, heavily as in my case they were encumber'd. But I am decidedly of opinion that you could not contend on equal ground with some of your tough-headed competitors without the risque of your life, or at least, of all that can make life valuable. The small value of the Fellowship is another weighty consideration, and tho' a hundred a year (which it appears it does not on the average exceed) would be a very comfortable addition to a curacy, yet as a time must elapse between your election and ordination, it is almost doubtful, whether it might not do you more harm by putting you out of the way of other things, than good by its own amount. This however, is a consideration only to be comparatively dwelt on—I mean in estimating the advantages of St. John's, in opposition to those of Trinity. I cannot but regret that you were not placed at the latter College from the beginning. But thus it is—that we cannot acquire experience till half its value is gone by.[1] If, however, your friends determine (which I hope will not be the case) that you should remain where you are, your best course is to proceed in that line of study, which combining the prescribed routine in a certain proportion with the more genial pursuits of literature, may at once give satisfaction to the rational demands of others and preserve your own mind and body in sanity. Without absolutely giving up all views to the Fellowship— pursue it rather as a contingent and possible, than as the necessary and final result of your labours. Omit nothing that may conduce to the obtaining it without injuring your more permanent and important interests. Do not expect it, and do not throw it away. So doing, you will satisfy yourself, your truest friends, and all reasonable people, who are not dazzled by the name of Fellow, which I suspect was the case in some degree, with poor dear Mama. I hope, you will [have] no occasion to exercise so many painful duties, but it is well to be prepared against the worst. As to the second point, namely, your dislike of the Johnian Society, few people are more disposed to make allowances for it than myself, but I am sorry my Oriel mischance should have any weight on your mind. If you do continue there, by all means keep in sight of the Superiors. But I need not dwell upon this—not only your habits of self-control, your elegance of mind and habits,

---

[1] Coleridge says even more pointedly: 'Experience, like the stern lanthorn of a Ship, casts its light only on the Wake—on the Track already past.'

your susceptibility to impressions of disgust, and the absence of all disposition to revolt against reasonable discipline, secure you from any real delinquencies, but your freedom from my nervous timidity, from that unfortunate mixture of fear and dislike with which I am apt to contemplate stern and authoritative characters, will always enable you to step forward in your own defence, and by exactly defining the extent of facts, leave no room for calumny. Do not, therefore, let any recollection of my misfortunes weigh a hair. Rather reflect, that however illiberally I may have been treated, the very possibility of such mistreatment arose from my own folly. And here you will perhaps permit me to give a short view of my own Oxford Life, which you will remember is to yourself.

With few habits but those of negligence and self-indulgence, with principles honest indeed and charitable, but not ascetic, and little applied to particulars, with much vanity and much diffidence, a wish to conquer neutralized by a fear of contending, with wavering hopes, uncertain spirits, and peculiar manners, I was sent among men mostly irregular, in some instances vicious. Left to myself, to form my own course of studies, my own acquaintances, my own habits—to keep my own hours, and in a great measure to be master of my own time; few know how much I went through, how many shocks I received, from within and from without; how many doubts, temptations, half-formed ill-resolutions past through my mind. I saw human nature in a new point of view and—in some measure—learn'd to judge of mankind by a new standard. I ceased to look for virtues which I no longer hoped to find and set perhaps a disproportionate value on those which most frequently occurr'd. The uncertainty of my prospects cast a gloom on what was before me. I did not love to dwell in the future, and gradually became reconciled to present scenes, which at first were painful to me. This was not a good preparatory discipline for Oriel. And indeed, from the first moment that I conceived the purpose of offering myself as Candidate, I felt that I was not consulting my own happiness. But duty, vanity, and the fear of being shipped off to Brazil—determined me on the Trial. You will scarcely believe that after the first flush of success, I was seized with uneasy melancholy—*triste augurium*— a feeling that I was among strangers, and a suspicion, not yet wholly removed, that my election arose in a great measure from the failure of my county opponents, and the vague appearance of Talent, rather than from that hearty conviction of my eligibility, which with their views would have been the only justifying cause of putting me on so severe a trial. A Feeling, something like yours with regard to St. John's, hung on me from the beginning. My engagements with St. Aubyn contributed (if it were only by taking up much of my time) [to prevent me] from falling immediately into Oriel Habits. And to tell the truth, I did not much like the state of a probationer, or submit as I ought to have done to a yoke of observances, which I sincerely think very absurd, and which I hoped I had escaped by being made a Fellow. I knew, I felt that I was subjected to a kind of espionage, and could feel no confidence in men who were watching me, tho' I had a better opinion of some of them—than subsequent experience has confirm'd. I thought most of them Bigots, ignorant deciders upon the conduct of others, conceited of their own dignity, and rather disposed to tyrannize.

The natural effect of all this on my mind was a tendency to resistance, and I was not bold enough to fight, or prudent enough to make peace. I was induced to fly, to shun the enquiring eyes which I ought to have met bravely, and to vent my chagrin in certain impotent, but I dare say not forgotten threats, of great reformations to take place in the College and the University when my unripe fortunes came of age. The complex effect of all this discontent and imprudence was, of course, self-reproach, inconsistency, quickly form'd and quickly broken resolutions, just enough caution to lose my reputation for frankness, increasing dread of my consocii—incapability of proceeding on any fixt plan, and an extreme carelessness whenever the painful restraint was removed.

You know the consequences. Now of these aberrations you will never be guilty, so you have not my fate to fear. Still it must be hard for you to live among bigots, minds at once coarse and narrow—but know well of yourself. I beseech you consider how far your previous impression and the common cant of the gayer and more ingenious, with the supposed analogy between St. John and Oriel, may not have given rise to your dislike, and whether some of your sources of uneasiness are not inseparable from an Academical life. Trinity, you will say has none of them. It may be so, but till you have been there you cannot be sure of it. I am not now speaking of Studies, or even of Society, these are points you may

ascertain. But I speak of a certain cold-heartedness—and confined feeling—which every body of fellows have more or less of.
College pride is as specific a feeling as Family pride and far
less connected with inward nobleness. This you will find—
let the discovery never prevent you from performing your
duty. Write to me when you please, *citius melius*. I think Mr.
Gillman has told you about the money for your bill, which
he will pay into the Bank if it does not exceed £30.

Father has been unwell—but is better.

Yours

H.

Southey's *A Vision of Judgement* (the Laureate's elegy on
George III) was published in 1821. It was natural for Mrs. Coleridge to give Hartley 'a hint to praise in her last letter', for she
and Sara (now 18) were still inmates of the Southey household at
Greta Hall.

LETTER 20

To DERWENT COLERIDGE, *St. John's College, Cambridge.*

[1821.]

My dear Derwent

Once in my life, I'll be as good as my word. I've just
finish'd a folio sheet letter to the *Maum*, in which I stated
that I would write to you this very day, and behold, this
very day am I writing. What a reformation! Not that I've
much to say, except to thank you for your last—(in which only
one sentence was absolutely illegible) to chatter an hour
upon paper, and talk worse nonsense than I could get any
body to listen to. To begin with complaints, I have been very
poorly for the last fortnight, with considerable oppression on
the chest, soreness, and difficulty of breathing, palpitation of
the heart, and a general debility of Body. I was at Highgate,
and at Mrs. Milne's (the kindest of the kind) during this
attack, from which I am now pretty well recovered. It is
a sad nuisance to be so susceptible of cold as I am. A month
among the mountains would make me twice the man I am
now, but I hope that will come by and by.

I dare say there was some symbolical, and some literal
truth in your tirade against strong Beer, but I much doubt
whether it is truth applicable to your own case. I don't
believe a word about your 'fading into the light of common
day', but I dare say you feel the poetic spirit flow more

tardily, not however, as your metaphor would seem to imply, from the exhaustion produced by some new and unnatural stimulus, but simply from the absence of those to which you have been accustom'd. Kindness, above all, female kindness, and the certainty of female praise and sympathy, an union of various feelings, hovering between love and friendship, towards more than one object—the admiration and encouragement of a woman of Genius—your own peculiar situation (I shall lose my Tea) in which much of anxious hope, was mingled with somewhat of a soft despondency, all together combined to form a sort of medicated atmosphere, of a bland exhilirator, disposing you at once to unrealize and to glorify your own thoughts, emotions, sensations—by enduing them with the universal of Poesy, by spreading a sort of color'd mist about your feelings, which added to magnitude, which it took away from the hardness of outline. Thus passion, gaining the permanence of thought, and thought the warmth and vitality of passion, you had but to add a tone, or rather to imitate in sound the silent harmony of your own imaginations, and the simple record of the goings on of your heart and mind came forth as sweet poems. Now, many of these excitements are removed. I can, therefore, easily believe, that your feelings, and the spontaneous processes of your mind do not so readily assume or admit a poetic form, as when they were themselves generated or impell'd, by Lakes, and Mountains, and Fair-hair'd women, and soft approving voices, and looks of love. But that your powers are impair'd, that you have lost any facility independent of your inclination, I will never believe. On the contrary, this loss may prove great gain, by obliging you to look abroad, to call out your imagination, to observe more, and invent more— all which I am confident you are capable of in no ordinary degree, but which you have not done enough hitherto. I allude solely to your poetry. You are not utterly wrong in your opinion of poetic reputation, but I do not think a young Poet ought to set out with an entire disregard of it. The wish to be popular infers at least a wish to be intelligible to the generality of mankind, and induces a writer to consult general sympathies, the effect of which wish on the mind of genius, will be the repressing of individualities, over-refinement, and self-indulgence, and a praedominance of the universal. For myself, I cannot pretend to an extraordinary reverence for that same public, that huge shadow cast by a multitude of tiny bodies, that cloud composed of various exhalations, where the fragrance of roses is interpenetrated with the vapour of Dunghills, but then, I respect their money and their patronage—and *that* the length of loyalty. Prometheus is in a great state of forwardness. He will extend over about 700 lines.[1] I am not displeased with him:—and he was honor'd with the mark'd interest with Miss Maria Battley. It is something in her way, and I think she knows something about it. But—truth to tell, I believe the praise of a Petticoat always puts me on particular good terms with myself, albeit I may be well acquainted with the fact that the Lady's sentence is far from final. It is a weakness, but—no matter. It's well to be able to please somebody, and the vimmin have much sway beneath the moon. My friend and pupil, C. Owen, has past his Littlego: an important event. And what do you think? I actually (what a tongue Fred Gunning has) was requested to compose a few lines for Miss Charlotte Owen's task, the subject Linnaeus—A sonnet was the result. Have you seen Southey's Vision of Judgement!!!!! *O Tempora, O Mores*—And is it come to this? And our dear good mother gave me such a hint to praise in her last letter!!! I came off, I think, pretty well, saying that I did not think it the *best* of S.'s poems. Seriously speaking, our late lamented Monarch did not deserve such an insult to his memory. And who, but a converted Revolutionist, would ever have dream'd of spurring the wind-gall'd, glander'd, stagger'd, bott-begrown, spavin'd (Oh—for the Complete Farrier) broken-down gelding, that has turn'd blind with facing year after year the same round of Court Compliments—who, I say, but Southey himself would have forced the poor old beast into the Hexameter long trot; and so mounted as on another Rosinante, set off in search of adventures, in the world of spirits? But upon my word, this is an awkward circumstance for Heroes and Poets, if they carry their squint eyes 'to Heaven or to Hell', as seems to be the case with poor Wilkes.

> If great Defoe be 'earless' still on high
> And Foote-like Vulcan, limps along the sky;
> If Horace coughing shakes the concave spheres,
> And taints the well of life with rheumy tears;
> If Virgil, puffing, climbs the sacred hill
> Raves, and recites, and blows, and stammers still;

---

[1] The published fragment including the conclusion numbers 622 lines.

His armless stump if famed Cervantes shews,
And Laureate Davenant, without a nose,
Snuffles the praises of the royal master,
And chides fair Venus for his sad disaster.

It would be inconvenient, no doubt. But as Milton is cured of his blindness and his Republicanism, we'll all hope for the best. What do you think of English Hexameters in general? They have some advantages, I think, in very wild descriptive passages—in gorgeous imagery, and where sound or motion is to be exprest; and may always be rendered pleasing, so [long as] you can pick your words with a due regard both to accent and quantity. Southey's scheme of governing them by accent alone, is not less faulty than that of Sir P. Sidney, who totally disregarded it. Some people talk as if there was no such thing as Quantity of syllables in English, which is nonsense. Take the two following lines:

I go to meet a maiden fair—

and

I'm gone to get a bit of fat—

which have precisely the same number of accents, disposed in the same places, but the former has twelve times, and the latter only eight. Is not the effect of the two very different? The prominence of Quantity, will I suspect, generally bear an inverse proportion to that of Emphasis. We observe it much more in languages with which we are imperfectly acquainted, as I do in French and Italian. Now I am inclined to think that Quantity must always be the ruling principle in Hexameters and that the mistake of Sir Philip was his not excluding words where the accent and quantity happen'd to differ, or, perhaps, his judging of length more by the eye and the Latin Prosody—and the ear and English pronunciation. To use a quaint, but not inapposite illustration—The Roman metres, in our Country, stand much in the praedicament of the Roman law: Accent is the common, Quantity is the civil law. Hexameters and Pentameters are the Admiralty Courts and Doctors Commons, where the practice must be directed by the Roman Code, and yet in conformity to the English. But when all is done, I think it would grow very monotonous before a hundred lines were well completed. The similarity of endings, the small range of words, the difficulty of observing any medium between a movement obtrusively mark'd, and one not perceptibly

metrical, or as it were, between dancing and loitering, and
above all, the appearance of imitation, the too great likeness
to what it is not, will I think, finally exclude it from Poems of
length. For *Gems* and fugitive pieces, wherever mannerism
is not a fault, whatever you may be allow'd to think more
of the workmanship than the work, I doubt not, but it may,
with much labour and an exquisite ear, be render'd acceptable. With regard to the double endings—they are neither
to be attacked nor defended on the same grounds as double
rhimes have been. The double endings of hexameter are
perpetual. Double rhimes are only introduced as a variety or
occasional convenience, and were therefore objected to, by
the advocates of perfect regularity, and as far as the Metre of
Pope and Dryden (long held up as the only perfect English
measure) is concerned, not without reason, a double-rhimed
Couplet appearing still more isolated than its brethren. I
have chatter'd so long about this, that I have no room for any
talk of this world. I have paid Bob's note and James and
Henry are delighted with their presents. Had James got his
move before you left? My Father was in better health last
Sunday than he has been for some time back. Miss Jane
Harding[1] ('whose head between her forks presages snow') is
staying with them. She is as like Mrs. Gillman as if she were
her petrifaction. There are said to be some women that
should be seen by daylight, and some by candle light, but
Miss Harding's proper light is the Aurora Borealis. She
seems like the essential form of an old maid, broke loose from
the *mundus intelligibilis*, the very entity and quiddity of Pru-
dism. Her approach chills the air like a floating lump of ice,
stray'd into the temperate Zone. She would be worth a mint
of money within the Tropics, but in our climate she's worse
than nothing. Like Wordsworth's Thorn, she looks as if she
had never been young, and, like his White Doe, as if she
would never be older. Mr. and Mrs. G. are well. They
would all send love I dare say. Mr. Montagu does so, and
Robert the like. He is busy, and my paper scant, or he
would drop you a line. How I hate to begin or finish a letter!
I hear nothing of the *when* between Miss Skepper and Barry
Cornwall,[2] but I should doubt whether that gentleman were
in a state either of health or purse, to make marriage advis-

---

[1] Mrs. Gillman's sister.
[2] Barry Cornwall (Bryan Waller Procter, 1787–1874) was married to Anne
Skepper in 1824.

able. Pray remember me to Worship. I cannot say, remember me to Henry. Do you ever see Townsend? Not much matter, tho' *entre nous* I believe our dear Sara likes him better than the generality of he-creatures. God bless her, and our excellent mother. I am afraid I should feel small penitence for my faults, if they were not affected by them. I have not room for a bit of politics.

Write to me soon. Damn the post duty. Let me know all about it and I will tell you more in my next. How do you manage with Tutors etc. Prenez garde.

Yours

H. C.

LETTER 21

To DERWENT COLERIDGE, ESQRE., *St. John's College, Cambridge.*

Grays Inn, August 27, 1821.

My dear Derwent

Do not think yourself obliged to me for this letter, tho I intend it for a very kind one. Don't be frighten'd now; I've no more intention of begging a favour than conferring one. I'm not going to dun you, nor to give you good advice—yet after all, I can't pretend to draw a bill upon your gratitude, for I have several motives for writing, that take precedence of that old-fashion'd one—kindness to you. You must know then, that I do not, in the course of the day, talk half as much nonsense as my health requires—in consequence whereof, so great an accumulation of that substance takes place upon my brain, that the vessels occasionally discharge their contents in my most serious conversation, nay, even in my gravest compositions. This truly mortifying accident occurr'd on the day whereon we parted, in the course of a very interesting discourse on capital punishment. Now, my present intention is (if I be allow'd to use a metaphor of no very delicate origin) to ruck off and clear my intellectual decks for action.

I am thoroughly convinced there is nothing so wholesome for mind and body, as talking Nonsense. Writing it is not half so good—it's like sending Sal volatile by the waggon with the cork out, but situated as we are, what can one do better? Nonsense, however, should never be written except to one's very intimate friends—good folks, whose careful memories can supply the proper looks and tones, and whose imaginations can restore our stalest good thing[s] to their original

freshness. Even a Pun does not look well on paper—it's so
like deliberate villainy, and then its orthographical imper-
fections are so open to the gaze of a censorious world. A lie
is still worse—without the solemn face, it is mere vapid im-
pudence. But a funny thing, that son and heir of laughter,
which never grows old, and may be as good a hundred years
hence, as at the moment of utterance, alas—alas—Pen and
Ink are its destruction. Woeful it is to reflect that of all the
wonders that you and I and the Maum have produced in that
way, not one can be of the slightest benefit to Posterity.
The words indeed, may be handed down from generation to
generation, like relic bones, and sacred nail-parings of the
saints (most of whom, by the way, never pared their nails at
all) but, ὀτοτοτοῖ, τότοι δά—they will work no miracles. The
wine will be drawn, and the bare lees be left this vault to
boast of. Two things, therefore, must the world despair of
enjoying—a printed Collection of our FUNNY THINGS and a
Polyglot Edition of Joe Miller—the latter by general confession, incomprehensible to all but John Bull, and the former to
all but our *single two* selves: like the Ladies Coronation tickets,
not transferable. This is a pity, but what remedy? Let them
be like the Druidical Mysteries, quae literis tradere nefas. *We*
shall never forget them. I don't know how it is, but I can
never laugh at any thing but what is exquisitely bad, and to
appearance, at least, purely accidental. Indeed, a praemeditated funny thing is worse than a praemeditated piece
of sensibility. Wit, to me, is hardly ever laughable, because
it is an exertion of the faculties—and humour, true humour,
is too nearly connected with thought. I may laugh at it at
first hearing, or so long as it has the effect of surprize, but
if it will bear thinking of, I can not recur to it whenever
my sides want a shaking. Few persons, I believe, enjoy the
humourous more than myself, and the higher the humour, the
greater is my delight, but as far as the mere excitement of the
risible muscles is concern'd, the coarsest drollery will answer
just as well. I never laugh now at Hogarth, or Fielding, or
Cervantes—or if I do, it is at their meanest jokes—unless in
sympathy with others. But at our old Funny things I can
laugh by myself for an hour together—nay, they furnish me
with a reservoir of laughter for all needful occasions. If ever
any of those jokes, 'which must be laugh'd at' are obtruded
upon me, I have but to recall the image of you, kicking about
the stone in my Aunt's Court, and complaining how you did

hurt yourself—(I can hardly write for˙ thinking of it) and I gratify the Joker to the very altitude of his ambition.

I have grown rather graver than I intended to be in the nonsensical department of this epistle, and by that means, extended it somewhat beyond its limits. Now let us be serious, very serious, my dear Brother. I have paid Monday and Slatter, and received some money from home—i.e. ten pound from dear Mother's own self, for Southey is at that Palace of delights called Netherhall. I shall have the £30 when he returns, which will be very convenient, for what with Monday's bills and what my last suit, which I felt myself bound to pay for, having been recommended to the tailor by Robert, most of the ten hath flown. Poor Maum shall not be the poorer for it, longer than I [can] possibly help, and I am very busy just now—several irons in the fire. Shall attack the German speedily. Papa has not been so well as I could wish, but is better.

Let me hear from you ere long. Do you find yourself lonely? I do, I confess. Robert is out all day, my other Friends are equally engaged and most of them seldom at home in the evening—and, what is worse than all, I know neither girls nor children. You must not be surprized if I should hang myself, tho' I have no determined thoughts that way at present. When I am thoroughly engaged in a course of profitable labour, I shall be better, I dare say. I am liable, too, to be annoy'd by trifles which don't concern me. That foolish business of the Milnes' made me blue-devilish for three days, and very cross to you, which I am sorry for. God be thank'd, it seems pretty well blown over. I cannot agree with you, that the M.'s are vulgar people, and was, I confess, a good deal nettled at the expression. Mr. Milne's temper and ill health are very tormenting, but his impatience does not betray him into vulgarity, tho' it may into rudeness. As for the Ladies, when you have seen as much of their excellent qualities as I have, you will make as large allowance for their faults. Not that I vindicate them, in the particulars to which we were alluding, or by any means assert, that either of them possesses Mrs. Gillman's fine tact in morals and manners: (by the way, a fine moral tact is a very different thing from a strong moral principle, and on this distinction your Idea of Gentility probably hinges) but then, I never knew any one else that did, tho' Sara very likely may—and is it fair to call worthy, and not unpolished females vulgar, for the want of a rare and unacquirable degree of refinement? In what rank can you calculate upon finding it? Surely not in the highest if the reports which descend to us groundlings are not destitute of foundation—not always in the upper-middle, for I think (under the rose) we need not quit our own Keswick fire-side to convince you to the contrary, and below the upper-middle, according to your own notions, it ought never to be look'd for. Can any man say, he has met with it more than once or twice in his life? That it is a very lovely and beautiful thing, I am joyfully ready to own—so is beauty, so is Genius—but all these are things which no one in any rank can be censured for wanting, except those who have thrown them away. Of the conventional manners of High-life I possess but a very scanty knowledge—and unless it were to hitch them into a story, I have little desire to know more—but these form no part of our present discussion. The little bickerings and tale-bearings of females of almost all orders proceed, if you will, from the vulgar part of human nature, but this is not the ordinary meaning of the word vulgarity, which ought never to be applied except to manners not beseeming the social condition of the person using them. One lesson, however, let us two divide from this unpleasant business. When you are closely united, by interest or gratitude, with a family, never be too intimate with their intimate neighbours. Quarrels will arise, both among the Genteel and the Vulgar, and in that case, your feelings are sure to be harassed, even if you are not drawn into the scrape yourself. I have been very diffuse on this subject, because it is one, both in its general and particular bearing, that my heart has much to do with. For the other, we will have it another time.

Your truly affectionate brother.

[H. C.]

Bob desires his remembrances—Will write to you.

From the beginning of Hartley's stay in London both his father and mother had been uneasy about him.

'Poor H.', his mother wrote to Poole, 'is preparing a volume of Poems for the press, but I fear is at loss for a publisher; he talks of writing for present support, but *what*, and *how*, Alas, I know [not]. It is impossible for me to have any peace of mind until he is in a regular way of providing for himself.'

His several contributions to the *London Magazine* were of a high quality, but they were not sufficient to support him; and his disappearances from the Montagus, (when he would wander off, leaving no knowledge of his whereabouts either for his friends or for his father) as well as his apparent indifference to his own welfare, led his father to seek a permanent situation for him. London or its environs, Coleridge felt, would serve only to drive his son from bad to worse, and almost in desperation he turned his thoughts northward. At Ambleside, the Rev. John Dawes, Hartley's old schoolmaster, still kept his school; and Coleridge, remembering Mr. Dawes's love for Hartley, asked him to take Hartley into the school with him as his associate. Mr. Dawes responded, asking Coleridge to send Hartley to Ambleside, but before doing so Coleridge felt honour-bound to give a full account of his son. The original of Coleridge's heart-rending letter, written in May 1822, has not come to light; but a long fragment (apparently a rough draft) of his letter still exists; and certain portions should be included here, for they afford a remarkably clear analysis of Hartley.

'Giving no trouble to any one—to no one opposing himself—happy from his earliest infancy, "a spirit of Joy dancing on an aspen Leaf"—to what better can I appeal than to Mr. Wordsworth's own beautiful lines addressed to H.C. six years old? From the hour, he left the nurses' arm, Love followed him like his Shadow. All, all, among whom he lived, all who saw him themselves, were delighted with him—in nothing requisite for his age, was he backward—and what was my fault? That I did not, unadvised and without a hint from any one of my friends or acquaintances, interrupt his quiet untroublesome enjoyment by forcing him to *sit still*, and *inventing* occasions of trying his obedience—that I did not without and against all *present* reason, and at the certainty of appearing cruel, and arbitrary not only to the child but to all with whom he lived, interrupt his little comforts, and sting him into a will of resistance to my will, in order that I might make opportunities of crushing it? Whether after all that has occurred, which surely it was no crime not to have foreseen at a time when a Foreboding of a less sombre character was passionately retracted, as . . . as "vain and causeless Melancholy"—whether I should act thus, were it all to come over again, I am more than doubtful. . . . Whatever else has been said—how far truly, and how far calumniously, I humbly leave it to my merciful God and Redeemer to determine for me—it will not surely be said, that the two Lads were left friendless, or under the protection of Friends incompetent, or whom I dared believe myself permitted to apprehend unwilling, to observe their goings-on, during their holidays or holiday-tides. Since the time of Hartley's first arrival at Calne, to the present day I am not conscious of having failed in any point of duty, of admonition, persuasion, intreaty, warning, or even (tho' ever reluctantly, I grant) of—parental injunction—and of repeating the same whenever it could be done without the almost certain consequence of baffling the end in view. . . . I appeal to God and to their own Consciences and to all good men who have observed my conduct towards them whether I have aught to condemn myself for, except perhaps a too delicate manner of applying their affections and understandings and moral senses—and by which, it is to be feared, I have in Hartley's case unwittingly fostered that cowardice as to mental pain which forms the one of the two calamitous defects in his disposition. . . . But let it be, that I am rightly reproached for my negligence in withstanding and taming his Self-will—yet is this the main Root of the Evil? I could almost say—would to God, it were! for then I should have more Hope. But alas! it is the absence of a Self, it is the want or Torpor of Will, that is the mortal Sickness of Hartley's Being, and has been, for good and for evil, his character—his moral *Idiocy*—from his earliest Childhood—Yea and hard it is for me to determine which is the worse—*morally* considered, I mean: the selfishness from the want or defect of a manly Self-love, or the Selfishness that springs out of the excess of a worldly Self-interest. In the eye of a Christian and a Philosopher, it is difficult to say, which of the two appears the greater deformity, the relationless, unconjugated, and intransitive Verb Impersonal with neither Subject nor Object, neither governed or governing, or the narrow proud Egotism, with neither Thou or They except as its Instruments or Involutes. *Prudentially*, however, and in regard to the supposed good and evil of this Life, the balance is woefully against the former, both because the Individuals so characterized are beyond comparison the smaller number, and because they are sure to meet with their bitterest enemies in the latter. Especially, if the poor dreamy Mortals chance to be amiable in other respects and to be distinguished by more than usual Talents and Acquirements. Now this, my dear Sir! is precisely the case with poor Hartley. He has neither the resentment, the ambition, nor the Self-love of a man—and for this very reason he is too often as selfish as a Beast—and as unwitting of his own Selfishness. With this is connected his want of a salient point, self-acting principle of Volition—and from this, again, arises his shrinking from, *his shurking*, whatever requires and demands the exertion of this inward power, his cowardice as to mental pain, and the procrastination consequent on these. His occasional wilfulness results from his weakness of will aided indeed, now and then, by the Sense of his intellectual Superiority and by the Sophistry which his ingenuity supplies and which is in fact the brief valiancy of Self-despondence. Such is the truth and the fact as to Hartley—a truth, I have neither extenuated nor sought to palliate. But equally true it is, that he is innocent, most kindly natured, exceedingly good-tempered, in the management and instruction of children excels any young man, I ever knew; and before God I say it, he has not to my knowledge a single vicious inclination—tho' from absence and nervousness he needs to be guarded against filling his wine-glass too often. . . . Whatever else is to be done or prevented, London he must not live in—the number of young men who will seek his company *to be amused*, his own want of pride, and the opportunity of living or imagining rather that he can live from hand to mouth by writing for Magazines, etc.—these are Ruin for him. I have but one remark to make—That of all the *Waifs*, I ever knew, Hartley is the least likely and the least calculated to lead any human Being astray by his example. He may exhibit a warning—but assuredly he never will afford an inducement.'

About the same time Coleridge also wrote to Hartley urging him to accept Mr. Dawes's proposal:

'You have tried—nay, that is scarcely true; but you have made the experiment of trying—to maintain yourself by writing for the Press—and the result—I do not know what conclusion *you* have drawn from it—has been such as makes *me* shrink, and sink away inwardly, from the thought of a second trial. A domestic Tutorship seems out of all question: and even if by any sacrifice of my political free-agency I could—which I have no reason to believe that I possess, or could obtain interest enough to do—procure you any situation abroad—you would not like it or set about to suit yourself for it. What remains but something of the *School* kind? If you have thought of any-thing else, let me know it. . . . If anything tries your temper here you ought to be glad of it, as an opportunity of disciplining it for the severer trials, which . . . you will meet with at Kes-wick, without the greatest caution on your part. To Mr. Dawes exclusively you must look and apply yourself—God bless you! While I live I will do what I can—what and whether I can must in the main depend on yourself, not on your affectionate Father,

S. T. COLERIDGE.'

Hartley made what protest he could, but his resistance was as weak as any arguments he could muster to justify remaining in London, and by the beginning of the year 1823 we find him at Ambleside, as assistant master of Mr. Dawes's School.

LETTER 22

To SAMUEL TAYLOR COLERIDGE

Thursday afternoon, 15 Clifford's Inn. [1822.]

My dear Father

You have probably ere this received Robert's letter, acquainting you that I am well in bodily health—I hope I may add, that I am in a sane state of mind. For what is past, it is irremediable, and I know you too well, to imagine that mere expressions of contrition, however sincere on my part, could afford you that consolation, which can only be derived from a rational hope with regard to the future. You must be aware, that the pain arising from the contemplation of a mis-spent past, is often the cause of continuance in misdoing, even after the temptations which first misled have lost their powers, and when the sophisms which have long deluded, appear in their true deformity. Without in the least degree, attempting to palliate conduct, which admits of no palliation, I will simply declare to you, that for a long time, almost ever since my return to Mr. Montagu's, I had been oppressed with an inward sinking, a despondency, which perhaps the more impaired my voluntary powers, because it did not visibly affect my health. I was in short afflicted with a sense of incapability, a dread of looking at my own cure. The more my faults became obvious to those most interested in me, the more I was possessed with that helpless consciousness of them, which conduces to any thing rather than amend-ment. Further than this, there has been no cause of des-pondency with which you are not acquainted. The going to Ambleside, in the face of such unfavourable sentiments on the part of some, certainly weighed upon my heart, and I felt a physical incapability of exerting the necessary authority, and preserving the necessary distance, among a set of boys, in whose number there must needs be found high spirits, and untractable natures. Boys of 15 are harder to govern than men of twenty, and yet, I can sincerely say, I did my utmost at Oxford to perform the duties of a tutor, and I did it in vain. I ought my dear Father, to have said this candidly, but I did not—it is past now. I was at the time I last saw you, in a state of mind and body truly pitiable. Thank heaven I am much better now, and with the recovery of health I have recover'd free will and hope. In regard to my future plans, I shall not decide till I have heard from you. It is my wish to make another trial of my talents in London. I know I can make more than a livelihood, and I have hopes, more than hopes of my own steady perseverance in the right path, but I will not be obstinate. Only let me say, that what with my past failures, what with the unavoidable weakness of nerves, and defect of that sort of sternness, which is a necessary supplement to kindness and attention in a

Paedagogue, I think schooling of all things, *possible*, the least eligible.

My kindest love to dear Mr. and Mrs. Gillman and Miss Harding and the children. I will finish Prometheus forthwith.

Believe, my dear Father

Your truly affectionate if not dutiful son

H. COLERIDGE.

LETTER 23

To JOHN TAYLOR COLERIDGE, *No. 2, Pump Court, Temple, London.*

Ambleside, Jan. 15, [Postmark, 1823.]

Dear John

This morning I received a letter, made up between my mother, father, sister, and Mrs. Gillman. I am not aware from its contents that you have received mine of the 2nd of January; but I suppose you have done so. I should not so soon have troubled you again, had not my father advised me to authorise you to transmit to him or to Mr. Gillman the sum of £15 on my account. I suppose this letter will be sufficient for that purpose. Whatever remains of the £300 when my present debts are discharged, I wish to be considered as my mother's property; and, if there be any formula which may be needful to place it at her discretion, I will, with your consent, and that of the fellows of Oriel, perform the same as soon as may be. I need not ask you how you like dear Sara—but I am really delighted at the prospect of her visiting Ottery. Fanny and she will be a lovely pair. I understand from the letter that you are now the father of two children— God bless them both—Sariola speaks fondly of them. It must have been a great delight to her to meet you all. Remember me kindly to Mrs. J. C. and to Henry—and believe me

Dear John

Your affectionate Coz.

H. COLERIDGE.

N.B. Should you see William Hart [Coleridge], whom by the way Sara does not seem to have met with, give my love to him—and tell Mr. Lisle that I have not forgotten his kindness, and the article on Aeschylus, shall shortly be at his service, if he thinks proper.[1]

---

[1] No such contribution of Hartley's has come to light—perhaps this is the beginning of a habit (so characteristic of Samuel Taylor Coleridge) of talking of literary works as written, which were only conceived.

76

Hartley was apparently quite happy in Mr. Dawes's Ambleside establishment, though occasionally he gives vent to expressions of despair and melancholy. Apparently, too, he managed for a time to avoid the temptation of wine and kept to his school duties with care and industry. He continued his spasmodic efforts to contribute to periodicals (for in November 1826 he began a series of essays in *Blackwood's Magazine*) and was invited to write an essay on poetry for the *Encyclopaedia Metropolitana*, but the article does not seem to have appeared.

The subject-matter of Hartley's letters now takes on the complexion of the country-side. Lost to the affairs of the world, settled in a small community where personal gossip becomes important, Hartley writes of what goes on about him. The persons of whom Hartley writes so charmingly have long since been forgotten, the identity of many of them being preserved only in his letters; but in this intimate, familiar correspondence his friends become our friends, and their activities become of interest to us. Yet the sad, introspective vein remains, and in every letter Hartley has something to say of himself.

About a year after Hartley came to Ambleside Mr. Dawes retired; but the school was carried on by Hartley and Mr. Suart. Later they determined on a school of more pretensions and took a larger house; but for causes quite beyond Hartley's control the school gradually became defunct about 1827,[1] and he was again cast adrift.

One of the most vivid pictures of Hartley at this time is one sent to Derwent by Mrs. Charles Fox, at whose home Hartley was a frequent guest in the years that followed:

'A numerous party had assembled one evening at Brathay Hall. Late in the evening I saw such a figure as I had never seen before glide noiselessly into the bright drawing room, small, dressed in black, with thick, long, raven hair almost on his shoulders, in such a manner as to fill up the space between, and to give the upper part of his form a peculiar preponderance over the lower. In his manner of approaching the lady of the house, his stiff, slow, silent bow, a sort of distressed shyness in his countenance, and a deprecating politeness, like that of the olden times, as I fancied it, and in his whole demeanour there was something strange and unusual. His humorous air of simplicity, his slow measured words, and general eccentricity of manners and appearance, was at first a signal for merriment. But that evening was the beginning of an affection which existed between us in uninterrupted continuance as that of a

---

[1] The date is only approximate, for there is no conclusive evidence to be found. Since there is extant none of Hartley's letters relative to the date of the failure of the school, Derwent's generality, 'after four or five years', must be accepted.

brother for a young sister, and was on my part fed yet more by the beauties of his moral nature, than by my high appreciation of his intellect and his genius.'

LETTER 24

To DERWENT COLERIDGE, ESQRE., *St. John's Coll., Cambridge.*

Ambleside, May 2, [1823.]

Dear Derwent

Long and anxiously have I hoped to hear from you, and, tho' God knows, I am not the man that should complain of your silence, I cannot but feel it as a privation—I am very dreary and damnably hip'd just now, and therefore, would not have you take every thing I may write in my present humour as a deliberate declaration of my feelings—but to tell the truth, I think you deserve to have a specimen of my low spirits, as a punishment for neglecting a very easy method of raising them. Considering indeed, my various and repeated failures, I have many, very many grounds of thankfulness. I am now fixt in something like a profession, with the prospect of obtaining orders[1] after two years, should I then determine on that course—as is certainly my present intention. I have found more kindness both here and elsewhere than I have earn'd. I have been deliver'd, providentially deliver'd, when I was hopeless of delivering myself; and, what is almost equal to all, I cannot find that either my cares or my follies have materially impaired my bodily or intellectual vigour. I receive kind and cheerful letters from father, and mother, and dear Sara. I am in no immediate pecuniary distress—I am free from embarrassment, and need not fear for my future independence. All these, and more than all these, are claims upon my gratitude. They do make me thankful and they ought to make me cheerful, if that word 'ought' and cheerfulness have, indeed, any connection. Why should I trouble you with my complaints—my blighted hopes —my premature winter of the soul? Let them rest with myself—And now for you. What are you doing? How do you agree with Mathematics? What honor do you hope for? Have you any designs on a Fellowship? If you should be so

---

[1] Hartley's plan to take orders never materialized; indeed, he later wrote: 'I do sincerely believe that the All Wise has suffered me to go astray in one path, as a judgment for my presumption in proposing to obtrude myself on another, that is most holy for those who are appointed thereto—most perilous and accursed to all others.'

fortunate as to obtain one, I should scarce advise you to become a resident. A Curacy in town, with your advantages of person and eloquence, would be an almost certain road to distinction, and eventually, to something more than honorable competence; but perhaps a private, or travelling Tutorship, in a family of rank, would as an introduction, be yet preferable. You have served your apprenticeship in that line—the manners requisite you either have, or will easily acquire—the yoke of society to you is light, you are acquainted, both by observation, and by sympathy, with the tastes of fashionable dilettanti—you know how to make learning presentable in good company, and your own appearance will remove some prejudices against it. Meantime, you would be acquiring knowledge of life, probably of foreign nations and languages, and establishing a firm reversion for yourself among the many good things, which patronage is proud to bestow upon Genius, if Genius is not too proud to earn and receive them. Remember, that it is to you that Sara will look. I must and will do my utmost—but all that I can ever do will be less than she deserves and requires. You, besides, owe her more for love than I do. You have seen her and Mama—What a pleasure must that have been! They said you were not very well. I trust you are now restored to perfect convalescence. The term of their absence from the North is daily shortening, still it seems long to me. Father speaks with delight of his daughter—and her Uncles are much pleased with her, as who is not? There is little news in this neighbourhood. Young Ladies hang on hand—a [small] country town, where the self elected censors go [against] all freedom of intercourse between the sexes, by prognosticating marriages as lightly as an opposition prophet prognosticates national ruin. Poor Green[1] the Artist is dead. He has left a large family unprovided for, or nearly so. Jane is an excellent young woman, and for many months during which he has been unable to pursue his profession, has been the stay of the house; but how little is it that a single female can do? They will, I trust, find friends, for they deserve them, and insensibility to distress is no fault of the age.

The Wordsworths, Mr. and Mrs., purpose a trip to the Continent.[2] They are now at Lee Priory in Kent. Miss

---

[1] William Green (1761–1823), water-colourist and etcher; specialized in portraying the scenery of the Lakes.
[2] The Wordsworths visited Belgium and Holland, the trip lasting from May 16 to June 17, 1823.

Wordsworth is but poorly. Dorothy is plain, but a sweet, simple-hearted Girl. Mr. Gee is about quitting the country, his sales have been today and yesterday. The Southeys whom I saw about a week ago are all well. Aunt Lovell is somewhat better than she used to be, but grown unhealthily large. Mrs. Bobson is as good-natured and as hot temper'd as ever; and Mr. Longmire as pleasant and as pompous. The Dicksons are leaving Old Brathay, much to my regret, for Mrs. D. is a great favourite of mine, and so is Eliza, and then there is such an angel of a Baby. Other folks are well—Mr. Dawes surprizingly so. He is not within, but I will venture to send his kind remembrances. John Marshal is gone, a great loss to me. I am shockingly off for contemporary male friends here; indeed, I have hardly an acquaintance of my own sex between 15 and 40. J. Wordsworth is entered at New College, Ox. with a silk gown, for reason which I have not room to explain. Pray do write if it is but half a dozen illegible lines.

Yours, etc.

H. C.

While Hartley was settling down to school teaching, his brother Derwent was going through his 'caterpillarage', as Coleridge later called it, a time when his orthodox opinions were shattered, with odd notions creeping in to take their place. His friends he chose among the more wealthy students, and he naturally drifted into the social life of the University.

One cannot forbear comparing Hartley and Derwent; one was odd, retiring, and self-condemning, a dreamer set in a world of fact; the other strong, aggressive, and self-possessed, a shrewd judge of worldly values. Both came to the university from the freedom of the north; one swam a little in the whirling sea of college life, only to be swept away by an unfavourable gale; the other drifted a short time in the current of undergraduate life, and then with the strokes of a swimmer came to shore on the crest of the waves. Hartley finally surrendered; Derwent was to lead a successful life. From the beginning it had been so; and in 1803 Coleridge, with prophetic insight, had written to Poole of his two sons, then seven and three years of age:

'Hartley is what he always was—a strange strange Boy— *"exquisitely wild"*! An utter Visionary! like the Moon among thin Clouds, he moves in a circle of Light of his own making— he alone, in a Light of his own. Of all human Beings I never yet saw one so utterly naked of Self—he has no Vanity, no Pride, no Resentment, and tho' *very passionate*, I never yet saw him *angry with* any body. He is, tho' . . . 7 years old, the merest child, you can conceive—and yet Southey says, that the Boy keeps him in perpetual Wonderment—his Thoughts are so truly his own. He [is not] generally speaking an *affectionate* child, but his Dispositions are very sweet. A great Lover of Truth, and of the finest moral nicety of Feeling—... yet always Dreaming....If God preserve his Life for me, it will be interesting to know what he will be—for it is not my opinion, or the opinion of two or three—but all who have been with him, talk of him as of a thing that cannot be forgotten. Derwent ... is a fat large lovely Boy—in all things but his Voice very unlike Hartley—very vain, and much more fond and affectionate—never of his Feelings so profound—in short, he is just what a sensible Father ought to wish for—a fine, healthy, strong, beautiful child, with all his senses and faculties as they ought to be—with no chance, as to his person, of being more than a good-looking man, and as to his mind, no prospect of being more or less than a man of good sense and tolerably *quick parts.*'

LETTER 25

To DERWENT COLERIDGE, ESQRE., c/o J. Moultrie, Esqre. Eton, Bucks.

[Postmark, June 24, 1823.]

Dear Derwent

Was there ever any thing like it? I have written a long and elaborate page upon half a sheet of paper, and now it's of no use at all. I can't copy it, for I would sooner eat my words than repeat them, and yet, I assure you, it was curiously penn'd, most quaintly composed of good set phrases, interspersed with sundry scraps of good counsel, very pithy and profitable. Well, it is gone—you will never look on it—suppose it all that is admirable, and by no means judge of it by what I may now write instead thereof. I am in a very idle, whimsical, prosing, versing, preaching, punning humour, and having this present 18th of June dismissed my pupils for the midsummer holydays, I will bestow some pages of my tediousness upon thee, little as thou hast provoked such return at my hands. Thou hast most certainly discover'd that brevity is the soul of wit—never was so short a thing so long in coming as thy most tantalizing epistle. Abortive births are generally too hasty—the mightiest animals have the longest periods of gestation—but thy brain, after an elephantine pregnancy, has dropp'd the moon calf of a mouse. Howsoever, I thank thee, and receive the favour as a civil dun accepts a promissory note in hopes of something better to follow. The first letter after a long silence is seldom full of matter; it comes sneaking like a poor penitent in a white sheet, with margins as wide as a new tragedy. The next, I expect, will be bold and voluble as a sinner freshly shrived, or a felon just acquitted, and ready to sin again with a good conscience. According to your direction, I burn'd your secrets, tho' had they been posted on the church door as bans are appointed to be posted by that choice morsel of Legislation, the late marriage act, no one would have been the wiser. Thou dost write the most incomprehensible cypher that ever baffled mortal curiosity. In the half sheet before mention'd were contain'd some prudent sentences on jealousy, which your own wit may restore with at least as much plausibility as Bentley has recall'd the true text of Milton so long obscured by that officious editor[1]—the luckiest creation of commentarian fancy. Yet I would really have you beware of the green eyed monster. You are framed to make women false; and tho' *cuckoo* is no longer so great a word of fear as in the olden time—yet all men may not be so liberal in their feelings as Lord Portsmouth or so desirous of having their horns exalted as his majesty. At any rate, was I disposed to act the part of Don Juan, I would choose a younger and less affected Julia than Mrs. P. [?] This is very foolish gossip—and very unsuitable to my present mastigophoric dignities. But beware - - - - I am sorry that you have been not well or not happy. I trust that even now the cloud has past away. That you feel at times a want of inward strength, of faith, of hope, and of fortitude, I rather lament than wonder: it is the common, perhaps the universal fine paid for the possession of extraordinary illumination—of lights not derived from the communicable intellect, of assurances which are of necessity their own sole evidence. The mind that depends on these visitations stands in regard to the ordinary understanding, as a Dial to a Clock—when enlighten'd it is certain—when unenlighten'd it is useless. There are periods of doubt, of darkness, of temptation, when the soul is proved—when nothing but the love of God and of man remains to support it; it is then that we discover our strength and our weakness, our dependency on divine aid, and the imperative nature of divine truth. It is then, that by patience we may prove

---

[1] Hartley refers, of course, to Richard Bentley's unsympathetic and atrocious edition of *Paradise Lost* (1732). Bentley later became the subject of one of the biographies in Hartley's *Biographia Borealis*.

victorious, and rise more safe than from no fall. You are not ignorant how severely myself have been tried. I have sunk under the trial—yet not so—as to have lost the power to hope against hope—to believe in spite of my own unbelief. When I review my past life, the soarings and stoopings of my spirit, the sad wreck of purposes and resolves that have perish'd almost before they were, and consider what I still am, and what power of spiritual growth remains in me, I often blush for what I have been, but oftener shudder at what I might have been. I am now not happy, but I am at ease, I am content, and I am cheerful. I have no hopes, and not many wishes, which lie at the mercy of chance, and I have a strength within me which is the more secure because I have learn'd not to confide in it. As our minds have hitherto run a similar course, may you take warning from my fall, and take courage from my recovery. You mention nothing with respect to your plans, either at College or afterwards, but I am informed that you have resign'd the pursuit of Academic honours. Were you so circumstanced, as to have a right to please yourself, I should almost congratulate you on this determination. At present, I will not blame, but I certainly regret it. Inability from ill-health is all-sufficient—but not a happy justification. But the world will think—and what is of more consequence, your friends do think—that your incapacity is closely connected with mental disgust, and that your easy departure from the line wherein you were embarked with the good wishes and evidence of such generous benefactors, denotes something more than mere infirmity of purpose. I do not myself say these things, nor do I accord with them—you are by Heaven appointed Steward of the health of your own mind and body, and can have no right to hazard either at the discretion of another. If you be sane in soul and frame, your worldly success is as certain as any uncertainty can be; still it behooves you to take care to give no unnecessary pain to your friends, and no unnecessary advantage to your enemies; and enemies every man will have who unites to Genius of no common order such graces and accomplishments as, being more visible than Genius, still more excite the envy of the dull, the frivolous, and the vain. Let me, my dear Derwent, advise you to be very cautious in your conduct to Father and to the Gillmans. When in their company be as little of a dandy, or even of a Beau, as you can. Write to them frequently and affectionately, and never argue with Mr. G. If he advert harshly to any part of my conduct, do not say much in my defense; his kind feelings soon return if his pride is suffer'd to slumber. Mother and Sara past thro' here and stay'd three days this week. Sara is well and the same sweet sylph as ever. Mother is, God bless her, not much more Jobish. Do write, to them, comfortably. I will forthwith concoct an article for your magazine,[1] tho' I would advise you, for appearance sake, not to do much for it till you have taken your degree.[2] John Wordsworth is arrived from Oxford. I spend part of the vacation at Rydal Mount. W. has been in Holland. John is laborious as an Ass. Dora is a sweet, good humour'd girl. Little Will is a bore. Fanny White is gone into Scotland. I am deem'd heretical for admiring her more than some others, but I think myself the best judge. I have taken lodgings at the house where Mr. Moy's old house [*sic*] —52 Guineas a year, board and washing included. The Dixons have moved from old Brathay to Field Head, a wilderness of a place for Mrs. D. and Eliza, who are great favourites of mine. Miss Marshall—George Crump's inamorato—has run away with a strolling player—a pity—but no wonder. A fine feast for the he and she tabbies of this most benevolent neighbourhood. Elizabeth Crump is staying with the W's. She is a kind-hearted young woman, but a little too apt to put on airs which only become a beauty of 16. Mr. Dawes is at [. . . ? . . .] All the young ladies would send their love to you, but it's too much trouble to ask. Give my love to Edwin.

[No signature.]

LETTER 26

To SAMUEL TAYLOR COLERIDGE, *Highgate, Near London.*

Ambleside, March 12, 1824.

My dear Father

Trusting to your liberal, and biblical commentator-like interpretation of the term 'week' I hope you will not think it necessary that I should begin this letter in the customary apologetic form—otherwise, I might save my own character for punctuality—such as it is—by antedating this epistle a few days, to bring it within the term specified in my last to dear Mrs. Gillman. However, notwithstanding my imputed

---

[1] This was *Knight's Quarterly Magazine,* where Derwent Coleridge contributed a number of items usually signed Davenand Cecil.
[2] Derwent took his B.A. at Cambridge in 1824.

radicalism, I have too much regard for the venerable institu-
tion of the post-office to shift my own negligence upon its
shoulders. You may conjecture, by this idle exordium, that
my qualemcumque animum is at least *in sano corpore*—would
that I were sure of its meeting you in like good condition. In
truth, as far as my single self am concern'd, I have occasion
for little besides thanksgiving. I am well in body, and prosperous in estate—that is, I have a moral certainty that my
gains are, and will be, more than equal to my expenses.
Personally, I have little to wish for, except your presence and
conversation, of which, the more deeply I reflect on any
subject, the more I feel the deprivation. My time is now so
completely occupied in tuition (from 9 in the morning till
8 at night) that I have not made any progress in the works
of which we have spoken together—but I regret this the less,
in as much as I am convinced, that with my present experience in teaching, I shall, when I obtain more leisure, (and
the time is not distant) be able to produce some thing
more useful, than I could have done at any time past. You
are probably aware of my engagement to furnish an article
on poetry for the Encyclopaedia Metropolitana[1]—I have
made considerable preparations for it, and hope it will not be
wholly unprofitable in other than pecuniary respects. Prometheus, tho rather squeamish at hic, haec, hoc, shall be
forthcoming ere long—But I cannot longer abstain from the
subject, which I fear has a painful influence in your thoughts
and which occupies no small room in mine—I mean dear
Derwent, and the present state of his *mind*—for as to his prospects and circumstances, they are such as we may and ought
to be content with. I think I know you too well to apprehend
your looking with an evil eye on any struggle, any temporary
dimness, or infirmity of the intellect in striving after truth.
If the search were promoted by pure love, and conducted
with honest simplicity, you would not judge harshly, tho'
for any length of time even to the end of life, it stray'd in
error. This worst mistake of a truth lover you would regard
with sorrow, not with anger, even were it a very inexpedient
mistake. I take for granted therefore, that you suspect, in
Derwent's present opinions, something improgressive, some-

---

[1] As far as can be ascertained, Hartley's 'Essay on Poetry' never appeared in
the *Encyclopaedia Metropolitana*. The two editions of the *Encyclopedia Metropolitana*
(1845–8) do not contain this essay; either Hartley did not complete his article or
the editors did not accept it.

thing alien and deadly to the love of truth; or, however you might blame or lament them, as prejudicial to his peace or his interest, you would regard them without hope and comfort. I fear that you imagine that Vanity rules his heart and soul, no less than his words, looks, and gestures—I do [not], and I cannot think this. If I know any one, if I can understand any thing, if I can distinguish good from evil, his heart of hearts is as pure, as loving, as noble—I will not make comparisons—but as any that I have ever long'd to resemble. That he is vain I cannot deny; but surely, you will admit a wide difference between the being vain, and the being *merely* vain—between vanity, as an incidental failing, and vanity, where it is the primary impulse of thoughts and feelings, and, if not a principle, instead of all principles— True, he is vain, and that may have led into imprudence, but it cannot have extinguish'd in him that ardour for the καλόν κἀγαθόν which I know that he possessed at least not much more than a year since, more zealously than any human being, except yourself, whom I have known. Indeed to the last day on which I conversed with him, he was an unhesitating upholder of the strictest system of morals and religion. How, and by what influence he has changed, I know not, but I confidently trust, with the faith of a Brother, and of a Christian, that the work of so many years, so many solemn thoughts, so many holy feelings, aided by all his happier recollections, all his early sympathies, cannot have been so effaced in a few months, that it will not outlast a momentary whim, or a few passing scruples. His misfortune is, that his intellect has no patience. He substitutes pos[itive]ness for certainty—and must always be positive of something. When his sentiments were orthodox, he had no notion that any thing plausible could be alleged against them. Doubts have troubled him, and he has not yet proved strong enough 'to hope against hope.' But folly, is, by its own nature, fleeting, and the good which I am sure is in him, is very hard to quench. I know not whether I have done much more at present than express my own opinion, founded however, on long and intimate knowledge, in this attempt, to mitigate the pain, which I hear from more than one quarter, you have suffered on D's account. It is my purpose to write to him soon, to draw from him, if I can, a full exposition of the state of his mind—and no endeavour shall be wanting to reclaim him, if my knowledge of his nature, in aught may aid me to effect it. How did you like Dora Wordsworth? She is a very pleasing girl—simple and affectionate; uniting her Aunt Sarah's[1] shrewdness to her mother's gentleness. Mrs. W. is now almost solitary, having only her son Willy with her. John is studying hard at Oxford—I read Thucydides with him at Xmas.—Mr. W. and his sister at Coleorton, are perhaps by this time in town. He has been translating Virgil[2]—into a sort of confluent couplet—or if the phrase be not a bull, rhiming blank verses. It is certainly, from the sample I have seen, a powerful work, but between Wordsworth's republican Austerity, and the courtly pomp of Virgil, the contrast is so wide, that I doubt, whether the more perfect correctness of sense, can atone in a translation for such disparity of mode. My dear Mother and Sara are, I believe, well—the latter engaged as hard as her eyes allow her. They were much grieved at the news of Mrs. Gillman's accident—I hope she suffers nothing from it at present. My best love to her, and to Mr. Gillman to whom I will write before very long. I have received a kind letter from Williams which I censure myself for not answering sooner. It is very long since I have heard from Jameson—how is he? I fear he has not received my last, which was [by] a private hand, and thinks that I have neglected him—

Your truly affectionate Son,
H. C.

LETTER 27

To JOHN TAYLOR COLERIDGE, *No. 65 Torrington Square,* or *Pump Court, Middle Temple.*

Ambleside, Feb. 12th, 1825.

Dear John

'Sera numquam est ad bonos mores via'

is the first scrap of Latin we learn, and perhaps the whole extent of Classic lore furnishes not a better. I hope my present epistle will not prove sera for our mutual advantage, tho' in truth I should be not a little ashamed of my tardiness, had I not a somewhat better excuse than procrastination, or even my engagements, multifarious as they are, to allege for it. The fact is—I had the misfortune to strain my thumb about

---

[1] Sarah Hutchinson, a sister of Mrs. Wordsworth's, although a favourite of Coleridge's, hardly ever receives praise from Hartley.

[2] As early as 1819 Wordsworth had completed three books of Virgil's *Aeneid*, and in 1824 he turned again to the subject. Coleridge rather frankly criticized Wordsworth's efforts.

the beginning of the year, in attempting to draw a pair of wet
boots upon wet feet, and have not been able to write without
considerable pain, till lately—and even yet I am very awkward, even awkwarder than usual about it—so you must not
criticise my penmanship. It is too late, I suppose, to wish you
a happy new year—but I may be allowed to congratulate
[you] on your Editorship[1] and your daughter. How I should
like to dandle your little Fanny! for I am as fond of Babies as
if I had twenty—perhaps fonder. It is, I believe, a family
failing with all the Coleridges. Of course she is a lovely child
—as every mother's, and most fathers' children are. My
Mother informs me that you wish to know what work I should
like to review.[2] I feel highly honour'd by your desiring to
enroll me among your contributors and will certainly do my
best to deserve the compliment. As to the particular Book,
I am ready to accept of any you recommend. Only, you
must remember, that I do not possess at present, and indeed,
have not ample means of acquiring that varied historical
and scientific information, much less that acquaintance with
existing circumstances and passing events, which tells so well
in a periodical publication. Like Plutarch I live in a little
town—tho' I cannot say that I am deterred from leaving it
by the same disinterested fear of making it less. Except a
newspaper, I see scarce any thing that speaks of things as
they are—and tho' I have access to far more good books than
I have time to read, they are not precisely the sort to make
an article of. My Uncle S[outhey] is indeed very kind in lend-
ing whatever I wish for, but I am not able to avail myself of
his Library on the spot, far less of the stores of his memory.
Classical literature, Criticism, Poems, Novels etc., I may do
well enough for; and if you can suggest any work in my
way, I will do my very best for you and for myself. I would
avoid all connection with religious or political controversy.
Should you see Mr. Smedley,[3] you will oblige me by asking
when the article on Poetry will be call'd for. I wrote to him
some time ago, in answer to a very polite note, and detail'd

---

[1] John Taylor Coleridge devoted much of his life to the law, eventually
becoming Justice of the King's Bench. Late in 1824 he succeeded Gifford as
editor of the *Quarterly Review*, a post which he resigned in November 1825, finding that his editorship interfered with his legal practice.

[2] John Taylor Coleridge had followed Hartley's career with almost a brother's
solicitude. It was he who finally obtained the £300 from the Oriel authorities; and
now, as editor of the *Quarterly*, he offered Hartley an opportunity to do review-
ing. Hartley did not, as far as can be ascertained, contribute anything to the
Quarterly Review.   [3] Edward Smedley, editor of the *Encyclopaedia Metropolitana*.

my plan etc., but have not since heard from him. Possibly my
letter was misdirected. By the way I did [not] then know
that he was a Clergyman. Pray apologise for my ignorance.

You are no doubt anxious to hear of the Bishop's safe
arrival among his many colour'd flock. I trust the W.
Indies will prove favourable to Henry's health.[1] It is rather
unfortunate that he should have quitted England without my
ever so much as shaking hands with him—but let us look
to a time when we may meet with joy as kinsmen. Mrs.
Patteson[2] has not past the Honey moon, tho' the fickle planet
has changed several times since she became a matron.
Frank [Francis George Coleridge] will shortly resign his
single blessedness. I hear he is prospering. May he continue
so to do. Derwent seems tolerably contented with his situation, and in a settled state of mind.[3] We do not hear from
him so often as we could wish. Sara's dear eyes continue
weak. I wish her mind were at ease, and that her health were
under skilful hands. Country Doctors are seldom able to
prescribe for disorders arising from delicacy of constitution,
however competent in cases of definite disease. For myself,
I am well in health—prosperous circumstances—my income
exceeding my expenditures, and as content with my business as may be—tho' 8 and often 10 hours, of Hic, haec, hoc,
δ, η $\tau\delta$ A B-ab—sometimes relieved by Arma virumque—
is not an absolute sinecure. Great boys are the least agreeable animals in creation. But I do not complain—save of
my lame hand, which will not let me write longer to you. If
I have omitted to mention any one, do not think that I have
forgotten them. I must not, however, conclude without
affectionate regards to your Lady; as for the little ones they
probably do not know of my existence. Remember me to
Ottery friends when you write, and give my love and duty to
my father, if you should see him,
and believe me, Dear J.
Your truly affectionate Coz.
H. C.

The following letter, probably written in 1826, is the first
addressed to Derwent at Helston, Cornwall, where, after taking
Orders in 1825, he had gone as master of the school. Much of

---

[1] In 1825 Henry Nelson Coleridge had gone to the West Indies to join his
cousin, William Hart Coleridge, recently made Bishop of Barbados.

[2] Frances, a sister of John Taylor Coleridge.

[3] In 1825 Derwent took Orders and became master of the school at Helston,
Cornwall.

the letter is concerned with periodical contributions, showing that Hartley was obviously trying to support himself by writing for the magazines; for during the next five years he published essays or poems in *Blackwood's*, *Janus*, *The Gem*, *The Literary Souvenir*, *The Christian Mother's Magazine*, and *The Winter's Wreath*.

Perhaps the most entertaining portion of this letter is that devoted to Wordsworth. Derwent had published in 1826 an essay on Wordsworth in the *Metropolitan Quarterly Magazine* (containing a passage on Wordsworth's later poems, highly offensive to S. T. Coleridge), and Hartley's own remarks on Wordsworth arose naturally from a consideration of his brother's essay.

The engagement of Coleridge's only daughter, Sara, to her cousin, Henry Nelson Coleridge (a son of Colonel James Coleridge), was at first objected to by Coleridge, mainly on the ground of consanguinity. Her marriage, which took place on September 3, 1829, was, however, a happy one. Many of the misgivings of the family were, as Hartley's remarks show, due to a dislike of Henry Nelson Coleridge's rather gay and flippant *Six Months in the West Indies*; but in later years Henry Nelson Coleridge, as friend, disciple, and Boswell of Coleridge, and friend and protector of Hartley, took an important place in the family.

LETTER 28

To DERWENT COLERIDGE, *Helston, Cornwall.*

[1826.]

Dear Snifterbreeches

Beg your Reverence's pardon—I had forgot that I was addressing a Clergyman—I hope you will not like this—my first epistle directed to you in that sacred character—at all the worse, for coming by the hands of a fair quaker[1]—who is bound in conscience to call your church a steeple-house, and, far worse, when you shall be installed, as I hope you will be, in a Daniel Lambert[2] of a Rectory, to refuse paying your tithes. Seriously, my dear Derwent, (alas, how hard is it for a wounded and self-reproaching spirit to be serious) I rejoice to address you in that holy function, which I trust, I had almost said, I know, you have not taken upon you, lightly or irreverently, or for mere motives of interest, but with due sense of all its aweful responsibilities. I can indeed conceive no situation more painful, more humiliating, than that of a man of subtle intellect and tender conscience, reluctantly

---

[1] This letter was delivered to Derwent by Mrs. Charles Fox.
[2] Daniel Lambert (1770–1809), keeper of Leicester jail, was the fattest man on record. He weighed at his death 52¾ stone.

and inefficiently performing your holy office, too good to
regard it as a mere trade, yet devoid of the faith, the love, the
consecration of heart, and soul, and mind, shining forth in
every act, and word, and look, which are needful to make its
ministration acceptable to God and profitable to man. You
will excuse me for saying, that I think parsons in general are
an ordinary set, intolerably vulgar when they are not gentlemen, and when they are, perpetually attempting to effect a
compromise between the gentleman and the parson. Their
whole demeanour is a solemn apology for the unfashionable
obligations of their cloth. There can be little doubt, that late
years have wrought a great reform in the manners of the
clergy, and that you will find fewer cassock'd huntsmen and
reverend toad-eaters than formerly. As for the fiddling
priest I have no objection to him, if he does not fiddle when
he should be otherwise employed. Music is as innocent a
recreation, as a Clergyman can pursue, and even safer for
him than for a layman, whom it exposes to many temptations from which the Clergy are guarded by their gowns. But
I regret that the title Priest should ever have been applied
to a Christian minister—Not to say how foully it has been
defiled by Heathen and papists, it is, as attributed to the
gospel ministry, an unscriptural term, for Priest, be it
remembered, malgré etymology, is the translation of ἱερεύς,
not of πρεσβύτερος. Now I recollect no instance of the word
ἱερεύς in the New Testament, applied to any Christian personage, except to Christ himself, of whose mediatorial office,
and atoning sacrifices—the Jewish priesthood was typical, and
once by St. Peter, to the whole church collectively. (1. Epist.
2 c. 9 v.) Now, the assuming to the governors and instructors
of the church, at any given time, the authority bequeathed to
the church universal in its permanent idea, is an error as
gross as that of those political Heretics who invest the individuality of a king with the majesty which inheres in a state,
and as much worse as popery, whether Roman, or English,
is worse than Toryism—I mean old Toryism, as it was professed by the worthies from Sancroft and Collier down to
Doctor Johnson; for Pittism is a modern and vulgar vice, of
no kindred to the venerable old superstition, which perhaps,
after all, was nearer the truth and certainly more pious, more
imaginative, more generous, than the whiggism of the
Lockians. But well a day—what am I prosing about?—
Running on upon subjects on which you must have firmly

made up your mind, when you perhaps would rather hear what I am doing, and how I am. Simply then, I am well. I have nearly finish'd a longish article for Ebony, part prose, part verse, entitled, 'The Old Batchelor', a signature, which signature by the way, I hope no one will interfere with. The article is bad enough, mainly silly, conceited, and impertinent; but it is fit for the company it is going into. I find great difficulty in acquiring the staid, philosophic style required for the Essay on Poetry. Magazine writing is bitter bad practice, and utterly destroys the faculty of grave, unimpassioned composition. Ebony owes me nearly 10 Guineas, which I wish he would pay. I must stoop to the necessity of dunning, perhaps the sight of my next article, which D.V. shall be off tonight, will relax his purse-strings. Do you ever see the Magazine? I cannot advise you to be a contributor. The book is always in hot water, and you may be answerable to public opinion for more than you write. This I set down among the casualities of trade, but it would much misbecome your profession. I wish you could get your hand into the *Quarterly*. The *British Critic* is as great a miser as Joseph Hume —a preaching, prosing, parsimonious, 5 Guineas a sheet old woman—My Grandmother review, the *British* which I once abused before one of the contributors (but if folks will scribble anonymous cant who is obliged to know anything about them?) is not worth *bribing*; whether it is worth writing for, I cannot tell—that depends upon pay. There are two or three other, exclusively clerical periodicals, with which you may do well to connect yourself. Poor Knight's *Quarterly* is defunct—no wonder—political economy is the worst subject a young man can write upon, and much of the matter was exceedingly flimsy. It was bad policy to attack *Blackwood*, who had shewn a favourable inclination towards it. I read your Lecture on Wordsworth. Very good, Sir very good indeed—especially the prefatory remarks, tho' I do think you have dealt scanty praise to Thomson and Cowper. Thomson, at least, did more for poetry, than any man between Milton and the present generation. He is not an imitator of Milton, unless writing bad blank verse, and using hard words can be call'd imitating him. As the poet of external, visible nature [he] is a complete original. As you do allude to defects in W. you might as well have had a rap at his gasconading prefaces, and that illtimed blundering Supplement, which is as full of sophistry and unfounded assertion as an egg's full of meat. Wordsworth's prose has done more to retard his fame, than the *simplest* of his poems. Why do you say nothing of the 'White-Doe'—so sweet, so beautiful? What a mighty genius is the Poet Wordsworth! What a dull proser is W. W. Esqre. of Rydal Mount, Distributor of stamps and brother to the Rev'd. the Master of Trinity! I hope we shall have the remainder of the *Recluse* ere long, and that W. will have the courage to let his poetical or philosophical creed stand on its own bottom, and not pursue the worse than useless attempt to disguise Spinoza in the ragged Surplice of a Westmorland curacy. You hoped in your last that I rydalmountified a great deal. I certainly shall do so more than I have done, but I have good, sufficient reasons for not being so intimate there as might *seem* advisable. What they are, I may some time tell you—I cannot tell my mother. N.B. You will see the propriety of not mentioning this in your letters to Greta-hall. Dear Sara, God bless her—I have neither heard from, nor written to her, lately, nor to Father either. *Entre nous*—I wish the dear girl had form'd another attachment. Worldly considerations apart, I do not think the author of the *Six Months' Residence*[1] the likeliest person in the world to accord with the exquisite tenderness and susceptibility of her moral and physical constitution. Ever[y] lover, who has had the education of a gentleman, must be delicate, but our Sariola will require delicacy in a husband. How could she indure the lot of Mrs. Gillman? Yet G. is a man of a noble nature. The *Six Months*, is very clever, and tolerably sensible, but there is a flippancy, a vulgarity about it, which I cannot esteem. It might have past in a magazine article, written in a feign'd character, but surely it suits not the accredited confidante and relative of a Bishop. Neither do I think he feels sufficiently the moral enormity of the slave system—tho' he has taken a just view of its political tendencies, and suggests many useful palliatives to the evil, which perhaps the wisdom of man cannot totally remove. At all events, he writes temperately, and practically—avoiding the coarseheartedness of the West-indian party on one hand, and the bravado of Macaulay[2] and such like spouting-club heroes, on

---

[1] H. N. Coleridge's *Six Months in the West Indies* appeared in 1826.
[2] Thomas Babington Macaulay, to whom Hartley alludes, was a contemporary of Derwent's at Cambridge. Coleridge wrote to Sotheby that 'The only uneasiness, I ever suffered on Derwent's account, was from some falsely called free-thinking opinions, which he had *caught* at Cambridge in the society of Austin, Macaulay, and some others whose talents and superior acquirements

the other. I am heartily glad you are fairly out of *that* set. I have made no allusion to your own engagement.[1] If you please you may tell me yourself about it. You know Mama's opinion—I do not agree with it. Had I been engaged, I never should have been the man I have been.

I must conclude—will shortly write again—but Mrs. Fox will be off. God bless you. Pray for your poor Brother.

Mr. Dawes dined with me yesterday—heard Mr. Harden's kind remembrances. Mr. Dawes is young and hearty and brimful of heart as ever. Owen Lloyd is his Curate—an excellent man, beloved by all who know him. Jonson Jackson has been at Ambleside. He is a well-looking, well-informed, gentlemanlike merchant—but his manners are cold. Billy Scambler is married—the only one of our school that is so. Herbert White distinguish'd himself at the capture of Bhurtpore—and is rising rapidly. He has written to me—his letters are admirable—he fully justifies your favourable opinion of his parts and nature, and has redeem'd the very natural if not excusable misdemeanours of his latter boyhood. The rest of that family are gone to town. They are a loss, for Fanny and Sophy were sweet girls, and had better heads and hearts too—than many with worse, gave them credit for—I must away—   [no signature]

After the failure of the Ambleside school Hartley settled in Grasmere (about four miles from Ambleside), first at 'the little rustic inn' and later with Mrs. Fleming, 'an elderly woman, the widow of a farmer, by whom he was regarded with motherly affection'. Without the steadying influence of a regular profession, he became more erratic, a wanderer dependent only on his own whims and desires. Wordsworth, living not far away at Rydal Mount, seems to have watched Hartley with pitying solicitude. To Cottle, Wordsworth wrote in 1829, 'You know he is not quite so steady as his friends would wish'; and Coleridge records, 'Wordsworth says—I lament it but have ceased to condemn him.' Diligently applying himself to composition at one moment, at the next Hartley was likely to wander off for days or weeks, finding shelter only as some kind-hearted rustic took him in. No one could keep track of him. His friends at first condemned, then grieved, and finally accepted Hartley as he was. His will was

were too well fitted to render their infidelity infectious'; but Derwent and Macaulay remained lifelong friends.

[1] Derwent was married to Mary Pridham in 1827. Although Hartley never met Derwent's wife, he seems to have been very fond of her; and in the years that followed she sought in various ways to show a sisterly attitude, sending gifts of clothes, &c., and writing long and affectionate letters.

congenitally weak, and circumstances dealt unkindly with him. The loss of the Oriel Fellowship and his inability to support himself in London may be laid to his door, but the failure of the Ambleside school was not, from all reports, his fault. Yet it was with a sigh of relief that Hartley left Ambleside, for the discipline of boys was alien to his nature. From boyhood Hartley had an instinctive horror of big boys. They persecuted him as a child, and even as a schoolmaster he feared them so much that at night he was wont to dream of his frantic efforts to discipline them and of the torture they caused him.

Among Hartley's many friends was John Wilson (known both as the Professor and as Christopher North), who combined the body of a Greek athlete with the mind of a strong-willed Scotsman. Wilson was as big and self-assertive as Hartley was small and modest; and with the rough affection of a giant he took Hartley in hand. Wilson not only insisted on contributions to *Blackwood's* (of which he was an editor) but even went so far as to *force* Hartley to prepare his essays.

'My father', says Wilson's daughter, 'had a great power over him, and exerted it with kind but firm determination. On one occasion he was kept imprisoned for some weeks under his surveillance in order that he might finish some literary work he had promised to have ready by a certain time. He completed his task, and when the day of release came, it was not intended that he should leave Elleray. But Hartley's evil demon was at hand; without one word of adieu to the friends in whose presence he stood, off he ran at full speed down the avenue, lost to sight amid the trees, seen again in the open highway still running, until the sound of his far-off footsteps gradually died away in the distance, and he himself was hidden, . . . Every one loved Hartley Coleridge; there was something in his appearance that evoked kindliness. Extremely boyish in aspect, his juvenile air was aided not a little by his general mode of dress—a dark blue cloth round jacket, white trousers, black silk handkerchief tied loosely round his throat; sometimes a straw-hat covered his head, but more frequently it was bare, showing his black, thick, short, curling hair. His eyes were large, dark, and expressive, and a countenance almost sad in expression, was relieved by the beautiful smile which lighted it up from time to time. The tone of his voice was musically soft. He excelled in reading, and very often read aloud to my mother. The contrast between him and the Professor as they walked up and down the drawing-rooms at Elleray was very striking. Both were earnest in manner and peculiar in expression. . . . the Professor's athletic form, stately and free in action, and his clear blue eyes and flowing hair, contrasting singularly with Hartley's diminutive stature and dark complexion, as he followed like some familiar spirit.'

While he was teaching at Ambleside Hartley was self-support-ing; but from the time he gave up the school he was always par-tially dependent on his family. His mother sent him small sums of money from time to time, usually through the medium of Mrs. Wordsworth; and she, as well as Mrs. Derwent Coleridge and Sara, provided him with clothing—indeed, his letters are full of acknowledgements for their gifts.

When Hartley left London in 1822 he saw his father for the last time; Sara never returned to the Lake country after her mar-riage in 1829, and Mrs. Coleridge returned only once (1831) after leaving the north with her daughter; Derwent saw Hartley but twice, once in 1843 and again on Hartley's death-bed. Thus Hartley was separated from his family, devoted as he was to them, throughout most of his life. Nor was his exile entirely voluntary. Every one felt that he should remain in the north, where he could be cared for. Wordsworth, indeed, wrote,

'It is far better for him to remain where he is—*where everybody knows him, and everybody loves and takes care of him.*'

But Hartley suffered over his separation, as the following extract from his note-book shows:

'I am far from all my kindred—not friendless indeed—but loveless and confined to a spot beautiful indeed—and dear— but where I am not what I might be elsewhere—where much that was dearest to me has been taken away—where I want a motive to strengthen my will—and worse than all—where I daily know myself my own heart's enemy.'

Hartley was, however, never friendless. Every rustic cared for him; and such families as the Wilsons, the Lloyds, and the Foxes watched over him tenderly. Mrs. Coleridge seems to have dele-gated to the Wordsworths her responsibility for her son when she left with Sara for London; and they, too, opened their house to him, tried to keep track of his wanderings, and even took charge of the small sums of money sent by Mrs. Coleridge for his needs.

LETTER 29

To ALARIC A. WATTS.[1]

Grasmere, May 3, 1829.

Dear Sir

Gratified as I was by the offered opportunity of enrolling myself among the Contributors to the Literary Souvenir, and

[1] Alaric A. Watts, to whom this letter is 'addressed, was the editor of the *Literary Souvenir* and the author of several volumes of poems, now forgotten. To the *Literary Souvenir* Samuel Taylor Coleridge also contributed in 1827 and 1829. Hartley's belated contribution, *Address to Certain Gold Fishes*, appeared in 1830. No further contribution has been identified.

flattered with the prospect of shining on your delicate paper, reposing betwixt your ornate covers, associating with the beauty and fashion of your most lady-like embellishments, and reading my name with others which 'the world will not willingly let die', you will easily conceive my disappointment and chagrin at the mischance or misdirection—which has caused two successive pacquets of my finest manufacture not 'to waste their sweetness on the desert air' but to slumber in their brown paper matrices among the secular lumber of a London Coach-office. My blundering Fate or fatal blundering—has I fear subjected me to an imputation of wilful neglect, and promise-breach, to which, in this instance I cannot plead guilty. That some copies of verse of which I have no transcripts, are by this miscarriage irrecoverably lost, is matter of little moment, but I am sincerely sorry, that, one whom, unacquainted as I am with his person—I should be proud to reckon in the list of Friends—should have occasion to suspect me of slighting his offers, or violating my own engagements. I should not have troubled you with apology or explanation, had I not hopes of yet being introduced to the excellent company which make their annual tour of the British Islands under your auspices. In plain terms—if my contribution would still be acceptable, I should be happy to send you a few compositions—which, if approved, may sally forth with the Literary Souvenir for 1830.

As to the quantity and quality, and that worldly consideration of price—we may easily come to an agreement. I expect the same remuneration which you afford to others of my standing. I suspect that prose will be more in request than verse—of which you will probably have an over supply. Either tales—or essays—ludicrous or serious matter—and as much, or perhaps more than you can find room for, is at your service. I pause for a reply—

and am Sir

Your sincere admirer

H. COLERIDGE.

P.S. Unknown as I am to you, and foreign as the subject may appear from present business, I cannot resist the temptation to thank you for the pleasure I have received from the perusal of many of your Poems. They possess a beauty of moral sentiment, a tenderness of moral affection, conveyed in diction so pellucid, and imagery so proper, that I fear not to assign them a place among those compositions which

H 97

being more loved than admired, sinking in the quiet depths
of human nature, without ruffling the surface, have done,
are doing, and will continue to do—a good work upon earth.
Many persons, some of whom now rest forever, have testified
to me their delight and profit in your strains. You may do
what may render you famous. You have done too much to be
soon forgotten.

LETTER 30

To MRS. SAMUEL TAYLOR COLERIDGE, *Greta Hall, Keswick,
Cumberland.*

The original of this letter has been mutilated, but fragmentary
as it is, it deserves inclusion here.

[1829.]

. . . . . .

I ought to tell you that the parcels etc. arrived safe. Many
thanks for them.

And so H.N.C. has prevail'd, and it is to take place in
August! Happy, most happy and full of hope am I! You, I
know, are always disposed to look with an eye of apprehension, if not of censure, on all matrimonial engagements, where
aught is left to be provided for by the bounties of Tomorrow;
and most certain it is, that the finest resolutions cannot take a
bond of Fate. Professional gains must always be contingent on
favour and circumstance, and children will not always wait
till there is room for them—still—there is a weary, wasting,
perennial evil in engagements indefinitely deferred. Moreover, in the case of the dear Namput (don't scold, I shall not
call her names when she is married) there is an urgent expediency in her acquiring a home of her own.

. . . . . .

her very innocent looks and sweet Christian tones, sweet as a
song of mercy, (to say nothing of the impossibility of the
Devil's approaching any dwelling whereof she is an inmate)
more than discharge all accounts but that of love, which love
alone can pay. But all this is as little to the purpose, as my
usual apologetic exordiums, upon which you once made so
severe an animadversion that I am determined in future, tho'
seven years should elapse between your question and my
reply, to use just the same formalities and informalities as if I
had answered by return of post. So now to business. Cuthbert [Southey], of course, is welcome to the shells, saving and

excepting such and so many of them as you shall think proper to carry to little Dervy.[1] How gladly would I see that little Animal, who, I hope, does not, either in body, soul, mind, spirit, nose, eyes, mouth, or aught else that enters into the composition of that drug of the creation, Man, resemble his sole paternal uncle. Uncle! I can scarce recognize myself under the title. To be sure, it is just the thing for an old Batchelor— and such was I foredoom'd to be—e'er the voice of the first halleluyah of the new-created Angels broke in on the eternal silence. My Brother gets a wife—well—my Sister is to have a Husband—well—I remain alone, bare and barren and blasted, ill-omen'd and unsightly as Wordsworth's melancholy thorn on the bleak hill-top. So hath it been ordain'd, and it is well. The world, knowing or unknowing, will have cause to rejoice in the ordinance, many, many centuries after our bodies are turned to unfeeling, unguilty, irresponsible earth, and when *we* shall be where there is neither marrying, nor giving away in marriage. But Cuthbert is welcome to the shells. I wish I could bequeath to him, along with them, a tithe of the pleasure, I have felt in arranging them (not perhaps according to the most scientific systems of mineralogy and conchology) on dear Wilsy's worm-eaten table, with that beloved check toilet-cover on it—oh! could I impart but a little of the pride, with which I used to exhibit these treasures, assigning them names and histories with the fearless inventiveness of unsuspecting ignorance. Could I disburse from the treasure of my memory, but one farthing in the pound of the mighty debt of happiness which I owe to dream-nourish'd childhood, and pay the dividend to the heirs and assignees of childhood. But I am getting entangled in metaphors, when I ought to be answering plain, matter of fact questions.

Let me assure you that your letters do not lie about, but are either carefully laid aside, or committed to the flames. Besides, were they plastered on lamp-posts with all the miscellaneous and elephantine communications of Quacks, Auctioneers, Bible Meetings, and the Humane Society! I do not believe that a single unauthorized eye would glance over them. What can be expected in a mother's letter to a son, but a doleful inventory of worsted stockings and too well known offences?—Tales not short, of ragged shirt tails—a sad recalling of neglected calls (Rydal Mount to wit, where I

---

[1] Derwent Coleridge's eldest son.

shall certainly call—let me see—before this day week) and sundries of wholesome counsel—which would sicken the indiscriminating stomach of surreptitious curiosity. Seriously speaking, I never, but once, had cause to suspect that any of your letters had been look'd at; that was long ago, I will not say by whom, but certainly neither at Elleray,[1] nor at Grasmere; and I have always taken care to prevent a recurrence of the accident.

Of course I need not tell you that Mr. Townsend call'd upon me at the Professor's, that he dined more than once at Elleray—that I dined with him at Low-wood—(the Dinner consisted of a very small Pike roasted—a small quarter of Lamb—a dish of peas—a Cranberry tart, etc.) that *I* wrote the critique on the Pilgrim to Compostella in Blackwood[2]— that both the Professor and I have read 'the Progress and Prospects of society'[3] and that we both of us admire it hugely —that my outward man is extremely respectable, except as far as relates to Coat; and a new Coat I must have, and probably shall have, before you can send in your veto. Also that I have sent a pacquet to Mr. Alaric Watts, part of which was taken, and part left; item, that I am constructing a long, laborious article upon Hogarth for the Magazine[4]—item, that I have received a letter from Mr. Hood's Brother, informing me, that Mr. Hood has declined the Editorship of that work —and referring me for payment to Mr. Marshall—No— 1. Holborn Bars, the person in whose name I was applied to for contributions to the *Gem*,[5] with the somewhat unacceptable information that said Mr. Marshall is a very mean, impracticable, disagreeable sort of personage, also recommending the *Court Journal* (which by the way, seems to be very good—for nothing—) as a channel for my communications, reserving my poor unworthy verses, which could confer no brilliancy on the *Gem*, to fill up the procession of the *Court Journal*. The *Court Journal* must pay uncommon well, before I will rank myself among its familiars.[6] It seems to be a mere repository

---

[1] Elleray was John Wilson's home in the Lake country, where Hartley was often a welcome guest.   [2] Cf. *Blackwood's Magazine*, July 1829.

[3] Hartley refers to Southey's *Colloquies on the Progress and Prospects of Society*, 1829.

[4] This was the third essay, 'Ignoramus on the Fine Arts', which appeared in *Blackwood's* in October 1831.

[5] To the *Gem* Hartley contributed two poems in 1829: 'She is not fair to outward view', and 'It must be so—my infant love'. Thomas Hood became editor of the *Gem* in 1829.

[6] No contributions to the *Court Journal* have been identified.

of vulgar tattle and fifth-rate gentility. Hood is seldom to be
recognized in its pages. In short, I would as soon have
nothing to do with it. Hood is going to publish a comic
Annual.[1] I wish his speculation may not prove a tragedy to
himself, and a farce to the rest of the world. He is a man of
real genius, and I wish him well. So much for literary matters. And after all this nonsense it will seem too sudden a
transition to speak of the Death which has taken place since
last we met. A good and happy Being has been removed from
the earth—one to whose kind heart I have been deeply indebted.[2] Often while reflecting on the abortive issue of those
cherish'd hopes, which open'd the purse-strings of my friends,
I have regretted the disappointment of the good Lady Beaumont, and wish'd that she might live to see that she had not
bestowed her bounty on an object utterly worthless and in-
grate. But she is gone, and if good spirits of the sainted dead
have any love or power to save for those that remain on
earth, earth may have cause to rejoice at what might seem
a more natural argument of sorrow, the departure of one
of the best of earth's inhabitants. You will receive this letter
by a private hand. Mr. Aychbawm is a Clergyman, private
Chaplain to Lord Grosvenor, who has kindly offered to carry
my burden—Would there be any impropriety in my directing
my next to General Peachey?

Has H.N.C. yet arrived? I hope, I trust, I shall, I determine that I will see him, before very long. If the *young
Couple*—(the Happy Pair I should say) spend the Honeymoon
in Grasmere, I will be near them. Mr. Wilson talks of visiting
Keswick shortly, in which case I shall accompany him. At
any rate, I will be present at the celebration—if I walk all
night, and all night again. In Justice, I ought to give her
away, but,

I remain,

Your aff. son

H.C.

N.B. Loves, remembrances, and respects, I bequeath to
pious purposes. It is formidably late, and they who think
themselves neglected, because I mention not their names,
must bethink themselves, that Night and Oblivion would

---

[1] Thomas Hood's *Comic Annual* was started in 1830.
[2] Lady Beaumont died in 1829. Coleridge, writing to Derwent of her death,
says: 'Poor Lady Beaumont has left me a Legacy of £50, which I shall send to
your Mother to lay out, as she thinks needful, for dear Hartley.'

have been married long ago, if they had not been within the forbidden degrees of affinity. I am not sure whether it is Sunday or Monday. So good night—a very good night to you all.

'Good go with *you*, *and only* night remain.'

LETTER 31
To MRS. SAMUEL TAYLOR COLERIDGE.

[1829.]

My dear Mother

You probably remember asking a few mornings ago, 'What I had to prey upon my mind?' and at the same time severely reprobating the wild and disponding talk I often indulged in. My answer, that I was not born to be happy, seem'd not to satisfy you, and my asserting that happiness was not the certain concomitant of virtue, appear'd to you little less than wicked. Now, disputes arise much more frequently from misunderstanding, than real difference: in the hurry of argument words are seldom selected with accuracy, and what is delivered as a fix'd opinion, is often little more than the imperfect expression of a feeling. So in the present instance, we dispute about happiness, and yet we are not settled about the meaning of the term. Permit me, therefore, to explain what I mean by saying, I cannot be happy; and at the same time to investigate, as far as I can, the primary and secondary causes of my present perturbed state of mind.

In the first place then, I by no means assert that I am incapable of enjoyment. On the other hand, I believe that I take pleasure in whatever pleases any body. I can take interest in any thing, however abstruse, however trifling or even common place it may be, that I see interests others. The world is not to me a barren wilderness; but it is a garden, thick planted indeed, but planted with forbidden fruit, and guarded by dragons. Were I a disembodied spirit, a thing to which no being was compared, without superior or inferior, and possess'd of powers unlimited, for good or ill, I doubt not that I should be active, benevolent, and happy. But all that is human is bounded; our life is all a fruitless effort to break the chain which only death can dissolve. The wider my sympathies extend, the more I feel my helplessness; the greater my faculties of enjoyment, the more conscious I become of the state of circumscription in which I exist, and it would be but poor consolation to a man bound and hand-cuff'd so that he could not stir, to know that he possessed the power of walking. Therefore, when I say that I never can be happy, I mean that I require a larger area, or in other terms, a greater degree of liberty than is compatible with the condition of humanity, which I nevertheless could not be content to enjoy for my particular self, unless those beings were participators which sympathy had made to me a multiplied self.

The proud man differs from the selfish man in this, the former requires that every thing should spring from himself, the latter that every thing should flow towards himself. There is a third character, that will neither be first nor second, but would fain stand alone, neither influencing nor being influenced by any one. Such, at some times am I, but my disposition leading me to love, and therefore of course to a wish to be loved, prevents my long continuing so. Thus I am perpetually kept in motion by two opposing principles, like attraction and repulsion in the Universe, neither of which I feel power to suppress; therefore, the happiness of internal quiet I cannot enjoy.

That there is a peace 'that passeth all understanding' attendant on good courses, I do not deny; this I hope may be mine; but it resides in the depths of the soul, and may co-exist with great tumult in thoughts and passions. The good man has an earnest of the bliss to come, but in the present world, full often sorrow and vexation of spirit.

The inward struggle, the yearning for unbiassed freedom I have described, produces an irritation that makes way for unpleasant thoughts and stirs up feelings not easily expressed or repressed, which find vent in wild paradoxes, the very strangeness of which, when uttered, serves to divert my mind from that brooding on itself so uncongenial to cheerfulness, by calling for all my ingenuity to defend them. Since they give so much pain, I will endeavour to keep them from your hearing, and to divest myself of gloom as much as possible in your presence. But of this be assured. He that made me, alone can alter me; but while I am, what I am, I cannot take for happiness, no, nor for virtue, what is ordinarily palm'd on us for such. According to the common cant, every person that is in no danger of the constable's staff or the Gossip's tongue, or if you like the phrase better, has a good purse, a good character, and, if any, a tolerably well behaved family, is well provided for both in respect to this world and the next. In reality he is a very *respectable* man, but not necessarily either a good or a happy one. As to virtue, I will not at present enter into a discussion on the subject; but for happiness, in the first place, I will venture to say that nothing is more absurd, than to suppose that it is something fixed and to all the same. Different men find their happiness in different ways; and excuse me if I tell you, that if I am to be happy at all, I must be happy in my own way; and that no one can or shall prescribe to me the road I am to pursue to it. I am well aware that entire dependence on other beings is neither an attainable nor a lawful aim. I am content to relinquish it. It is in two things that I shall chiefly seek for comfort; in the improvement and extension of my own energies, and in the sympathy and affection of such of my fellow creatures as I shall find best suited to me, and to which I can best adapt myself. To those whom I love, I will give up all, provided they ask it of my free love, and not as by their own prerogative. I claim, and will maintain my claim, to be sole judge of what is my duty; that which I hold to be such I hope I shall not neglect, but am determined never to betray. With regard to the human objects on whom I build my hopes, who or what they are, or may be, I shall say nothing. (You must be aware I am speaking of such as I may choose or chance to connect myself with, not of those to whom I am bound by nature or gratitude.) The selection of them is a privilege I hold dearer than my life, and will never surrender. My pleasure, my comfort, my labours, my life, I will devote, if need be to you, and to my father, but never will I exclude from my heart that human creature which that heart welcomes, let its recepton cost me what it will.

You have now heard the worst, and I think having made this declaration, I shall proceed in my duties with more alacrity. The charge of desperate indolence you have brought against me with some appearance of reason; I am resolved, and it shall be reasonable no longer. Whatever may be unpleasant in my temper or manners I will strive to correct, tho' the task will be more difficult than that of throwing off apparent sloth, as I have to struggle against natural irritability in the one case and against want of common sense in the other.

However you may judge of me, I still shall remain

Your affectionate son

H.C.

LETTER 32

To DERWENT COLERIDGE.

                  Begun August — Finished August 30, [1830.]

My dear Derwent

The only possible excuse I can utter for not having sooner written to thank you for your acceptable present of apparel, was the hope of announcing better tidings with regard to St. Aubyn[1] than at last I can give. We will begin therefore, with that business at once, and then, I know not how long I may scribble about other matter, postage being out of the question—a saving which may possibly reconcile your orthodoxy to receiving the pacquet from the hand of a Quaker. Some weeks ago I had a letter from St. A. confessing the debt, with much apparent candour, and desiring to be inform'd of its amount and circumstances. I replied, with perhaps more gushing of kindness than some folks might think suitable to the case, not even alluding to the two letters which I had previously written and of which he had taken no notice, but simply desiring him, at his earliest convenience to transmit the money to you. That he has not so done, is I fear, but probable. In your hands, I therefore leave the business, much thanking you for taking such an ungracious deal of trouble upon you. I do not now think that St. A. requires any forbearance from me; he is, or ought to be, rich, and whatever weakness of toleration I may have for such as from imprudence or even self-indulgence, contract debts without the means of discharging them, I profess none for the wilful neglect of payment, when ample means are at command. By no means, however, incur any expense on your own part, nor run the risque of offending any whom your heart or interests would preserve or acquire as friends. I do not deserve it of you, and you as a husband and father, have duties of far greater moment than the facilitating my relief from the penalties of my own folly. If the money can be recovered, it is our Mother's. At all events, I am determined to be free from pecuniary obligations to her before Christmas, well knowing not only the privations she necessarily undergoes from the narrowness of her income, but the poison which such worldly dealings mingle with the pure streams of affection. The sense of obligation is the bane of gratitude, and hard it is to love

---

[1] St. Aubyn was the student whom Hartley had tutored at Oriel; apparently Hartley had not been remunerated for his services.

either one's creditor or debtor, as Child should love a mother. And now for more agreeable matter—

Fearful I am that I have not congratulated you in prose or verse on your happy change of condition. At all events, double gratulation, tho' to the happy couple, somewhat of a bore is not, like anabaptism, a heresy; albeit, there are, or have been, if the world lie not, happy couples, to whom gratulation at three years end would sound ominously ironical as the mistake of old Elspeth, who drank to many more such merry meetings, at her grandson's funeral. But not so to you, I trust, and doubt it not: for although married life cannot be an unwaning honey moon, (it would be tiresome if it were) nor a wife always continue the Fancy's queen, nor a husband be, all life long, a Lover, yet I can believe that when love has been originally wise and innocent, it strengthens with time, and bestows on every age, its appropriate blessing. Tho' causes, even more irremovable than poverty, must, I fear, constrain me for ever to the heart-solitude of celibacy, I am a great advocate for marriage. Married people are in general, better than single ones; they are the less selfish because attention to self-interest is become a more obvious duty; they are far more pious and conscientious, know themselves better, and feeling the intensest anxiety for the moral purity of each other and of their offspring, they experience, what batchelors seldom more than half believe, the infinite importance of purity in itself. But it is a good joke for me to be prating to you on these points, with all the insolence of an article writer. Often have I strain'd my imagination to construct for my own mind's eye a perfect image of *your* beloved Mary, but there is a shadow, a reminiscence that baffles still my efforts, a figure which I know is not, cannot be the true one, always presents itself instead. You perhaps recollect the only rememberable lines in Prior's Solomon[1]—that very respectable poem, which nevertheless, is rather too like one of Mrs. Fry's Newgate-made Quakeresses to be quite so moral as Mat meant it to be. Yet it is an excellent copy of verses, the work of no common genius, but of a man worse both in head and heart for being a Batchelor and a Politician. Well, but the line is:

'And tho' I call'd another, Abra came.'

I do not desire you to describe my Sister in Law. Prose de-

---

[1] Hartley refers to Matthew Prior's *Solomon on the Vanity of the World*, ii. 1. 363.

scriptions create no images, and poetical ones many, but all false. Nothing but deformity can be accurately described. In vain would you schedule her perfections, tell the very hue of her tresses, and communicate to your style the lustre of her eyes, scientifically delineate her facial angles and tell with arithmetical exactness the length, breadth and thickness of every feature. I should be never a whit the wiser. I could give you a long list of causes of the inefficiency of verbal description, but as you will probably read them in my next article (if so secular an abettor of Mother Church as Maga [*Blackwood's*] is admitted within your walls) I shall spare you the catalogue at present. I hope, some time, and not long hence to see the *ipsissima*, that would convict every idolon of falsity. But the little Dervy, the small cretur, the *homunculus* that hath invested me, all unworthy as I am, with the respectable character of Uncle—what wonders are there in him? Whom is he like? I cannot say. But I know what you Papa's and Mama's are like. You are like those conjurors, who pretended to confine familiar spirits and behold futurity, in a clear, transparent piece of chrystal. For what on earth, more pure chrystalline, more innocently insignificant, than the Face of an Infant, that mere abstraction of humanity? Yet, God bless it, the good gossips hold it up to the light (as if it were a bottle of Claret) to the infinite discomfort of its small eyes, and with noticeable inconsistency, in one breath pronounce it 'a little beauty' and yet the very moral of the very ugliest of all its ugly Aunts, Uncles and Cousins. Nay, find more prognostication in the knobs of its skull and the elevation of its forehead and the arc of its eyebrows, and the spherical angle of its eyes, and the balley-corns of its nose (and what I think of no small importance) the interval twixt nose and upper lip, and the cycloid of the open mouth and the conic section of the shut lips, and all the projections, concavities and convexities, of the under lip, chin, and chops, than the Kephanonomantists could in the head of a Donkey, or the Talmudists in Urim and Thummim—But little Dervy, my little Nephew, what kind of little darling is he? Infants, tho' not deform'd, may be described. Is his hair black, like all ours? As far as my recollection goes, Sara, that is to say, Mrs. Henry Nelson Coleridge, is the only light-hair'd Coleridge I know. Are his eyes grey like his Grandfather's? I may add, like his Grandmother's also? I might anatomize him with interrogatories—one thing only I hope,

i.e. that he is in nothing, Soul or Body, like his Uncle. I mean,
as far as his Uncle is himself (and not a genuine Coleridge of
the West); and that, if possible, he may have the address and
self possession of his father, his grandfather's genius and
love of truth, his grandmother's self-denial, his Aunt Sara's
iñnocĕncĕ of heart (but no male creature *can* retain that), and
as much of the good-nature, cleverness, courage, and, since
some defects all mortals must have, even as much of the
sympathetic vanity of the Coleridges as will not interfere
with his more solid virtues. But, Heaven bless him—I almost
wish I were more limited in space. I might not then torment
you with a few scraps of sense swimming like force-meat balls
in a huge tureen of Nonsense.

I may perhaps enclose herewith a few lines to my unknown
sister-in-law, and Nephew; but, as they are not yet written, I
make no promises.[1] I doubt not that you sympathize with me
in rejoicings at our dear Sara's nuptials. As a brother, I
could have wish'd, had such been the will of Heaven, that
she had chosen a richer man, and that a richer man had
chosen her, for she would have well become the highest
station, and is not, of all the women I ever saw, the best
adapted to make the most of a small income, but then, tho'
a love match may not be always prudent, it is always wiser
than a match without love, and what the strictest self-denial,
the utmost frugality consistent with an honorable appearance
in the world can accomplish, they both will do—and Henry
has a fair course before him. Most glad am I, at all events,
that she is out of the house of bondage, and a house of bondage Greta-hall was to her, not by any fault, far less from any
intention of its proprietors, our excellent Uncle and Aunt, but
from her own excessive, I might almost say, morbid delicacy.[2]
Tho' she could not but know, that both she and our Mother
were doing daily services, much above the price current of
reciprocal favors, and that their presence was a perpetual
motive of good and kindly feelings, tho' they knew that their
absence would be regretted and the house never look like

<hr/>

[1] The poem, 'To My Unknown Sister-in-law', as given at the conclusion of
this letter differs considerably from the published version. Cf. *Poems* ('Muses
Library'), p. 79.
[2] Whatever may have been Sara's feelings about Greta Hall (and perhaps
three families of Southeys, Lovells, and Coleridges made a crowded and com-
plicated household) she owed much to her uncle, Robert Southey. She enjoyed no formal schooling, but he taught her several languages, directed her
reading, and really educated her; and she remained ever grateful to him.

itself without them, an uncomfortable sense of obligation, always lay like an incubus on their gratitude. They were afraid
to move, to speak, every wrinkle of that blood-ill-temper
which disorders not diminishes Aunt S.'s benevolence, even
sometimes the young lady airs of our Lady Cousins, seem'd
to their feverish apprehensions like a warning to depart. But
N'importe, she is I hope, a happy wife, and will be ere long a
happy mother. You have probably seen Henry's book on
Homer.[1] It is wonderfully clever, does him much credit. I
thoroughly sympathize, (hang the word it's always intruding)
with his admiration of the old bard, tho' by what subtlety
of logic he reconciles this admiration with his theory of the
Homeridae, I cannot tell.[2] The Galaxy is a stale illustration,
but it should be remembered that the Galaxy is made up of
very little stars. He does not, indeed, pledge himself to the
theory of Wolf and Heyne (a theory which, if I did not abhor
puns of all sorts, and particularly good ones, I should pronounce Wolfish and Heinous), but he states all the arguments for it, and little or nothing against it, except indeed a
hint, that it is not quite certain that the Greeks in the age of
Homer were without an Alphabet. I will not trouble you
with all my own reasons for rejecting the hypothesis, tho' I
mean ere long to trouble the public therewith. But first, as
to the Identity of Authorship in the Iliad—Who has ever
discover'd a single argument against it? There is something,
I believe, about a Pylaemenes, whose father, or whose self,
laments after he is dead. Ulysses, or Diomed call'd Dolon,
Dolon, before they knew his name was Dolon. Such instances might be brought to disprove the authenticity of any
writing, sacred or prophane. Then there is a Poem about the
Cid, very like Homer's Iliad, only not so moral, which is
known to have been written by one man; therefore, Homer's
Iliad was written by twenty. An epic Poem as connected as
the Iliad might be made out [of] the different ballads about
Robin Hood; therefore, the Iliad might be made out of
different ballads about the Trojan War; therefore, what a
sorites—was so made. There must be better arguments for
the position than ever I have heard, or Henry has advanced,
or our Father would never have advocated it, as we both have

[1] i.e. H. N. Coleridge's *Introduction to the Study of the Greek Classic Poets*, 1830.
[2] Coleridge, like his son-in-law, Henry Nelson Coleridge, was a strenuous
advocate of the theory that the *Iliad* was composed by several authors. Both
James Fenimore Cooper and Sir Walter Scott record his remarks on the subject,
and twice in the *Table Talk* Coleridge is quoted as supporting the contention.

heard him do, tho' *entre nous* a German fancy goes a great way with him, and had he been, like me, an almost daily reader of Homer, he would have been as thorough a believer in him as I am. Henry has certainly produced arguments for the posteriority of the Odyssee to the Iliad not a little startling—yet they do not convince me. The identity of manners, moral characters, the very idiosyncrasy of manner in the Author, the manifest and conscious superiority in both poems of the Author to the age and actors of his narrative, overweigh the discrepancies of mythology, which furnish the strongest, indeed the only ground for doubting the Iliad and Odyssee to be the works of one and the same Man. Henry beats me sadly in scholarship, and has access to more books, and of course nothing can be further from my purpose than to enter into controversy with him. He wishes me to review his little volume in Blackwood.[1] Could I obtain admission, I would prefer the *Quarterly*,[2] or why not do it [for] both if I could but disguise my style, as easily as my hand, and surely he must be a bold man who would swear to my MS. for 3 lines together. I should in a review, be altogether laudatory for dear $\Sigma \acute{a} \rho \xi$[3] her sake, who should not by right have married an Author or a Barrister, since she cannot bear to have any of her friends spoken or written against.

Of course I don't think of connection in this epistle. Thank you for your excellent razors—could my chin speak, as I read in the papers that someone has made his play a tune, how eloquent would be its gratitude. I appeal to all living *barbarians*, nay, I invoke the shades of all beards that ever were shaven, from the hairy excrement of the Macedonians reaped by order of the Son of Ammon, to the moustaches of the British heroes, extirpated at the bidding of William IV (whom God grant long to reign) whether shaving, even tho' the razor were forged by Vulcan and tempered in Styx—be not a bore—a bore!—a crying sin—an unnatural crime. Did not Moses forbid males to assume female attire, and what less is it, to expose our chins in female nakedness? Thanks, nevertheless, for your razors, and all things appertaining thereunto. I thank my dear sister-in-law for the silk handkerchief, which for her sake and yours, I take pains to dispose

---

[1] As far as can be ascertained, Hartley never wrote such a review, although in his letters he continued to discuss his plans for its composition.
[2] None of Hartley's contributions to the *Quarterly* (if there were any) has been identified.　　　　　　　　　　　　　[3] Probably meant in fun for $\Sigma a \rho a$.

about my jugulars in such a manner as to bear the least resemblance to a halter. Thanks for your coats, etc., which if they do not make me look much like a Gentleman, at least persuade the world, that I have the spirit to *prig* a gentleman's wardrobe, and therefore, am not 'A poor petty-larceny rascal without the least genius.' The trunk came very opportunely at the commencement of the general mourning—A practice, by the way, I wish were confined to our sex. It is little matter what men wear—most part of us look well in nothing, and such as ever look well, look genteel enough in black. Elderly women, too, with delicate white-linen, and close caps framing their gray locks and venerable faces are reverend in their bombazines, and sad-coloured satin, but while women can be pretty, let them be as pretty as they can, tho' all the kings in Europe were gone to Davy's locker. Talking of Kings, ought we to be glad, or sorry, for the late events in France? Perhaps, ere this letter reach you, we may know better. But it is, and long has been, my fixt opinion that, if any cause authorize resistance to establish'd authority, such cause is to be found in the attempted extinction of the popular voice—that such purpose existed on the part of Charles and his jesuitical advisers, few will dispute, and not many will demur, when I express my belief, that some ulterior plot against the freedom of souls and bodies was design'd by the insane aggression, but, truce, perhaps I speak 'to a willing bondman'. We never quite agreed about politics even in the fervour of our mutual indignation against Queen Caroline's persecutors. My opinions have not changed. Perhaps, it were well not to take up paper about it.

Of Westmorland and the *old familiar faces*, what shall I say? All are not gone—but most are changed. The Rydal Mount family perhaps the least of any, tho' W.W. to me seems yearly less of the Poet, and more of the respectable, talented, hospitable Country gentleman. Unfortunately, his weakest points, his extreme irritability of self-approbation and parsimony of praise to contemporary authors are much *in statu quo*. This is a little ungrateful, for he always applauds my attempts; but what he would do, if they were favourites with the public, no matter. They were all hugely belly-ached with Townshend's articles in *Blackwood*, which was almost as silly as the articles themselves. C. H. Townshend[1] is a pretty man, with

---

[1] Chauncey Hare Townshend (1798–1868), the poet, had met Hartley many years before at Keswick.

a pretty Lady, and divers little dogs, who has written some very sweet verses, and is altogether a man whom one may talk with, and love; but how, with his maidenly face, and his soft lisping voice, he could set up for a critical assassin—A Satyrist of the 'reigning Vice', a writer of Tragedies of the Satanic school—it caps me. But Gentlemen Writers seldom hear the same harsh truths that we of the trade, have injected into us. They are sure of as much admiration as they want, among their own set—and it's little a Man sees or hears of the world in the inside of his own carriage. John Wordsworth, a truly respectable Clergyman, and Rector of Moresby, a Parish on the coast of Cumberland—Patron Lord Lonsdale —is about to be married to Miss Curwen, a very amiable young Lady, quite pretty enough, but whether rich enough I have my doubts, as old Capricorn left his estates much encumbered—which I am sorry for, since Henry Curwen is a most excellent, right-hearted, and right-minded man, and John Wordsworth is so truly estimable, and so much what a Minister of the Gospel should be, and withal, so unlikely to fall foolishly in love, that I am sure the woman of his choice must be what a minister's wife should be. Dora, as sweet a creature as ever breath'd, suffers sadly from debility. I have my suspicions that she would be a healthier matron than she is a Virgin, but strong indeed must be the love that could induce her to leave her father, whom she almost adores, and who quite doats upon her. I am afraid there is little hope at present of another portion of the *Recluse*, but it must delight every lover of mankind to see how the influence of Wordsworth's poetry is diverging, spreading over society, benefitting the heart and soul of the Species, and indirectly operating upon thousands, who haply, never read, or will read, a single page of his fine Volumes. Of the Southeys I now see comparatively little. Uncle is the same—no, not quite the same: years have not left untouch'd his heart, the years cannot render him less fit for heaven, but time and death, and perhaps a continuance of mental labour, not always genial or nutritious to his better part, have robbed him of that joyous, ardent, hopeful, heaven ward soaring Spirit he once had. He is despondent, pardonably, yet I must say, culpably despondent with regard to the great interests of human nature, and seems to me by his writings (for I venture not at our brief and distant interviews, to question him personally), to be with all his no-popery zeal, in great danger of becoming a R. Catholic. Nothing but his acquaintance with the impositions, immoralities, and diabolical cruelties of the Church of Rome prevents it, and what man knows as much of them as he does? Of course you have read his colloquies—and with delight—but delight mingled with sorrow, that so much beautiful truth should be intertwined, and in a manner, interpenetrated with so much dangerous error—so much historical research accompanied with so much inconsiderate assertion, such extensive and kindly observation of human life unsupported by a profounder knowledge of human nature. The fictitious communion between a living Poet of the 19th century and the ghost of a Courtier of the 16th is not a happy form for such momentous arguments. It might have done well enough for a single dialogue, but two bulky volumes of ventriloquism and falsetto is too much in all conscience—like this voluminous letter of mine, you will say. Edith May[1] is a very fine young woman, gifted with strong sense and womanly virtues—but cousinship apart—She is not a woman for me. She never makes me rejoice that I am a Batchelor, or lament that I am doom'd to die so. She is too patrician—too fashionable—She looks, speaks, feels, more like a product of the exclusive circles, than the daughter of a lake-poet. I wish Uncle had a daughter like Dora or our own dear Sara. Bertha is a mild, amiable young lady, too near heaven by the altitude of a chioppine— and Kate the sweetest faced little creature I ever saw—In very truth, I am afraid to look at her. Cuthbert is a nice little fellow enough, but rather too childish for his years. It is fearful to think of him, as he may turn out in the wicked world. It is just such indulged, innocent, creatures as he, that are the easiest dupes of vice—liable to be shamed out of their negative virtue—made impudent by the revulsion of excessive modesty—who learn in their fresh-man's term to think drunkenness knowing, and a maidenhead unmanly and unnatural. But let us hope better things, let us pray that his father's good Angel may spread the wings of protection around his head, and that he be not tempted above what he is able. So much for kinsfolk. Now for old Neighbours. Mr. Dawes is as hale, young, positive, and noble-hearted as ever— he has only one pupil, who bids fair to be a Shakespeare as far as small Latin and less Greek can make him so. Owen

---

[1] In the lines that follow Hartley mentions Southey's four children, Edith May, Kate, Bertha, and Cuthbert.

Lloyd is become the Pastor of Langdale, and the diligent, satisfactory performance of his sacred duties has a very favorable effect on his spirits—he is cured of the blues—but very anxious about his friends in France, who, I dare say, are safe enough if they keep out of the range of shot. However, it is perfectly natural. Do you recollect the pretty Miss Moss, Miss Jane Moss, who gave us Sugar-candy? She is now the wife of the great Sugar-maker Brancker,[1] an amazingly rich man, who has bought Croft-Lodge—pull'd it down, and built it up in a style which neither Vitruvius, Palladio, Inigo Jones, Piranesi, nor Sir Jeffrey Wyatville ever dream'd of, even in a night-mare, or under the influence of opium—It is a good house notwithstanding. (I don't mean it is good with tumbling down.) The chimneys, tho' not agreeable to taste, are 'wind-pipes of good hospitality'. It is a genial mansion, where one always meets with welcome, genuine kindness, and a great deal of strong English sense and humour, liberal politics, correct notions of ecclesiastical polity, good dinners, enough and not too much good wine, and excellent bad puns. Mrs. Brancker is a sweet little woman, but like too many sweet little women, in bad health. Our old hostess, Mrs. Robinson, is still to the fore—and I am afraid likely to survive her son, who is going fast down the hill. The Hardens have been for some time abroad, but are returning in September, greatly to the joy of Ambleside and its vicinity. Harden continues the same happy, honest Hibernian as ever and Mrs. John gets rather more Scotch—but without detriment to her heart—which was always the best part of her. Jane is a fine girl, very religious, and her religion is good as far as it emanates from herself, but I'm afraid a few drops of sulphuric acid have been infused into the pure milk of the word, by that abstract of ugliness, that incarnation of Calvinism, that strong minded woman—her aunt Rankin, with whom I fell in hate at first sight. Allan is married to an agreeable young Lady and Jobby wedded to Mr. Simeon's Skeleton sermons. John William, after being the rudest of all possible Cubs, enter'd, somewhat precociously, into his puppyhood, but so much the better, it is over the sooner, and he is now a gentlemanly youth, with considerable talents, and tasteful pursuits. When at Elleray last summer, I frequently saw your old Friend Mrs. Machel—but I was not the star beneath whose influence the sorrowful Nyctanthes

---

[1] James Brancker was one of Hartley's warmest friends.

would unfold her petals or shed her perfume. Seriously, she is the last woman, whom I should have supposed capable of holding such converse, of cherishing such sensibilities, of writing such impassion'd and imaginative language, as her correspondence with you brought forth. The utter want of sympathy, of understanding sympathy, for James, who could feel with her, can only feel, has driven back her thoughts into the center, and only peculiar spells can charm them back again. I should conjecture that Christopher North was no particular favourite of hers, for always reserved, she seems doubly so in his presence, and perhaps, with all her literary tastes, would not wish to exchange her Furness Squire for an Edinburgh Professor. Of Professor Wilson you can have but little recollection. If you knew him, as I know him, you would love him—as all must who know him well—however they may differ from the politics of Kit North, Tickler and the Shepherd, tho' their imaginations refuse to quaff Toddy at the Noctes, and their sensibility be wounded by the critical polemics of Ebony. He is a living confutation of the dogma, that Scotchmen are deficient in humour or generosity—but perhaps the want of tact and delicacy imputed to that nation, have not been wholly supplied by his Oxford breeding. It is, in fact, a defect which no breeding can remedy, tho' the high polish, or rather varnish, of fashionable life may conceal it. Refinement is a deceit[ful] word. There is a fining pot for silver, but there is none for human souls. I do not mean by this, that Wilson is ever offensively coarse or regardless of the feelings of others, nor even that the defect of which I speak appears in his conversation, at least in the presence of females, but now and then, it peeps out in his writings—especially when he means to be pathetic—his pathos is too much like brandy in port wine. Sometimes, too, he commits the crying sin against all taste of speaking amorously of eatables—e.g. 'the voluptuous breasts' of Grouse. This of course is a joke, but it is an unpleasant joke—it affects the mind differently from what it is intended to do. But all this is nothing to set against his multitudinous goodness—to man, woman, child, bird and beast. Mrs. Wilson is an excellent lady, still pretty and young looking in the face —tho' somewhat rotund in person. She has three daughters and two sons—all nice creatures in their way—the eldest son, a fine handsome youth, without many in-door studies, tho' he draws well—the second boy (who is rather too obviously the father's favourite) a mild, simple, truth-loving, and diligent lad—whom I loved as well as I can love a lad—for they are to me of all created beings the least likeable, as companions—an antipathy, which constituted one reason of my failure as a teacher. Maggy, the eldest daughter, is a bold, clever, lady-like amiable tall belle—with a good deal of her father's humour, a very sweet voice, an aversion to study, and a cruel delight in tormenting the Tutor—a pious Meenister of the Kirk of Scotland, who hated her most devoutly and the worse, because he would have fallen in love with her if he had dared. Sorry am I to confess that I sometimes discharged the battery of my own theological reading upon him, in defence of episcopacy, and in execration of John Knox, much more to please Maggy and Mary than in the hope of bringing him over to our truly apostolic establishment. Mary is a very sweet and gentle, rosy dimpled lassy—English in heart, and Scotch in accent—of a full, squeezable figure, and so comely a height that one regrets that she is likely to outgrow it. Then there is the little rosy darling Jane, the general patroness of the dumb creation, in whose cheeks the bronze of Phoebus looks ten-times brighter than the hectic flush of Misses, who are constrained to take care of their complexions, and whose figure is the prettiest for a child I ever saw, and will be beautiful in the grown woman, tho' these devilish contrivances called back-boards and stays never violated her little body—and her only calisthenics are the wild motions prompted by her own happiness. Dear me—la—what a deal I have written—and not half got through. You remember Chucky Doro—She is now Mrs. Benson Harrison—the mother of some sweet children—the same happy, plump, ever smiling, never excursion-reading creature she ever was—yet a most excellent wife to a man double her own age—but rich—which is everything. I grow every day a greater admirer of money—and heartily despise myself for being poor. I should not have troubled you with this long catalogue of acquaintance, had I not thought you would be interested in all that passes on the banks of Winander—I could write a sheet (a la Blackwood) about a thousand things, but must draw to a close—with a few words about my literary plans. Not to trouble you about Magazines and annuals, where what I write or shall write is not worth your precious time and invaluable eye-sight, I trust, D.V. to produce two Volumes of Miscellanies in prose and verse—consisting of such portions of what I have already publish'd, as I think worthy preservation—the Prometheus—and a good many essays, tales, etc., serious and comic, that have not yet seen the light.[1] I have also long ponder'd on a Poem, which could I execute up to my conception, would perhaps take rank with Pollock's *Course of Time*.[2] The subject, if not the title, Idolatry—and likewise a brief treatise or tractate or pamphlet to be entitled—The Freeman's faith—the end and scope of which is to prove, not only that civil and religious liberty are strictly consistent with Christianity (which has been explicitly denied by Infidels, and virtually by professing Christians) but further that there was little real liberty before Christianity, that there is none now out of Christendom, and that all the true freedom on earth has either grown out of Christianity, or is founded on principles which imply the great truths of Christian revelation, and render probable the great facts of Christian history. I would tell you more about it, but I must write no more to night— my eyes ache—and so with thanks to Fred Mont for his little remembrance, tho' a purse is not of much use to me—any more than spectacles to a blind man—and a kiss for Derwent Junior—and kind—remembrances they cannot be—and respects are too cold—and compliments too insincere—and love too warm—good wishes too general—let the word kind find a substantive in the lexicon of your Mary's kind interpretation, for to her it is meant, and universal greeting to all your flock, to be delivered next Sunday, immediately after the first lesson.

I am,
You know what.

Next morning. Please excuse this tautological, unconnected, silly, irreverend scrawl—and read no more of it at a time than suits your leisure and pleasure. I wish you could see Grasmere at this moment—the lake smooth as a silver shield for the most part, but freshen'd by partial currents of air which give relief and coolness to a somewhat sultry and electric atmosphere—one single boat rests on its oar or steals from one bass fishing spot to another. The woods are wearing now their darkest green, a hue less lovely to my eyes than the lustrous, transparent verdure of the spring. So true is Wordsworth's observation (somebody has borrow'd my

---

[1] No volumes of prose or verse were published at this time.
[2] Robert Pollok's *The Course of Time* was published in 1827.

Wordsworth, and I'm like a Jack Tar without his tobacco pouch) that the older we grow, the more we become attach'd to things that typify Youth. Yet this ripe manhood of the year is beautiful still. The sun is shining bright, and yet there is a sombre tint in the air, that blends and modifies the lights and shades—the shadow'd clouds drag slowly over the mountain sides, and the smokes mount slowly as a solemn hymn to Heaven. Jupiter has been unusually pluvious with us—and the good folks are unromantically anxious about the hay day. Friend Fox and his Lady are truly good people and the Widow Carter is goodness itself. I cannot deny a growing partiality not only to Quakers but to Quakerism. This by the bie—Pray write some terrible high church and King book—and get a good fat living—tho' be sure you leave yourself a hole to creep out, should Liberalism be in the ascendant—so that you may turn handsomely and without the imputation of ratting. Remember the Ten Bishops—the Conversion of St. Bob (Peel I mean) which should be observed in the Roman Catholic Church instead of the Conversion of St. Paul.[1] The Spinning Jenny may be canonized as well as Catherine's wheel—or—if engines of Torture are fitter for consecration than machines of trade—the Papists may e'en worship the Tread mill—Pshaw, I would have a new clause in the Commination—Cursed be all they, that make religion a pander to party, and celebrate incestuous nuptials between the Church and the State. But this is heterodox in the west, enough to fright the multitude of Cornish boroughs from propriety. Once more adieu—You must excuse Verse for the present or I shall not finish my article for Ebony.

Friend Fox was gone, irrevocably gone, when I carried the above scrawl'd papers to Dale End. But he left his *better part* behind, and through her gentle conveyance you will probably receive them, when I know not. Should any business sort of concern arise, you may perhaps have a few lines before. I presume, for at this moment I have only presumptive evidence, that Mama is with Sara. When last I heard about her she was at T. Poole's, Stowey, the best of Batchelors, the redemption of Country Gentlemen—the glory of Somersetshire, the antagonist pole to Sir Thomas Lethbridge—Appropos—What a pity that Sir T. Lethbridge is not in Parliament.

---

[1] In 1829 Peel introduced a Bill granting Catholic emancipation.

Representation is not, ought not to be local. It is enough if each interest, each caste and denomination of society are adequately represented. Now, I hold that the Blockheads, a large, powerful, exceedingly respectable, undeniably loyal, and almost exclusively orthodox class were never so well represented as by Sir Thomas—who contrived to be a mere and complete Blockhead, without ever ceasing to be a gentleman. No man can say that Sir T. Lethbridge ever made a fool of himself—far less a buffoon or blackguard, he seems always to have made the best of the brain which niggard nature allotted him. Why did he rat? As a pro-catholic, I always rejoiced in his opposition—as a friend to human nature, I lament his defection. When a man has nothing to recommend him but his honesty, no fraction is vulgar enough to express his worth, when he has ceased to be honest. Well, as Time allows, I will give you a Sonnet—but mind— not to be so severely criticized as you used to criticize my poor efforts. Many are the Sonnets, Songs, Epistles, Elegies, *jeux d'esprit*, humourous and sentimental articles, that I have either strangled in the birth, and murder'd as soon as born, for fear of you. Verily you were the most most merciless, perhaps because the honestest critic I ever met with. But now for the Sonnet.

> Can Man rejoice in joys he may not know?
>   Yes. Brother, truly I rejoice with thee,
>   And with thy Wife, whom much I long to see,
> And often try to picture, so, and so,
> Right glad my fairest fancy to forego
>   For one slight glimpse of her reality;
>   Yet what she is, or has been, or may be,
> (Since human nature has its ebb and flow)
>   You still must be, or live with half a heart—
> And I, whom Nature curst before she made
>   As loving you, have in her bore a part.
> My naked thoughts by you are fresh arrayed
> In wedding garments—and my fancies base,
> In their mean selves, from you desire a grace.[1]

Ah me—I am ill at these Numbers. Do you remember the metrical correspondence we held in the old happy days? I hope these to you are happier—but to me—Well, you are an ordain'd minister—but I fear you will never do for me what

---

[1] This sonnet has not previously been published.

Moultrey [*sic*] did for me, or church wife or baptize babe of
mine—but there is one service—the sublimest our church has
authorized—which you or some one else will have to read
over me—and—were I fit to die, I should say, the sooner the
better, but unfit as I am to live, I am far more unfit to die.

Dear Derwent—

At length I must bring this voluminous epistle to a close,
for Mrs. Fox is on the eve of departure. She is a most sweet
woman, tho' under seal of silence be it spoken, a very wet
Quaker indeed. I wish you could see her two little girls,
the quickest, little, witty, affectionate darlings in the world.
Our poor friend Longmire is no more. Peace to his soul,
and may his infirmities perish with his mortal part. Habits,
first arising from the nature of his business and aggravated
by introduction to the society of men a little above him in
rank, and far below him in every thing else, have broken a
constitution never robust. I fear that his affairs will be found
in much disorder, for he was latterly impaired in memory.
Mrs. Robinson, who bears up as well as can be expected,
intends to sell the premises; but is apprehensive, I fear justly,
that they will not fetch a high price. However, the recent
alteration in the Beer Trade will make malting a plausible
speculation. She will not be in want, but will not be opulent.
Of all God's creatures, old women bear privations the best,
but she shall not want what is required to make her comfortable. You have probably heard of the decease of Mrs. Lloyd
—after an illness of only ten days. She has not left a better
behind. Never did I know so much true Christian fortitude,
and such judicious beneficence coupled with so kind and soft
a heart. I am no general lover of strong-minded women, who
go about doing good, as it is call'd. They are often coarse
natures, who think compassion a weakness, and utterly insensible to any sorrow that is not absolute physical suffering;
moreover they do a great deal of mischief—more even than
your inconsiderate givers, who are bountiful from impulse;
for they encourage tale-bearing among the poor, and teach
them, the only vice, alas, which too many have to learn—
Hypocrisy. But Sophia Lloyd was proof that no virtue is
inconsistent with pure goodness. She is blessed in her children. Grosvenor at least and Owen are such, that I wish it
had pleased Heaven to make me such a man. Willingly
would I give up whatever Genius I possess, tho' now I have

few pleasures but what arise from intellectual exertion, no
hope but what is sustained by the consciousness of intellectual power, no means of subsistence but the revenue of my
invention, nor any prospect of doing good in my generation,
but by the communication of truth; yet were it possible to
exchange my imagination, fancy, or whatever I possess of the
Poet and Philosopher, for the confiding faith, the purity of
heart, and the zeal and love of Souls which constitute the
simplest Christian pastor, I would gladly sacrifice every prospect of fame, and even of fortune—tho' to you I scruple
not to say, that if health be spared me, I can easily acquire a
competence much more ample than I could have expected
in the Church—especially as I am physically unfit for the
duties of tuition, except it were of very young children. Owen
is gone to France to bring over his sisters—they are said to be
partial to French society and French manners—which is to be
regretted, since their continuance in that country without a
mother must be out of the question. Mr. Lloyd is better than
he has been for many years. How I should like to see him
again. I can hardly understand the attraction which has so
strongly attach'd me to him—perhaps it is, that he is the only
man of talent and sensibility to whom I could feel myself
superior in strength of will—no boast certainly. Once more—
adieu. Let me hear from you at your leisure—and be particular in describing my Nephew.

To my unknown Sister in Law.

Mary, our eyes are strangers, but our hearts
Are strongly knitted in strong bonds of love
For one, whom love of thee hath sanctified—
The wilder wanderings of his youthful thoughts
For thee he curbed—for thee assumed the yoke
Of humble duty—bad the world farewell,
With all its vanities of rhyme, and prose,
The secular pomp of gorgeous eloquence,
The victory of worldly warfare—all
That charm'd his soul in Academic bowers
And turn'd his footsteps from austerer paths
Of science absolute, and reason pure.

Not small the struggle and the sacrifice
When Men of many fancies, daring minds
That, for the substance and the form of truth
Delight to fathom their own bottomless deeps,

Submit to creeds authentic, positive laws,
Appointed rites and ceremonial duties,
And he, that Pastor of a Christian flock,
That is no Hireling, drudging at a task
Ungenial, nor intruder bold and vain,
Unhallow'd, unanointed self inspired,
Of all men hath the greatest need of love,
To keep his thoughts, his hopes, his heart at home.
If human speech have aught of holiness,
Three names contain its utmost sanctity
And all we reverence is exprest at once,
In Husband, Father, Minister of Christ;
Or if a holier title yet there be,
That word is Mother.
      Dearest Sister, I
Am one, of whom you doubtless have heard much
Not always well. My name too oft pronounced
With sighs despondent, sorrow, meek reproach,
And recollection drear of blighted hopes
By lips that fain would praise, and ever bless me.
Yet deem not hardly of me. Who best know
Most lightly censure me, and who believes
The dark inherent mystery of Sin,
Doubts not the will and potency of God
To change, invigorate, and purify
The self-abased heart.
      Good-night. E'en now
Perhaps thou art sleeping by my brother's side
Or listening gladly to the soft, sweet breath
Of thy dear Babe—While I must seek a couch
Lonely, and haunted much by visions strange,
And sore perplexity of roving dreams—
The spectres manifold of murdered hours—
But yet—Good Night—Good be the Night to thee
And bright the morrow. Once again, Good Night.

It would be very easy to improve these lines, but as they came to me, so I send them to you.

Whenever we meet again I shall have great difficulty in reverencing your Reverence in so reverend a way as reverend reverences ought to be reverenced. I shall infallibly be calling you Snifter-breeches—or scrawling Derwent is a Dunce, in your sermon covers—or telling that cleanly and humourous tale of 'Good Gracious, you absolutely have blown your nose in your night-cap.' What a subject for Wilsy would that make—What noble confusion and picturesque disarray in the drapery—What anger, surprize and disgust in mother's countenance—and what open-mouthed stolid impenitence in yours! The story serves one good purpose at least—I can always laugh at it—when ever it is proper to laugh—hence I never disoblige a bad punster by looking grave at his efforts to be witty.

You probably have little time for literary labours or I should advise you to write for the Quarterly Theological. It is a very staunch, orthodox work—not ultra in politics, and seldom or never contains any thing which your character would suffer from having imputed to you. I know no other periodical, in which as a Clergyman you ought to dabble— tho' the Quarterly, under Lockhart's management, is very different from what it was under Gifford, whose benevolence (for he was said to be a most benevolent man) certainly did not trickle through his pen. I do not think our cousin John did himself much credit by some of his articles in that work— he is—in truth—rather too Devonshire to be quite clear-sighted on some subjects. An excellent Man truly, and of no mean genius—but apt to mingle his politics and religion with matters in which they have no concern. But this by the bie. Among the visitors to the lakes this season was Mrs. Hemans the Poetess. She is an agreeable woman—but not unconscious of her reputation—looks, dresses, and talks with a certain aim at effect, which tho' the most excusable of all foibles, is not the most commonly excused. What a blessing is stupidity! Besides its other advantages, it confers the reputation of good sense, good breeding, good nature, good politics, good faith, good works—never if you would pass for a thoroughly good sort of man, and a finish'd gentleman, say any thing above the capacity of the dullest man in company—especially if the dull man be older or richer than yourself. Avoid the conversation of famous conversationalists. They cannot bear to be outshone, and in the tierce and carte of logomachy, you are the most formidable opponent I ever encountered. Argumentation is quite your forte, but rather suffer yourself to be beaten, than win of a logician that hath a good living at his disposal. It is perhaps, better to make a feint of resistance, than to acquiesce with every word. Depend upon it, the surest means to make great people pleased

with you is to put them into good humour with themselves.
It is actually more than bed time—So, diddle-diddle-dump-
ling-Whack row de dow.

LETTER 33

To OWEN LLOYD.[1]

[1831.]

Dear Owen

My letters generally begin with an apology for not having
written sooner. This should begin with an apology for the
occasion of writing at all. I am well aware, that on Saturday
morning, I exprest myself with a very foolish degree of
vehemence on points whereon I knew well enough that you
differ widely from me, and without that respect which is
always due to your sacred calling, when vested in a person,
who, as you do, feels its sacredness. The fact is—I mention
it to explain, not excuse my violence of language—that I was
irate at the sneering manner in which Mr. B. H. spoke of
Whately and of Arnold—men whom I should deeply revere
had I never known them, for their uncompromising zeal
in the cause of true Christianity—and to one of whom at least
I feel indebted for greater kindness than I ever deserved, or
can ever hope to repay. Perhaps too, the mere mention of
their names recalled to my mind certain passages in my own
life, the recollection of which is not likely to produce tran-
quility of spirit: wherein the conduct of Whately (I like him
better by that name than by his present title of Archbishop)[2]
was strongly contrasted to that of other and it may be, more
orthodox personages. Yet I cannot think that my words, in-
considered as they were, implied any reflection upon the
church of which you are a worthy Minister. I only meant to
declare my conviction that the Church would be far more
efficient, and its ministers more beloved, more respected and
therefore more powerfully useful, if the State had no lien
upon the Church at all. But we shall understand each other
better if I explain, as briefly as I can, what I do, and what
I do not mean by that separation of Church and State for
which I contend. Politically speaking, I am much more a

---

[1] Owen Lloyd, a companion of Hartley's school days at Ambleside, was the
son of Charles Lloyd. Hartley wrote two poems on the death of Owen Lloyd,
'A Schoolfellow's Tribute to the Memory of the Rev. Owen Lloyd' and 'Epitaph
on Owen Lloyd' (cf. *Poems*, 225 and 238), which are a testimony of his friendship.   [2] Richard Whately became Archbishop of Dublin in 1831.

Tory than a Whig, and least of all, a Democrat. Believing that the exercise of political power never has, or can have, a favorable effect on the moral Being of Men; that the strife of politics tends to weaken or pervert the holy charities which should constitute our happiness on earth, and to divert our energies from that Hereafter, for which alone we were created rational and accountable creatures, I hold it best that those prerogatives which are necessary for the safety and order of society should be placed in a few hands, and that to them, power should rather be an inheritance than a conquest. To the 'powers that be' I profess an unresisting obedience, not presuming to judge of the expediency of their particular measures, as long as those measures respect only the things of this world—so long as compliance is merely disagreeable and not sinful. Incommodum without peccatum can never justify resistance to constituted authority. So far at least, my opinions are scriptural. But I cannot discover, from Scripture or Reason, that civil Governments have in Religious matters any authority at all. Christ has himself in this regard absolved his disciples from the most sacred of all allegiance: 'He that loves Father or Mother more than me, is not worthy of me'—therefore, *a fortiori*, we may conclude that he who fears King or Parliament more than the Truth, which is Christ, is unworthy of his Saviour. But what is truth? So said Pilate and would not wait for an answer. That it is every man's duty to determine for himself, only respecting the determinations of others so far as they supply the materials of right judgement, the means of just induction, and for this purpose, I confess I would rather like the religious experience of the simplest old woman than the decrees of all the legislative assemblies and ecclesiastical councils that ever made the air unwholesome by their congregated absurdity. Even the Ispe dixit of a King, or of a Pope should have more weight than the compromise of a multitude, authorized or unauthorized, for the opinion of a multitude is the opinion of nobody—a thousand bipeds will sometimes agree upon a question, and not one of the thousand have a better reason to render for it, than—'Every body thinks so, so it must be right.' My conclusion, therefore, is that as neither Kings nor Parliaments, absolute or limited, septennial or annual, reformed or unreformed, can alter the essence of the Almighty, or prescribe the issues of his grace, that they confine their legislative activities to matters within their own compass. Let them see that the country is well guarded against foreign aggression, that person and property are as far [as] may be, safe from the attacks of the assassin, the incendiary, the plunderer, the sharper, that the humble, well disposed labourer shall not be tyrannized over by unions or combinations (a duty of government very grossly neglected of late) let them, in short, secure the conditions of moral civilization, and leave the souls, for which they cannot legislate, and would, if they could, legislate most absurdly and wickedly, to the one, sole Sovereign of souls, who appoints and needs no Viceroy over him. You say, my dear Owen, that Christianity lies at the root of all civil obligations. What Christian doubts it? There should be no classification of duties. All are alike religious and absolute. But I cannot see any good reason for consecrating any particular duty more than another. To refer every act and thought to the Father through the Son is true religion—to forge the signature of God to individual obligations is at best ἐθελοθρησκεία and to make any indifferent action a sin or a duty by an express act or vow, is a presumptuous infringement on the prerogative of God. No man has any right to make that sinful to himself, which the Almighty has left discretiously to manhood. Perhaps, you may allege the use of a Marriage Vow—but I deny the inference. Marriage does not make that sinful which before was indifferent. It makes that lawful, (I mean in the religious sense) which without it would be sinful. It does not constitute, but removes a prohibition. It is, in fact, no more than a law of nature, confirm'd by revelation. For no man ever loved a woman but he wished her to love him and him only—and if a woman do love a man, as any man worthy of the name would be loved, she has a determined will and an indefeasible right to be the sole object of his conjugal affection. How ignorantly have the Philosophers, and Fathers, and Schoolmen, and Protestant Divines, and Utilitarian Moralists prated—as if Love and Chastity were contradictory propositions—and Marriage a sort of amnesty, an indulgence for sin by anticipation. How much more wisely, aye more chastely, have the Poets always spoken. The Man who never loved knows not what chastity is, and all that is said in the Bible against fornication, must appear to such a man, mere nonsense. Better to suffer any agony of soul, to know that providence has decreed one 'single to live, and unlamented die,' to be aware as I am, that nature has let the Devil set his cloven foot upon your face, and made you the abhorrence of every sweet and lovely [woman], or that Fortune had thrust you into such an uncomfortable corner, that any man with the least generosity of spirit, would rather die for love in the said corner by himself, than tempt any poor female to half starve in it with him—better—but

Breaks off thus: no conclusion or signature.

LETTER 34

To MRS. SAMUEL TAYLOR COLERIDGE, *No. 1 New Square, Lincoln's Inn, London.*

Grasmere, Feb. 6th, [Postmark 1831.]
My dear Mother
You have, I am afraid, been long thinking that your last delightful letter, written on dear Sara's birth day, should have obtained a more prompt return. That letter was indeed a comfort to me—I have read it again and again; it was the first of yours for many years which I could bear to read twice—I may say the first since the Oriel Business; for even while I had the school and your letters were for the most part full of encouragement, I had a presentiment that it would never do, and therefore your commendations seem'd like reproaches put out at interest. There is none of my delinquency for which I feel so much remorse, as for my foolish compliance with the advice of some well-meaning people who knew nothing of me, in consequence of which—poor Suart was induced to embark in an undertaking ruinous to himself and injurious to his creditors. For all the duties of a Preceptor, except the simple communication of knowledge [I am] as physically unfitted as dear Papa for those of a horse-soldier. For a Teacher who has to deal with Females or young Men, it may be sufficient if he can engage attention, but the master of school-boys must be able to command it, and this is a faculty not to be acquired. It depends upon the voice and eye and nerve. Every hour that I spent with my pupils was passed in a state more nearly related to fear than any thing else. How then could I have endured to be among unruly boys from 7 in the morning till eight or nine at night?—to be responsible for actions which I could no more control than I could move a Pyramid? Strange it may seem, but I have an instinctive terror of big boys, perhaps derived

from the persecution I suffered from them when a little one.
If I am at all unwell or feverish which, thank Heaven, is
much seldomer than I have deserved, these are always at me
in my dreams, hooting, pelting, spitting at me—stopping my
ways—setting all sorts of hideous scornful faces at me—op-
pressing me with indescribable horrors, to which waking life
has no parallel. You have often wished that I had been bred
at a public school. I have not the least doubt that the fagging
and maltreatment of these places would [have] driven me
frantic mad, even to see it. It may often be a Man's duty to
persevere in a profession to which he feels a strong disinclina-
tion, but no man ought to enter on a line of life, for which he
is conscious of an insurmountable incapacity. In my own
case, the difficulty was so far from diminishing by use, that
the increasing disorder of my nerves made it every day
greater. Hence you may conjecture the cause (I mean it not
for a palliation) of the unhappy irregularities into which I
latterly fell. But enough and too much of this. I have a
better excuse than ordinary for my long delay'd reply. I
wish'd to answer your 'comfort with thee-like' to tell you that
I was paid for my labours, and had made a proper use of my
earnings. Now it happen'd that I never heard of the parcel
for a month or more after it was sent, and was perilously
alarmed lest it should have miscarried; for foolishly enough,
I had not seen it book'd myself. At length, however, a welcome letter from the Professor with an enclosure of ten
pounds, assured me that all was right: and that ten pages of
my Article (Ignoramus on the fine arts) were to be in the
February number.[1] I have not yet seen the bo[ok] (we are
block'd up with snow—I have not been able to get even to
Rydal Mount since February came in and the coach is
stopped) but ten pages cannot be much more than a third
of the paper. The rest will appear in March, and of course
will produce another remittance; but I am sorry for the
delay which doubtless is owing to the confounded Politics
that they stuff the Magazine with, to the great annoyance of
Ladies and Liberals; and not much to the satisfaction of sensible Tories, for they are often so coarse, abusive, and inconsistent, that they cannot do much good to the cause they profess
to support. This is justified on the plea that the So call'd
liberals are still worse—but they forget that the democratic

---

[1] The three parts of 'Ignoramus on the Fine Arts' appeared in the February,
March, and October 1831 numbers of *Blackwood's Magazine*.

publications are calculated for the Tap-room, while contrary opinions will be read or listened to only in the parlour. Aristocracy without gentility is an insult to the People. But I am diverging again.

Most of the money, I paid to Mrs. Fleming;[1] with the rest I discharged some old bills, only keeping a few shillings for the pocket. Miss Wordsworth, kind creature, said she would wait for the next vessel. I must write to Henry himself in a day or two, so shall say no more of literary matters here. As I have three good flannel waistcoats, I do not perceive the necessity of purchasing any more at present: by next year I shall be quite rich and out of debt, even I hope, more than out of yours. I did not quite understand you about the thirty pound for which Sir J. St. Aubyn advised Derwent to draw. I had a very polite letter from my quondam Pupil, promising to do the honest thing. I told him in my reply to remit the needful to Derwent, but I shrewdly suspect he has done nothing of the kind. This was the money of which I spoke to Sarah Fox (I love to speak of her according to the fashion of her own gentle society) making a little too free with the American [vice] of Anticipation. That sweet little *woman* (she has two darling tiny ones) conveyed a letter for me to Derwent, three times as long as his longest sermon, but his various vocations and avocations have not allow'd him time to repay me with a word, not so much as Amen. I hear he is, or has been in London, so I need not say more about him or his. And now for my dear little Matron of a Sister and my unknown nephew Herbert.[2] How I should like to see the Madonna and her Babe. 'Is he wean'd?' I almost hope he is, for I see stronger women than Sarinda sadly pull'd down by the little tugging Piggy-wiggies. And yet, a babe at the breast is such a picture: nay—such a reality of sympathetic bliss, that it must be heart-rending to subject the darlings to their first taste of worldly privation. I have prosed and left no room for a Sonnet, even if I had one; but the fact is, I have had so many Babies to write about that I can say nothing appropriate to my Nevvy and I hate to repeat myself. When I write to Hal I may perhaps be in a more poetic vein. I think the verses to little Miss

---

[1] Mrs. Fleming, with whom Hartley lived at Town End, Grasmere, until her death in 1837.

[2] Sara's son, Herbert, was born in 1830. After winning a double first class at Balliol College, Oxford, he became a distinguished philologist and an early contributor to the *Oxford English Dictionary*.

Fleming[1] the best I have written, at least in versification and expression. She was born on Sunday. You probably saw the Tea-table in B.[2] but it does not look so well in print as it sounded when Elizabeth Warde listen'd to it. Ladies' praise makes one overrate one's nothings sadly. However, it was not too bad to keep company with Delta and other periodic rhimers in the same luminous miscellany. One cannot select one's company in a stage-coach. I had a letter from Elizabeth the other day, to which I must soon reply. Uncle Southey, you know, is come home. I did not see him as he passed—indeed such hasty meetings only tantalize and flurry. Edith, I hear is better, and going to be married. I hope her husband will be a Bishop—and even that will not give Eney a Title for which I cannot help thinking she was born. You know I suppose that she is the *lofty beauty* of the Sonnet. I will write, I think, to Aunt Lovell. I can make the freest with her, and perhaps it may amuse her. My friend Archer is gone to Ireland, his native isle, but talks of returning. He is a fine creature, perfectly mad about Wordsworth and Joanna Baillie, and, tho' we hardly ever thought alike, we sympathized admirably. I hope the Rydal Mountians are not hindered by the weather, which certainly has a design against all our lives. I will see them as soon as stirring is feasible—but I am not quite so well as usual myself. Don't be alarmed, however, it's only a slight cold. We had a sight of Christmas dances—And one does get cold on such occasions. It is of no use to cross—you could not read, so with Love to Hal and his wife,

I remain your brat

H.C.

Mrs. Carter is gone—for which I am truly sorry. She wishes to purchase Pa's works, but I must talk about this to Henry. Mr. Brancker is in Liverpool. I will shortly write to Father—Love and duty if you see him.

LETTER 35

To MRS. SAMUEL TAYLOR COLERIDGE, *Hampstead, London.*

Rydal Mount, April 16, 1831

My dear Mother

I enclose you a bill—twelve months after date—which I received this morning from W. J. St. Aubyn. It will be at

---

[1] Cf. *Poems*, 67, 'The Sabbath-Day's Child.'
[2] Cf. *Blackwood's Magazine*, March 1830.

your own discretion to get it discounted or no. I am now writing at Rydal Mount. As Miss Wordsworth has the pen in her hand I need not tell you any thing about them. I will look over the clothes, but I am in no want of any thing but pocket-handkerchiefs and trowzers. Miss W. was kind enough to send me a message, offering to pay any bills that might be pressing, but except a trifle to T. Troughton, (who has been dangerously ill) and £1-16 to a Bookseller at Kendal (which is shockingly old, and was almost forgotten, till I received a nudge in the shape of a dunning letter) there is nothing imminent. Early in May, if not sooner, I shall receive a remittance from Edinburgh, which will set me entirely free from debt, except to yourself: and you shall be paid and over-paid when the poems are publish'd. What is the gross amount of your claims? This £10 will, I hope, do something towards liquidating them. I am rather flurried, and cannot recollect all I ought to tell you, but I shall pay Henry my long promised letter, and send a sonnet to little Herbert, in a day or two. Thanks for Swing[1] and the *Athenaeum* which is very welcome, and well worth Two-pence, tho' you must excuse me warning you not to write in it, as you sometimes did in the *John Bull* from Keswick—no, not a word, for the simple monosyllable 'well' cost a neighbouring Gentleman five pounds. I will look over the clothes; an old coat, waistcoat and continuations, I gave away to the children of poor Aggy Micchle, my late Washer-woman, who is dead, leaving several small children and one almost an infant. There are some more things not wearable, which I leave at the disposal of Owen Lloyd, as good an Almoner as could be chosen, and an exemplary Pastor, notwithstanding that apparent want of dignity on which you were so severe—

> But Dignity's my detestation
> Like Dirt, and Distress, and Damnation.

I will send you the list required, at the first convenient opportunity. I spent a few days with Mrs. Carter at Ullverstone—good old Lady, she wears herself out with acts of kindness. I am afraid she will not be at Grasmere this season. She talks of a journey to Cornwall, where I hope she will find her and our relations well, and the rotten boroughs disfranchised. I am a Reformer, but not a Fatalist. I had nothing to do with

---

[1] H. N. Coleridge's *The Genuine Life of Mr. Francis Swing*, 1831.

Chantley, and don't know who had. I am not quite a month
in arrears with Mrs. Fleming. I mean, it is not a month since
I paid all that was due, leaving a small balance in their hands.
I received £20 for the two parts of 'Ignoramus', the third is
forthcoming. But literary matters I reserve for Henry. Dod-
a-bless a little soul—does it read Greek with its good man of
a night? Lord love it. You see she never grows any older in
my imagination. But she is a sweet creature. Is the little one
weaned? And how is he going on? I am sincerely glad that
my Father is in his be[tter] way. I will write to him, perhaps
to Mrs. Gillman first. Mrs. Carter is desirous to possess my
father's Poems, in the shape they were last produced in. If
they be sent down to me, I can convey them to her, and price,
carriage, etc., will be duly paid. I must contrive to get all
my father's works myself. I have none of them but the
Aids to Reflection, which I rejoice to see a new Edition of
announced.[1]

With best love to Sara and Henry,
I remain, Your dutiful son,
[No signature.]

P.S. Will look over matters and send just account, when I
have done the article I am about, which I must go home and
labour at directly, and try to write a more eloquent style
than I have perpetrated in this epistle. You will probably
see Mr. Wordsworth, and Dora, William, etc. I hope I shall
see or hear of the Keswickians ere long. They are well at
present.

Archer is returned.

LETTER 36

To MRS. SAMUEL TAYLOR COLERIDGE, *No. 1 Downshire Place,*
Downshire Hill, Hampstead, near London.

Grasmere, October 10, 1831

My dear Mother
    I deserve it, and yet to hint the possibility that a son could
outlive his affection for his mother, and such a mother, is
sufficient reproach for a fault great as mine. You cannot,
do not seriously suspect this, for if you did, no profession,
scarce any performance of mine, could exorcise the evil
spirit from your soul, for dead affections have no earthly

---

[1] The second edition of Coleridge's *Aids to Reflection* appeared in 1831.

resurrection—it is vain to puff at the cold ashes of extinguish'd love, to galvanize the corpse of tenderness to a
mimicry of posthumous life. But no, my mother, I never
ceased to love you, tho' times have been, when that love was
more remorse and agony, proclaiming aloud the duties which
it gave no strength to perform. You have not experienced
as your main sorrow, what it is to fear the voice, to shrink
from the eye of offended love, or you would know that any
thing rather than indifference occasion'd my absence when
you were paying your last visit to Rydal Mount;[1] and, after
all, that absence was not wilful, for I did summon resolution
to return, and expected to find you still, but you had departed
just a day. I do not allege this as a palliation of my wandering, but simply as the fact. With regard to my long silence, I
have nothing to say, but that I have been always intending
to write daily, and hourly, but then I thought such an article
or such a page might be finish'd, and you would like to hear
that it was done, and that I received the money, and then,
I thought I would write to Henry and could not tell what to
say about his Homer. My review has been deferred, because
Professor Wilson got the start with his articles upon Sotheby's
translation,[2] and then I was at a loss about his pamphlet,
(which, by the way, I have never received, tho' he mentions
sending a copy for me) and lately, I have had a nasty troublesome cold, cough, and influenza, which has kept me within
doors (the weather has been doleful). I'm getting better and
truly was never so bad but what I might have written, but even
you may understand how much even slight illness increases
the reluctance to set about any thing, which has been delay'd
too long to come with a very good grace at last. Well, here,
half gone, and nothing done, but really your reproach,
gently as it was expressed, has brought strangers to my eyes.
Now for business. I need not tell you how acceptable the
parcel was, and how useful most of the things. The shoes fit
beautifully, the white trowzers ditto. Flannel waistcoats,
which I have begun to wear, are all that can be desired. The
Surtout and brown trowzers can be taken in, an operation
which my dear mother, you had better, in case of sending
another parcel, leave to be done here, for those nice blacks are
a leetle too tight—you must have taken measure from the
living skeleton—I am, however, obliged to you, just the same.

---

[1] Mrs. Coleridge paid her last visit to the north in the summer of 1831.
[2] William Sotheby's *Polyglott Georgics* was published in 1827.

I am sorry that the *Athenaeum* is no longer publish'd in such
a shape that I can get it, for it is well worth two-pence. I can
hardly say as much for the *Carlisle Patriot,* which is a dear
two-penny worth of waste-paper at a fortnight old, seeing it
is nothing but waste-paper 'in its newest days.' Still it is
pleasant to receive any thing which you have handled. I
have an opportunity of seeing papers enough at Mr. Withington's, the present occupant of Allan Bank, a most worthy
Englishman and Tory of Falstaffian dimensions, who has been
extremely kind and hospitable to your humble servant. At
this present, I am sorry to say, he is beleagu'd by an old enemy,
the Gout. Mrs. Withington is a charming woman and has
some dear little children. Oh, how I should like to see my
little Nephews, both of them, I know not which of the
two I would rather choose. If I understand aright, Sara
and her spouse are gone to Ottery without the Bab. Is this
so? I hope they don't alarm themselves about threats and
[. . . ? . . .] flags. Half a dozen blackguard boys may
placard a whole city, and then exult in the 'reign of
terror' they have created; but there will be no insurrection
which a posse of policemen may not put down in an hour.
The people are not desperate yet, they think that it will
be all the same in a few sessions. My own opinion is, that
nothing but a rebellion can prevent Reform.[1] But hang
politics—I wish you were all safe among the hills, where we
talk of Reform as coolly as of the last conflagration, or the
Comet that in the year 1834 is to singe the earth with its tail.
But this levity is rebuked by the thoughts of my Father's
illness. I must, I will write to him, and that forthwith. I
have written to Hood by a private hand, and directed to
Henry's Chambers. I suppose the letter will be safe—no
matter, anyhow. I'm going to send him a pacquet. Have
you seen my last in Blackwood, October? I have been
paid for it £10. There is another in hand; how provoking
not to be able to work at the beginning of the month. I
should have earn'd enough to pay off all my debts—that to
yourself excepted. However, I must fag the harder now I am
well. As soon as I hear of Hal's return, I will write again,
to him or to Sara and enclose a sonnet to the Darl. I am
too stupid just now to make a good 'un. The Wordsworths
are expected to-day. P. Wilson has been here—kind as

---

[1] This refers to the agitation preceding the passage of the Reform Bill in 1832.

ever. Spent a week with him—never had any man a truer friend.

> Your affectionate,
>
> H.C.

I have paid those two bills without troubling Miss W.

N.B. You will think it strange I should not mention Dervy, but it is not because I have forgotten him or his. He never writes to me—but indeed I cannot expect it. I will write to him, nevertheless. I hope Edith's intended is a man of fortune. Her sphere is decided fashion. I should think her fitter for a palace than a rectory. Little Kate is a Darling, and actually condescended to dance with me when they were over here—so did Bertha. I don't think the Winter's Wreath is out yet—I should certainly have heard. It is probably advertised. I will send you a copy when I get one. I have contributed largely, and been paid in part only.[1] God bless us both and all. This is a sad hurried scrawl. I will soon write again, when I am less agitated.

LETTER 37

To MRS. SAMUEL TAYLOR COLERIDGE, *No. 10 New Square, Lincoln's Inn Fields, London.*

February 17, [Postmark 1832.]

My dear Mother

It is no small comfort to receive a letter from you which I can bear to read again and again, and it is only of late years that your Epistles have been of that quality. Even in my happy school-days, the receipt of a pacquet from Keswick, was always an alarm—bad news or good advice, anxiety or lamentation, were bitter ingredients in the cup. At that time, too, to write a reply was the most fatiguing of bodily exertions; so very disagreeable was the manual act of penmanship, that to scrawl an extra copy would have been an intolerable nuisance, and a very severe imposition. I almost wonder, indeed, that I ever acquired a facility in the use of the pen, which I never had, till I became an Author. I know many persons, not otherwise indolent who still hate the business of writing as much as ever I did. At College, your letters were indeed most kind, and as far as concern'd myself, sufficiently cheerful; but then they were darkened with complaints to

---

[1] Hartley contributed a number of items to *The Winter's Wreath* in the years 1829 to 1832.

which I could administer no consolation, and beset with questions, which I might perhaps have answered more accurately had they been put with less uneasy solicitude. After my brief triumph and ultimate failure at Oxford, reproach was well deserved, but not therefore salutary; questions which it was right for you to ask, were not on that account easy for me to answer: even in the brighter intervals a gloomy presentiment hung over me, which made your qualified congratulations seem more reproachful than downright objurgation. But enough, all this is past, and I trust that henceforth our communications will be regular, and if not joyful, serene. Sara's happy marriage, Derwent's excellent conduct and pleasant prospects will, God willing, be a source of increasing comfort to you, which I will not poison, but, as far as in me lies, will endeavour to enlarge. But now to business. Your last, agreeable as it was in the main, spoil'd my dinner, and my day's work; and instead of commencing my letter as you directed, I set off instanter to Rydal Mount, (where my visits have not been infrequent). Sorry I am to say that I did not see Miss Wordsworth. She is slowly, very slowly convalescent. The rest of the Family well, barring Dora's detestable toothache, against which I would gladly read all the anathemas in Tristram Shandy, if it would do her any good. Mrs. W. seems remarkably flourishing, and does not grow older. Indeed, both she and her excellent husband belong to that class of persons, who look very old at thirty and very young at sixty. I believe myself to be of the number. Mr. Wordsworth I cannot conceive to have ever been a youth either in mind or body. Miss Hutchinson looks ten years older than her sister. I have seen younger looking women of eighty. As far as my observation goes, Mothers, if they enjoy tolerable health and ease of mind, bear age much better than old Maids. But of all the cruda viridisque Senectus (Sara will translate for you) of all the *old boys* that ever I saw, commend me to Mr. Dawes. I cannot bear to think of his ever dying, nor do I think he ever thinks of it, other than as a human certainty himself. Happily he never believes, that he had any serious illness, but ascribes his confinement to the Doctors, who would bleed him when nothing was the matter. Of what took place, while all were in such trepidation for his life, he manifestly has no more consciousness than if it had taken place before he was born. His memory and teeth are the only parts of him that seem to testify the lapse of years. He is extremely happy just now, having let or lent (but I believe he refuses all compensation in money) part of his Cottage to his quondam pupil Herbert White, who is now at home on leave of absence, a noble creature, with a lovely wife. I have just been spending a day or two with them. I flatter myself I am a favourite with both. Mr. Dawes takes his meals with them, and insists on paying his share of all expenses. Yet this man, of whom I have known more unostentatious unacknowledged acts of disinterested munificence than of any other (Uncle Southey and Professor Wilson excepted) has been called a Miser by his maligners, and maligners he has, I know not how or why, except, perhaps, because, having been urged by his friends into a profession, for which he had no inclination, he is rather uninspired in the reading-desk and pulpit! Truth to say, he is not a good Parson, but he is an excellent Man. How I have been prosing about nothing—Not a sentence but that about Miss W. to the purpose. I have an article sent to Blackwood which has not yet appear'd. These detestable Politics jam up the periodicals cruelly, and I who could flourish away to some tune, am constrained to leave that most profitable subject untouch'd because I would not willingly contradict the opinions of my family and friends, and cannot coincide with them without wounding my own conscience. Not that I am an advocate for the Bill, but neither am I an advocate for things as they have been, and I have nothing to propose, but what would be, tho' much less democratical, even more radical! But of this to Hal—to whom also all other literary matters. Glad you've seen *Winter's Wreath*. Got £10. Have several offers of work, some of which shall accept; others must think about. A schoolmaster wants me to puff his establishment. Can't do it. Poor old Dr. Bell. What will he do in Heaven, where I suppose all Education is suspended.[1] Wish he'd left Uncle and Mr. W. more, and unincumbered with conditions. A few thousands in trust for me, would not have been amiss. I am not in want of respectable wearing clothes, but must have a hat and a company suit for the summer. My shirts are properly kept in order—Drawers, Stockings, Cravats abundant. Handkerchiefs—might do with some. I have a very good frock Coat, which you sent last, and the trowzers are wearable, but tight things have a sad secondhand look.

---

[1] Andrew Bell (1753–1832) founded the Madras system of education.

D[erwent] had sent me his sermon.¹ It is very good. Glad to hear his dear Mary is better. How the population is increasing—Summat mun be done. Dear Father—I had a letter from Temple, who was much delighted with the interview. I will write to him, not much about myself—that he can learn from others, but about things in general, which will break the ice more comfortably. Best love to him, the Gillmans, Hal and Sal. Mr. Dawes' respects. Dora, Mr. W. and Mr. Quillinan² gone to Keswick.

From your affectionate Son,

H. COLERIDGE.

In the spring of 1832 Hartley had an opportunity for regular employment with a publisher at Leeds. Through his numerous prose and verse contributions to the magazines and annuals he had acquired a literary reputation, and F. E. Bingley invited him to undertake a series of biographical studies. In order to carry on the work with greater facility, he determined to settle at Leeds, about seventy-five miles distant from Grasmere; and the results of his stay there (his *Poems*, and his *Biographia Borealis; or Lives of Distinguished Northerns*, both published in 1833) must have been highly gratifying to him and to his friends.

His mother was extremely dubious of the wisdom of his going to Leeds. Knowing his utter irresponsibility, and feeling that in the Lake country he was at least among friends who would look after him on his wanderings, she feared that he might come to grief among strangers at Leeds. The fact is that she, like every one else, had ceased to believe Hartley capable of self-management. Hartley, however, was more sure of himself, and he seems to have spent the months in Leeds soberly and industriously. While there he lived with Mr. and Mrs. Bingley, until the advent of a second Bingley baby forced him temporarily to seek lodgings elsewhere. He and Bingley got on well, for Hartley was happy, as always, in a domestic circle of which a baby was a member. Yet Hartley found Leeds a lonely place—despite the diversions of urban life—and when he returned to Grasmere in the summer of 1833 it was with almost unmingled feelings of relief.

The business arrangements between Hartley and Bingley were simple enough. Hartley was to prepare at regular intervals a series of biographies of distinguished Lancashire and Yorkshire 'Worthies', in return for a remuneration of £200; and Bingley was to pay £50 for a volume of poetry, to be followed later by a second volume.

¹ *The Circumstances of the Present Times, considered with a view to religious improvement. An Advent Sermon.* By Derwent Coleridge, 1831.
² Hartley refers to Edward Quillinan, who in 1841 married Wordsworth's daughter, Dora.

When the *Poems* appeared in 1833, the volume was well received. In it are included many of Hartley's best sonnets and lyrics—in fact had he published nothing beyond this slender volume, his fame might well rest on it alone. The *Worthies*, too, won almost unlimited praise from the reviewers. The work consists of thirteen biographies, containing studies of Roger Ascham, Richard Bentley, Captain Cook, and others, and although discursive, they form a charming literary product. Walter Bagehot in his essay on Hartley Coleridge, says of the book:

'This Biographia is actually read: a man is glad to take it up, and slow to lay it down; it is a book which is truly valuable, for it is truly pleasing; and which a man who has once had it in his library would miss from his shelves, not in the common way, by a physical vacuum, but by a mental deprivation.'

Unfortunately, Bingley was not a good business man and in 1833 he went into bankruptcy. The *Northern Worthies* had progressed as far as the thirteenth number, and only one volume of *Poems* had been issued. 'My brother', writes Derwent, 'returned to Grasmere, [in the summer of 1833] and, after considerable delay and negotiation, was released from his engagement, through the intervention of an invaluable friend, Mr. James Brancker, to whom my brother had already been indebted for much judicious kindness during his residence at Croft Lodge, near Ambleside, and who continued to the end of his life to regard him with affectionate interest.' Hartley, glad to be free again, returned to Mrs. Fleming's, where he remained until her death in 1837, when he took up his abode with the Richardsons. Save for a brief visit to Sedbergh, Hartley lived in Grasmere the remainder of his life.

It is a curious fact that Hartley Coleridge, whose name is almost synonymous with desultoriness, should have been able, under the right circumstances, to produce such a quantity of literary work in scarcely a year. In a different environment from that of Grasmere, with more opportunity, encouragement, and intellectual stimulation, he might, perhaps, have done full justice to his genius. As it was, the conclusion of the Leeds affair marks the end of what might have been a successful literary career.

LETTER 38

To HENRY NELSON COLERIDGE, *No. 1 New Square, Lincoln's Inn.*

April 15, [Postmark 1832.]

Dear Henry

This must needs be a very brief epistle, for I have not a great deal to say, and I have a great deal to do. But in the first place, I did write about the business you mention'd—

Secondly, I did not receive an answer till yesterday. Blackwood expresses much admiration of the Fletcher Letters,[1] but
thinks their republication at this time would not be just the
thing—requests me to use my influence to induce my Father
to compose a similar series, expressly adapted to the present
juncture—referring to the former, so as to get his foresight
and insight in the clearest point of view, and vindicate his
claim to the character of a political prophet—And this I
think myself would be the more excellent way—but, alas,
is our dear Father now capable of composing any thing without danger to his health, especially upon an irritating subject,
which he can scarce handle according to his convictions,
without setting all the Σφῆκες of the press in array against
him—Bow-wow-wow—the little Dogs and all—but however
—'Tom will throw his head at them,' and they shall find that
it is a head with horns on it. By the way, I had a dreadful
alarm yesterday morning—a letter with a black seal. I was
told it came from London, and never took thought to look at the
postmark, but ripp'd it open in agony—when behold—it was
a very innocent epistle from Ebony, containing the news I
have communicated above, with an explanation of the non-
insertion of my last article and exhortation to produce something excellent. People should never use black wax unless
they are known to be in mourning—it is like a passing Bell.
I have got a job out of Yorkshire—namely to revise a
Biography of Yorkshire and Lancashire Worthies. The first
sample I received yesterday—containing the lives of Andrew
Marvel and Bentley; it seems to be—but no matter—I am
to have 6^d [?] for my trouble and my name—and I shall take
special care to distinguish my workmanship from Mr. Dove's[2]
—the Compiler, who has gratuitously inform'd me, *per episto-
lam*, that he is a Whig and a Dissenter—terms all but synonymous with conceit, ignorance, presumption, and vulgarity.
On Wednesday the eleventh, I return'd from a very pleasant
visit to Keswick—my kind and excellent Uncle ask'd me to
fill up Bertha's vacant space while that lofty Maiden was at
Rydal. Of course, when she return'd to her home, I was
obliged to return to mine. I found them all in as good spirits

---

[1] Hartley refers to S. T. Coleridge's eight 'Letters to Judge Fletcher' on the
Irish Question, which were published in the *Courier* between September 20 and
December 10, 1814. They were not republished until 1850, when Sara Coleridge included them in *Essays on His Own Times*, iii. 677–733.
[2] 'It appears that the execution of this design had been previously entrusted
to another Editor, Mr. John Dove.' Preface to *Northern Worthies*, 1852.

as I could expect, that is to say—Uncle joyous in his goodness—Aunt sometimes smiling—Edith always witty when
she's out of pain—Aunt Lovell enduring her painful lot most
admirably—and Aunt Eliza,[1] the same good, quiet, orderly
governess-like, humble creature she ever was—I wish she
would not behave so much like a poor relation—It is what I
am sure is not the wish of her sister, still less of her sister's
husband. It may seem strange, if at this time of day I assert
that my esteem and affection for Southey has been much
enlarged by a single week's intercourse, and yet such is actually the fact. His excellences heretofore have been held up to
me as example—it is no wonder, therefore, if I look'd at them
with a distorted vision. Now I have seen [him] as he is—
with love, with veneration, with humility. Dear Hal—I have
a vast deal to say to thee about many things which I must
defer till I have a private hand to convey my pamphlet—
mean-while you must not be angry if I contradict your
Lycanthropic Lesen, very flatly in print—All's fair you know
—and I must Defend Old Homer.

The Maum requests me to answer queries about cloathes,
and sends no queries to answer. With respect to the parcel, it
will be acceptable when it comes—but I am not in a hurry. Of
course, I must have the things she mentions—Linen etc., are
in good care, and diligently mended. I have rather more at
present engaged for than I can comfortably do—but I will do
it—So you must excuse short letters. I have learn'd Italian,
and must learn German—which I am learning with the
assistance of a kind German Lady. This will please Father,
who was always desirous that I should study that language.
Would to God I could do some thing better to sustain his
declining years. Do not let him think that I neglected to
write to Blackwood about the business—for it was not the
case. My delay in writing arose simply from expecting of his
answer, which I have reported above. I am setting about the
Prometheus. When it is done, I will send him a copy; till I
have some such recommendation present, I cannot venture
into his presence. I wish I could announce Miss Wordsworth's recovery, of which I cannot bear to resign all hopes—
but I am afraid she is not much better.[2] I shall be rejoiced

---

[1] Eliza Fricker, Mrs. Coleridge's sister.
[2] In 1829 Dorothy Wordsworth was stricken with a serious illness. She
partially recovered, but three years later suffered a relapse, and for the remaining twenty-three years of her life was an invalid.

to hear of Sara's accouchement—I rather wish it may be a Daughter. Did you ever see Mrs. Derwent, or Derwent's Sermon? I hear that she is good and pretty and think that it is *pretty* good.

I thought I could not have fill'd a page—lo—I must needs conclude—with dear love to Mama—and Shorty—and the Sweet

Yours truly—

H.C.

LETTER 39

To MRS. SAMUEL TAYLOR COLERIDGE, *1 Downshire Place, Down-shire Hill, Hampstead, London.*

Leeds, July 24, [Postmark 1832.]

My dear Mother

At the risk of keeping the press waiting, I take up my pen to set you at ease as much as lies in my power. The parcel arrived safe. The things will be very useful—the shirt fits, but is rather too gay for so old a Gentleman as I am grown. I can get the things altered, but I have thought it necessary to get a new black suit—those you sent will do well for every day. My dearest Mother, my conscience smites me for not having acknowledged your kind gifts, but some allowance must be made considering that I have to write eight, nine and ten hours a day to keep up with the press. I expect the printers' devil every moment and the Devil a bit shall I have for him. With respect to my quitting Grasmere and coming to Leeds, I assure you, I did it from a sense of duty, in order that I might relieve you from the burden of my maintenance, and discharge the great debt I owe you, and assist both you and my father.

The work in which I am engaged is a history of the worthies of Yorkshire and Lancashire. Were it not for the expence, I would send the Prospectus, but it may come the next time Mr. Bingley sends a parcel to town. It is to come out in 12—5 shilling parts—perhaps more than you can afford to pay. I am to have two hundred pounds for my labour. Mr. Bingley is also about to publish my Poems, for which I am to have fifty pounds. I am also engaged to assist in a Magazine, for which I shall be handsomely remunerated. It is monthly, and as it costs only one shilling, you may per-haps manage it. I ought to be scribbling the introductory article at this moment, for it should come out to morrow. It

is entitled, The Academic Correspondent.[1] The editor is
Mr. Fenton, Mrs. Green's Son in Law. It may be had of
Simpkin and Marshal, or any other book-seller, I dare say.

If you can get us any subscribers for either work, pray do—
among your wealthy friends I mean.

Understand distinctly that I involve myself in no pecuniary
risk in connection with any of these works. I had no time to
consult you. If I had not gone, the work, to which I was
engaged must have fallen to the ground, to the great loss of
the Proprietor—nor could I have had resolution to quit had
I deliberated about the matter. If you think rightly you will
approve of what I have done. I am comfortable; my host
and hostess are very young married people, highly respectable, and very religious. I shall give them no unnecessary
trouble—they have a lovely baby.

And so, dear Sara has got an Edith—dear creature—I
wish I had time to give it a sonnet. I hope she will speedily
recover from her confinement. As soon as ever our terrible
hurry is over, I will write a long letter to Father, also to
Henry and to the Wordsworths. I am going to write to
Greta Hall, to request my Uncle to give me some information
about authorities for the Lives, which I am sure he both can
and will give me.

My very best love to all and every one, not forgetting my
niece and nephew. I have a sonnet written to the latter but
have not time to transcribe it. Excuse this scrawl—Your
letter which I was dreading has made me very nervous. How
I shall scrawl about Irish Education, I can't tell, for if I
don't write better than this, the Printers will print every word
wrong and I must be half the night correcting the proof.
Don't be alarm'd. I am less in temptation at Leeds, where I
know no *public house people*, than at Grasmere, where, however, if duty and interest permitted, I would much rather be.
I have acted for the best, have made a sacrifice of my inclinations, and am well satisfied with myself. I begin to know
what hard work is. It is not amusing, but it will be something
better. God bless you all.

The Cholera is very destructive among the poor here—
indeed, the wonder is that any escape.

We observe very much the same regimen as Mr. Gillman
recommends. I am glad to hear that James is going on so

---

[1] To the *Academic Correspondent* Hartley contributed an essay, 'Irish Education', in 1832.

well. It is quite time Henry G.[1] should do some thing, but it is not easy to tell what. I am not so ill off that can scrawl. Kiss the dear Babes and their Mother and believe me—

Your affectionate

H.C.

Write soon, or I shall think you are angry.

LETTER 40

To W. FELL, *Ambleside, Westmorland.*

Leeds, October 16, [1832.]

Dear Fell

I avail myself of the opportunity of Tom Green's visit to the lakes, to send you a few lines, which will be more than commonly stupid, in consequence of my having a confounded head-ache and a bad cold. I also enclose you a copy of the first number of the Yorkshire Worthies. If you can procure any subscribers to that work you will be doing the cause a good service. The second number will appear, if all be well, on the first of November. It will comprize the lives of Anne Clifford, Countess of Pembroke, Roger Ascham, Bishop Fisher, (these are all printed), Mason the Poet, and Sir Richard Arkwright. Upon the whole I have been very well, and as far as it is possible for me to be so, very industrious— at least rather hard-worked. I cannot say that Biography is just altogether my forte, for I don't at all excel in plain statement; neither, in the haste with which the work is to be got out, is it possible to hunt out for original facts, or collate original documents, even were they always accessible, which is far from being the case. Moreover, there is nothing in the world so difficult as to write good plain prose, in a style which attracts no notice for itself, but sets off the sense to the best possible advantage. For myself, I find it easier to write simply in verse than in prose. When I compare Southey's biographical style with my own, I confess I am almost driven to plunge myself over head and ears in the slough of despond. Wordsworth would say, and Archer would say after him, that Magazine writing spoils a man for every thing else: but I do not exactly agree to this. A good style would do as well for a Magazine as a bad one. The truth is, that simplicity is a great gift, and the imitation of simplicity is the worst of

---

[1] This refers to the two sons of the Gillmans at Highgate.

affectation. Every school mistress you know, tells every little brat whose nose twangs as if it was the Hell of Bumble-bees, to read as it speaks, not aware that to read either as you do or as you should speak, is one of the most arduous achievements of elocution. The same, mutatis mutandis, holds good of writing. It is easy enough to write colloquially or familiarly, that is, to introduce into your composition a quantum suff. of needless expletives, solecisms vulgarisms and impertinences, (oh las and ah buts, egads and damnes) and fancy that you are quite at your ease, and that your book or epistle differs in nothing from elegant conversation—but fie fie this is affectatious. But there is no occasion to make this here letter a literal translation of Cicero *de Oratore* interlarded with St. Augustine's Confessions. So wishing that you may [find] any thing to like in the Worthies, I leave it to its fate—only if you could get it into the society. I have little to tell you about myself or any body else. I am very comfortable. Mrs. Bingley is a very pretty little woman and has a very pretty baby: so she and I go on very well, my fondness for babies making amends, in the eyes of Mothers, for a multitude of sins. I know very few people in Leeds. Those whom I do, seem to be good natured, hospitable plain folks. The walls of course now plastered with Election puffs and squibs, the newspapers rancorous against one another, but, as far as I can see, the business does not create half so much private dissension, as did the far-famed Westmorland Election.[1] I have heard Mr. Sadler[2] speak in the Cloth-hall-yard. He is a very fine-looking old man, with a white-head, an intellectual forehead, and a gentlemanly lower countenance—his voice is pleasing, though his tone is slightly Yorkshire. It would be hardly fair to judge of his powers by a speech before such an audience, and that too very imperfectly heard, but I really cannot say that it at all came up to my preconceptions of Sadler as a high-minded philanthropist, and a philosophic politician. He gave himself out as the exclusive champion of the operatives, and endeavoured to make them think that his opposition to the Reform bill was solely because it disfranchised the pot-wallopers! This might be so far true, as that

---

[1] Hartley refers to the Westmorland election of 1818, when Wordsworth, in support of the House of Lowther, published *Two Addresses to the Freeholders of Westmorland*.
[2] Michael Thomas Sadler (1780–1835) was at this time the parliamentary leader for the cause of radical working men.

his principal objection to the Bill was the precedent it gave for disfranchisement, tho' I confess I think this the very weakest ground on which it could have been opposed, but at any rate it was not the whole truth. He dwelt earnestly upon the ten hours bill, for which I should be disposed to give him a vote if I had one, which, thank God, I have not, and I hope never shall, till the Ballot is establish'd. But enough of Politics. A Sunday night or two past I heard an old woman preach—mind, an actual old woman, in a quaker close-cap and petticoats: she performed quite as well as the generality of old women who so indelicately array themselves in inexpressibles. The Sunday before I made an attempt to hear a very famous preacher from Derby, whose name I forget, but the Chapel was so crowded that I could not effect an entrance. I just caught a glance at her however, and heard the tone of her voice. She was young, and by no means ugly, but her tone was rather too like that of a stroller actress in a love scene. There was no attempt or disposition to insult or ridicule either of these Evangelistes—which considering that many of them must have been attracted by mere curiosity, and were very distantly related to the classes in which courtesy is supposed to be indigenous, was a favourable symptom of national manners, and though I would not gladly [see] any woman I cared much about turn preacher, I do heartily rejoice in that perfect freedom, which allows all to preach, and compels no one to listen. But Tom is here, and I must conclude. I did intend a shot at Mr. Brancker which I will certainly give him at an early opportunity. I must request you to present him with the copy of the Worthies, and my Compliments, hoping to hear a good account of all in your vicinage. I must also request you to give the little book to Herbert White if he be still with you—if not to Mrs. White, that the enclosure may be sent to him. My kindest respects to Mrs. Claude[1] and her little ones, and tell her I intend her a Christmas present. If I can get away a week, I will trouble you with my presence at that time. Pray write and let me know how the summer has gone with you.

Yours truly,

H. COLERIDGE.

---

[1] Mrs. Claude, the widow of a Liverpool merchant, was a relative of Mrs. Fell's. The Claudes lived for a time in the Lake country, and with them Hartley was on terms of intimacy. A good many of his letters to them have been preserved.

LETTER 41

To MRS. SAMUEL TAYLOR COLERIDGE, *Downshire Place, Hamp-stead, London.*

[Postmark Leeds, November 19, 1832.]

My dearest Mother and Sister

This comes to assure you that I am not dead either of Cholera or, what is more likely, of hard work. I know very well that I ought to have answer'd your letter immediately, and Hal's long before now, but some how or other, I have not. Better late than never. The truth is, that I have so much writing, and am so hurried, that I like to let the pen alone whenever I can, and besides, to tell the truth, I have not escaped an epidemic cold which has been gangin amang folk—but I am quite better now. I mean quite well. Could I, however, have conceived that I could have afforded my dear Sara a moment's ease, or in anywise calm'd her disordered nerves, I would have written whatever it had cost me, and I have been intending to write daily and hourly. I do rejoice that she has at least got the worst over, but it is a sad thing she should have such Frickerish nerves. I know not whether those, or my father's disordered stomach is worse; though I can certainly say rather more of nervous than of dyspeptic disorder, for my own nerves from seventeen till after twenty were dreadfully weak, in fact I was a martyr to the Blue Devils in my youth, and there sprung the root of my misdoings. God has been exceedingly merciful to me; and my fellow creatures exceedingly kind, or my condition had been far worse than it is. I am now, I may say, content with the present, as knowing my state to be far better than I deserve, and not without hope for the future. Literary employment agrees both with my mind and body, and I am happily free from that morbid anxiety about fame, which torments men far wiser than I. If I get praise, it is well—it helps to sell a book, and as long as my scribble sells, I shall not want an employer or sufficient remuneration. If I be abused through thick and thin, I owe no forbearance to the abuser, and shall find an opportunity of repaying him with interest. If nothing at all be said, but that would be provoking. We have just finish'd the second part of the 'Worthies' containing the Lives of Lady Anne Clifford, Roger Ascham, Bishop Fisher, Mason, and Sir Richard Arkwright, (the last composed chiefly of extracts from Darwin,

147

Wordsworth, and the Library of entertaining knowledge).
Have you seen the first part yet? If Hal takes it in, you will get
a sight of it. I would be obliged to you to puff it as much as
you modestly can, but I by no means expect you will much
admire it. I shall never be a Biographer like Uncle. To
morrow, God willing, the first sheet of Prometheus will be
put to press with a dedicatory sonnet to my Father.[1] I shall
not include any ludicrous poems excepting one which you
have never seen, which has a very serious meaning and conclusion. If there be any others which you or any body else
objects to, they shall be thrown aside.

I will write to Hal as soon as he returns and probably to
Father before you see him. Dearest love to Sara, and the
dear little ones. Alas—the Post. More in Dad's letter.

Your truly affectionate Son,

H. COLERIDGE.

N.B. I am writing at the shop, and there is a bothering fellow making a noise in it. The Baby is a sweet creature. O
that I could see yours my dear Sara, and before long I will
see them. In a week's time I shall have all arranged about
money matters, and then I will tell you all about it.

LETTER 42

To MRS. SAMUEL TAYLOR COLERIDGE, *No. 1, Downshire Place,*
   Hampstead, near London.

Leeds, Christmas day, 1832.

My dear Mother
   Your last brought melancholy tidings. I should have
stolen a quarter of an hour to answer before, but really of

---

[1] Apparently the plan to include the 'Prometheus' in the first volume of
Poems was changed, for it was never published during Hartley's lifetime. The
'Dedicatory Sonnet' to S. T. Coleridge was included in the first volume (the
second volume never appearing), and is given below:

> Father, and Bard revered! to whom I owe,
> Whate'er it be, my little art of numbers,
> Thou, in thy night-watch o'er my cradled slumbers,
> Didst meditate the verse that lives to shew,
> (And long shall live, when we alike are low)
> Thy prayer how ardent, and thy hope how strong,
> That I should learn of Nature's self the song,
> The lore which none but Nature's pupils know.
>
> The prayer was heard: I 'wander'd like a breeze',
> By mountain brooks and solitary meres,
> And gather'd there the shapes and phantasies
> Which, mixt with passions of my sadder years,
> Compose this book. If good therein there be,
> That good, my sire, I dedicate to thee.

all earthly tasks I am the worst at consolation, and to attempt
amusing under your, I hope not present circumstances,
might seem to indicate an insensibility to sufferings, perhaps
the severest to which a virtuous being can be condemned to
endure. God grant, that you may have less need of consolation. I hardly dare bid you a merry Christmas! Indeed
merriment was never much to our dear Sara's taste—even
[less] than to yours. She always, at least after her sylph-like,
capering childhood, seem'd to partake much of the stillness
and quiescence of Aunt Southey's nature. You, however, if
you were happy, and not nervous, would have no disinclina-
tion to innocent fun, and Hal I am sure, is meant for a merry
fellow. (Indeed John is the only *grave* Coleridge of the
Devonshire breed), but alas, he will not be merry now, unless
a great change has taken place ere now, which may the
Giver of all good grant, if it be his pleasure.

The little ones, however, Lord love them, will be merry
Christmas day or Good Friday, if they be well. How I long
to see them! But your affection mistook me in supposing
that I had any fixt plan for coming to see you just now, much
as I should like it. I am tied by the leg to the Worthies, and
am not sure that I shall accomplish a fortnight's holy day for
half a year to come. Mr. Bingley and I have now a sign'd and
legal agreement—I am to receive £250 certain for my labour,
and if the work succeeds, an additional £50; but this rests
on Mr. B's honour. I must mention that the whole addition
to the £200 originally bargain'd for, was proposed by Mr.
Bingley himself. For this remuneration I am to furnish the
press with the matter for forty printed pages—which amount
to about seventy two long pages of my scribble, or twelve per
day—no light work let me tell you, and the poems going on
too—but I am well content to live by labour and on the
whole, do not regret, for my own sake, my not having enter'd
a regular profession. Were I now but twenty, and thought
myself at liberty to follow my own free choice, I should certainly prefer the situation of a literary operative to any other
which I could be, unless I could obtain some active and useful situation, as Librarian, or so forth. Of this indeed, I am
not without some dim hopes at present. But enough of this;
I am at all events most thankful to the Almighty that he did
not allow me to consummate my offences by assuming, without *his* call or authority, the function of his minister. Yes,
my dear mother, right thankful I am that I am a layman—

not that I the less revere the true pastor of God's Sheep, wherever he is to be found. My reverence for such a clergyman as Owen Lloyd is greater than I can feel for any other character on earth. By the way, I have to thank you for Derwent's sermon. I am glad it pleased his congregation. I hope it will please the Bishop, or some other of the dispensers of the loaves and fishes. I long to see Derwent, John Wordsworth, and Owen Lloyd, with an excellent living a piece, and I think Derwent has the best chance of the three, if *he play his cards well*—but there's the rub. I have strong and fervent and thankful hopes that better times are approaching for meritorious servants of their Saviour. I am sorry that Hal don't like my sentiments in the Worthies, but if it comes to that, neither do I like all his in his publications. It can't be help'd. If, however, I have ever spoken with unbecoming levity of aught which any good man holds sacred, I repent. I am confident in the goodness of my cause, and know that it needs no questionable weapons. I am going to eat my Xmas dinner to day with Mr. Henry Rawson, one of the most respectable gentlemen in Leeds, brother to George Rawson whose name you may chance to have seen in the newspapers as chairman to Macaulay's committee. I met Mr. Macaulay at the table of a member of the same family—he was very gracious and spoke of his remembrance of Derwent at College. I can't say I was smitten with him at all—he does not seem to be a Liberal of the right, i.e. of the Xtian philanthropic sort. He is not a Clarkson. He is, however, perfectly a Gentleman and this, you Tories will say, is something for a member of the Reformed.

Our election has gone of [f] very quietly, only a little scuffling on the day of nomination. Some of the *respectable* supporters of both parties really seem to think it worth while to dispute about who began the fray; as if there were not plenty of blackguards on both sides! The business does not seem to have created that dissention and rancour in private life which attended the Westmorland Election. By the way, *Lord and Colnel* are in for Westmorland. This will please the Bard. I really plead guilty for not having written to that family since my removal, but then the pen is so seldom out of my hand. I hope my father's lucid interval continues. Love to him and the Gillmans. I never had any thought of including ludicrous poems in the present vol. As Mrs. Bingley is on the eve of confinement, it becomes necessary for me to change my

abode, at least for a time. I have procured them at Mrs.
Mason's, the same Elizabeth Green to whom I addressed my
Valentine,[1] at a guinea a week, for which Mr. Bingley is
answerable. It is as [cheap] as can be expected in this place.
The suit of clothes, hat and boots, and my washing have been,
or are to be paid by Mr. Bingley—of course set against my
account. I am afraid that the Flemings have applied to Miss
Wordsworth for money before now. I wish you would send
me down the account of how matters stand between us. I
will do my best to pay you all. Just at this moment, I would
rather, if it could be avoided, not request Mr. B. to advance
any large sum, for he will have to pay my lodgings and washing weekly, and has had considerable demands upon him
owing to the expence of the Worthies, and failures among
those connected with him in business. But all will be well.
The baby walked for the first time to day, by nown self. Dod
a bess it. We are cruelly thick in this small house; for my
lodgings are not quite ready for my reception. I rather feel
in the way, but they are very kind, and do not make me
feel it.

With best wishes for sweet Sara and kind love to all
                    I remain, Your affectionate Son,
                                              H. COLERIDGE.
P.S. We have had Edwin Atherston[2] lecturing here—he
call'd on me, and was the means of introducing me to the
Rawsons and other primates: he is a good-looking, good-
natured man, and plays well on the Piano-forte and organ.

                        LETTER 43

To HENRY NELSON COLERIDGE, *No. 1. Downshire Place, Hamp-
    stead, London.*

                        Grasmere, Sunday, Sept. 29, 1833.
Dear Henry
    Think not my long silence wholly without excuse. I have
been waiting for intelligence from Leeds, which might have
enabled me to give a more full, true, and particular account
of my affairs than in lack thereof I can now engage to do. I
will, however, delay no longer, and as it is lawful to heal
on the Sabbath day, I will, instead of subjecting myself to
the infliction of another of our semi-evangelical ministers

---
[1] Cf. *Poems*, 103.
[2] This is Edwin Atherstone (1788–1872), author of *The Fall of Nineveh.*

interminable discourses, do my best to heal the anxieties, which my dear Mama must feel about my present condition. In the first place then, I must tell you that I have not left Leeds in debt or in disgrace. The immediate cause of my quitting, was Mrs. Bingley's going to seaside with her parents for a month, taking her two little angels and the nurse with her. Bingley, therefore, prudently enough, determined to shut up his house and lodge at his father's, giving me as he expressed it a *holy day*. It was not absolutely made up at our leave-taking, whether I should return or not. Mrs. Bingley, whose heart I had perhaps won by my fondness for her dear babes, was evidently desirous that I should, but I certainly shall not do so, unless he should determine to resume the publication of the 'Worthies'; in which case, I think myself bound in honour and conscience to fulfill my engagement, which I could not do without the use of a public library. And now, dear Hal, let me tell you, that however ill I can afford to bear any fresh accumulation of blame on my own over-laden shoulders, I beseech you to impute to me solely and entirely, the fault of his opening your letter, and his subsequent passionate reply. It was written, as he confessed, in anger. As for the fines, he never had the least intention of enforcing them, and I knew well enough that the condition was only like the pound of flesh in Antonio's bond—Bingley being no Shylock but rather too little of a Jew for his own interest, in fact one of the best natured, best-hearted, and not one of the strongest headed boys, for he is hardly more in age, that I have ever met with; and if through an irregularity of mine, he should permanently suffer, I should think no repentance enough to atone for the crime. There is one thing, however. His old Dad in Law can't last for ever: and when it shall please heaven to take him, there will be an excellent windfall. But this is very little to you. More to the purpose is— that the third part of the work which I have completed entitles me to a third part of the price engaged for—which together with the 50 for the Poems will surely cover the expence of my board for the time I was there, and the divers et ceteras he disbursed on my account, including washing, postage, two suits of black clothes, two hats, a pair of boots and a pair of shoes. I have earnestly desired him to send in his account, but he has not yet done so. Don't you write to him—it will do no good, and may provoke him to be hard upon me. The paper's done, and I have not said half—if

I cross you won't be able to read—but I will write to Mama on Thursday, and tell all things herein omitted. I have received the greatest possible kindness from Mr. Brancker who generously presented [me] with £5 and ordered six copies of the Poems, which—damn it—they have never sent. It is a blessing to society when such men acquire riches.

God bless dear Sara—her Mother—her Babes, oh that I could see them. It is a strange dispensation that I, who so little deserve it, should enjoy almost unvaried health and she should be so afflicted. But He, the All-good, chasteneth whom he loveth, and trieth the silver in the furnace, and uses sickness and trouble to wean those from earth whom he has predestined to Heaven. I will write to Father, perhaps to night—but wholly on literary subjects. I cannot bear, at this first breaking the ice of years, to enter abruptly on any secular affairs. I am composing an article for *Blackwood*. Perhaps you could procure me employment on some of the London Periodicals, or suggest some book likely to sell. The Poems, I believe, have not done so far amiss. The Review in the *Quarterly* I must thank you for. It is far too laudatory for my stomach, and I have pretty strong digestion. But why, in the Devil's name cannot they review my book, gentle or semple, without a fling at poor Wordsworth,[1] who by the way

---

[1] *Quarterly Review*, vol. xlix, 1833. The review reads in part: 'We are not aware of any instance in *our* literary history of the son of a great poet achieving for himself the name of poet. Here, however, is such a claim advanced by the son of Coleridge; and, weak and merely imitational as many of the pieces included in this volume are, we are bound to say that we consider its author as having already placed himself on high vantage-ground, as compared with any of the rhymers of these latter years. From the locality of the publication, *Leeds*, taken together with various melancholy allusions in the verses themselves, we are compelled to believe that the fate of this gentleman has not been such as his birth, education, and talents, with the well-won celebrity of several of his immediate connexions, might have been expected to lead him to. What his actual situation may be we know not; but we are grieved to hear the language not only of despondency, but of self-reproach bordering almost on remorse, from one who must be young, and who certainly possesses feelings the most amiable, together with accomplishments rich and manifold, and no trivial inheritance of his father's genius. . . . It is an old saying, that the oakling withers beneath the shadow of the oak; and perhaps had it been the happier destiny of this lady's 'poor kinsman' [referring to Hartley's sonnet, *To a Lofty Beauty, from her Poor Kinsman*] to spend his early manhood under the same roof with the 'father and bard revered' to whom he dedicates his little book, we should never have been called upon to announce a second English poet of the name of Coleridge. If he will drop somewhat of that overweening worship of Wordsworth which is so visible in many of these pages—so offensively prominent in the longest piece they contain [*Leonard and Susan*]—and rely, as our extracts show he is thoroughly entitled to do, solely upon himself, we are not afraid to say that we shall expect more at his hands than from any one who has made his first appearance subsequent to the death of Byron.'

is sadly afflicted in his eyes? I must now conclude. My trunks will come in a day or two. I am well off for clothes. Thank dear Mother for the parcel, and Aunt Eliza for the Handkerchiefs—Love once more to both. When Miss Smith returns to town, I will send a huge article of a Letter, in which all things shall be made clear, if not satisfactory. Till Thursday Adieu—

Yours truly

H.C.

LETTER 44

To MRS. SAMUEL TAYLOR COLERIDGE, *No. 1, Downshire Place, Hampstead, London.*

Grasmere, Monday, Oct. 7, 1833.

My dear Mother

Not knowing whether you have or have not, seen my letter of last Sunday to Henry, I must run the risk of repetition as to the most important details thereof. I did hope, before this time, to have been enabled to tell you more than is therein contained, but as I have not heard any thing from Leeds, I can only give you the same general information as I gave to Hal, which I shall endeavour to exhibit in the most comprehensible form.

You say, kindly, far too kindly, that you will not reproach me for any transactions at Leeds: but perhaps you are not aware that with regard to my finally quitting Leeds no reproach whatever is due. I left, neither clandestinely, nor in debt nor in disgrace—not in debt, at least, to any person but Bingley; and I should think, if matters were fairly arranged, not to him. For see, there are on his side £10, which he gave me, to pay a few pressing debts, when I left Ambleside, £5, which I afterwards sent to Ambleside, two suits of black clothes, two hats, one pair of boots, one pair of shoes, my washing during the time I was at Leeds, my lodging at a guinea a week during the time I was at Mrs. Mason's, and my lodging and board at his own house for the remainder of my sojourn. If to this be added postage, and some few shillings, not twenty I am sure, you see the whole of my debt to him. *Per contra*; there should be, one third of the sum engaged for as respects the 'Worthies,' the Poems, and some little jobs of which we never made any account. By the way, I should have added, the expences of my journey to Kendal etc. to my debtor account. On the whole, I am sure there is no fair, debt on my side; for as to the *forfeitures*, he will never exact them: though they would make me a little delicate about urging payment of the arrears on my side of the balance. Before quitting, I once and again desired him to give me in my account, and have done so again since my return to Westmorland, but I have never yet received it—which I the less wonder at, as divers copies of the 'Worthies' and the 'Poems' sent for at the same time and also by various other channels, particularly six copies of the Poems for Mr. Brancker, (whose name I have mispelled in the verses on his birth-day)[1] have never been forthcoming. I do not know what to think of it. But voilà. Mr. Brancker is going into Yorkshire to visit his brother-in-law, (the Gentleman by whom I was so hospitably entertained near Bradford) and promises to investigate the matter and do the best for me. That he will act kindly to me I have no doubt, but I hope he will not be *brusque*, (as he sometimes is to a degree, which combined with his reforming politicks makes him no great favourite with *Dora*) for it sometimes happens that an over zealous friend, like the grateful Bear that knocked out the eye of the Sleeping Hermit, while endeavouring to brush a fly off his face, does more harm than good. But I have put [you] in possession of the real facts of the case (tho' perhaps some of them will make 'damn a few' at me)—for you will agree with me that the truth is best in every possible emergency. I doubt not, that if all and every transaction of my life were fairly divulged, even to you, or to my best friends, however much you might find to blame (and much God knows there has been) you would be delivered of many vague fears and uncircumscribed suspicions, which cast a darker shadow over my image in your heart, than the worst known act of my sad existence. But this is sad talk. Never had man a kinder, better, more generous friend than Brancker has been to me. I must tell you, that soon after my arrival in Westmorland, he presented me with a Five pound note, in the most delicate way possible; in such a way indeed, that you yourself could have felt no pain in accepting it, considering that £500 would be no great outgoings for him: and I doubt not that were money needed for any feasible plan, and I were relia-ponable, he would be quite ready. In truth, he has all the generosity,

---

[1] See *Poems*, 97–101. In the 1833 edition the name is spelled 'Branker'.

all the hospitality, all the independence which should belong
to a man who has made a princely fortune by his own skill
and industry: and may well be forgiven, if he have not quite
all the polish of a man bred up from infancy among those
who had nothing to do but refine their manners, and very
little of the servile smoothness of a tradesman who has his
fortune to make out of shillings and sixpences, dropped into
his till by customers, whose self-importance he has called into
consciousness by booing—booing for their custom. I am in
no immediate want of clothes: all my shirts, etc., flannel
waistcoats, drawers (beyond what I brought for immediate
use) are on the road, and will be here in a few days, together
with my papers: the books and heavier articles are still at
Leeds; but excepting a few of the former, as Shakespeare,
Homer, and Pindar, Henry's Homer, and my Father's
Reflections (his poems, I have brought with me) which may
come in a parcel along with the Poems and Worthies which
Troughton has ordered, I seriously doubt whether they are
worth the expence of Carriage. The old rags I am sure are
not. But at all events, I can get them when I choose; they
were not detained for debt, or *ought at that rack*. The new
shirt fits to admiration; but I am in no immediate need of
shirts: indeed I hardly remember when upon the whole, I
have made so respectable an appearance as to the outward man as I do at present in a party. Parties have been
numerous, and I seldom left out. How often have I longed
for dear Sara, and her sweet little ones! When shall I see
them? I hope they are not the least like me! I find myself
absolutely unable to picture either of them to my imagination. This is not the case with regard to little Dervey, of
whom I have a most distinct portrait in my brain, not at all
like the original I dare say, but still it is vivid and substantial
enough to love and caress. This is not difficult of explanation. Of Henry's infancy, I knew nothing. Sara was always
so completely unique, so perfectly a Fairy, a being belonging
neither to time or space, so like the etherial vehicle of a pure
spirit, a visible soul (I remember once when she was sitting
at the Piano-forte at Greta Hall she told me I was a *visible
fool* for saying so) that I cannot image any thing like her,
which is not completely the same. 'There is nothing like the
Moon, but the Moon.' But Derwent retained a baby's face
longer than any one I remember; he was, as my Father said
'A fine *representative* Baby' and any painter might have

drawn a hundred babies from his Idea, all like 'yet oh! how different'. Perhaps this is all Greek or worse, to you. For dear, dear, tiny Sara, I fear it is too painfully evident that she has a *body*, and a body that is a sad burden and torment to her sweet soul. Yet the last news I heard through Mrs. Wordsworth afforded a gleam of hope. I do not, I dare not, I will not despair. I will try to write her a most entertaining letter by the time Miss Janetta Smith returns, for she has promised to convey a pacquet for me. I am constructing an article for next *Blackwood*, which I hope will bring in £10. I cannot say, at present, I absolutely decline your kind offer of paying my lodging and washing for the next half year, but I will do my best to render it unnecessary. It is now, and has been for some months, too late for the forthcoming annuals, and if not were not, I have never had any correspondence with, or applications from, the present Editors. The 'Winter's Wreath' is no longer published. But on literary matters I will dilate more at large in my next to Henry. Thank you for the parcel, and thank Aunt Eliza for the handkerchiefs—the pattern is elegant, and does great credit to her taste. Is she still within hail? If so give my kindest love to her. She was always a real favourite of mine, and so is Aunt Martha. I received the *Quarterly* from Mr. Murray. If praise could do me any good, there is enough of it: but I know nothing of that 'overweening worship of Wordsworth' which I am warned against. I admire, nay revere, what is great, excellent and beautiful. And excellent in Wordsworth—that is five sixths of his works—but I am not, and never was a convert to his peculiar sect of poetry. At all events, no man but himself could realize his ideas. I flatter myself the Volume has sold tol lol. Dora finds great fault with its shape: a fault chargeable solely on my own bad taste for it was my selection, and I cannot, for the soul of me, see any thing the matter with me. Howsomever, I succumb to Lady-judgements and will do better when next I have the opportunity. I dined yesterday at Rydal Mount, and met a far better reception than I deserved, indeed as good as I ever could have deserved. Dora is looking, I think, unusually well; and Miss Wordsworth, though very feeble, better than I ever expected to see her again. Poor Mr. Wordsworth is all but blind. He bears his affliction with wonderful cheerfulness. I read to him my own Life of Roger Ascham all the afternoon. I will often go and read to him. My very best love to dear Sara. I would pray for her, if I thought my

prayer would be of any avail. The prayer of a good man
availeth—but—
>   I remain dear Mother,
>   Your truly affectionate Son,
>   H. COLERIDGE.

P.S. I have written to my father, but the letter waits
transcribing, and I find that in my hurry, I have not said
enough about the Gillmans, nor about you. Indeed, little
about any thing but Homer. I do not mean to say much
about matters, this bout to him. The letter is only an ice-
breaker.

I had a delightful kind letter from Mrs. Fox the other day
—giving a charming account of Derwent and his family. I
wish that dear good Lady would not say quite so much about
my Genius, but Quakers are the greatest of all possible
flatterers.

LETTER 45

To MRS. HENRY NELSON COLERIDGE, *1 Downshire Place, Downshire Hill, Hampstead, London.*
>   Greta hall, March 24, [Postmark 1834.]

My dear Sara
It was a sweet consolation to hear that your old playmate
and cousin bride had seen you, and that you were at least
well enough to take pleasure in the meeting: nor could the
good tidings have transpired in a more fitting place than this
identical parlour, where, changed as most things are, there
are still some lingering relics of old times, of the happy times,
which 'have left a joy for memory'—times, which are the
most invaluable possession of my heart, and, paradoxical as it
sound, the better for being flown. There is much and true
philosophy in a saying of Farquhar's, though he puts it into
the mouth of a ruined rake and fortune-hunter, that 'past
pleasures are best'—'Not e'en the Gods upon the past have
power.' To walk with reverted eyes, to live in the days that
are gone, is commonly accounted to be the natural propensity of old age, or the acquired indulgence of affliction. For
myself, I remember not a time when it was not so with me.
Distant hopes were never the stuff of my day-dreams. If, in
childhood, or, as was more frequently the case, in the turbu-
lent period of transition betwixt boyhood and adolescence I
sometimes felt in haste to be a man, no anticipated delight, no

definite purpose, or indefinite yearning mingled with my
angry impatience. The idle wish arose merely from a horror
of restraint, a sore antipathy to counsel. Yet, in my earliest
childhood, I was not without a sense, a praesentiment, that I
was enjoying more freedom than I could ever expect again,
tho' I rather envied the dirty ragged boys who were not made
to change their stockings when they got *wet shod*, and if they
had pennies given them were allowed to spend them in Gun
powder and little cannons. I believe that obstinacy or the
dread of control and discipline arises not so much from self-
willedness, as from a conscious defect of voluntary power, as
fool-hardiness is not seldom the self-disguise of conscious
timidity. You will not wonder, I hope indeed, you have too
much sense to wonder, (or be shocked at any thing) that I
regard all the reforms wrought on these premises as un-
favourably as the staunchest Conservative can regard the
Reform'd Parliament. Even the *Conversion of Paul* seems to
me little better than apostasy. The organ room is out of tune,
not at all comparable to what it was with its bare walls,
whereon the Damp had played the Geographer—mapping out
Ejuxrias and Eutopias, with shores embayed, and winding
rivers long and wide, and forests vast of mouldy greenery,
sharp jutting capes to cleave the long-backed waves; what
time my cousin Robert [Lovell] and myself On fiddle hight of
Caledon did play Broad Scotia's Ancient Music—Poor dear
Wilsy's kitchen—but of this I cannot bear to speak. Besides I suppose you know the changes well enough, though
some have taken place since your departure. But there are
worse alterations than these. Snouderumpater's chair and
little table no longer occupy their custom'd nook. You are
no longer the shorty. Edith's queenlike form is seen no
more; and alas, the Church-yard is full of our hopes and
affections. But enough. Uncle is still the same—quite as
good—and sometimes quite as funny and light-hearted,
though assuredly he has more frequent fits of silence and
abstraction; and I am afraid he looks gloomily on public
affairs. And what do you think of the 'Doctor'? And what
do you think of Lockhart's wise conjecture, that I—even I
—Hartley Coleridge, assisted by my father, am the author
thereof? A great compliment doubtless. It is a book! a book
indeed. It must be delightful to every one, and yet there are
some touches that can only be felt by a few. I do, I confess,
like the Pantagruelism and the narrative, and the love, better

than the good advice, or the religion, or the politics, which may be all very good in their kind—(altho' *entre nous*—the sort of sectarian Church of Englandism which it breathes is any thing but—no matter) but the contrast beneath the serious and comic parts seems to me too sharp. I mean to review it in *Blackwood*,[1] and shall throw out some sapient innuendoes respecting the author, just to lead wiseacres astray. I shall insist upon it that it could be written by none but a Clergyman, a Doncastrian, a valetudinarian, a great Tra-[veller,] a man who had experienced disappointments in Love, probably an Oxonian and a senior fellow. Of course the A. I. chapters must be regarded as altogether fabulous or allegorical: and I shall prove by irrefragable arguments that the Bhow-Begum is the Church. But Uncle is just going out, so I must end with thanking you for your letter. Tomorrow I shall most likely return to Grasmere and my labours. All here send their best loves to you all. Commend me to Mama and Henry. I shall write to both of them anon.

God bless you, and be thank'd for the improvement in your health.

H. COLERIDGE.

On July 25, 1834, about a year after Hartley returned from Leeds, his father died at Highgate. The news, though intimations of Coleridge's mortal illness had been received through the Words-worths, came as a severe shock to Hartley; for until the receipt of the unhappy tidings he had promised himself amendment for his father's sake. Now his shortcomings, his indolence, and his weakness of will seemed monstrous. He wrote long letters of condolence to his family, which show a broken and contrite spirit. Hartley loved his father—indeed Coleridge inspired a full measure of love in each of his children—and the letters on the occasion of Coleridge's death are pathetically sincere. Nor were his letters Hartley's only expression of grief. In two sonnets, one written not long after Coleridge's death, the other thirteen years later, Hartley records his admiration for his father.

---

[1] Two articles on Southey's *Doctor*, 'The Doctor. First Dose', and 'The Doctor. Second Dose', may, from internal evidence, be ascribed to Hartley. See *Blackwood's Magazine*, August and October 1835. Concerning the authorship of the *Doctor*, the reviewer remarks: 'Of all the ignorant guesses yet made, the most senseless is that which mutters the name of Hartley Coleridge. His papers in Maga, signed Ignoramus, and his Sonnets, show that he has genius and talent of a high order; but we, who know his wit well, know that he has no power over its expression to shape or modify it after the likeness of any other man's speech.'

If when thou wert a living man, my sire,
I shrank unequal from the task to praise
The ripening worth of thy successive days,
What shall I do since that imputed fire,
Extinct its earthly aliment, doth aspire,
Purged from the passionate subject of all lays,
From all that fancy fashions and obeys,
Beyond the argument of mortal lyre?
If while a militant and suffering saint,
Thou walk'dst the earth in penury and pain,
Thy great Idea was too high a strain
For my infirmity, how shall I dare
Thy perfect and immortal self to paint?
Less awful task to 'draw empyreal air'.

Still for the world he lives, and lives in bliss,
For God and for himself. Ten years and three
Have now elapsed since he was dead to me
And all that were on earth intensely his.
Not in the dim domain of Gloomy Dis,
The death-god of the ever-guessing Greek,
Nor in the paradise of Houris sleek
I think of him whom I most sorely miss.
The sage, the poet, lives for all mankind,
As long as truth is true, or beauty fair.
The soul that ever sought its God to find
Has found Him now—no matter how, or where.
Yet can I not but mourn because he died
That was my father, should have been my guide.

Coleridge had been a deeply affectionate and solicitous parent.
The force of circumstances early drew him away from home, but
his letters are full of tender messages to and about his children.
Hartley he loved particularly, possibly because his eldest born
was so utterly unable to stand alone in the world. In 1829, Coleridge had written to Sotheby:

'What Queen Mary said, on the loss of our last stronghold in
France, that if her Heart were opened, Calais would be at the
core, I may say of my poor dear Hartley.'

And one year later he added a codicil to his will, in which special
provision was made for Hartley's material comfort.

'Most desirous to secure as far as in me lies for my dear son
Hartley the tranquillity indispensable to any continued and
successful exertion of his literary talents, and which, from the
like characters of our minds in this respect, I know to be especially requisite for his happiness, and persuaded that he will
recognise in this provision that anxious affection by which it is
dictated, I affix this codicil to my last will and testament; and

I hereby give and bequeath to Joseph Henry Green, Esquire, to Henry Nelson Coleridge, Esquire, and to James Gillman, Esquire, and the survivor of them, and the executors and assignees of such survivor, the sum whatever it may be which in the will aforesaid I bequeathed to my son Hartley Coleridge after the decease of his mother, Sara Coleridge, upon trust. And I hereby request them (the said trustees) to hold the sum accruing to Hartley Coleridge from the equal division of my total bequest between him, his brother Derwent, and his sister Sara Coleridge, after his mother's decease, to dispose of the interest or proceeds of the same portion to or for the use of my dear son Hartley Coleridge at such time or times, in such manner, and under such conditions as they the trustees above named know to be my wish, and shall deem conducive to the attainment of my object in adding this codicil, namely, the anxious wish to ensure for my son the continued means of a home, in which I comprise board, lodging, and raiment. Providing that nothing in this codicil shall be interpreted as to interfere with my son Hartley Coleridge's freedom of choice respecting his place of residence, or with his power of disposing of his portion by will after his decease according as his own judgment and affections may decide.'

LETTER 46

To DERWENT COLERIDGE, *Helston, Cornwall.*

Grasmere, August 1st, 1834.

Dear Derwent

We are both alike—both fatherless children. I never felt before—how much we are brothers. Would that I could but see you, talk to you, were it but for a single hour—O Derwent, we have sustained the greatest loss which Time or Death can ever inflict. I never felt, never acknowledged, the value of a father, and of such a father, till I knew that I had no Father. To you this loss must indeed be sore, and you must derive a consolation from the very depth of grief, for your grief is pure and holy; you may remember that the thought of you was a comfort to our dear Parent, that dying, he might yet be glad to live in you, that if you were separated from him, it was by great and happy duties. For me, I can only hope that no painful thought of me adulterated the final out gushing of his spirit, that if he breathed a prayer for me, it was a prayer of comfortable love, foreseeing, in its intensity, its own effect.

I feel, I know, how utterly incommensurate my grief to its

occasion. Friends think they have nothing to do but console. Perhaps other people do, or think they do lament the departed enough. I declare that I reproach my own heart for its unfilial insensibility. All the sorrow I feel were scarce adequate to the loss of an affectionate dog. In times past I have shed tears, hot, scalding, painful tears for mere nothings, and now I cannot weep, though now my Tears might be a second Baptism, washing my soul from sins of many days.

But this day, I saw a mother and a father parting with their child, for six months only—and they wept—and I could have wept with them—and why? They had no cause, no hint of grief, and yet I envied them not their hope, but their pregnancy of sorrow. And yet why Sorrow? It was his wish that he might so meet death, as to testify the depth and sincerity of his Faith in *Jesus.* And was he not, while life and breath were granted him, a powerful preacher of Jesus? For myself I can speak, that he, he only made me a Christian. What with my irregular passions and my intellect, powerful perhaps in parts, but ever like 'a crazy old church clock, and its disordered chimes': what but for him I might have been, I tremble to think. But I never forgot him—no, Derwent, I have forgot myself—too often—but I never forgot my father, and now—if his beatified spirit be permitted to peruse the Day book of the Recording Angel, to contemplate the memory of God which forgets nothing, in which the very abortions of Time, the thoughts which we think we never thought, the meanings which we never meant to mean, live everlastingly—if he may look in that book, or rather, if an intimate knowledge of its contents be consubstantiated with the essence of his Beatitude, then will he know that among my many sins, I was not one that I loved him not; and wherever the final bolt of judgement may drive me, it will not be into the frozen region of sons that loved not their fathers. That I did not pray with him when he uttered his last prayers, that I partook not with him the blessed sacrament, that I heard not his last words, I shall ever regret; for I had not, as you have, imperative duties to withhold me, and had I known— but what use is it now to say what I might or would or ought to have done? He is gone—gone from earth for ever, and to whom can I pay the huge debt of duty which I owe him?

Dear Derwent, I have long been planning a letter to you, a letter that should have been in a far different strain from this. You have had your troubles, sickness and death have more than once been your enemies, and you best know whether the necessity of daily exertion be a dead weight on the afflicted spirit, or whether the daily round of duties, dutifully performed, be not rather as 'pools of water' in the desert. I would I could see your surviving little one. Dear little Dervey! I live in hopes of seeing him, and you! But I lived in hopes of seeing our dear departed Parent. But for my own deraye, above all my soul-withering procrastination, I might have seen him, might have comforted him, might have been enriched with the fulness of his wisdom; of which, alas, some fragments only, abide in my memory. But if we are never to meet, if I am never to see your Darling, may the intermission of our hope be my departure from this world, and oh—may I be fitted to join our blessed Parent, and wait for you all in the patience of the Lord.

I cannot enter now on many things of which I have long desired to speak to you. I shall—D.V. soon put forth a second volume; though half, more than half, the pleasure I expected from its publication is departed. God help us—it is a sad piece of vanity, when a great spirit is departed from the earth, to think of one's own silly verses; and yet, I shall finish Prometheus half as well as if he, who praised the commencement so far beyond its deserts, had been alive to judge it. Heaven grant I may never write what he would not have approved on earth, or may not approve in Heaven. Dear Derwent, we have still one Parent left, one that has long been in fact a widow—let us do all we can to make her old age secure and comfortable—to turn her sorrow into joy.

With best love to my unseen, I will not say unknown Sister, and darling Nephew,

I remain, Dear Derwent,

Your ever affectionate
BROTHER.

Dear Sara—I fear this shock will throw her back. Henry says she was slowly recovering.

I don't recollect whether Praed[1] or any of your friends are in this dumb and radical Parliament.

---

[1] Winthrop Macworth Praed (1802–39), one of Derwent's college friends, was elected M.P. for Great Yarmouth in 1834. The authorized edition of his poems was edited by Derwent Coleridge in 1864.

I cannot write, or rather you could not read were I to write, lady wise, across and diagonally—or I could say as much again. But it would not be the Sun and Chequers—at least the Sun would be totally eclipsed. You have never told me what you thought of my Poems.

LETTER 47

To MRS. SAMUEL TAYLOR COLERIDGE, *No. 1 Downshire Place, Hampstead, near London.*

[Postmark, August 4, 1834.]

My dear Mother

Though from Miss Hutchinson's report, I had too much reason to expect the sad event announced in Henry's letter of last Friday, and though I cannot say that I was much surprized, yet so little had I prepared my mind for the loss that it fell upon me as the fulfilment of an unbelieved prophecy: and even yet, tho' I know it, I hardly believe it. I do not feel fatherless—I often find my mind disputing with itself—What would my Father think of this? And when the recollection awakes that I have no Father, it appears more like a possible evil, than an actual bereavement. You may perhaps have felt something like this on first hearing of the departure of distant friends. I am sure, I do not express it well. Yet had I been forewarned by that mysterious presentiment, that shadow which the Future still throws before, I could not but feel that something was coming. Nightly I dreamed of my Father and had a daily an especial longing to see him. But this is sad talk and vain. Henry, God bless him, bid me write comfortably to you. Whence can that comfort be derived, if not from the consideration that he departed in the faith of Christ, with the Holy Spirit conducting his soul through pain to victory? But this I need not say to you. When we mourn for the dead, we mourn but for our own bereavement. We believe, or strive to believe, that they live for themselves and for God, but for us the dead are dead. It is common on these occasions to dwell on the shortness and uncertainty of life. I know not why—but that is not the moral I draw from death. I rather grieve that it was not I, that I was not like Kirke White, called away in my youth, that my beloved Parents did not close my eyes, that my death should have been the only sorrow I had ever caused them, that when they talked of me, they might weep tears of tender

joy, thinking of what I might have been, and no painful
thought of what I had been, ever jarred

> The silent melody of thought that sings
> A ceaseless requiem to the sainted Dead;
> That so the sharp wound hid within the Heart,
> May grow a spot most finely sensible,
> To each good impress of the hand of God
> Till Death no longer seem'd a terrible thing,
> But like a blithe and long wish'd Holy day—
> That frees the spirit, weary of the school,
> And discipline of Earth, once more to join
> The friends and kindred of their happy home;
> While the all-Father with a look benign,
> Praises the task, imperfect tho' it be,
> And blesses all in their love, and his own.

Dear Mother—this is a sad attempt at verse—and it may
seem to you, to evidence small sense of my orphan state that
I should choose such a vehicle—but I have so long used myself to express my deeper feelings in metre, that I find a
difficulty in expressing them in prose. I hope I shall soon
have a letter from some of you—full of detail: I wish to
hear every thing about my poor dear father, his very last
words, all and every thing, and particularly about the
funeral. Of course he is buried in Highgate Churchyard.
Did James Gillman perform the service? Who were there?
How does Mrs. Gillman take it? I must and will write to her.
You may be sure that I have written before this reach you—
I have written a long, long, very long letter to Derwent. Did
Father say any thing of each of us?—but ah, Mother, how
little worthy was I of such a father—how inadequately did I
value him—and how little adequate is all the feeling my poor
heart has left to suffer for his loss! I reproach myself, bitterly
reproach myself, that I do not lament him more—not that it
could do him any good, but I am afraid I now appear a
strange monster to have wept so little. I cannot weep. This,
I suppose, is constitutional. My eyes burn, but I do not weep
naturally, tho' like a popular preacher, I can talk or even
write myself into tears. But what avails? Better were it, could
I make a resolve, firm as destiny, that my future life should
be such as my Father's Spirit may behold with satisfaction,
if Spirits know aught of what passes on earth. At all events,
Dear Mother, I have one Parent left to whom my whole duty

now devolves; for I have no ties but those to which I was born. Dear little Sara, how does she sustain this? Any good hearing of her would [be] a sunbeam. I wish I had red ink. The Rydal Mount Family have been very kind to me. I shall go there to morrow. I have been preparing a pacquet for Henry, including a Sonnet on Sara's short lived twins. It shall come when I think you are a little calm. Yet what more calm than death, and the reflections which death begets in a Christian Mind? To him—that is gone I owe it, and it is better than any inheritance, that in my worst aberrations I never ceased to be a Christian, at least I always found myself a Christian on my return—that is—I always did and do believe that I ought to be a Xtian—

Which that God may make me,
Is the sincere prayer Of your affectionate Son.

H.C.

P.S. Of course I must have a mourning—I shall consult about it at R.M. Love to H.

From the time he returned to Grasmere from Leeds until his death in 1849 Hartley lived a contented, even if aimless and unproductive life, planning much but doing little. His hair turned grey prematurely, and in middle age he seemed like an old man. The eccentricities that had been merely tolerated in his youth were now almost unnoticed by his friends, and he became a universal favourite. Those who were his intellectual equals looked after him as best they could, for he was, indeed, an elusive sprite with his numberless wanderings and disappearances; but it was the sturdy Westmorland and Cumberland yeomanry who were his special guardians. One and all they loved him, and wander where he would, he was always among friends. They seem to have treated him as though he were from another sphere; and it is amusing to record that years after Hartley's death, when Canon Rawnsley went about the country-side seeking anecdotes about Wordsworth, he was constantly hearing of 'li'le Hartley', as they familiarly called him. Hartley's opulent intellectual gifts —his eloquence, his passionate outbursts, his poetical effusions— were at the service of all. He had, indeed, a 'young lamb's heart', as Wordsworth had long before noticed; and with little children, particularly little girls, he was most tender. Tennyson,[1] Spedding, Wordsworth, and other celebrities praised Hartley; and every

---

[1] Tennyson writing to Derwent after Hartley's death says: 'I met poor Hartley one night at the Salutation Inn, Ambleside. I preserved no details of his conversation. I only remember that he was full of humour and of kindliness with a flow of eloquence, which must I think have somewhat resembled his father's.'

written account left by casual summer visitors to the Lake country (Caroline Fox and Aubrey de Vere), and by residents such as the Briggs and the Claudes, bears witness to the innocence and sweetness of Hartley's nature.

To present an adequate picture of Hartley and do justice to him would require a separate treatment, but the descriptions quoted below will perhaps illuminate the letters which follow. W. E. Forster, writing to his father in 1838, says:

'Hearing from Kendal that Hartley Coleridge was staying at Sedbergh I wrote a note to him, asking him to take tea with me as Sarah Fox's relation. He came very kindly. The next day was rainy and most dull was the prospect, but happily I met H. C. in the street and he spent the day with me, and read me several of his unpublished sonnets. It was such an intellectual treat as I never had before. He is a strange compound of eccentricity, immense power of reasoning and imagination, amiability, simplicity, and utter want of self command—I should think his conversation was equal to his Father's, in fact those who know him think it to be so. Never heard anything like it. If I could have taken it down, I might have sold it very high. . . . O pray let me send a £5 note to Sedbergh—Coleridge is fat, one sided, about 5 feet high, eyes dark, hair grey and black, he is a most strange looking mortal, and worth observing if thou meetest him.'

Thomas Blackburne, writing to Derwent after Hartley's death, gives a most interesting series of impressions:

'Hartley never, or very seldom, remembered what he had written. . . . It was his custom to put aside what he had written for some months, till the heat and excitement of composition had effervesced, and then he thought it was in a fair condition to criticise. He seldom altered. "Strike the nail on the anvil," was the advice he often gave to me. Roger's poetry he called bakers' poetry, from its superfine polish. He never kneaded, or pounded his thoughts; they always came out *cap-à-pie*, like a troop in quick march. To see him brandishing his pen (the very recollection of which has made me sadly blot this page) and now and then beating time with his foot, and breaking out into a shout at any felicitous idea, was a thing never to be forgotten. The common method of keeping up the velocity, by muttering and remuttering what is written, and using one line as a spring-board to reach another, was not the method which he adopted. His sonnets were all written instantaneously, and never, to my knowledge, occupied more than ten minutes; when he once challenged me to a match, and exceeded that time, he tore up the paper; and yet a rapid, continuous, oral discourse he told me he never accomplished. . . . Those who had only seen him in the careless dress that he chose to adopt in the lanes—his trowsers, which were generally too long, doubled half-way up the leg, unbrushed, and often splashed; his hat brushed the wrong way, for he never used an umbrella; and his wild, unshaven weather-beaten look—were amazed at his metamorphose into such a faultless gentleman as he appeared when he was dressed for the evening.'

Still another correspondent wrote to Derwent:

'It is no uncommon thing to see an old man with hair as white as snow; but never saw I but one—and that was poor Hartley—whose head was mid winter, while his heart was as green as May.'

Only two things broke the uneventful tenor of these years, the school-mastering at Sedbergh and the preparation of the critical introduction to *Massinger and Ford*; otherwise Hartley's existence was but a succession of births, marriages, and deaths, interspersed occasionally by picnics, parties, or excursions; and more than any of his letters, this group is but a record of Hartley's mind and character.

LETTER 48

To MRS. HENRY NELSON COLERIDGE, *No. 1 Downshire Place, Hampstead, near London.*

Grasmere—Day before Easter Sunday [Postmark, April 21, 1835.]

My Sister dear, and dearer now than ever
    Since I am one of a poor family,
That like an old and thunder-stricken tree
    War with the winds, with desperate endeavour—
A few leaves clinging to the age-warp'd boughs,
    A small knot on a lower branch together
    Wooing with kindred smiles the captious weather,
Taking all good the sneaking time allows—
    And one poor leaf, that ventures to put forth
In the chill aspect of the boisterous north
    High in a bare and solitary branch,
A single tree upon a mountain side,
    Rooted in desperate patience to abide
The downfall of the threatening avalanche,
Since you, and I, our brother, and our 'Mother',
    Need most of all the love of one another,
Strange must it seem, that with a love so strong,
    I have been mute, so very, very long.
I fear, alas, you deem my heart is rotten
    And all my childish love of you forgotten—

And better 'tis, sweet Sara, you think so,
　　Than all I am by bitter proof to know;
But I'll not pester thee with thoughts unholy—
　　Come let us sing, Away with Melancholy—
'Tis true I have a heavy debt to pay,
　　But I may yet recover my leeway,
And for a sample, now I think upon it,
　　I'll send your Ladyship a promised Sonnet.[1]

But born to die; they hardly breath'd the air
　　Till God revoked the mandate of their doom.
A brief imprisonment within the womb
　　Of human life was all their destined share.
Two whiter souls, unstain'd with sin or care,
　　Shall never blossom from the fertile Tomb,
Sweet buds, that not on earth were meant to bloom,
　　So swiftly Heaven recall'd the spotless pair.
Let Man, that on his own desert relies,
　　And deems himself the creditor of God,
Think how these Babes have earn'd their Paradise,
　　How small the work of their small Period;
Their very cradle was the hopeful grave,
　　God only made them for his Christ to save.

There 'tis—'tis very bad, methinks you say—
　　But there it is, bad be as it may;
'Tis true, as Papers have the news retail'd,
　　That my poor foolish Editor has fail'd;
I'm very sorry, but not much astonish'd,
　　Like most rash boys he was enough admonish'd;
He'll blame me much: and troth, I must confess—
　　I am to blame for his foolhardiness.
He thought in me he had a mine of gold,
　　My talents known, my weakness all untold.
But well it is, that his Papa in law
　　Won't let the lad want plenty, for the maw,
Else should I sorely grieve for his sweet brats,
　　Not being one of those Aristocrats,
Who think poor people's children noisome weed,
　　And that the rich alone have right to breed.
Talking of this, my Sara, what d'ye think
　　(To ask the question is but waste of Ink)

---

[1] For the sonnet see *Poems*, 180. The lines as given in Hartley's letter differ
slightly from those in the published version.

Of Harriet Martineau's political novels?[1]
Fine food, forsooth, for starving paupers' hovels—
No doubt, 'twould much improve the poor's behaviour,
  And make them happy in their low conditions
To teach them all to disbelieve their Saviour
  And make them infidel Arithmeticians.
Were I woman, I should blush for shame
  That such a thing should bear a woman's name.
I hope however, that the scribbling elf
  Does not at all times understand herself.
But now to business—I've not had a word—
  From Bingley or his assignees, I heard
The news quite accidentally from Troughton—
  Or to this day I had been left to doubt on—
I have not written, for I know too late,
  In business still to blunder is my fate,
But I've applied for counsel to my anchor
  The wealthiest of my worthy friends—Jim Brancker.
Who now, *tant pis*, is gone to Liverpool
  For fear his sweating sugar furnace cool.
I'll nothing write for Fraser's Magazine
  Nor any work so brutal and obscene—
To lend it aid, is not to Heraud's credit:
  Hal, if he likes, may tell him that I said it;
But ask him, pray, your Hal I mean, if I,
  Could get a corner in the Quarterly.
But perhaps it will be better, if I write,
  To Lockhart, who will pay the bill at sight.

Best love to Mother; now I've broke the ice
  I'll send another letter in a trice;
Tell her I'm working now for Blackwood, and
  Have three amazing articles in hand—[2]

But really I must dismount my rocking horse of a Pegasus,
and add a few lines in humble prose. I never heard from the

---

[1] It is amusing to find, that as Harriet Martineau despised Hartley, so he despised her. When later he met her, he found her personally even more objectionable than in print. Charles Macfarlane records the following conversation: 'I chanced to mention old Miss H.M. "What! do you know her too?" said Hartley. "Only by sight," was my reply. "Then," said he, filling his glass to the brim, "suppose we drink d—n to her! I abhor the woman as a woman, and I detest her rampant irreligion and all her principles." '

[2] Hartley probably refers to his articles on the *Doctor*, although only two appeared. There are a good many articles in *Blackwood's*, which one would like to attribute to Hartley, but concerning which there is no objective proof of authorship.

Oxford Lady, and can't guess who she can be. A letter I certainly have had within these few last days, from the quondam Mary Harris, now Mrs. Barnard, but nothing to the purport which Mother mentioned. I am not sure whether more than 500 copies of the Poems were printed. Bingley sometimes talk'd of a thousand. If only 500, I think they must be nearly sold off. I am extremely sorry that I did not see Bertha and Kate when they were at Rydal. I was staying with John Wilson Jun. at Elleray, and did not hear of their being there till too late. Poor Aunt[1]—I am deeply sorry, but I must say, not at all surprized. May God put a speedy end to all our troubles—For hers, I fear, there is but one. Best love to Hal and the darlings—This is a terrible scrawl of a letter, but you will think it better than none. I must ascertain some[how] or other whether any of the annuals are going, for I have things which will just suit them.

Your affectionate Brother

H.C.

LETTER 49

To MRS. SAMUEL TAYLOR COLERIDGE, *No 1 Downshire Place, Hampstead, London.*

Grasmere, May 16, 1835.

My dear Mother

Your parcel by kind Mrs. Wordsworth of course arrived safe; the contents, particularly the handkerchiefs, will be very useful. I am quite delighted with the sweet little one's sweet little book.[2] It is such an image of the tiny self—not perhaps as married life, and alas, sickness and sorrow have made her now, but as she was in those happy years when her Idea was shaped in my heart: an idea which will never be effaced till my own dissolution, and perhaps not even then. Could I see her now, that Idea would doubtless continue to modify my perceptions of the present, and something of the Numpet, the Fay, the Sylph, the Invisible, would enter into my internal representation of the pensive Matron. When I dream of Derwent, (which is almost every night) he always appears the same boy that he was when our quarrelling was complained of by some good officious people as a nuisance, and I shall have some difficulty, when we meet, in always bearing in mind the Rev'd, the Papa, and the Paedagogue.

---

[1] About this time Mrs. Southey's mental difficulties terminated in insanity. She died two years later, in November 1837.

[2] Cf. Sara Coleridge's *Pretty Lessons for Good Children*, 1834.

The Sonnet[1] is exquisitely pathetic. Of the pretty poems I think I like those best which relate to natural History. The little Fables are charming, and have tended to reconcile me to a sort of composition for which I had before something like an antipathy. Sarinda's are among the few Fables I ever read which appear to me to be natural. In ascribing speech and a certain portion of reason to what we call dumb and irrational animals, or even to Trees, Flowers, Gems, brooks, or mountains, the Fabulist only uses his just prerogative: but beyond this, nature should not be contradicted: the real habits of animals should be carefully observed, and they should not be described as performing human actions to which their natural actions have no imaginable analogy or resemblance, as for example card-playing, fiddling or shopping. The ancient fables attributed to Aesop, Phaedrus, Pilpay, Avienus etc., are emblems or [. . . ? . . .] allegories rather than Fables, most probably suggested by the Zoographic Hieroglyphics of Aegypt. The Lion, the Fox, the Ass, etc., are mere pictures of abstract qualities, as power, craft, stupidity. Other tales, in which beasts and birds compose the Dramatis Personae, are to be considered as burlesque satires, intended to make human actions and passions ridiculous, by ascribing them to the brute creation. Such are Spenser's Mother Hubbard's Tale [1591] (none of his best productions)—the old popular Tale of Reynard the Fox, (What has become of my Father's copy of it?) and the once admired children's books, *The Peacock at Home, The Lion's Masquerade, The Cat's Gala, The Lobster's Voyage to the Brazils* etc. which, though sufficiently humorous and entertaining, are not, I suspect, very wholesome aliment for children, whose sense of the ridiculous is generally, quite strong enough of itself. On the other, Roscoe's 'Butterfly's Ball'[2] and Mrs. Trimmer's 'Flapsy and Pecksey'[3] (which I am glad to see so kindly mentioned in the Doctor) are exactly the sort of Beast stories which I think the wee 'uns may be the better for reading. But I dare say all this is very uninteresting to you, who were never fond of critical discussion, or discussion of any sort at any time, and least of all when you are anxious for information of a more household interest. I am afraid that we small fry of the press are about the worst letter-writers in the world.

---

[1] The dedicatory sonnet to Sara's *Pretty Lessons*.
[2] See Wm. Roscoe's *Butterfly's Birthday*, 1809.
[3] See Sarah Trimmer's *Fabulous Histories*, 1807.

We always smell of the shop so confoundedly, and will be
scribbling about literature or politics, or mayhap metaphysics, to people who would rather hear news of their friends or
economics of the wardrobe. Before, however, I have done
with Sara's book, I must discharge the vials of my indignation upon that frontispiece. What rascal drew, what radical
engraved it? A radical he must be, for such are all under-
strappers of the fine arts, all Flunkies of science, and Laz-
zaroni of Belles lettres, as well as Quack Doctors, Pettifogging
Attorneys, Itinerant Lecturers (Mr. Silk Buckingham[1] to
borrow) and the most part of worsted Blue-stockings. I am
glad that the Darling's book has sold. A good many copies
have been disposed of in this neighbourhood. Mine I have
lent to Mrs. Claude, a very sweet woman, and most kind
friend of mine, with whom I am studying German, which
will be a very valuable acquisition and may be turn'd to
account both in an intellectual and pecuniary point of view in
many ways. It was always my dear Father's wish that I
should acquire German, though I know there are those who
wish he had never learn'd it himself. I have none of his works
except the *Remorse*, the three Vols. of Poems, and the *Aids to
Reflection*. This is sad. The *Table Talk* has been reviewed
both in the *Edinburgh* and *Quarterly*, but I have not read
either review.[2] I might have done so, but I wish to read the
Book itself first. I hope *Henry has been very, very, careful as to
what he has recorded.* Dear papa often said things which he
*would not himself have published: and I have heard him utter opinions
both in Religion and in Politics not very easy to reconcile with what he
has published. Any thing of this sort would be welcomed with a
savage* exultation by such miscreants as begrudge Southey the
just reward of his manifold labours for the benefit of his
species and the honour of his Maker. You would hardly
believe that such there are, but so it is, though the respectable
of all denominations rejoice that his severe trials are not to
be aggravated by anxiety about the wherewithal.[3] Of his
works, I have none but *Madoc* and the proof sheets of *Kehama*. I dined yesterday at Rydal. Mr. Wordsworth is wonderfully cheerful, all things considered, and Mrs. Wordsworth,
angelic as ever, is a model of calm resignation, tho' her

---

[1] James Silk Buckingham (1786–1855).
[2] Coleridge's *Table Talk*, edited by H. N. Coleridge in 1835, was reviewed in
the *Edinburgh Review*, lxi. 129, and in the *Quarterly*, xcviii. 1.
[3] From 1835 Southey enjoyed a pension of £300, granted by Peel.

own health is far from what one could wish. Poor Miss Hutchinson, naturally despondent, is sadly knock'd down. I never saw a human being look so old. I wish I had any thing comfortable to say of Dora. I hope that a journey southward, which is contemplated may be of service. Miss Wordsworth continues much the same—only the *hask* weather, any thing but like May, is against her. William has just left them. John, his wife, and daughter Jane are there still. It is a little beauty, but very shy, at least she would not take to me at all. I read 'Yarrow Revis[ited]'—and some of the new Poems[1]— very sweet, but can't talk about them here, for I've more to say than I've room for. All send their love. You need not send any coats at present, for I am in no immediate need, having had two done up for every day and there is another which will turn nicely when I want. Of trowzers also I am well. Waistcoats wear out worse than any thing. When I get a remittance from *Blackwood* I will get a new hat, but my present is not by any means bad. I have an old one which I wear sometimes in wet weather which must have given offence to somebody—Hang 'em—I have not heard a word from Bingley or his Creditors, and am I think, well advised not to take the first word. Mr. Brancker, one of the kindest of men, promises (from no solicitation of mine) to befriend me to any reasonable extent in getting the copy right of the Poems out of their hands, but of course, if they demand the second volume I must give it them. But they will do no such thing when they find they have a man of business and a long purse to deal with, and not such a Greenhorn as your feckless brat. I am busy about transcription among other things at present. Tell Sara that the Article for the *Quarterly* shall *not* end in smoke, but I do not know what subjects are unoccupied or what books to review, or rather what to take as a Text. I wish to meddle only with subjects of literature. My best way will be to write to Lockhart. Professor Wilson is expected on his way from Edinburgh to London. I wish I could send you a pacquet by a safe private hand.

Best love to Hal, Sal, and the Darls,

Your affectionate Son,

H.C.

I hope you will be able to read the crossings. I have but just time to get in Post to night.

---

[1] *Yarrow Revisited, and Other Poems* appeared in 1835.

LETTER 50

To MRS. SAMUEL TAYLOR COLERIDGE, *No. 1 Downshire Place, Hampstead, London.*

Saturday—I don't know what. [September, 1835.]

My dear Mother

You may be sure that I opened your last with fear and trembling, and all the anticipations of an evil conscience— and was most agreeably surprized to find so little scolding in it. I will not, however, detain you with excuses, but to business at once. Perhaps I cannot tell you any thing more comfortable of our friends at Rydal than that Mrs. Wordsworth is gone to visit her son and daughter-in-law at Workington. Mr. Wordsworth is, all things considered, wonderfully well— I have often seen him lately, sometimes on his walks, sometimes at the Foxes,[1] and sometimes at his own abode: (the day before yesterday, he call'd upon me—what think you for? to borrow a razor as he had not shaved that morning, and bethought him to call on the Parrys). Dora is not worse, I wish I could say she was much better. She has the same sweet smile as ever, and all the good spirits that can proceed from a kind and innocent heart in an afflicted body. (Miss Wordsworth is, I suppose, more comfortable as to her bodily feelings—suffers little or no pain, and is grown fat, but her memory is gone—so they say, at least, for I do not now see her. She never leaves her room.) I hope Mr. Wordsworth feels some consolation in the complete victory of his poetic fame. He may at least feel assured, that no Great Poet ever lived to see his name of so full an age as Wordsworth has done. His last volume is exquisite. Now it is sad bathos to begin about jackets and shirts, but such was the order you prescribed, and I am bound to obey. Of shirts, I have abundance. Mrs. Fleming's Grand daughter does my mending—(I don't say that she *mends* me). As some little recompense, I gave her some of the silk I have got at Funerals to make herself a bonnet, and she has hemmed the rest into neckcloths for me. You *must* be aware that it is unfit for making waistcoats, breeches, etc. I believe I have now about twenty pair of Trowzers, about 9 of which are whole and respectable—three or four may be darned for work days—the rest incorrigible

---

[1] Mrs. Sarah Fox of Penjerrick, Cornwall, and her daughters, Caroline (the Diarist) and Anna Maria Fox, who spent several summers at Grasmere.

reprobates. But perhaps Mrs. Fleming may turn some of them to account for her grandsons. I have a tolerable comely suit for great occasions. Nevertheless, the coat etc., you speak of, will not be unacceptable, if you can send them conveniently about Xmas. Remember, however, that blue does not turn well, and turning coats is rather expensive. Those you have sent fit me exactly, for I am so deep—i.e. so far from the breast to the back bone, that I have known coats of much larger men, that would not button over me. Believe me, it is not in the Corporation. I have no lack of Flannel waistcoats, stockings, or any other article of attire. By the way, I am afraid I never thank'd Sara for her very kind present to my legs. I always feel mighty genteel when I have got them on. Bless a soul. I also feel very elegant in the shoes you were so kind as to send me. In that present you have, according to the adage, got the length of my foot. They say every one has a pet part of their body—and I confess, if I could be conceited of any thing about my ugly little carcase—it would be of my little feet. At least they prove, that I am not stunted or runted, that I am as big as ever Nature intended me to be. They will serve me for dancing shoes, so long as my dancing days continue, and perhaps rather longer. I think the wardrobe is dispatched. Mr. Parry has not yet received the Number of the Quarterly containing the Review of my book[1]—but I got a sight of it the other day at Mrs. Claude's. I am, of course obliged to the author; but I really think if he had been rather less brotherly, or cousinly, or call it what you will, it would have been all the better. He lets the cat out of the bag. It looks too like a family concern. I think the praise excessive, but let that pass. I should have wished him to treat the sentiments, which you said gave him pain, with no more ceremony than if the name Dan O'Connell instead of Hartley Coleridge had been on the title page. I am afraid I shall not treat his Homeric scepticism quite so ge[nerously] in my article on epic Poetry. As to the Thucydides, I cannot think it exactly the book for me—considering how little access I have at present to classical books, and how little I know of those critical niceties, on which the merits of an edition of Thucydides must hang. I think a book might have been selected more in my way. But if I had Arnold's Thucydides,[2]

---

[1] Hartley refers to Henry Nelson Coleridge's review of the *Northern Worthies* in the *Quarterly* (liv, Sept. 1835, 330).

[2] Thos. Arnold's *Thucydides* appeared in 3 volumes between 1830 and 1835.

which I have not, nor Mr. Wordsworth either, I would set about it. I delicately hinted the thing to Dr. Arnold himself when he was here—but he said he had no copy. Hal has taken Lamb to himself. He had a good right to do so—but *that* would have suited me. I am rejoiced to hear of Sara's book coming out with worthy illustrations. It is so like the dear self. I wish she could have gone with Henry to Devonshire. In that case, you must all have acknowledged that the Reform Bill has done *some* good. I received this morning a Cornwall paper giving account of the silver salver and H.'s inscription. Good—Good—I dare say Derwent doats upon his Emily.[1] I wrote a long letter to him the other day to which Mrs. C. Fox appended a few lines. The Foxes are most kind creatures; it is a delight to have them here. Their man remark'd that I was very like my brother. I have a great deal to say about 'Table-Talk' and other things, but in a day or two I shall be able to send a pacquet by private hand, wherein I shall write to Sara, fearing Henry may not be returned. I come on famously with my German. Mrs. Fleming is in bed, or she would send her best respects. Bless you all and the dear little ones.

I remain
Your affectionate Son
H. COLERIDGE.

LETTER 51

To HENRY NELSON COLERIDGE, *No. 21 Downshire Hill, Hampstead, London.*

Jan. 11th, [Postmark 1836.]

Dear Henry

To put Mama out of her misery at once, I never had, and have not, the least intention of complying with Bingley's proposal. I took what I really think was the wisest course. I did not answer his letter at all but wrote to my excellent friend Brancker, stating what Bingley had said, with my own objections to the scheme, of which the strongest, as I plainly told him, was my Mother's aversion to it. This was, indeed, only due to Brancker for his kind exertions in my behalf on a former occasion with which you are not unacquainted, and besides, I know that he is both able and willing to bring the

---

[1] Emily Frances Gillman Coleridge was born July 6, 1835, and died June 13, 1836.

matter to the best conclusion. However, I only requested his advice. He has, however, done more than advise: as you will best understand, by an extract from his last letter to Mrs. Claude (of whose little ones he is guardian, and almost a father) which she, good creature, immediately transcribed and sent to me. Luckily it arrived at the same moment with Mama's parcel, and saved me from a flutter which might have made me incapable of answering directly:

'Tell Hartley that I am in correspondence with Bingley about his affairs, and I hope to come to a satisfactory conclusion probably this week, when he shall hear from me; meanwhile tell him not to write or interfere.' Now, Hal, I would lay a wager you are laughing to yourself and thinking that I like the past piece of counsel better than all the rest. However, you shall be informed of the result as soon as I know it myself, and I doubt not it will be agreeable. Here, Hal, you see the influence you possess as a Tremensian; no one, not even Bingley, would have thought have [of?] continuing the work had it not been for your panegyric.[1] I may at least thank you for my fame, such as it is. Dear *Snouderumpater* charged me with being rather ungracious, if not ungrateful, in my remarks on that business. Nothing could be farther from my feelings. In fact, I had then only very slightly run over the article at a friend's house; on reperusing it carefully, I find more of the *Ars celare artem*, more proper fault-finding, than I at first observed. Still I think the praise excessive, but you are a good natured fellow, and it might not be insincere. I don't however, quite know what you mean by saying that my life of Roscoe was written as a duty, any more than any other life. Except on the subject of criminal jurisprudence and of slave-dealing, I expressed not even a general agreement with his political sentiments, and said, quite as plain as need be, that I consider his pamphlets weak and flimsy, hardly deep enough to be called sophistical. Of the elegance of his mind, the variety of his acquirements, the urbanity of his manners, and the kindness of his heart, I never heard but

---

[1] Hartley remarks elsewhere: 'The very panegyerical, not to say puffing article in the Quarterly about the Worthies had the effect of inducing Bingley (the Bookseller) to send me an invitation to resume the work, but on terms which I could not have accepted even had I not known my dear Mother's disapprobation of my returning to Leeds. For once in my life, I acted prudently—wrote to my excellent Friend Brancker who has completely emancipated me, so that I am at liberty to publish a second volume where I can find the best market—of the Poems I mean. This is a great relief to my mind.'

one opinion, even from his political enemies. I have certainly
heard another version of his conduct as a man of business, but
in a matter, of which I should be an incompetent judge, even
were I better acquainted with the facts than I pretended to
be; I was not to blame in speaking tenderly of a man so much
beloved, and so recently departed. It is not my fault if other
scribblers are made of sterner stuff. On the very important
question as to the baaing or vaaing of the Greek sheep, I succumb to your superior learning. The argument, with honest
Rogers' leave, is an absurd one, for no animal sound is capable of being spell'd, any more than a whistle or a peditus.
The Cock does not really say Cock-a-doodle-doo, nor the Dog,
Bow, wow. Even Cookoo does not to my ear convey the cry
of the bird so call'd, though it denotes it as well as any combination of letters can do. Animal sounds admit of musical
notation, not of orthographic writing. But I cannot agree
with Mitford[1] that the pronunciation of the Modern Greeks
is even a clue to that of the ancient occupants of the same
country. The modern population of continental Greece is in
a large proportion Schlavonic, and you might *me tantum judice*,
as well seek at Paris for the pronunciation of the ancient
Kelts, or the Romanized Gauls, as at Athens for the orthoepy
of the Dores or Iones. Besides, it is pretty certain, that the
pronunciation of the Greek letters must have varied considerably in the time between Homer and Quintus Calaber
(why do you call him Quintus Smyrnaeus?) in the space
between Magna Grecia and Marseilles on the west and the
Greek settlements in Bactria to the East. But the question
is unprofitable, for the truth can never be discovered. It
would be a great convenience certainly, if there were a pronunciation of the ancient tongues common to all Europe;
for an English and a foreign scholar can hardly understand
each other in Latin; and it were well to give to each vowel
a distinct sound, but beyond this we cannot expect to go. I
know not on what part of my book you found your suspicion
that I undervalue classical learning. I have asserted its use
and dignity very plainly. I have assigned to its professors
an honourable station in the Republic of Letters. I do not
even disparage the minutiae of verbal criticism. They are
good in their way, though I do not think the study very
edifying to the soul or emollient to the manners of those who

---

[1] William Mitford (1744–1827), author of a *History of Greece*.

pursue it as their main object. But dancing may be very pretty exercise, notwithstanding that one would not choose to be exactly like a Dancing Master. The Classics will I hope, always form a considerable part of an *Academical* education, but for the great class, with whom study must at any early age give way to active employment and become at most the resource of leisure hours, I do think learning Latin not the wisest course in the world. And now that we are on this tack; what makes you think that I dislike your 'Table Talk'? I might have fears lest it should be Mali exempli—fears which Allsop has shewn not to be wholly groundless. I might tell Derwent, that the book gave me no feeling of my father's manner, which it does not pretend to do, but the execution of the work I greatly admire, and Derwent well observes that it were sad indeed if so much excellent criticism, so much moral, religious, and political wisdom were to perish with the lips that uttered it. I have not seen Allsop's book.[1] I think he deserves a trimming, though I should hardly suppose he would insert any thing but what he thought was proper for publication; and any letters he may possess are most likely on philosophical topics. He has probably the excuse which another has not of knowing no better.[2] To some people, vanity, and a chance of money-making, are potent temptation. You will laugh and swear when I tell you that I have received a communication from Tait requesting me to contribute to his Magazine, and proposing for a subject 'Recollections of my Father'. The letter was not from the radical Editor himself, but from a Mr. Smith, who *does* Asia and America for the Ency. Brit. whom I never saw but once in my life. I need not consult you about a proper answer. Do you think Massinger would be a good subject for the Quarterly? The Family Dramatists, published by Murray, might serve for a heading. I need, I suppose, say no more about that publication, than that Massinger is a fitter subject for that sort of expurgation than most of his contemporaries,

---

[1] In 1836 Thomas Allsop's *Letters, Conversations and Recollections of S. T. Coleridge* appeared, a work which was highly offensive to the Coleridge family. The allusions to Wordsworth and Southey, as well as to Coleridge, were of a private and often painful nature, and certainly should not have been made public at that time.

[2] Hartley refers to De Quincey's article on Coleridge, which appeared in *Tait's Magazine* in September 1834. De Quincey gives a good many details of Coleridge's family life (including the misunderstanding with Mrs. Coleridge) and he goes to great lengths in an attempt to prove Coleridge's plagiarisms from the German.

as the objectionable parts generally admit of easy separation. I must praise Gifford[1] for his services as an Editor, and need not say much of my very low opinion of his abilities as a Critic. Or what say you to Retzsch's Illustrations of *Macbeth*,[2] which might furnish occasion for an ingenious if not very profound examination of 'Ut Pictura, Poesis' which is not more than half true? But I must conclude, the rather as I shall have occasion to write again in two or three days, and have to shave before I can take this to the post. Miss Wordsworth is, I fear, much the same, nor likely to be much better. There are, I fear also, small hopes for Aunt. Dora improves. Mrs. Parry is a sad sufferer. Why are good people ever ill? It is a sad mistake in education to persuade young people that virtue will exempt them from suffering, or turn the world into a happy valley. The trick is soon found out, and then they think with Brutus—'Virtue, what art thou but a name'—and a bore? An excellent paper might be written, 'On the inutility of lying, considered as a mean of moral improvement.' I am delighted to hear that Sara goes on so well. Give ten thousand loves to her. Mama never says any thing about her own health. I will write to Derwent soon. We have had an unusually gay Christmas. I had Sweet's 2d. Ed., a bible, and Worthies. I know not how to get a Janus[3] but could learn. Love to the dears.

Yours, in great haste
H.C.

LETTER 52

To MRS. SAMUEL TAYLOR COLERIDGE, *No. 27 Downshire Hill, Hampstead.*

Grasmere, Jan. 18, 1836. Raining Cats and Dogs.

My dear Mother and Sister

After posing for some time which of you to address, I have determined, like the widow'd queen of Chrononhotonthologos,[4] to have you both. But this is not a proper strain to commence with, considering the solemn subject of dear Henry's last letter,[5] which with its black seal and edges, almost made me faint (I am not exaggerating, I was as sick as

---

[1] Gifford edited Massinger's plays in four volumes for Murray, in 1813.
[2] Cf. F. A. M. Retzsch's *Outlines of Shakspear, Macbeth*, 1833.
[3] In 1826 Hartley made four contributions to the *Janus*, an annual.
[4] See Henry Carey's play by this title.
[5] H. N. Coleridge's father, Colonel James Coleridge, died in 1836.

death) lest something should have happened to either of you. Right glad I am that I did not hear of the letter, before I saw it, though, after all, a few moments' recollection might have suggested to me the probability of the case, as you had all mentioned poor Uncle's moribund state in every letter. Perhaps I was less affected by the announcement coming as it did, like a relief to me, than I ought to have been. But the actual decease of persons whose recovery has been long despair'd of, comes to the distant but as the confirmation of something past. Henry himself appears to consider it in the same light, and I knew too little of my Uncle to be much affected at his departure, otherwise than as death is always awful to a Christian mind—(for independent of the judgement to come, death seems to me at the worst a bore, like the breaking up of a merry Saturday night's party by the uninvited intrusion of the Sabbath, and to the great majority of mankind, the best thing that could happen.) But it was not on this that I began to write, or I should not have begun in so light a strain, but to inform you, that by the kind offices of my excellent, though radical friend Brancker, I am quite disentangled from all engagements with Bingley, and at liberty to publish what I choose, where and when I may, with the counsel of better men of business than myself (without which dear Mother you won't catch me making any bargains in future) think proper.[1] The process of this matter you will better understand, when, on Henry's return, I send up copies of the letters, either by Mrs. Parry's parcel or along with the article for the Q. which, D.V. shall be ready in *three weeks* at farthest. Meanwhile you will be satisfied with a few extracts—1st from Mr. Brancker's favour of the 16th. 'By the enclosed letters you will find you are quite emancipated from the thrall of the Leeds' Bookseller, and you will see too in what position the Copyright of your Worthies and Poems remains. I do not believe him quite about the London

---

[1] Bingley's letter to Hartley on this occasion (misdated by Derwent January 1833, and which undoubtedly belongs to the year 1836) will be of interest: 'Having been informed by your friend Mr. Brancker that you feel no inclination to resume the editorship of "The Worthies", and that your mind is not at ease respecting your promise to furnish me at some time with MS. for a second volume of poems and a pamphlet, I beg to state that you need no longer consider yourself under any engagements to furnish me with MS. either for the aforesaid volume of poems, or for any other work. But although I shall never call upon you to redeem any engagement that you have entered into with me, I shall consider myself both honoured and obliged by the offer of any of your MS., either now ready or in embryo, for publication.'

House who are wishing to purchase them—at all events the matter is so placed that I think you are sure to hear before any such bargain is concluded, and if they should go into *reputable London Hands*, it may probably be the best thing that can happen for you, as they would most likely open a communication with you for their continuance. Perhaps it may be prudent to consult Mr. Wordsworth on the best move you can next make—he knows more of these matters than I do, though as far as business arrangements go, probably I am more used to it than he.' So for Mr. Brancker—the sublineations are his own. The following sentences I need not copy, as they refer only to his joy, in which he takes it for granted I sympathized at the result of the Liverpool municipal elections, which you care nothing about, or if anything, would deplore what he rejoiced at. By the way, in this matter of politics there is a remarkable coincidence between my position and Brancker's, for all his family, his father (still living) included, are high Tories. But he differs from me in having been the successful man and the upmaker of his house, so, though not absolutely above family censure, he cannot be taken to task and haul'd over the coals, as I was more than once in my life at Ottery and elsewhere. Perhaps too, Hal would suggest that Philosophical and Academical Conservatism is a very different thing from high corporation Pittism, and that Brancker's choosing to differ from his relations, was very different from my presuming to disagree with mine. But on this head, permit me to say, that my Father's opinions on many points of public import were considerably different during the years wherein I last conversed with him, from those which Henry has recorded. He admitted the necessity of a reform in parliament, and though I could never have imagined that he could have much admired little Johnny Russell's unprecedented piece of stupidity and blundering, call'd 'the Reform Bill', I thought he would have been thankful, as I am, for any thing which got rid of the idolized abominations of the old system, not as better in itself, but as necessary, transitory, and, at least, making room for something better. But this is a wearisome digression to you, and you will think that I am, as good Mrs. Robinson used to say, 'Aboon wi' mysel,' and hardly know what I am writing— which is not very far off the truth; so light hearted am I at the removal of the burden which has weighed down my powers, and render'd me a dead weight to you, my dear Mother, for so long, that it is not very wonderful if it makes me a little light headed also. But to return—The passage which Mr. Brancker does not quite believe, is as follows—'The Copy rights of the 1st vol. of poems and of the 3 parts of the Worthies do not exactly belong to me (Bingley) but I am empowered to negotiate a sale. The person to whom they do belong is not willing to fix a price, but will be glad to listen to any proposal that may be made. A London House has applied to purchase, and the same reply has been made in that case as in yours. If, therefore, Mr. C.'s friends can make up their minds as to what price they will give, I shall be glad to hear, etc.' To this Mr. Brancker replied, and kindly sent me the extract from his letter dated January 16th, 'I am not prepared to make you any offer on the part of Mr. Coleridge's friends for the two Copy rights, nor do I think it likely that one will be made. I trust, however, they will not be disposed of to strangers without being previously offered to Mr. Coleridge at the trade price.' I daresay you will agree with my friend's scepticism, and think him perfectly right in leaving the Copy rights alone till there is some plain speaking about whom they belong to. Besides he has paid £20—(and never once alluded to it in his letter to me. I only gather the circumstance from Bingley's demand and acknowledgement) to free me from all engagements as to the second vol.—and this is far more than I had any right to expect. All this trouble (there must have been three letters at least, to say nothing of the money, which to him is not perhaps very much) this excellent man has undertaken without solicitation from me or mine, (I merely asked his advice) and that too at a time when his own health is not good, his wife on a sick bed, and in the midst of multitudinous business, both commercial and political, for one who has no claim in the world upon him, except it be that his poor Lady used to give me Sugar-candy when I was a little boy at Clappersgate, and she, the pretty Jane Moss, had no thoughts of being Mrs. Brancker. I hope he will be back in April, as he promises. I might not, perhaps, have said quite so much about his excellences, which you could easily enough have deduced for yourselves from his conduct, but that I am afraid, my dear Mother has sometimes suspected me of being insensible to kindness, thinking favours things of course or no more than my due (nay, nay, Mother, you never thought me quite such a fool as that, either). I recollect for instance your once saying, that you

supposed I considered gratitude no virtue because I said one
Sunday when I had no appetite for church, that I did not see
why I should go to church the more because Lady Beaumont
was at Keswick. If my dear Mother, you had then reproved
me for want of prudence or decorum, you would have done
right, but gratitude had nothing to do with the case, and
besides, then I did not know the value of kindness, so well as
I do now. Sometimes I may have said things about dear
Uncle to you, which I should have [been] very angry if any
body else had said, but then—it was when you used his name
as a reproach to me, or advanced his conduct or opinion as
a rule. Now if you want to make a man hated, hold him up
as an Example. It is an extraordinary proof of the loveliness
of Southey's character, that though his name was rife in every
objurgation and every admonition I received, I never could
help but love him. Dear Uncle, he has his trials in this
world—four lovely children taken from him, two of them at
the most interesting ages—and one with little warning (for
dear Herbert always bore a prophecy of early death in his
pale face and bright eye—it was not the natural brightness
of childhood—prophecies are never intelligible till they are
fulfilled) and now—poor Aunt! I long to see them, but I
know not how far a visit at this time, even for an hour would
be agreeable—It has been such an unmerciful day of rain
and wind that I have not been able to get to Rydal since I
received the agreeable ultimatum (which was late last night).
I shall, of course, consult Mr. W. about what is next to be
done. I should have written to some of you before I did, but
knowing the matter to be in good hands, I hoped you would
hear nothing about it at all, till I could announce the settlement. Dora is gradually improving, but Miss W. remains in a
state from which I fear she will not emerge till she feels 'that
Death with her is dealing'. There is something consolatory
though melancholy in the reflection how few persons perish
without a revival within. Mr. Wordsworth looks older but
keeps up his spirits wonderfully; his character, like his poetry, is
much softened by age. I know not how Derwent can think his
last volume poor and degenerate. This is, indeed, nothing like
the Ode on Immortality, or the finer parts of the Excursion,
there is neither the same profundity of thought nor the same
solar warmth of feeling—but there is a vein of tenderness,
sweetness, and beauty which is almost new. It is natural for
an old man, and such our revered friend now is, to withdraw

alike from intensity of intellectual exertion and perturbation of feeling. My father could not have written the Ancient Mariner at sixty, yet who will say that his Genius declined? The Genius was there as mighty as ever, but the frame could no longer endure to set it a going. Most delightful it is that Wordsworth has opened for himself a path so well suited to his declining years. I do wish, however, that there had been a little less of Lowther Castle, and that he had not call'd poor old Lady Lonsdale a *Nymph*.[1] As for the Politics— No doubt you have heard of Miss Senhouse's happy union with Squire Pocklington—What a name—Edith changed for the worse,[2] but from Senhouse to Pocklington. What a declension! By the way—how is Edith's darling? I wonder if she is at all fond of it. I cannot imagine that queen-like creature having any thing to do with clouts, nightcaps, and other unsightly and anti-aristocratic utensils which are entailed upon maternity in the lower and middle orders. She decidedly should have been a countess, and had nothing to do with the bantling, except when it was brought in with its finest lace cap and muslin robes, when she thought fit to be interesting and madonna like, and to shew that the Noblesse are not incapable of natural affection. We have had a gay Christmas—the festivities are now pretty well over. I meant to describe some of them but have left no room. Miss E. Carlton is married, and now the Revd. Mrs. Bates—her brother is about to marry Miss North. You know that both the Miss Whites are spliced—with revolution moving upon earth and comets whisking their tails about in the sky—what the Devil can folks be thinking of. Thank you for the collar. I forgot to say any thing about Giles's bill—but I have nothing to say except to thank you. If it was not paid before, all's right. Mr. Dawes is well. I dined with him last week. Love to ... Bless a Soul. Your affectionate son and brother. . . . .[3] of writing this small hand.   H.C.

LETTER 53

To HENRY NELSON COLERIDGE.

Grasmere, May 8, 1836.

Dear Hal

Returning on Friday evening from a pleasant party at my

---

[1] See 'Lines written in the album of the Countess of Lonsdale, Nov. 5, 1834'.
[2] Edith Southey, who married the Rev. John W. Warter.
[3] MS. blurred by stamp.

excellent friend Mrs. Claude's, I found the pacquet from
Snouderumpater, for which many thanks. Mr. Wordsworth's
journey enables me to send you this sabbath-breaking scrawl,
free, gratis, for nothing. You will hear from him a more
accurate account of the good afflicted than I can give you.
Suffice it to say, that their patience, fortitude, and cheerfulness are a spectacle for men and angels. I never in truth
had so high an opinion of the family before. In their days of
health and happiness, there was something exclusive in the
closeness of their union, and the ladies exhibited a degree of
jealousy about the bard's fame, with which I could not
altogether sympathize, and, moreover, they were somewhat
too apt to 'season their fire-side with personal talk'. Poor dear
Miss Hutchinson, without a spark of malice in her heart, had,
from the perfect faultlessness of her own life, a good deal of
intolerance in her head, and yet, she could forgive in persons
whom she liked, much greater derelictions than she censured
in those to whom she was indifferent! Of all my friends, of
whom God has given me so many more and better than I
have deserved, she has [been] the only one in whose manner
I observed a marked difference, indeed, though she never
surceased her good wishes for my father's son, I am afraid she
did not latterly regard me with any degree of pleasurable affection. I believe politics had some little to do with this coldness.
Not that she was so illiberal as to dislike people for differing
from her own opinions, (she certainly and naturally liked them
better when they agreed) but hers was pre-eminently a one
sided mind. Had I been an out-an-outer, she could have
understood it, but my mixture of old cavalier toryism and
German liberalism, (for I never was, and never talked like
a Frenchified Jacobin or Yankee republican) puzzled her,
and she was rather shocked at my almost total disbelief in the
existence of political integrity in any sect or party, to which,
nevertheless, the time gives too much proof. But she is gone
where these things trouble not, where I hope, no rumour of
earth reaches and no memory of earth remains.[1] A knowledge of what is doing below would make any spirit, not
possessed of omnipotence and omniscience and absolute self-
sufficiency, miserable even in Heaven. But, perhaps this is
heresy. I know not what induced me to teaze dear Sara with
my politics in my last long letter. I must have expressed my-

---

[1] Sarah Hutchinson, Wordsworth's sister-in-law, died June 23, 1835.

self ill, for nothing could be more remote from my intention than to accuse you of misrepresentation or suppression in regard to the public opinions of ὁ μακαρίτης. All I said was, that his was a many sided mind, that it had chanced that I had seen it under aspects probably less frequently developed in latter years, and though I well know that he never would have approved of the measures called reforms, and still less of the manner and spirit in which they have been carried, his conversation when I was last in the habit of hearing him authorized me to think that he did perceive the necessity of deep and vital changes, not in servile compliance with the spirit of the age,—(an odious phrase) but to approximate the practice of the constitution to its Ideal and final cause he certainly did hold, or I grievously mistook him, that though the government did work well according to the money getting commercial principles of the economists who assailed it, it did not work well morally, did not perform its duty to God or to the divine in Man, did not supply those demands of human nature, which are at once rights and duties. He did express strong indignation against the selfishness and short sightedness of the governing classes, a selfishness modified and mollified indeed by much kindness and good-nature,—but not controlled or balanced by any clear principles. He utterly condemn'd I know, to his latest hour the system which considering men as things, instruments, machines, property, does not in effect make them so. Though he never held that happiness is the legitimate end of human existence, he thought comfort, competence, national free-agency, a kind and paternal treatment of the many, which alone can render a duteous, filial loyalty possible—are the essential conditions of a healthy state either of individuals or classes. I cannot, moreover, help thinking, that though at no time of his life a Jacobin or a revolutionist, he was in his youth at the period to which my earliest recollections of him extend, a great deal more of a republican, and certainly, much more of a philanthropist and cosmopolite, than he appears to have been distinctly aware of in his riper years. I recollect being somewhat startled and terrified at the exulting tone in which he spoke of the French Revolution long after its true character had appeared. He was, as far as his nature allowed him to hate any thing, a king-hater, and a prelate-hater, and spoke of Charles 1st and of Laud with a bitterness in which I never did and never can sympathize.

He also, but read not this to Mama or Sara, did even when I was last with him at Highgate, speak very harshly of the political subserviency of W.— and S.— Indeed I am most happy to see by the Table Talk, and by the testimony of his will, that ere his decease, his heart was fully reconciled to those excellent men, from whom he was for a while cruelly alienated by the ill offices of inconsiderate tale-bearers—perhaps a little aggravated by the injudicious praises of others—who dwelt upon their virtues in a way that sounded a great deal too like an implied reproach of his merely corporal infirmities. There is, moreover, I am afraid, a jealousy in friendship as well as in love— and —certainly was apt to consider himself as my father's only true friend. Many, and many a time have I pleaded, almost with tears, for my dear Uncle, and I think it very hard, that I should have been represented to my mother as a detractor from his moral and intellectual greatness, because I did not and do not, admire any of his laureate poetry—(except the epicedian on the Princess, which is beautiful) nor agree with all his Articles in the *Quarterly. Entre nous,* I think he has retained, even in his ultra-toryism, and high-churchmanship, the fundamental error which made him, in the heat of youth, somewhat of a revolutionist; he expects a great deal more from positive institutions than God ever intended they should produce. You cannot make men moral, religious, or enlightened by Law. Law has done its best, when it prevents the evil-disposed from being mischievous with impunity, and leaves no pretext for any man to take the Law into his own hand. The first, not highest duty of a Government, is to constitute and maintain the state, to defend the national existence and the public honour; the second, to keep the peace at home, to give security to person and property, and to protect religion and morality from insult or oppression; the third, to promote the healthy circulation of property by a well-regulated taxation, and, as far as may be, to prevent individuals from growing rich by making or keeping others poor, to see that private wealth is not increased without a proportionate increase of public wealth. These I hold to contain the sum and substance of the duties of a state—out of which duties arise the just prerogatives of a state, and the just obedience of the subject. No individual, no multitude or combination of individuals, be their rank, education, or usefulness what they may, have any right to set their private will, interest, convenience, humour, or opinion against the will of the State embodied in law, but the law should never represent the will, inclination, or interest of any individual, or any class, but should be the passionless exponent of practical reason. As to the distribution of powers and functions, it is plainly absurd to lay down any general rule, or to assert the absolute unconditional right of any man or number of men to a legislative voice, but certainly, that does appear to me to be the best condition of society, in which the citizen is never wholly merged in the subject, which gives to every adult, not indeed direct political power but a political existence, a public character, which attributes to every man a something beyond his bare human being. It seems to me a great solecism to allot political privileges or franchises to any man from which others of equal rank, property, occupation, and education, are excluded—the effect by the way, of the blundering ten-pound qualification—about the worst that could have been devised. You will understand that I allude to privilege and franchise emanating from and referring to, the central government, not to the chartered rights of self-governing bodies, as the Universities and the Church ought to be. With regard to these, it is sufficient that their privileges do not infringe on the common rights of citizenship, far less intermeddle with the imprescriptible duties, duties subjective, and therefore rights objective of men to their own pure reason and their immortal souls—which are called—I admit by a very ineligible phrase, the rights and liberties of conscience.

Prerogatives may and must be given to certain bodies and certain persons, perhaps are most conveniently given to an hereditary first-magistrate and an hereditary peerage, but these prerogatives should always be correlative to duties, should be larger than the efficient performance of the necessary duties requires. To aristocratic privileges, apart from legislative or conservative functions, I am a decided enemy. In his private capacity, the rich man should have nothing more than the poor man but what he pays for. Sumptuary laws, which confine certain luxuries of dress, diet, amusement, to certain classes, are hateful—they break down the sanctity of home if strictly executed, and if as in our precious Universities, they are generally suffered to sleep, they are incentives both to extravagance and to deceit. They degrade and demoralize the trading class, and introduce a hungry, cringing, impudent race of contraband dealers. You yourself would hardly defend privileges which entitle a nobility or Clergy to exemption from the common operation of law—which allow, and in a manner encourage, the aristocracy to oppress, wrong, and defraud their inferiors. I believe the odious privileges of the French nobility and Clergy to have been a great cause of the ferocity of the French Revolution. Little of this kind exists in England —the exemption of the Clergy from military service and onerous civil offices, of course, is perfectly right, and the personal irresponsibility of the King, is perhaps essential to the Monarchy, but the exemption of real property from the payment of debts seems to me a dishonesty which no expediency can justify—and I see no reason that a peer should be believed on his honour, while the commoner is impiously required to wager his soul. I rejoiced with the angels in Heaven to find that my revered parent thoroughly sympathized with my abhorrence of the present system of administering oaths. I hope all oaths, at least all but the oaths of witnesses in criminal cases, will be speedily abolished. I hold that no private individual is entitled to disobey or evade any law, simply because he finds it inconvenient to obey it, or because he thinks it unwise or unnecessary, or because he was not himself consulted in the making of it, so long as it does not enjoin what is sinful, or prohibit a positive duty, or compromise the natural rights of parents, husbands, and wives etc., or forbid what though not an absolute duty to all, may be necessary to many, as marriage. But then, the law, to claim obedience, must respect matter that is the proper subject of legislation—matter in fact, terrene and secular. I am as decidedly for an established and well-endowed church as you are, but I would have it an independent establishment, a complete self-government, assoil'd from all earthly business, save the care of its own property. I would have the church policy purely spiritual, the state policy merely and absolutely secular—I am far enough from a radical. There is only one point, a mighty one to be sure, in which I do agree with the Radicals, that religion should never operate as a political disqualification, that no act of the Church, or any Church, should require a civil sanction, and no act of the State a religious sanction—that marriage for civil purposes, as legitimacy of children etc., should be *bonâ-fide* a civil ceremony—(I would not certainly admit the performance of marriage by dissenters to be any necessary part of the legal tie); the civil ceremony should be obligatory on all, and all should be at liberty to seek the blessing of the Minister where they expect to find it. With Marriage, as it is a symbol, a mystery, a moral and religious bond, I hold that the state has nothing to do; as marriage is a matter of decency, the world have a right to a pledge, and visible proof, who are and who are not married. It is the business of the State, as far as may be, to prevent sham, clandestine, or very hasty and premature marriages, to regulate the relations of property and the law of inheritance, but it should never compel the performance of any religious rite, or suffer the civil concerns of any man to be compromised by its omission. Of course, the same observations apply to the registration of infants, etc. I hope the Lords, the Bishops especially, will not oppose the Dissenters' Marriage, or registration acts; it is high time for the Church to cast away every thing that is merely formal, non essential, or dubious, and take a *firm* stand on the vital points of Christianity. (I am glad my father continued to disapprove of the Athanasian creed). But with the Marriage and registration bills, I think that concession to the Dissenters ought to stop. They have no right to legislate for the spiritual concerns of the church. All parish business should be disjoined from vestries, and dissenters should be excluded from them—indeed, none but regular communicants should be admitted. But mind, I will not have a single communion profaned to a test. But how I am running on—tired as a dog—and not said a word to the purpose. I shall very shortly send the article on Macbeth. I fear it will be so long that you will be obliged to curtail it. I shall have a good deal of Greek to quote. I hope it will be sufficient to refer to the passages, as none of them are from uncommon books, and writing Greek is so very laborious and slow a process, to me, nor could I be sure of correctness as to the accents. I shall give my own poetical translation, also, of the scenes which Schiller in his translation of Macbeth has substituted for the original witch-scenes.[1] He has altogether mistaken in my humble opinion, the true character of Shakespeare's witchcraft—but the verses are pretty. I hope you did not write the article on the Original in the last Quarterly but one, as it contains a very unfeeling allusion to poor Charles Lamb. There is an Ass writes for the Quarterly—who is he? You need not tell him that I said so.

---

[1] For Hartley's translation of *Schiller's Translation of Macbeth* see *Poems*, 288-9.

I shall write to Moxon at Rydal Mount, after talking to
Mr. W. The £5 was for an article in the Edinburgh Encyclopaedia about Sinclair the letter founder.[1] It was paid me by
Sinclair himself. My garments are all right and tight, some of
them rather too tight, for your Coats will not button over my
breast—not that I am grown fat, but I am very deep from the
breast to the back bone. I thank Mama for the stock—but
shall not wear it in Summer—they are hot and stain one's
shirt, and I have silk neckcloths plenty—the gloves are very
acceptable.

Owen Lloyd has lent me an essay on Faith by my Father[2]
transcribed by poor Charles Lloyd. It will probably make
a good addition to your forthcoming volumes. I will transcribe it tomorrow, and Mr. Ball, an excellent Quaker friend
of mine, who is going to London on Tuesday, will take
charge of it. I will also send some marginal notes from the
Andersons, though you will probably see the propriety of not
publishing the whole of one of them, as it contains opinions
and certainly expressions which my father would not
latterly have approved. I have been reading Von Raumer's
England.[3] He speaks highly of the Table talk and of my
father, though some of the sentiments are at variance with his
own. But I really must conclude as I have a few lines to
scribble to Sara. What would Sir Andrew Ague-cheek say to
such an immensity of a scraitch on the Sabbath.

Your affectionate Coz-

H. COLERIDGE.

N.B. I have read Taylor's Philip Van Artevelde.[4] It is
admirable.[5]

It was the wish of the Coleridges, particularly the immediate
family, to counteract the impressions created by the unjust
publications of de Quincey, Allsop, and Cottle, and every one
turned to Hartley. He promised an essay on his father, to be prepared as an introduction to a new edition of the *Biographia Literaria*
(1847). Delay after delay followed, and though for years Hartley
speaks of the essay as nearing completion, it was never forthcoming, the supplement to the *Biographia Literaria* being prepared

---

[1] The British Museum catalogue contains only one edition of the *Edinburgh
Encyclopaedia* (1830), in which no essay on Sinclair appears.
[2] Coleridge's 'Essay on Faith' was included in the fourth volume of the
Literary Remains, p. 425.   [3] F. von Raumer's *England in 1835*.
[4] Henry Taylor's *Philip Van Artevelde* was published in 1834.
[5] At the bottom of this letter Hartley has penned a note to his sister Sara,
which is omitted.

by Henry Nelson Coleridge and Sara. Fragments of Hartley's essay on his father have been preserved and were published in the *Publications of the Modern Language Association.* ('Hartley Coleridge on His Father', E. L. Griggs, December 1931.)

LETTER 54

To MRS. SAMUEL TAYLOR COLERIDGE, *21 Downshire Place, Hampstead, London.*

Grasmere, August 21, [1836.]

Dear Mother

Though I have not a very great deal to tell you, yet recollecting my promise of the 4th anent, to write again within a fortnight, I prefer breaking the Sabbath to breaking my word. My principle object, however is to apologize for the very hasty, blotted, and rather testy epistle which I wrote upon the spur of the moment, in much mental agitation, and very considerable bodily pain, having a rived heel, the result of new shoes, which had blistered sadly; and when nearly well, were rubbed once again by the necessity of putting on shoes, and walking (very fast) to Rydal to breakfast with the Judge,[1] (for Dr. Arnold's note reach'd me only just in time). Moreover, being obliged to go with shoe-heel down, I had run a thorn into my foot. All this, which must appear almost ludicrous to you, accustomed as you are to serious maladies, is now quite better, and I am indeed remarkably well. I call'd at Rydal Mount yesterday and ask'd if they had aught to say, but nothing except love. I am afraid all there, is more in *statu quo* than we could wish. Mr. Wordsworth is better than could be expected and his spirits wonderfully good, all things considered—he is busy about his poems, which is good for him. Mrs. Wordsworth as kind and sweet, almost as cheerful as ever—but, alas—she looks very, very aged. Dora, dear creature, too manifestly tries to seem as well as she can, without much success. Mr. Quillinan, Willy and John (not the Rev. but Ap. Richard), are there. They had nothing new from Keswick. I wish the Doctor may do some good. Talking of Doctors, there is another volume of the Doctor forthcoming. What a wonderful energy of intellect, that can produce such a work under such circumstances. And yet, it is possible, that poor Uncle finds a relief in writing happy nonsense. He says he cannot now bear to write serious poetry. It is

---

[1] John Taylor Coleridge became a Justice of the King's Bench in 1835.

a fact, which, to a person unacquainted with human nature, might seem a paradox, that the most famous works of humour have been written by men in distress of mind, body, and estate, and that tragic writers (dramatic and narrative) have been generally men of light hearts. In further illustration of which fact, it may be remarked, that young Poetical Novelists deal much more in the pathetic, the gloomy, and the terrible, than those of more advanced years. My father was young when he wrote the Three - Graves; Wordsworth was young, when he wrote the Female Vagrant, Vaudracour and Julia, and the more affecting passages of the Excursion: and I believe Southey would now shrink from the terrific imagery of Thalaba and Kehama. King Lear was one of Shakespeare's earlier plays —Twelfth night was his last. I think I perceive in Wordsworth's last volume, a decided inclination to the playful, the elegant, and the beautiful; with an almost studied exclusion of the profound feeling and severe thought which characterised the offspring of his middle age. This can be the only reason why Derwent thinks these poems *poor* and *degenerate*; for they are as perfect, perhaps more perfect, in their kind than any of their predecessors: but the kind is less intense, and therefore, incapable of that unique excellence which the disciples adore. My taste is more Catholic, and I am delighted, yea thankful to God, to see such freshness and loveliness of imagination, in a man upon whom old age has descended not without its attendant trials and sorrows.

I hope the dear Travellers are by this time safe at their destination. Thursday, the day prefixed for their departure, was an abominable pourer here. I hope it was better in the South, as Henry with his cruel cold, had to go on the Dicky. Devonshire will be a new scene to Herbert and Edith. They will be smothered with love. I hope Sara will not be the worse for her journey; Mrs. Woollam, who has had some experience, thinks she will be a great deal better for her rustication. God grant that it may be so. I wish you could have gone with them, for you will be solitary in their absence. The Judge looks no older to me, than when I saw him sixteen years ago, only greyer. He is very unlike a Judge, at least unlike my conception of a Judge, but then I never saw a Judge before, except when dressed in character. The wig, and scarlet gown, I daresay, will make him judgematical enough. Frank looks much older, but then he is so—he is greyer than myself and I shall be quite white in a few years.

This is a family disease. Is Derwent at all grizzled? Poor dear Derwent, how I long to see him. I am much distressed to hear of his wife's weak state—the loss of Emily is a hard trial. I shall now write to them. I have not yet done so since their affliction, not out of procrastination, for I never intended it, but because I think new sorrows are best let alone. Mere sympathy, condolence, does but add grief to grief. I can give no comfort which his Xtian mind will not better supply, and to attempt to divert, while the wound is young, is impertinent mockery. Now, it may please him to find he is not forgotten, and I may possibly help to give a new impulse to his thoughts. I suppose the parcel, containing my transcriptions for Henry, is lost—and I must do it all over again. This is provoking—for I hate transcribing, and the Essay is pretty long, and besides, it is Owen's property, and I have kept it an unmerciful time. But there is no remedy. I shall send the article on Macbeth, direct to Lockhart, which will save you expense—and to defer it till Mrs. Woollam's return might miss the Quarter. Indeed, it will be so long that I am afraid it will need clipping. About the Essay on my Father, I will write to Hal himself. If there is a coat or frock which you can send by Mr. Woollam, it will be useful at Christmas. Have you got my Quintillian? If so, send it by the same hand. The Aristotle etc., I intend for my Nephews in due time. I am going to dine at Mr. Parry's on Tuesday. You will be sorry to hear that Mrs. Parry's weak health has determined them to offer the villa for sale. I do not think they can easily find a purchaser, except at a great loss: for it is a house which it will require a large income to keep up, and there is so little property pertaining. They are excellent people and will be a loss to the neighbourhood. Mr. Brancker is just returned from Liverpool; I am going to call on him. Mr. Dawes is wonderful and as good as ever, though his very unevangelical, and somewhat blue principles make him very unpopular with a certain set. I often have to fight his battles. He is a plain spoken man, and shews the worst to the outwards. Mrs. Fleming's best respects. Pray give my grateful remembrances to Mr. and Mrs. Gillman, if you see them. I ought to have written—I will write to Mrs. Gillman.

I remain, dear Mother
Your truly affectionate
H.C.

LETTER 55

To JOHN TAYLOR COLERIDGE.

[Grasmere. October, 1836.]

Honoured Kinsman

I shall be most happy to wait on you at four.[1] Indeed, were I quite sure of finding you at home, I would come much earlier that we might discuss matters at length.

As to the prefatory essay, I have been consulting about it with myself. I should not shrink from the task, were [it only] my father's character as a poet, a Critic, and in general a literateur (will it not offend his manes to be characterised by a French word?), but I am hardly capable of arguing his philosophy at present. Indeed my opinion is that no view of it should be attempted, till his remarks are all before the public.

Yours truly,

H. COLERIDGE.

LETTER 56

To MRS. SAMUEL TAYLOR COLERIDGE, *Downshire Place, Hampstead.*

Rotha Some place—Oct. 28, [1836.]
Deep snow, is it so with you?

My dear Mother

One of your dear old phrases, recorded I doubt not, in the lingo grande, was between hawk and buzzard. Now I have been exactly between Hawk and Buzzard with regard to you and yours, and, my dear Mother, but I—[*sic*] for some months past. You would, therefore, naturally excuse me for a little confusion of memory, seeing I am but a bat, fluttering between Hawk and Buzzard, owing my safety only to a compact between the two aristocratic Accipitres, never to feed on carrion. But now, Mother, for the application of the Fable. I should have written to Henry, long before now, indeed, as soon as the Judge shewed me, not his epistle, for that I never saw—it was sent to Keswick, but the extract from his epistle— of and concerning the introduction to the *Biographia Literaria*. But first, concerning the said introduction, I must tell you that it is doing, and will by the time this letter reaches you,

---

[1] John Taylor Coleridge had taken Fox How (the Arnold residence in Grasmere) from the end of the long vacation, after Dr. Arnold had returned to Rugby.

be done; that is, the outward walls will be completed, for I shall have a great deal to transcribe—which may take a week longer: 2d. If Derwent has, as Henry mentioned it was his intention to do, written any thing on the subject which may be producible when the Biograph. Lit. 2 Edi. is published, I should for many reasons wish it to take precedence of mine. I do not state this in order to excuse myself from a labour, which under other circumstances I should have declined, because my article will be complete before I can hear anything about it. But I do think, that an introduction from the 'Rev. Derwent Coleridge, M.A., Head Master of Helston School, etc., etc., etc.' would have more weight with that portion of the public whom Henry would best like to please, than plain Hartley Coleridge. Besides, Derwent was much more with S.T.C. in his latter years, is a much superior scholar, in every respect fitter for the task. At the same time I acknowledge that he has not so much leisure to devote to the subject. I dare say, indeed, that when his school is over and he is fairly in his arm-chair and slippers, he does not take up a pen very willingly, or if he does, it would rather be to add a few notices for some ponderous work of learning: to collect the metal whereof to cast a cannon, some centuries hence, than to pound up sulphur, charcoal and nitre to make a squib for immediate explosion. So, I suppose though I cannot do the thing as it ought to be done, I know nobody likely to do it better, and so—but what think you of a Sonnet for the commencement?

If, when you were a living man, my Sire,
 I shrank unequal from the task to praise
 The increasing worth of your successive days
What shall I do, when your celestial fire,
Its earthly fuel extinguished, higher, higher,
 Purged from the passionate subject of all lays,
 From all that Fancy fashions or obeys,
And every breeze that eddies round the lyre
Is altogether what I dreaded most?
 No genius could aright the likeness paint
 While upon earth an erring, suffering saint,
The best of earth, was all that you could boast
 That best to honour if my will was faint,
How shall I praise you in the heavenly host?[1]

---

[1] This form of the sonnet differs considerably from the one included by Derwent in the edition of Hartley's poems. Cf. *Poems*, 111.

I shall alter if not improve this much before it is committed to the press, but I send it to you, to convince you, that my mind is in it and that I am really about it. When it is done—it will be sent off immediately, carriage pay'd, (for I expect £5 for another job) not waiting for the long deferred arrival of Mrs. Woollam—What a dear little Angel Katty Woollam is!!! Owen Lloyd has just gone out of the room, for perhaps you do not know that I am now writing at Mrs. Claude's, and suggested some improvements in the Sonnet, which I shall avail myself of. He desires his kindest remembrances. He is much better. But how is dear Sara? I have sometimes wished that I had a magic necklace, or picture, or barometer, or something or other, that could inform me how that dear little one was going on from day to day, and from hour to hour—And yet, what use would it be of, unless I also possessed the gift of healing. The prayer of a good man availeth much. But I am not a good man.

Mrs. Fleming has set aside a shirt for a pattern, the collar [and] wrists, of which I perfectly approve. You will make whatever alteration fashion requires, for you know how ambitious I am of setting. Tho' I seldom suffer any pious regret at the departure of any of my fellow creatures to be interrupted by any intrusive congratulation of selfishness, yet I am almost afraid, that the death of the living Skeleton who died of corpulency at New York would have given me a more unmingled pang, if I had not hoped that you would no longer make use of him as a measure for my necks, wrists, etc. *Est Modus in Rebus.* Sara will tell you—There's reason in roasting of eggs. (By the way, I never tasted a roasted Egg.) Are there no characters on the Stage but Falstaff and Slender? I am not certainly so bulky as the King that Eglon slew in his summer parlour, but neither could I be drawn like a piece of bride-cake to dream upon, through a wedding ring. The fact is I am neither fatter nor thinner, though a great deal shorter, than a gentleman ought to be. Also Mrs. Fleming says—and so say I—that I have not enough worsted stockings for the winter. I think Mrs. Fleming's youngest Grand daughter whom I call the Paddock, a sweet little girl, who has learned to knit in the Prussian fashion introduced by Mrs. Claude—(I don't know—at least, I can't explain the difference between this and Wilsy's old way of knitting. I can however, see that it is different.) I think however that the Paddock could knit me two or three pairs of winter-stockings if we had the material, but I am not certain that I can spare any of my immediately incoming five for this purpose.   In 3 weeks' time I expect £10 or £15 from a Magazine and then I could see about it, but I am a wretched shopper, and could earn money—though you rightly think I am too slow about that—easier than know how to lay it out to the best advantage.   The profits of the article for the Quarterly I wish to be considered as so much back.   I have not far from ready a volume of Sonnets on Scripture Subjects[1] which may perhaps raise the greater part of my year's lodging.   My Essays, which include those already printed, and those in hand, would make at least two Octavos.[2] The Prometheus and other miscellaneous Poems shall follow ere long.   I could publish forthwith a volume of comicalities such as the Mince Pie[3]—etc., but perhaps these are better scattered in periodicals.   But I do sweat and roar to think, dear Mother, that you and Sara—not perhaps the *only* persons on earth that I care for, but perhaps the only ones that care much for me, though by no [means] the only ones that have been kind to me and for whom I am bound to pray—but I am provoked that you should be tormented by this evocation of evil spirits by D. Q., Cottle,[4] Allsop and Co. —though I cannot say I feel much anger at any but the first— the rest may plead idiocy and dotage in their defence.

Yours

H.C.

P.S. Find I've said nothing above about any thing you care for except my old stockings.   The Rydalians are well on the whole—Joanna 'that wild-hearted maid hath returned to us' about 10 years older than she was 29 years ago.   Dora has been out on horseback, Sir C. Bell and Sir B. Brodie having given horses.   Saw Cuthbert.   He looks tired [?].

---

[1] Derwent, in his edition of Hartley's poems, remarks: 'It was the intention of the Author to have published a series of Sonnets and other short Poems, exclusively on Scriptural subjects, as a Christmas present. The greater part of the pieces in the present collection were written with this design, (which, as explained in the Memoir, was never executed,) about ten or twelve years before his death.' (*Poems by Hartley Coleridge*, 1851, ii. 312–61.)
[2] No collected edition of Hartley's essays was published during his lifetime. Derwent brought out *Essays and Marginalia*, in two volumes, in 1851.
[3] 'Mince Pie' was published in *Blackwood's Magazine* in February, 1828.
[4] Hartley must have referred to the advance notices of Cottle's *Early Recollections*, &c., as the book itself did not appear until 1837.

LETTER 57

To MRS. SAMUEL TAYLOR COLERIDGE, *Hampstead, London.*

My dear Mother   Grasmere, Nov. 6, 1836.

Mrs. Woollam's departure has taken me by surprize. I could not let her go without a few lines, though I have nothing of importance to add to my last, to which by the way, I expected an answer ere now. I received a newspaper to day, which informs me that you are living, but I am cruelly anxious about dear Sara. I hope to God she is at home by this time, and Henry too. I dare say he would be very happy in the enumeration of the poor radicals he has struck off the rolls, if something nearer to his heart than even Toryism did not damp his self-congratulations. Mr. Woollam not coming is a disappointment to me—perhaps to you also. I am resolved never in future to send compositions by private hand. If they be worth any thing, they must be worth carriage. I was at Rydal a day or two ago. All much at one. Of course, I do not now see Miss Wordsworth, but I heard her, which I had rather not, for to be anywise witness to distress one cannot relieve is unprofitable pain. And yet not altogether unprofitable, for the very fact that the All good should have permitted such an intellect to fall into confusion, proves how little we ought to value ourselves on intellectual endowments, apart from our moral use of them. Perhaps the dispensation which seems to us so severe, is really merciful; God has tied a bandage over her eyes, while she is passing the awful river, which he will remove when she has arrived upon the happy shore. There has been much sickness among my friends hereabouts—no great wonder—for the weather is ferocious. I never knew it so bad at the time of year. We had a thick snow on the 29th October. Poor Mrs. Brancker has been very ill indeed. Do you remember the pretty Miss Jane Moss who used to live in the cottage next to our home at Clappersgate? She is Mrs. B. and pretty still, though sadly faded with continual sickness, arising, I have heard, from injudicious treatment in her first and only confinement. She never had a living child. I believe her husband would be a happier man, and perhaps some people might think, a more judicious, that is to say, less political man, if he was a father— but he is a father to Mrs. Claude's children, who are four sweet girls and a noble John Bull of a boy, whom she will have enough to do to manage. The loss of a parent is ever a misfortune—a double misfortune if the parent be of the child's own sex. Still I think it is easier to supply the place of a father than of a Mother. Perhaps I have some know-ledge of what it is practically to be without a father. It is not easy to knit together links once broken. I fear I was not what I ought to have been to my father, any more than to you, but it is very cruel in people whom I never injured to publish my father's natural complaints of my delinquencies to the million whom they concern not—still worse to promulgate what can do no credit either to the living or to the dead, and must convey very false impressions to the public, (What the Devil have the public to do with it?) and most infamous to assume the character of author of the publication of what the Traitor has no moral right in, garnish'd with nonsense which is certainly peculiarly and absolutely his own. But this is foolish, for it can only irritate both you and myself. But I owe Master Allsop a licking. To be sure, he has the excuse of idiocy, which De. Q. could not plead. How could [my father] unbosom himself to such a man? Alas, the wisest of us are not invulnerable to flattery. I hope the dead know nothing of what passes below, or [my father] might be sorely vexed in spirit to hear that a Pagoda had been erected to his memory in which the feelings of his best friends were to be immolated to the partnership of himself and Cobbett! !¹

---

¹ Allsop's *Letters, Conversations and Recollections of S. T. Coleridge* deserves all that Hartley says of it. The book, which is addressed to Allsop's children and was apparently intended for their moral education, consists mainly of the stupid stringing together of Coleridge's letters and conversations, interspersed with Allsop's own advice and observations. A sample of the moral council follows: 'Moral courage, my dear children, the daring to suffer the present evil, be it an expiation for the past, or as an offering or a testimony to convictions, not *lightly* attained, is always its own great reward.' This fragment of wisdom follows an agonizing letter from Coleridge containing personal references to Hartley and Derwent, who are very thinly disguised by Allsop under the initials 'J' and 'E'.

Moultrie's amusing sonnet, 'To the Anonymous Editor of Coleridge's Letters', merits inclusion here:

A gibbering ape that leads an elephant;
A dwarf deformed, the presence heralding
Of potent wizard, or the Elfin King;
Caliban deigning sage advice to grant
To mighty Prosper in some hour of want;
Sweet Bully Bottom, while the Fairies sing,
Braying applause to their rich carolling,
But feebly typify thy flippant cant,
Stupid defamer, who for many a year
With Earth's profoundest teacher wast at school,
And notwithstanding dost at last appear
A brainless, heartless, faithless, hopeless fool.
Come, take thy cap and bells and throne thee here,
Conspicuous on the dunce's loftiest stool.

There is one passage in Allsop's book, which involving a direct attack upon my Cousins, the Judge and the Bishop, and an implied one on my Uncle and Mr. Wordsworth, I shall certainly notice in my essay.[1] I cannot undo what is done, but I think it incumbent upon me to shew that I do feel for the honour of my family and my friends, and it is only prudent to let the bags know that we are not to be stu[ng] with impunity. This, my dear Mother, is a long and uncomfortable digression grown out of Mrs. Claude's family. One of her daughters is as beautiful a creature, [...? ...[2]] excepted, as I ever saw. She must have been married very young—for her eldest daughter looks older than herself. I wish my father had known her—they could have talked German so well together. By the way, I am growing a famous German myself, which is good. When I can translate German I need never be out of work. I have been dining with Mrs. Claude to day and am now sitting in a room without a fire—the climate any thing but tropical, and the hour waxing late—so with my best of love to all—I trust Sara is by you to receive it—

I am, dear Mother,

Your affectionate

ΣΝΟΥΔΕΡΥΜΠΕΡΙΔΗΣ.

LETTER 58

To MRS. SAMUEL TAYLOR COLERIDGE, *Downshire Place, Hampstead, London.*

Grasmere, Dec. 26, 1836.

Thank you for the Almanac.

Dear Mother

Your kind package came to hand this morning, which was most acceptable for all its contents, but most of all, for the dear note in Sara's own hand, which gave me hopes, sadly

---

[1] The attacks are as follows:

'Wordsworth one day said to me, when I [apparently Lamb] had been speaking of Coleridge, praising him in my way, "Yes, the Coleridges are a clever family." I replied, "I know one that is." '

To this conversation Allsop appends a footnote:

'My amiable and kind-hearted friend said here less than the truth, at least as I understand it. Cleverness was not at all a characteristic of Coleridge, whilst it happily suits those to whom Wordsworth alluded, who are or have been clever enough to appropriate their uncle's great reputation to their own advancement, and then to allow him to need assistance from strangers. No one who knows the character or calibre of mind, whether of the Bishop or the Judge, can doubt, *ceteris paribus*, that the one would still have been a curate and the other a barrister, with but little practice, had they borne the name of Smith—had they wanted the passport of *his* name.'   [2] MS. cut here.

frost-bitten by your very unwelcome addition about her re-
newed ill-health. God grant that things may be better when
this reaches its destination. Mess—but I was in the seventh
heaven at the sight [of] her bird-like pen—too full of herself
to pay much attention to any thing so remote in comparison,
though in itself near and dear, as her very lively description
of Frank's and Edward's darlings. I had run down stairs to
tell Mrs. Fleming the good news before the bad caught my
eye, and I said little about the letter, for why damp her congratulations? It is, however, a great comfort that you are
yourself somewhat improving. I do wish, and trust that you
have not such a killing winter as we are threatened with in the
North. After an autumn of almost incessant, cheerless rain, with
have [*sic*] the Scotch variation of snow, wind, and water frozen
in the washing stand. God be thank'd, I keep quite well, and I
believe our friends at the Mount are not worse than usual, but
it is savage with old rheumatic people, among whom I am
sorry to say, that Mr. Dawes—(who when well, has the
person of a man of forty, though I suspect him to be nearly
double of that age) has had a sharp attack. He cannot bear
to see any body when he is unwell. I hope he is so far recovered that I shall meet him at Mr. Brancker's, where I am
going to keep Christmas day, yesterday, the Christmas day
de jure, being Sunday. I believe I have two parcels to acknowledge—certainly two letters. The stockings that came by
Mrs. Parry's parcel fit admirably—so do the Trowzers and
silk-neckcloth. By the way, I have five or six good silk neck-
cloths so you need not think of sending any more. I think
I told you that I gave the scarf which I received at poor
Miss Hutchinson's funeral to little Dinah. You could not but
approve of it, for she does many a job for me, besides constant waiting, but I hope I give no more trouble than needful.
I say I think I told you, for really, if you had not twice complained of the omission, I should have thought that I had
acknowledged the 'Remains',[1] but I suppose I only intended
to do it. I am, on the whole, greatly pleased with them.
There is little in the book that is new to me. Some of the
marginal notes can hardly be intelligible to any but those
who are familiar with the books in which they were written,
and a few contain opinions not strictly consonant with
my father's later judgement. But Henry has performed a

---

[1] H. N. Coleridge's edition of Coleridge's *Literary Remains* appeared between
1836 and 1838 (vols. i and ii, 1836; vols. iii and iv, 1838).

laborious task, with infinite care, industry and skilfulness. I
wish he may approve as highly of my essay on my Father's
character as a Poet, a Critic, and a literary Man—for I
think myself incompetent at present to enter deeply into the
merits of his philosophy. I can only state my thorough
accordance with his Xtianity, to which, under God, I owe
my own. I did intend to have explain'd my plan to Henry in
a long letter, but as the Parries leave us next week (I fear
for a long period) by which time—God willing—I shall
finish the Essay itself. I will say no more at present. But I
must return to the parcels. Both the shirts fit very well; one
I shall wear to day. Indeed, I have it on. I don't quite
understand the peculiarity of the Collar. I suppose it consists
in the slip inserted in the back. However, it does very well.
The Coats are very acceptable. The shoes a great deal too big.
You know I have lady-like trotters. Perhaps I may manage
to exchange them with my shoemaker. It is time to dress, and
I must call at Rydal as I go. Mrs. Fleming may, perhaps, get
some of her children or grandchildren to write you a few
lines against the pacquet, some time when I am out—to
offer to do it myself would not be suitable. She is pretty well.
I am not in imminent want of any thing, have shirts and
drawers enough to be doing with—though to be sure some
of the old uns 'are diabolical'. The white gloves are very nice
—they need not be washed, but may be cleaned with that
universally applicable substance—India Rubber.

Thank the little Darlings for their loves and kisses. I
believe it will be too late ere this comes to hand—to send compliments of the season. Besides I am afraid you will not have
a very merry Xmas, though I hope a happier new-year. I
must conclude—With best love and wishes to Sara, Henry,
and above all, yourself,

I remain, my dear Mother
Your grateful and affectionate
HARTLEY COLERIDGE.

P.S. I suspect the Article in the Edinburgh in which I was
kindly mentioned was written by James Spedding, who has
just written to me about a volume of Poems to be published
for the benefit of the family of a literary man, who, he says,
he does not know, but requests me to contribute a sonnet or
other short piece.[1] I had a former application on the same

---

[1] The memorial volume mentioned above was *The Tribute*, which was got
up for the benefit of Edward Smedley's family, and contained contributions by

head. I shall send some translations from the German and Italian, for I dare not put anything original of mine by the side of Wordsworth, Henry Taylor, Tennyson, and others, who are also contributors. James Spedding is in the Colonial Office. Does Henry know him? Perhaps not, for James is of *our* side. Not a radical, however. I thank him for his selection—for I think it the best thing I ever wrote. Mrs. Claude is at Liverpool, for the health of her eldest daughter, who is in a very puzzling state of nervousness. She is a loss to me for the present. I fear Aunt Coleridge is in a state from which her relief will be a blessing. I have not heard lately from Keswick. Trust that Uncle S. will be the better for his journey. You will be glad to see him and Mr. Wordsworth too. Glad to hear better account of dear Mary. How I long to see Derwent! ! But I shall be positively too late, and if I don't mention every body—you think I don't love them.

In the early part of the year 1837 Hartley went to Sedbergh, in Yorkshire. His friend, the Rev. Isaac Green, assistant master of the school there, having fallen ill, Hartley supplied his place for a few months; a year later, on the sudden death of Mr. Wilkinson, the headmaster, he returned to assume the duties of headmaster from the late spring until the midsummer vacation. Here Hartley found a school already well organized, where it was not his problem to establish discipline. Thus, freed from the vexing responsibility which had marred his experience in the Ambleside school, he was this time eminently successful. Two accounts of Hartley at Sedbergh have been preserved, which present charming pictures of a unique, though effective schoolmaster.

'I first saw Hartley in the beginning, I think, of 1837, when I was at Sedbergh, and he heard us our lesson in Mr. Green's parlour. My impression of him was what I conceived Shakspere's ideal of a gentleman to be, something which we like to have in a picture. He was dressed in black, his hair, just touched with grey, fell in thick waves down his back, and he had a frilled shirt on; and there was a sort of autumnal ripeness and brightness about him. His shrill voice, and his quick, authoritative "right! right!" and the chuckle with which he translated "rerum repetundarum" as "peculation, a very common vice in governors of all ages", after which he took a turn round the sofa—all struck me amazingly; his readiness astonished us all, and even himself, as he afterwards told me; for, during the time he was at the school, he never had to use a

---

Tennyson, Landor, and others. Hartley did not contribute, though he mentions several times his intention of doing so.

Dictionary once, though we read Dalzell's selections from Aristotle and Longinus, and several plays of Sophocles. He took his idea, so he said, from what De Quincey says of one of the Eton masters fagging the lesson, to the great amusement of the class, and, while waiting for the lesson, he used to read a newspaper. While acting as second master he seldom occupied the master's desk, but sat among the boys on one of the school benches. He very seldom came to school in a morning, never till about eleven, and in the afternoon about an hour after we had begun. I never knew the least liberty taken with him, though he was kinder and more familiar than was then the fashion with masters. His translations were remarkably vivid; of μογερὰ μογερῶς "toiling and moiling"; and of some ship or other in the Philoctetes, which he pronounced to be "scudding under main-top sails", our conceptions became intelligible. Many of his translations were written down with his initials, and I saw some, not a long while ago, in the Sophocles of a late Tutor at Queen's College, Oxford, who had them from tradition. He gave most attention to our themes; out of those sent in he selected two or three, which he then read aloud and criticised; and once, when they happened to agree, remarked there was always a coincidence of thought amongst great men. Out of school he never mixed with the boys, but was sometimes seen, to their astonishment, running along the fields with his arms outstretched, and talking to himself. He had no pet scholars except one, a little fair-haired boy, who he said ought to have been a girl. He told me that was the only boy he ever loved, though he always loved little girls. He was remarkably fond of the travelling shows that occasionally visited the village. I have seen him clap his hands with delight; indeed, in most of the simple delights of country life, he was like a child. This is what occurs to me at present of what he was when I first knew him; and, indeed, my after recollections are of a similarly fragmentary kind, consisting only of those little, numerous, noiseless, every-day acts of kindness, the sum of which makes a Christian life. His love of little children, his sympathy with the poor and suffering, his hatred of oppression, the beauty and the grace of his politeness before women, and his high manliness,—these are the features which I shall never forget while I have anything to remember.'[1]

'On the 29th of May, the boys having been for some reason balked of the expected holiday, revenged themselves by "stripping the hollows bare of spring", and adorning the school-room with extemporized arbours, pleasant to the eye, but as obstructive as might be to the business of the afternoon. Among other devices, the largest bough was set up tree-wise by Hartley's

---

[1] *Memoir*, cxiv.

desk, and the exercises which awaited his perusal were suspended on the topmost twigs, well out of his reach. Hartley,
however, contrived, by getting on a bench and using a hooked
stick, to filch them down, and many were the jokelets which he
vented on the exercise-tree and its unripe fruit. The mischievous boys had anticipated a storm; they found sunshine; and
Hartley was a double favourite ever after.'[1]

LETTER 59

To HENRY NELSON COLERIDGE, *Downshire Place, Hampstead,*
London.

Sedbergh, March 27, 1837. Revd. I. Green's.

Dear Hal

Were you not surprized to hear that like Tate's King
Lear, I had resumed the rod of empire and recommenced
Paedagogue? It is indeed, a step, I little expected of myself,
and which considerations of mere gain would hardly have
induced me to take, so little agreeable were my recollections
of my former rule. But the desire to relieve the mind and
body of a worthy young man whose sufferings, full as much
mental as bodily, remind me somewhat of what I have
imagined of dear Sara's, and a half feeling that a temporary
change of scene and occupation was growing needful to my
own health of mind, overcame my natural terror of a Hobby
de hoy—I engaged, however, under the express understanding that my functions terminated with the lessons; for I know
myself both morally and physically incapable of exerting
authority or enforcing discipline, and when I find the
animals above my hand in school—(I never meddle out of it)
I must resign. As yet, they are personally respectful and I
have never lost my temper—I believe, indeed, that the disposition to anger decreases with increasing years, unless
ill health occasion bodily irritability. The employment is
not laborious, nor very exhausting, and the superior master
is present should an appeal be necessary, but as I have only
the lower classes to hear, there is not much interest. I am,
however, amused with various sorts and sizes of stupidity,
and as a psychologist, I expect great improvement from the
opportunity of observing the negative quantities of the human
intellect. Snouderumpater requests me not to be sarcastic
with the dull boys, because it will make me unpopular. Now

---

[1] *Fraser's Magazine,* June 1851.

I hope I have too much Christian feeling to make mere slow-
ness of understanding a subject of ridicule, even if it were a
good one, which it is not. For nothing which is not admired,
cried up, or idolized either by its possessor, or by the public,
or at least by some clique or party. [sic] Were I sarcastic at
all, it would not be on dulness, but on cleverness. I am well
aware that when I was myself at school, I was much addicted
to call my co-mates and fellows in the awkward squad,
dunces etc., but then they were my superiors in the play-
ground. I never cut up the little boys, however dense they
might be. A man, however, who is capable of stern dignity
of demeanour should never joke with or upon those whom
he is set over, not so much because jesting gives offence or
even that it provokes retaliation, as because it betrays vanity,
and a vain man has little chance of being respected, unless
he can make himself feared. As school is over by four o'clock
or sooner I have plenty of time for composition, and should
have finished the Essay long ago. I *will* finish it in a fortnight—See if I do not; but truth to say, I hope I shall satisfy
you better than I am able to satisfy myself. My dear Father's
greatness is not only too large for my comprehension, but in
some parts too high for my apprehension—not that I cannot
understand him, but I cannot realize many of his ideas. I
have inherited, it may be, a certain portion of his subtlety of
understanding, but I lack—what in him I most revere—the
power which finds in the acts of the pure reason a permanence—truth—beauty—and supersensuous life. He said himself that every man was born an Aristotelian or a Platonist. I
think I understand that, but it is possible that a man may be
a Platonist κατὰ πνεῦμα, in faith and hope and desire, and an
Aristotelian κατὰ σάρκα, the natural, I may say, inevitable
operation of his mind may be Aristotelian, and yet, he may
be conscious that there must be certain Platonic truths essential and possible, which he cannot integrate with his self-
constitutive individuality. But this is *nihil ad rem*, because I
do not intend to discuss my father's Philosophy at all, except
in connection with his Ideal of Poetry. I certainly shall make
the essay something more than a review of his Poems. For
I shall call it—Coleridge the Poet. Now I conceive that the
poems he has written, admirable as they are, do but indicate,
or to use a word of his own—in his own sense—symbolize
himself as a Poet, and that very imperfectly. My plan is as
follows—First, I shall disclaim all pretensions of taking the

height and measure of his mind, in its completeness, not on the ground of my own incapacity, for it is a bad kind of Egotism to be talking to the Public about one's own incapacities—but on the plain common-sense argument, that such an attempt were premature till his philosophical remarks are publici juris. 2nd. I shall state my reasons for choosing his poetical character for my theme: 3rdly—Give my Idea—of a Poet—what therein essential—what accidental—how far dependent on the idiosyncracy, mental and physical, how influenced by circumstances, collateral studies etc. Under this head I shall examine how far S.T.C. the Poet was influenced by S.T.C. the Philosopher, and clear him from the imputation of being a Metaphysical Poet. Undoubtedly in some of his early poems, he did versify Metaphysics, but then he ceased to be a Poet at all—for his then Metaphysics, from which by the way, I derive my pretty Christian name, were not very poetesque—(a word we want confoundedly) but his maturer taste acknowledged that this was riding his hobby-horse out of the road, and all his poetry is no more metaphysical than all ideal poetry must be. There certainly is such a thing as Metaphysical Poetry; but as far as I know, Wordsworth is the only Metaphysical Poet; Davis [John Davies?] was only a Metaphysical versifier, Lord Brooke only a metaphysical aphorist, for his tragedies are hardly verse at all. Henry More was a Poet and a Metaphysician, but his poetry and his metaphysics are curd and whey—like the Drama and the Poetry of Euripides and of Fletcher, both of whom were Poets and Dramatists, but neither of them a Dramatic Poet—for their Drama is not poetry, and their poetry is not Drama—But I see [I] must conclude, or else I shall leave no room to satisfy our good mother's anxiety about my toggery.

All I can say on the subject is, that I am well in Coats—but ill in trowzers; therefore, must have a new pair. My Ambleside tailor is paid—how—I shall explain in my next. Have got a new pair of shoes. Have read Derwent's speech —Very good, but not the line of argument I should have taken. Quite agree in execrating the proposed robbery. Little in Mama's last about darlings—wish I could see them. Glad you've got house in Park. Sorry obliged to leave Hampstead. Make best excuse you can to Mama for not writing before. Send Coz letter with packet.

Your affectionate etc.
H.C.

While Hartley was at Sedbergh in 1837, his excellent hostess, Mrs. Fleming, died. His mother, who, now as always, seems to have regarded her son as a helpless child, was solicitous about what arrangements he could make for board and lodging. 'It is natural to think', she wrote to Hartley on July 8, 1837,

'that you would have written on the news of the death of poor Mrs. Fleming, whose departure from this vale of tears is so much regretted by your anxious mother, as most certainly by yourself. . . . I was sorry to infer [from Mrs. Wordsworth's letter] that you could no longer expect a home under that roof. Nothing was said about the books, cloathes, etc.—which you left there, but, doubtless you have had some intimation of these matters from the heirs or executors of your late poor friend. Mrs. Wordsworth seemed to think you intended to stay where you are, [Sedbergh] but she will see, from my letter, that you intend to stay till midsummer. . . . Do not keep me in suspense about your future plans, as I cannot be easy till I know what you mean to do. I hope you will not think of a public house as in the instance of poor J. Bell's house, which you made your home so many years. I suppose there are persons in Grasmere who would be glad to have you, if only for the sum paid for your board—but I guess it is not very easy to meet with a home for you so suitable as your last.'

Fortunately, Hartley was able to make his home with a young farmer and his wife, William and Eleanor Richardson, who watched over him tenderly, and with whom he stayed until his death in 1849.

LETTER 60

To MRS. HENRY NELSON COLERIDGE, *10 Chester Place, Regent's Park, London.*

[Postmark, September 7, 1837.]

My dear Sister

Thank you for your Fairy Tale,[1] which I [have] not yet read, so cannot praise. It will, however, make an excellent text for a review, in which I can do it ample justice without letting the cat out of the bag. I was right glad of all your letters, for I was growing anxious about you all, although the news is not quite so good as I could have wished, it is not on the whole, worse than I anticipated. I am now comfortably settled,

---

[1] Sara Coleridge's *Phantasmion* was published in 1837. In this fairy tale Coleridge's daughter shows that she inherited to no little degree the imaginative power of her father.

and trust to get a great deal done. I certainly find the Essay a very nervous and puzzling sort of affair. Whether I shall execute it to your satisfaction I know not, but I am sure I cannot do it to my own. It were indeed, no very hard matter to review the poems, somewhat more intelligently than they have ever been reviewed before: but you must be aware, how imperfect an examen of the departed's powers, even as a poet, the most ingenious analysis of his printed verses must be—considering that he ceased to be a writer of poetry before his mind was settled, indeed when it had only given indications of its final tendency. Few however, as his poems are, I think they exhibit three distinct phases, not perhaps strictly distributable in order of time, yet capable of the painterly classification of first, second, and last manner. The first include most of those call'd juvenile poems, in which little more is attempted than the expression of tender feelings, under beautiful images in sweet versification. These do not appear to me to differ much from other juvenile poems, except as they are better, and better and worse is no generic distinction. There is much love, much melancholy, but of a very nightingalish sort—now and then a good deal of anger— and a great deal too much personification. These are but the flower bud of his poetic nature, while it remained a part of his individuality. I think the 'Lover's Resolutions' the best of this class. 2nd. His attempts to embody in poetry his philosophic mind and moral aspirations, as they existed in his early manhood, e.g. The 'Religious Musings', 'Destiny of Nations', 'Fears in Solitude', etc. 3rdly. The products of his pure imagination—emancipated from his individuality— 'Genevieve', 'The Ancient Mariner', 'Christabel'.[1] The 'Remorse' forms the transition between the second and third classes. Now this is easy work enough, but to shew what S.T.C. was as a Poet, recourse must be had to his prose, we must ascertain what were his principles of poetry, and this

---

[1] In one of the fragments of the Essay on his father, Hartley comments on *Christabel*:

   'What shall we say of Christabel? I know it was my Father's favourite child— the fondling of his genius, the child in which he recognized himself most and finest. It is not the alcohol but the virgin honey of Poetry. It is a fragment, no doubt, but more of it—like more honey—a thing that has no predefinite shape, could only have been more of the same sort.

     The inspiration of a visitant breeze
     That played beneath a burden of perfume
     Resting and panting in a narrow room
     Exalted in fancies—fair and sweet as these.'

cannot be done without going at least so far in his philosophy
as his doctrine of Ideas. However, I will do my best, and I
don't despair of making a very readable article, which I
should think quite good enough if it were about any body
but my father.

I am glad that Herbert is taught to sow. Make him use
his hands and his eyes as much as you can. The studies and
occupations of a child cannot be too objective. As to Edith's
Latin I shall say nothing. No rational creature can dislike
any individual female for classic attainments. You are a
sufficient proof that they are consistent with the most
feminine and matronly excellence; but I confess I think a
woman none the worse for wanting them and should be sorry
that Hic-haec-hoc—and ὁ, ἡ, τό—should ever become essential
to the Lady. Where the faculty exists, it should be cultivated,
but I do think it a great waste of youth, in nine instances
out of ten, to devote to dead, aye, or living languages. There
are more good books in any one language than life is long
enough to master. My recent experience in schooling has
very much confirm'd my previous heresy on this head.
There were not above three boys among my pupils to whom
Latin will ever be of any use, except, perhaps to thrust them
into professions for which they have no vocation. But
with regard to males, a custom is establish'd which perhaps
cannot yet be safely violated. I hope no such custom
will ever tyrannize over your sex. God bless them both—I
long to see them, but my candle is in the socket. Adieu till
tomorrow.

Tuesday Morning, Sep. 5.

You will be glad to see that I am up, have been so for
nearly two hours and breakfasted, though it is but just nine.
I am indeed very much amended of my old slug a bed
habits, though perverse destiny orders it, that if ever I do
indulge, I am sure to have intempestive callers. This always
happens if I go to bed earlier than usual. I soon fall asleep,
wake about two in the morning, tumble about in great discomfort of mind and body till six and then drop off again.
But in general I am up by eight. I sometimes take a snooze
after dinner, which saves time. I prosed so last night, that
I have not left myself room for half what I have to say. Tell
Mama that there is no hurry about the Sedbergh bills. Mr.
Green would not hear of my paying them at all; but it would

be far more than a fair remuneration for my trouble should
he discharge them; but they can wait till I make some money,
or rather, I believe he has already paid them along with the
boys' accounts, and I can pay him or his father. I had a
letter from Mrs. Isaac yesterday. She says her husband
has resumed his duties both in school and church, and is
decidedly better. I forget whether I told you that the little
Caroline who was coming into the world when I wrote a hurried letter by Mr. Upton, is my God-daughter. I was taken,
I confess, by surprize, supposing I had only to stand proxy,
for I am not without scruples as to my own fitness for a
sponsor. Shirts will not be unacceptable though I am in no
urgent need. I have two or three for out, and anything clean
does for in. The dr[awers] I must get. Tell Mammy that I
have plenty both of black and white neck-cloths; indeed the
latter I never wear, for I never see them worn by any but
clergy and old gentlemen. Grasmere is not full of company,
but there are a host of Cants—and Oxons at Ambleside and
Bowness. I am only acquainted with one of them, a nice
little man who has lent me the *Lyra Apostolica*,[1] and a delightful work of Professor Sedgwick's on the Cambridge studies,[2]
in which he attacks Locke and Paley as unceremoniously as
our dear Father was wont to do. Seldom have I read in any
recent work, so much calm, genuine Xtian piety, strong
philosophic sense, and sound morality, expressed in genuine
mother English. I am fully rewarded for my labors at the
school by even two interviews, which, however, I hope will
not be the last. The P. is now at Whitehaven about Coal.
He has been to look at those disastrous pits where so many
lives were lost. I fear that the loss is such as Mr. Curwen can
ill bear. John Wordsworth is desirous of taking pupils, his
income being nearly reduced to the proceeds of his living.
I saw Mrs. Wordsworth yesterday with her little Grandson—a fine child. She desired her etc., but had nothing
to say. The *Lyra Apostolica* is, I suppose you know, a joint
work of Keble, Newman, and others of the same manie. I
do not like either the poetry nor the theology, but that is
neither here nor there. I hope your high-church Parson will
not persuade you that Mrs. Fox is out of the pale of salvation,
or that dear little Berkley[3] is in Gehenna. I am anxious to

---

[1] Newman's *Lyra Apostolica* was published in 1834.
[2] Adam Sedgwick's *A Discourse on the Studies of the University*, 1833.
[3] Referring, of course, to Hartley's brother Berkeley, who died in infancy.

see Derwent's sermons, and yet more to see himself, and his wife, and little Derve—though whenever we meet—God grant it may be soon—there are certain subjects which must be taboo'd. Not but what I am ready to hear and read all sides: but I never will again trust myself to *vivâ-voce* disputation on religious or moral topics. What I have to say I will write. Our late Curate, a very amiable young man who fancied himself an evangelical, but was in heart a pure simple primitive, though weak-headed Christian, is no more. He went to Ireland on a three-week's visit to his mother, and expired of a short illness under her roof. He was much beloved, though not very much listen'd to—at least he made no disciples. It is hardly possible to evangelize the rustic population of Westmorland. Kendal, indeed, is full of religions, with no lack of unreligion—in Grasmere there is little of either. Our present Minister (Curate) makes himself very unpopular by his brusque manner of subpoenaing the natives to church—and yet more deservedly by the presumptuous judgements he passes upon the dead, while they are yet scarce cold in the grave. He is an Irishman, a new-ordained militia officer. Poor Mrs. Parry was so ill, that they were obliged to quit Grasmere, with little chance of returning, after a very short stay. Mr. Brancker is not in Parliament. He might have come in for Kendal if he had chosen—but it is as well as it is. I do not weep for Hume's defeat, though I do laugh at Sir J. Graham's. Aunt Eliza's loss of franks is the only evil I know attendant on the ousting of R. Waron. But hang politics. Hal will have an opportunity of striking a lot of radicals of[f] the register—hope he will find all well at Ottery. Will finish Prometheus, tho' not hopeful of its making a hit. You are probably aware of the death of Mrs. P. Wilson—a sad loss, and also that Mrs. Narver's sufferings are at an end. Poor Mrs. Claude is in trouble about her eldest daughter, whose mind is affected with I am afraid, small hopes. She is in Liverpool. No hope, I am afraid, of Aunt. Uncle is wonderful. There is a baby in the house. My host and hostess are young. P. handkerchiefs I would do [with]—Love to all and each. Hope Mama is better—by the way she makes herself ten years older than she is—i.e., 77. I shall be forty one in a [fortnight].

Your affectionate brother

H.C.

LETTER 61

To HENRY NELSON COLERIDGE.

[1837.]

Dear Henry

The enclosed Sonnet is not, of course, for the public eye—
I leave it to your own discretion to read it to Mama, or Sara,
if you think it will not set old wounds a bleeding. I have my
doubts as to the former, besides the allusions would perhaps
puzzle her. Not a word in prose or verse will I ever publish
that can be tortured into a reference to our domestic affairs,
or even to my own circumstances. Lockhart gave me a lesson
for that. I regret and resent the appearance of several pieces
in my first volume. One Sonnet which Sara has (if she have
not prudently destroyed it) having slipt by mistake into the
printer's hand, I peremptorily ordered to be cancelled, and
I wonder that I did not the same with regard to the lines
addressed to Mary Derwent.[1]

As for the thing on the other side, over and above the more
pressing reasons for keeping it to ourselves, I know it is very
open to Criticism. I protest I would not show it to Wordsworth on any account. His austere taste would be mortally
bored with the confusion of Astrology, Mythology, Scripture,
and Hylozoism it exhibits—and perhaps some people not
quite so particular in matters of composition would be horri-
fied to find Moses between the Dioscuri and the Anima
Mundi. But in my Sacred Sonnets intended for the Religious
World, I have avoided any thing that can give them a pretext for setting up their backs, though I shall not win golden
opinions from all sorts of men or women either—at least not
from the admirers of the *Lyra Apostolica.* I shall enclose
a specimen or two.

I could not thank you in prose for the great reconcilement
you were the means of effecting—the peace and comfort and
universal charity you gave to the last days τοῦ Μακαρίτου. You
caused him to die in good will with all men—save the
Reformers and the dissenters—happily unconscious what
a pack of resurrection rascals were hovering around his
deathbed.

Yours truly

H.C.

---

[1] Cf. Letter 32, 121–2.

To H. N. COLERIDGE.

Kinsman, Yea—more than kinsman, brother, friend—
O more than Kinsman, more than Friend or Brother
My Sister's Spouse, Son to my widowed mother,
How shall I praise thee right and not offend?
For thou wert sent a sore heart-ill to mend:
Twin-stars were ye—Thou and thy wedded Love
Benign of aspect, as those Imps of Jove
In antique Faith commissioned to portend
To sad sea-wanderers peace. Or like the Tree
By Moses cast into the bitter pool
Which made the tear-salt water fresh and cool—
Or even as Spring, that sets the boon Earth free
Free to be good, exempt from winter's rule
Such hast thou been to our poor family—[1]

LETTER 62

To MRS. SAMUEL TAYLOR COLERIDGE, *No. 10 Chester Place, Regent's Park, London.*

Grasmere, January 13, 1838.

My dear Mother

It is somewhat late to wish you a happy new-year, and shamefully late to answer your's and Henry's pressing and too kind letters. I shall not, however, occupy half my sheet with unavailing excuses, but simply say that my silence has not been occasioned by asthma, broken-neck, rheumatic-fever, or arrest, and that I have a great-coat, which though not very handsome or fashionable, is quite good enough to wear in the dark, and moreover, I stir very little in bad weather. But now I will answer your questions *seriatim.* I am in no imminent want of stockings or drawers. The shirts I shall receive most thankfully, though I have quite sufficient change, and Mrs. Richardson is a diligent mender. Four I appropriate to great occasions. I have a good suit of black— of which I am tolerably careful, and two or three every day Coats and trowzers, which are good enough to sit by the fire in. A kind Lady, Mrs. Greenwood,[2] has made me two excellent flannel waistcoats. You must understand that her

---

[1] Cf. *Poems*, 135.

[2] The Greenwoods were among Hartley's most intimate friends in the Lake district, and to them, especially little Mary Elizabeth, he addressed many of his poems.

younger son is my Pupil. I have got a new hat, though my old one is very decent. I shall, therefore, reserve the new one for Church, or such times as I have to walk with Ladies— for any hat is good enough for evening parties. The Rydalians are pretty well. Mr. Wordsworth's eyes considerably better. I am sorry that you suffer so much in that way. Some time ago, I was apprehensive that my own sight was failing, but it is now completely restored, at least as good as ever, for I never could read small print long to gether without pain. I have a pair of Spectacles, presented to me by a middle-aged Lady, but they magnify too much. I only use them in cases of necessity. John Wordsworth was over for a few days, and I saw him: he was well. I hope he may succeed in getting pupils. He is a sound Classic, a sound Divine, and an excellent man, but I am afraid he is not possessed of that sort of shewy—alamode knowledge which is most coveted by wealthy parents. There is at present, resident in Ambleside, a Frenchman who has two pupils at high rates—one of them a Baring, a very fine young Gentleman indeed. I cannot thoroughly understand the principle on which so many of the affluent entrust their sons, and still more their daughters, to Foreigners, who often can teach little besides the accent of their native language. I have no especial allusion to Monsieur Galippe; who, though thoroughly French, is a very gentlemanly, well-educated, and apparently amiable man— I believe a good Mathematician. But he does not seem to know very much of the *best* literature of his own Country, and cannot be very deep in the Greek, Roman or English. Of course he is militaire, and was upon that perilous 'journey to Moscow' which dear Uncle hymn'd so exultingly.[1] Of course I do not sing the verses in M. Galippe's company. But this reminds me—that I ought e'er now to have spoken of the Departed, and of the survivors. Poor Aunt [Southey]—I trust it is well with her. A melancholy close was hers, of a day never bright, even when the sun shone most serenely upon it. Never knew I a Being—in whom a pure and benevolent Spirit was so little joyous. A morbid sensitiveness to pain and an almost apathy to pleasure, an intellect sensible, and not uncultivated, but of little activity, sink beneath afflictions which coarser minds cry out in a few weeks, and in which livelier natures might, after the first pangs were over, discover topics of hope and consolation. Doubtless

---

[1] See Southey's *Voyage to Moscow*, 1813.

they have wept, but their tears would be of comfort, though not of joy. Kate is expected at Rydal on her way South. I think, on several accounts, it will be better for me to defer a visit to Keswick till the Spring, when I shall have finished several works I have now on the anvil—made some score of pounds etc. There are besides the essays (not *memoirs*) two or more volumes of essays, criticism etc. of my own, a volume of Sonnets (nearly complete), on sacred subjects, two or three articles, and D.V. *Prometheus*. But of this I cannot speak with certainty, so difficult is it to recommence any work of imagination after any interval. I do not think it would have been possible for my father to have continued Christabel, had his health been ever so joyous, and the reception of the poem ever so encouraging. He might, indeed, have written a great deal more about Christabel and what he wrote could not but have been valuable, but it would not have harmonized with the fragment—the joinery would have been too apparent. I never knew a work, in which there was any continuity at all, that was successfully continued. But I forget, you have no interest in critical questions, and I have to catch the post. I write this letter to relieve your fears, and deprecate your wrath. The next shall follow in less than a week, not unaccompanied with Christmas gifts of some consequence—among the rest, a review of *Phantasmion*, an essay of my Father's on Faith, which I transcribed once before, and sent by private hand to Mr. Green; somehow or other (by no fault of my friend the bearer) he never got it, and a portion at least of the long expected.

I have not much to say of my lodgings—only they are very comfortable. I like not my host and hostess the worse for having a baby, a fine, crowing little fellow and my Godson. Mr. Dawes is well, a marvellous man for his years, straight as a Grenadier—at a few yards distance, you would not suppose him more than forty. In this he differs from Mr. Wordsworth, who, for so temperate a man, looks very old indeed; but he never could, never at heart [have] been young in his life. Mr. Brancker is here and well. N.B. not in Parliament, which some people think quite as well. I can't quite understand what I ought to do about the Copy right of *Borealis*, but I certainly made what I supposed to be a legal transfer of it. If Hal will explain, I will do the needful—and mean time, will make enquiries. God bless dear Sara—and you all—I am now doubly anxious for her. May she get well over it.

I had not heard of Aunt Edward's decease, but being not unexpected, it shocked me less than the sudden information of Mr. Poole's.[1] A great loss to Mankind is he. Uncle Edward, I suppose will not long survive. One by one, my old friends drop away, and though I want not well-wishers, nor active benefactors, I feel painfully how few are left of those who were bound to me by nature, or a parent's memory.

Happy new year to the children.

Your affectionate Son,
H. COLERIDGE.

I will write to Mary to thank her for the shirts etc. Don't think I forget Derwent, but I must positively endue my greatcoat and be off.

LETTER 63

To the REV. ISAAC GREEN, *Sedbergh.*

Grasmere, Good-Friday—or rather Saturday—A fine night.
[Endorsed April, 1838.]

Dear Isaac

I need not tell you that I was much affected by the sudden decease of poor Mr. Wilkinson. I had heard, indeed, of his illness, but never suspected any thing worse than a bad cold which would only require a little nursing and was absolutely staggered when Gilbanks stopped the Coach to inform me that he was no more. I suppose you did not yourself apprehend an unfavourable termination of his complaint till a short time before the last. I am not one who looks upon death as an infliction on those that die—but it is often a sore misfortune to those that survive. Mr. W. has left a large family, none of whom can yet help themselves; some arrived at the age when paternal control and protection is specially needful: but I hope his circumstances will prove such as to furnish a comfortable provision for the widow and her offspring. You do not probably yet know who will succeed him in the school, or what changes will take place under the new regime, but I think there can be little doubt that the new sovereign will gladly avail himself of your ministerial services, if you are disposed to continue them. Most likely there will [be] several removals among the upper boys. I think the time allow'd for the appointment of a Master rather scanty, but as the choice lies in one College—where there are probably expectants

---

[1] Coleridge's old Nether Stowey friend, Thomas Poole, died in 1837.

enough, it is not likely there will be any delay in filling up the vacancy. So easy a Master as Mr. Wilkinson will not be found in a hurry. I have heard that it [sic] was a good deal annoyed at the mischievous pranks of the hoaxers—and no wonder.

The advertisement of the drowning was a great deal too bad. I had a pretty strong inkling that Master Bouske was at the bottom of it. You are doubtless inform'd of the death of the elder Mrs. Greenwood—a great relief, considering the helpless state in which she has existed for some years past, but it has brought before my mind the possibility, aye certainty indeed, of an event, which if I live to see it, will leave me in a manner alone in the world.

I am no news-monger, and am in a very stupid humour, and besides I am like to be in the situation where Adam was when his candle went out and for the same reason. I hope the Priestess of Lucina, (Mrs. Dodgin) will find Mrs. Isaac in a promising way, and that she will get well over her approaching trial. Had your house been in a less busy and agitating state I think I should have paid you a visit, as I might possibly have helped you in the school; but under existing circumstances I am afraid I should be in the way. Might I trouble you—at any opportunity—to send me a copy of the Verses on . . .[1]—which I do not possess in their corrected state?

Give my love . . .[1] and a kiss to my little God-daughter. Remember me kindly to Mr. Upton and his family—are any of them likely to change their state?

How comes on the chapel? How is Mr. Wilkinson of Howgill?

Believe me—yours truly

H. COLERIDGE.

LETTER 64

To MRS. SAMUEL TAYLOR COLERIDGE, *10 Chester Place, Regent's Park, London.*

Sedbergh, May 25th, 1838.

Dear Mother

Your last but one arrived just as I was in the act of packing up: when I had literally not a moment for scrawling—yet I did take it to Rydal Mount and meant to have answered it, as soon as I was settled. But one thing or another intervened,

---

[1] MS. erased.

and the treacherous weather inducing me prematurely to assume my summer array has given me such a cold in the head that my eyes and brains are but just sufficient for the necessary work of the school. The old song couplet 'a light heart and a thin pair of breeches' but a thin pair of breeches has given me a heavy and an aching head, without making my heart much lighter. Yesterday was a whole Holy day, begged, and you may suppose granted, without much difficulty, on pretence of the Queen's birth-day. In consequence, I thought myself quite well last night and this morning, but the plaguey Greek letters have brought on the pain in my noddle again, though I must say the boys were remarkably good. Don't alarm yourself, my dear Mother, I have not been, and am not, seriously ill; but I rarely escape a cold about this time, and colds admonish Caesar that he is a man, and me that I am a man past forty. My eyes are not inflamed nor bloodshot, but they feel as you may have sometimes experienced after a sleepless night, though I sleep very well. I believe it is more owing to coughing than any thing else, but the cough has now gone—the weather is fine, and I shall be quite well in a day or two, but mean while, I think it prudent to avoid much unnecessary reading and writing. This letter is strictly necessary, but you will excuse it being rather short. I will write to Henry about the book when quite bobbish. I brought all my father's works (which I have at least) and intended to work hard at the Essay, volume of Poems, etc., but could not do any thing for the last week. With respect to the Extracts, the best possible mode of publication would have been in connection with editions of Hooker, Jeremy Taylor, etc. I have some thoughts of proposing an edition of Shakespeare in which my dear father's annotations should be included.

Mr. Green was not so ill as I expected to find him, but is far from strong. He and I have the whole business of the school on our hands, as the new master does not come till after midsummer, at least not for good. Mr. Green could not be chosen Head-master—The school is in the gift of John's Col. Cam. and of course goes to a member of that Porcine body. Mr. G. was of Queens' Col. Cambridge. But with his precarious health, it is not probable he would have proposed himself had he been eligible. I now occupy the Head-Master's place. I find my Pupils, if not over diligent, very respectful and tractable, but I meddle not with discipline further than is necessary to keep order at lesson times. The boys have been in general quiet since Mr. Wilkinson's death, which was very unexpected. He seem'd a strong and healthy man this time last year. He has left a widow and eight children—I am glad to say—tolerably provided for, though as there are six girls—there will be enough to do. Neither of the boys is yet capable of any employment, nor do I think that either of them could possibly pass at either University, for they are particularly slow—a mortifying thing for poor Mr. W. that his own boys should be the worst learners in his school. His widow looks very melancholy and sorrow-smitten. She quits Sedbergh next week, as the house belongs to the school. Mr. W.'s Mother is still living.

I was sorry to hear of poor Sara's failure—but as she has recovered tolerably, we must consider it a good job of a bad one. Mrs. Green is threatening again—she is a heavy sufferer in pregnancy, and far from as [patient] as some folks under similar circumstances. I cannot think of troubling her about stockings which I do not immediately want; besides, nothing whatever is to be got at Sedbergh—the most shopless place— for a market town—that I ever saw. If Mr. Evans (who has promised to do the needful for whomsoever Mr. Green might engage as assistant) comes down with the stumpy before I return, I can get some at Kendal—not that bought worsted stockings are ever good for any thing. By the way, the £1–2s. was for a hat. I have got the surtout and do not want any clothes immediately. I have white-trowzers etc. enough, but the frock will be acceptable. I don't think nankeens look well on old gentlemen.

I am writing very shockingly ill and can't help it. Excuse me if I have omitted any thing of moment. I will write again as soon as ever my noddle permits. Sorry for the death of Mary's mother. Death's shafts fly thick. What a number of my young friends are gone, and of the elder those that remain must go. God's will be done—I shall be sadly desolate in the world. Dear love to Sara—I have a bone to pick with her but no matter just now. Love to Kate if she is still with you. I guessed as much of Bertha. Glad you're likely to see Uncle. Sorry about Herbert's throat, but don't apprehend any danger. Obliged for Newspapers—Cost penny at Grasmere. Nothing here. Paper always useful. Henry etc.

I remain your affec. Son,

H.C.

LETTER 65

To MISS MARY CLAUDE.

Dear Mary   [Sept. 1838.]

I do not send you this Sonnet because I think it worthy of its subject. Indeed, hastily got up as it has been, it is hardly worthy of its author. But knowing your partiality for the person to whom it is addressed (in his clerical capacity I mean) I thought you would not be displeased to see that Heretic as I must needs appear in his eyes—I hold him in high honour. Besides, I would fain send you some thing, and what can a poor scribbler send but his love and his verses? The first you would hardly accept, the latter you may deign to look at. The first line is literally true. Fearing a collision on points that should never be prophaned by casual angry disputation, I could never screw up my courage to call upon Mr. Faber,[1] though I had just come to a determination when I heard he was gone. He has made some converts, I believe, to the High Church—he certainly made a Polish Countess whose name I can neither pronounce nor spell, cry out in an audible whisper, Ah, ma Pauvre Eglise, by his reflections on Popery. But I am afraid he has prevail'd on nobody to fast upon Fridays. But you have enough of controversy at Liverpool, if you choose to listen to it, which I very strongly disadvise and remain, Dear Mary, Yours truly

H. COLERIDGE.

To the Reverend Frederick Faber.

I fear'd to meet thee, for I know too well
I am not all, in will, or work, or creed,
Which thou demandest of the chosen seed:
Of mind too volant, perhaps too proud to dwell
A settled inmate of a lowly cell,
In that time-hallow'd temple, founded deep
By holy sages, that in glory sleep.
Yet, by our common faith I love thee well.
Bold art thou in thy function, as the seer
That call'd upon Jehovah for his flame,
Yet in thyself as meek as womanhood,
And modest as the virgin face of shame:
Stern to thyself, as God were all severe—
To others kind, as he were only good—[2]

---

[1] Frederick William Faber (1814–63), who after a distinguished career at Oxford, had taken the pulpit at Ambleside. He later followed Newman into the Catholic Church.   [2] This sonnet has not been previously published.

I find too late, that the first and eighth lines end with the same word. But perhaps you will excuse this defect. Let no unfriendly eye behold it.

LETTER 66

To MRS. HENRY NELSON COLERIDGE

Greta Hall, February 23, 1839.

My dear Sara

Here I am in the old dining room—which with the exception of the original study is the least alter'd of any room about the house. Well might Mother ask—what would Jacky and Wilsy think could they rise again to see what work has been made at Greta-Hall!! There is no need to say, considering who has made it, that it is good work in the main, but nevertheless, it is melancholy work in my eyes. Perhaps it is partly the weather, which is, as Uncle has call'd it half a dozen times, *rascally*. There is nothing sublime or satanic in its depravity—rascally is the very word. Hard, harsh, uncomfortable, mirky frost-melted rather than thaw'd by sleety rain—a patchy covering of ragged-dirty snow—the mountains looking like great black giants badly white-wash'd—the trees reduced by the late tempest to more than wintry bareness—the ever greens, whose verdure is always of a sombre cast, cold, grim, and rusty—hardly one indication of approaching Spring at a time when I have often seen the gardens all in a glow, the birds and insects busy, the buds bursting with the pimply parturition of vegetable life, the rathe primrose, and the starry celandine 'telling tales about the Sun'. In plain speech, it is a very late season, and I can't help thinking, that the sky and the earth who are certainly in the agricultural interest, are consumedly in the sulk at corn-law agitation. I confess, I rather miss, the uncarpeted vacancy of Wilsy's parlour and Papa's study—though, they are furnished with the best of all furniture, good books. Now I am as impartial in my tastes for books as the old Toper in 'Gammar Gurton' in regard to Ale. Give me but enough and good enough, I care not 'whether it be new or old'. But in this house, one is reminded of the apparent paradox of the late Lord Liverpool, which attributed want to superabundance. It weighs upon the spirit to see so many excellent writings and to know how few of them any individual can ever read, but it is still more distressing to reflect how many of them I might have read—which I have not life before me to read now. For the present visit, I shall confine myself chiefly to referring and abstracting, mainly too from the Theological and Daemonological works. I have brought over a box full of MSS. and have been inflicting sonnets and other verses on Kate and Bertha without remorse. I have not yet ventured to tease Uncle with any thing, though I would fain consult him, but I know that he is not fond of being read to, and thinks, perhaps truly enough, that I read my own poems, at least, very badly. But you will be anxious to know something about the living beings of your own fireside, for so it once was. Alas, how many blank-spaces in the circle! Uncle's health appears wonderful for a man of his years and exertions. Even his face does not confess more than fifty—his hair is much thicker than mine (which is soliciting Macassar) and very little, if at all, greyer—he is as erect as ever, and in walking, carries his head in the old position, which one might think he had learned by swimming—he walks at such a pace that I find it difficult to keep up with him, but then my respiration [is] much affected by cold, especially snowy weather, so that I could walk twenty miles in the dog-days with less painful fatigue than ten in such weather as this. His daughters think that he is thinner, but I don't see how that can be. He always seem'd to be at zero as to *embon point*, but I know that the bones and muscles do contract with age. Mrs. Fleming, who was as straight as an arrow as long as she went about, remark'd that her gowns were growing too long for her. Altogether, Mr. Southey is the youngest looking man of his years I ever saw, except Mr. Dawes, who is, indeed, much older, and looks it in the face, though his amazing muscular power, which seems very little impaired, gives his movement an appearance of yet greater vigour. I cannot yet observe any striking decay of Uncle's memory. Extempore recollection was never in him a conspicuous talent; he did not cultivate it but relied upon his pen, and we are hardly aware how much the natural faculties are weakened by artificial aids, or how much more may have been preserved by oral tradition before the gradual use of letters, than would appear credible at present. The only material change I remark is in his spirits. He is not low indeed, but he is silenter than ever, and now and then seems absent or at least abstracted, and self involved, which I never knew him before. Of course I am and shall be careful not to intrude upon

him, or weary him with long speeches, far less with unnecessary questions, or disputation of any kind—when I cannot
agree I will hold my tongue. He is much quieter, but flashes
of the *Doctor* break out ever and anon, and on the whole, I
hope he enjoys no scanty measure of that calm satisfaction,
which results from a life well-spent. That he has 'the peace
that passes all understanding', it were irreligious to doubt.
Happiness is an unmeaning word—perfect bliss is not for
this world, and joyousness is for youth alone. I think he is
quite right in his *choice* though I never saw the person.[1]
Should I judge of her by her writings, she must [be] a goodly
sample of womanhood. The picture now before me indicates
a comely person in the cool of the afternoon of life; and (a
strong recommendation in my eyes) that the Lady is fond of
dogs. Bertha is, I think, pretty well, the existing nature
of things considered. I like her intended much, and they
behave remarkably well for persons in their situation. Kate
is very pale and feeble, but I think, more beautiful than ever.
The pensive expression suits her cast of features well—the
severest test of Beauty. Features must be unfortunate indeed,
if liveliness, animation, levity, the indices (often deceptive
enough) of a light and gladsome heart, eager to please,
will not make them attractive. How plain a French woman
can afford to be, and yet have all the effect of prettiness.
But placidity compels the face to speak truth about itself.
Beauty in death must be absolute beauty, and beauty in
repose is but the next degree. Moreover, apart from all
physiognomical considerations, nothing is so disagreeable to
me as dull animal solemnity, seriousness without thought-
fulness or sensibility. I wish, however, that dear Kate did
not look quite so pensive—particularly when she smiles.
Better weather of which there is some promise to day (the
former pages were written yesterday) (Feb. 22nd) will enable
her to take fresh air and exercise; but I am afraid the
approaching separation distresses her in prospect. I am
commissioned to tell you that Bertha's marriage takes place
(D.V.) on the 12th of next month.[2] Kate received your long
letter yesterday morn, and sends thanks and love. Its contents on the whole were agreeable, but I am sorry to hear
that Henry is not quite 'the thing', and that he cannot take the

---

[1] Southey was married to Caroline Bowles in 1839. The marriage unfortunately caused considerable dissension in the Southey household.
[2] Bertha Southey married her cousin, the Rev. Herbert Hill.

best means of setting himself to rights. Very sorry indeed that Lady Patteson should be such a sufferer. I do not quite understand all you say about James' movements, and John's settlement at Heathcourt. But I hope all will be for the best. I am as anxious as any body for my friends' well doing though I confess, some persons are more curious about the items. By the way, I wrote to the Judge a few days ago, chiefly on account of a young clergyman who wants a chaplaincy in Australia. I could say little about him, except that he was a friend of mine, and very orthodox. As far as I understand yours to Kate, you have not made up your mind as to Herbert's school destination. On such a point, I would not venture even on a suggestion. As to the detail, I have little experience, and on the general principle, I have much, that to you would appear heretical prejudice. But I certainly agree with Mr. Lonsdale, that there is no more danger in 500 boys than in 20—I should say less. In a large number, the better and the worse break up into sets, and with common prudence, a little guidance, and a good instinct, a well-disposed youth has more than a chance of becoming [a] member of a respectable society. In a small school or college (I can myself speak to the latter) there is a sort of Hobson's choice—and a fearful probability that the worst, at least the most knowing, and audacious, will be the ring leader—the Demagogue, the glass of fashion. There is nothing of which boys are so much ashamed as innocence. How is Miss Fatima Full-moon? Poor Aunt Lovell is just gone out of the room. She is upon the whole better than might have been expected, but not so well to day, as she was yesterday, when she was quite in high spirits. She looks old. But so do we all, though I think every Mother likely to bear age well, at least in the face. She says little of her own ailments to me, and was never a great complainer about her own health. I have not yet alluded to the Departed, and know not whether I shall, except to Aunt Lovell.

I ought to have acknowledged the receipt of the 'Church and State'[1] and 'Italy'. The latter I have not read much of, except the notes, which are cockneyish enough. But 'the old Proverbs hath it—You should not look a gift horse in the mouth'. I am often ready enough not to look at a *gift book* any where at all. The 'Church and State' I read ἀμυστί—uno haustu and shall read it again and again, though I confess

---

[1] Coleridge's *Constitution of the Church and State* was first published in 1830.

it does not remove my scruples and difficulties. It has given me many new lights but it has not 'scattered the rear of Darkness thin'. It is, however, an admirable work, and needs deeper study and meditation than I have yet bestowed on it. I have also read Mr. Gillman.[1] Mama in her last ask'd me—How I liked it? It is not always just exactly easy to say in a single sentence how you like a book. With regard to that book, I must deeply love and revere—the intensity of affection, the almost religious zeal, the affection of the friend, the zeal of the convert, the gratitude of the disciple—which appear in all the book, and in every part of it. Unlike some others, Gillman has shewn no inclination to set himself in the foreground, or to blazon the extent to which ὁ μακαρίτης was indebted to him. It is a good hearted, noble minded book, but it is not a well-written or well constructed book. There is, however, less in it which one would wish out—than I apprehended. Uncle has never seen it, and I have not offered to lend him it, which I certainly should do, if I thought it would give him pleasure. I had designed a long description of consecrations, confirmations, bishops, and several sonnets (already written) on those occasions, but as that sort of thing will keep—and post won't stay.

With best love to Mother, Husband and Bairns,

I remain, Dear Sara,

Your affectionate brother,

H.C.

Early in the year 1839, at the suggestion of James Spedding, Moxon, the publisher, requested Hartley to prepare a biographical introduction and a critique for an edition of Massinger and Ford. Hartley at once consented, promised a manuscript at an early date, and then fell into his old habits of procrastination. Moxon in desperation applied to Wordsworth, that the bard of Rydal might exert his influence on Hartley. Wordsworth's letter on this occasion certainly did not reassure the publisher; and perhaps the failure of Moxon and Hartley to come to terms over other works may have emanated from the unsatisfactory experience in the case of the Massinger and Ford.

'Not being able', Wordsworth wrote on February 24, 1840, 'to meet with H.C. immediately on receipt of your letter, I wrote him a note a couple of days after and told him its contents. I have since seen him, and done all I could. And now let me give you, in respect to him, a piece of advice, once for

---

[1] *The Life of S. T. Coleridge*, James Gillman, 1838, of which only one volume was published.

all, viz., that you *never* engage with him for any *unperformed* work, when either time or quantity is of importance. Poor fellow! he has no resolve; in fact, nothing that can be called rational will or command of himself as to what he will do or not do; of course, I mean, setting aside the fundamental obligations of morality. Yesterday I learned that he had disappeared from his lodgings, and that he had been seen at eight o'clock entering the town of Kendal. He was at Ambleside the night before at eleven o'clock, so he must have been out the greater part of the night. I have lately begun to think that he has given himself up to his own notions, fancies, reveries, abstractions, etc. I admire his genius and talents far more than I can find words to express, especially for writing prose, which I am inclined to think (as far as I have seen) is more masterly than his verse. The workmanship of the latter seems to me not infrequently too hasty, has indeed too much the air of an Italian's *improvisatore* production.'

The edition finally appeared in 1840. The critique is lacking, but the biographical introduction and the footnotes, though often discursive and quite irrelevant, are delightful.

LETTER 67

To EDWARD MOXON

Grasmere, March 30, 1839.

Sir

Through my excellent friend, Mr. James Spedding, I received notice of your proposal respecting the lives of Massinger and of Ford. I immediately communicated to him my ready acceptance of the terms, which are more liberal than any on which I have hitherto been engaged, except perhaps for the Edinburgh Janus, an annual which did not live to be biennial. Of my style of biography you are perhaps not wholly ignorant, should you ever have chanced to look into my 'Biographia Borealis', a blustering title, as the 'Doctor' says, of which I am rather ashamed; but it was hastily adopted, 'The Worthies of Yorkshire and Lancashire' being inapplicable to the portion of the contemplated work which circumstances allowed me to execute at the time. With regard to Massinger, I should conjecture there are few facts to be added to the few that Gifford has detailed; for Gifford, however defective in taste, seldom failed in research; moreover, Massinger seems to have passed his life in the obscurity, and, alas! in the penury and brevity of a smoky winter day.

It would be to little purpose to swell the narrative with anecdotes of his patrons and contemporaries; but of the characteristics of his genius, his *peculiar* excellence, I am not aware that anything satisfactory has been written, except a few valuable points in the Remains of S.T.C.[1] On these points alone can I promise any originality. With Ford I am less acquainted; but in both lives you must put up with a paucity of facts. I hope you will not complain of superabundant criticism. I do not know to what limits I shall be restricted; but I suppose I must not much exceed the length of Procter's 'Ben Jonson.'[2]

As the edition is to be confined to single volumes, the notes, if any, must be few; though I think each play should have a short introduction, setting forth the time when first acted, source of the story (when either ascertained), etc. Dr. Ireland's moral applications, evidently copied from those in Croxall's Æsop, may well be dispensed with. What had his reverence to do with profane stage plays? I think I can borrow Gifford's Massinger. I shall be obliged to you for Ford, likewise for Ben Jonson, who is a huge favourite of mine. I don't think his biographer, Barry, *entre nous*, has done him half justice. Of his poems, which abound in grand moral truths and powerful thought, sometimes finely, sometimes, it may be, quaintly illustrated, but always expressed in sterling English, a better sample might have been given than a few songs, one of which, passing pretty in its way, is hardly fit for modern lady-singing, even by ladies who warble Tom Moore with perfect innocence; you cannot misunderstand old Ben into propriety.

I believe Mr. Spedding said something to you about a collection of Essays which I propose to publish. I was not ignorant that the consent of former publishers must be obtained; but I do not apprehend any difficulty on this score, especially as the number contained in any one periodical are too few to compose a respectable volume. Most appeared in works now defunct, as 'The London Magazine' (Taylor and Hessey), 'The Janus', and 'The Winter's Wreath;' the others will be worked up into a new shape, and the greater number will be unpublished; but I will do nothing clandestinely. I should like to know on what terms you would undertake publication, as also of my second volume of poems, which,

---

[1] Cf. *Literary Remains*, i. 108–13.
[2] Cf. Procter's (Barry Cornwall), *The Works of Ben Jonson, with a Memoir of his Life*, 1838.

D.V., I would wish to appear in the current season. Were I informed on these points I might authorise my friends to take steps for the recovery of the copy-right of the first volume, which I believe is nearly out of print.

A speedy answer through the Colonial Office would much oblige,

Yours sincerely, though unknown,

HARTLEY COLERIDGE.

P.S.—You will probably not deviate much from Gifford's text, which appears to me as good in most points, as is likely to be obtained. Should any consideration occur to me, I will take the liberty of submitting it to your judgement. Pray remember me kindly to Mr. Procter. I have not forgotten his kindness some nineteen years ago.

LETTER 68

To HENRY NELSON COLERIDGE, 10, *Chester Place, Regent's Park, London.*

Grasmere, October 24, 1839.

Dear Hal

Though in extreme haste to finish my job for Moxon, which is just on the nail, I must not let a post slip without answering your just-arrived—for with me in epistolatory responsion, a miss is as good as a mile—and dear Mother may be anxious. Her too literal interpretation has led her into a slight mistake; when I said 'you will see me soon', I only meant that my work would soon be out. I was somewhat startled at your first mention of the 'dim rumour' which I feared might have come from some misinformed busy-body in such a shape as to vex and alarm mother; for she is (I hope, not sick, but)

capable of fears
Oppressed with wrongs, and therefore full of fears,
A Widow, husbandless, subject to fears
A woman naturally born to fears.

I had certainly no definite intention of coming to London at any prescribed time, though a great wish to see you all once more, and my little nephew and niece—whom I have never seen at all, nor can I call them distinctly before my mind's eye. Sara's and Ganny's elaborate descriptions of the Darlings, as such descriptions always do, bamboozle the esemplastic power. Young Derwent I seem to see in feature, hue, and limb, but of course the image is far enough unlike the original. I had I thought, an authentic likeness of Mrs. Trollope[1] 'in my mind's eye, Horatio'. I had pictured her not *exactly* a *Lady*, but an excellent, genteel, comely fine-Lady, handsome though not lovable, somewhere about the July of her age. By the Holy Power, she is a mighty respectable, comfortable looking dowdy, weighing 13 stone at the least, some five and fifty—some thing between a house-keeper and a Land-lady, but not the house-keeper of a noble house, nor the Land-lady of a first rate hotel. Her voice is particularly unaristocratic and unintellectual, just such a muffled squeak as you may hear from the female occupant of one side of a stage-coach, when—with importunate civility proffering her silver-topped Brandy-phial. I must in justice state that Mrs. Trollope bears no indications of brandy, and that her expression is rather good than otherwise. I must also mention that I only once saw her for a very short time, along with Cyril Thornton Hamilton,[2] a man whose military stateliness of exterior (*me tantum judice*) does more than justice to the gentility of his mind. But who would [have] expected to see Her—who hath glittered in the Court of Vienna—'like a Lady from a far Countree'—sinking into an imitator of Boz? Fair ones of Cincinnati, Ye are well avenged! I took this shabby scrap of paper, because I thought I should not have time to fill a bigger, and here I have been filling up a whole side of it with Mrs. Trollope! I am truly obliged to you for your ready offer of bed and board, but cannot accept it till my present work is fairly off hand, and some others beside. Moxon seems to be a very liberal publisher; his terms for these 'Lives of Dramatists' are 25 guineas per sheet—the sheets are pretty close to be sure (you may see the size in Barry Cornwall's Ben Jonson or Campbell's Shakespeare) a[nd] I deal largely in note—but still it is good pay. I am restricted to four sheets for the two lives. Moxon is disposed to publish my Poems, giving a certain sum, for the first Edition, leaving the second—should such be call'd for—for the subject of a fresh bargain. About the specific sum he said nothing, nor did I, wishing for your advice and assistance in business-matters. We also talk'd about purchasing the remainder of

---

[1] Frances Trollope (1780–1863), mother of the novelist, published in 1832 her *Domestic Manners of the Americans*, a book highly offensive to Americans of that day.

[2] Hartley refers to Thomas Hamilton (1789–1842), who published *Cyril Thornton* in 1827.

the 1st Vol—and also of the 'Worthies'. I think I could rely on Mr. Brancker's assistance—if needed. But of this and other matters, more in my next when I have set the last hand to Massinger and Ford, which will be about the week end.

It was a cutting phrase to say that I had deserted the Biographia; neglected would have been hard enough, but perhaps I deserve a cut. I will finish the Essay, if it be not too late. Poor Gillman! But by Mother's last was I inform'd of his death.[1] Mother thinks she told me of it, but I cannot find it directly mentioned in any of her letters that have arrived, though I find allusions which I did not understand. I shall certainly write to Mrs. Gillman—I wish the letter may be a consolation, but letters of consolation in such cases are pure impertinence. I waive all mention of Derwent's Sermons,[2] till I can read them with my whole heart and mind— only I greatly approve of the form in which he has put them —as a succession of Essays—The pulpit of a country parish is no place for controversy, nor can any disputed point be fairly treated in the compass of a sermon. Glad to hear of his health and prosperity, but not *very* glad that his Mary has commenced a *maternal career*. She does not seem lucky therein, any more than dear Sara. There is some likelihood, the Dr. thinks, of Bertha. Hill is a good fellow. I would have gone to Rydal to make enquiries of the Hills, Wordsworths, etc., but it rains cruelly. What a year—Talking of rain, I would thank Snouter to send the mackintosh and stockings as soon as possible. I could hardly go to Keswick, should I be so disposed, when work done, without them.

Kindest loves to all,

H.C.

LETTER 69

To EDWARD MOXON.

Grasmere, March 12, 1840.

Dear Sir

My dear and honoured mother has informed me that you have transmitted to her your liberal remuneration for my introduction, for which I am truly grateful; it is considerably more than I expected.[3] I regret that I did not adopt, in the

---

[1] James Gillman's death occurred on June 1, 1839.

[2] Cf. Derwent Coleridge's *The Scriptural Character of the English Church, considered in a series of sermons; with notes and illustrations*, 1839.

[3] Hartley in writing to his mother on March 13, 1840, says: 'It was always my intention to have left in your hands whatever Mr. Moxon paid, after

biographical notices of Massinger, the same brevity which I effected in the life of Ford. I should then have left myself room for a critical analysis of their several dramatic and poetic merits, for which I have much material written, much more than I found it possible to compress into the few pages which your limits would have allowed in addition to what I had already occupied. As it is, I hope you are not dissatisfied with my work, though I cannot expect you quite to overlook the tardiness of the performance.

Mr. Wordsworth called upon me this morning, in company with Mr. Baron Field.[1] The latter informed me that you had applied to Mr. Cary for the Beaumont and Fletcher, but that he declined appearing as the double of Mr. Southey. Mr. Wordsworth was of opinion, that those authors could not be properly treated by any one not acquainted with Spanish literature.[2]

I see, by advertisement, that you have given Vanbrugh, Congreve, and Co. to Leigh Hunt.[3] He will make a good thing of it, if he takes care not to smuggle in any socialist heresies, for which Vanbrugh, at least, in his 'Provoked Wife,' hangs out such tempting loops. Nothing more or better can be said in defence of these writers than what Lamb has said in his delightful essay on the Old Actors; which is, after all, rather an apology for the audiences who applauded and himself who delighted in their plays, than for the plays themselves. It would be indeed unjust to conclude upon the evidence of the 'Confederacy' or the 'London Cuckolds,' that all the husbands east of Temple Bar were horned cattle,

---

deducting the sum of my debts, and a couple of pounds for contingencies; but, perhaps, your arrangement is best. I find it, however, awkward to be absolutely without cash in pocket. It sometimes necessitates borrowing, and occasions more expense and folly in many ways than it spares. Whatever I earn is, in fact, due to you as a debt. I trust you will never more have to be at expense on my account, and that I shall do something for the support of your old age. Moxon has paid magnificently—£20 more than I expected. I am glad the job gives satisfaction, though it was somewhat tardy in the finishing, and may seem abrupt in the conclusion.'

[1] Baron Field (1786–1846), the friend of Lamb, Wordsworth, and others, was a miscellaneous writer of some distinction.

[2] Hartley in writing to Moxon on September 18, 1839, had asked for this: 'I am afraid my delay on the present occasion will not recommend me to future employment; but if Mr. Southey's health does not allow him to fulfil his engagement as to Beaumont and Fletcher, I shall be glad to relieve him. At the same time, as being ignorant of Spanish, from which most of their plots are derived, I cannot do it as he could have done—nor can my name bear the same weight.'

[3] Leigh Hunt's *The Dramatic Works of Wycherley, Congreve, Vanbrugh, and Farquhar. With biographical and critical Notices*, 1849.

or that people would always act or approve in real life what
they laugh at upon the stage. But Lamb always took things
by the better handle. A severer moralist might conclude
from the indifference or positive pleasure with which we read
and behold the representations of sin, that we have little
abhorrence of sin apart from its painful consequences—here
and hereafter. Besides, Lamb's defence of Congreve is like
my dear father's defence of the attack on Copenhagen[1]—
unavailable to the doer, however available for the deed.
It was the defence which Congreve himself set up against
Collier. He stoutly maintains his pious purpose, in a manner
that might have suggested Byron's

> 'If any one pronounce the tale not moral,
> I tell him—if a clergyman—he lies.'

Believe me, sir,
Your obliged,
H. COLERIDGE.

LETTER 70

To JOHN TAYLOR COLERIDGE, *London.*

Ambleside. May 12, 1840.

Dear Sir John
Our correspondence has been so intermittent and unfre-
quent, and my sense of your mighty importance in the state
which has appointed you to the highest duty (one excepted)
that a subject can hold, is so strong, that it is not without
hesitation, fear—I might almost say—reluctance—that I now
address you. I appear in fact in the character of an M.P.
who has a petition to present—in the prayer of which he has a
friendly and collateral interest, but the import and result
whereof he must be content to leave 'to the wisdom of the
house.'

I understand that a vacancy has lately occurred in the
list of commissioners of bankruptcy—which is in your power
to supply—and that Robert Temple of York, Barrister is an
applicant. As he is a particular friend of mine, to whom I
am obliged for kindness, originating, I believe, in affectionate
esteem; as I hold him to be a thoroughly honest man, and in
the best sense of the word, a Gentleman—and I know him to
be a not unintelligent admirer of my father ὁ Μακαρίτης—and
as I myself love him with a friendly love, I can sincerely

---

[1] Cf. *The Friend*, Section I, Essay 10.

say that by conferring the office upon him, you would delight me. Of his claims, or professional qualifications, of course I know nothing. People are sadly mistaken in thinking that poor relations have any influence with their powerful kindred. It is quite as much as a lost sheep can expect, that the *graced* members of the flock shall continue to take any, the least interest *in them*; for the goats to expect that we shall have any interest with you—is rather too bad.

I am not sorry that Derwent has been disappointed in his application for the City of London School. He is not the man either to succumb to, or to winter with, purse-proud vulgarity, far less to submit to ignorant dictation in a matter wherein his own reason, integrated with his faith, as Soul with body, and vitalized by his conscience is, should be, and will be, his controlling and commanding spirit.

It may be, that between your *vocation*, and your numerous *avocations*, you have not seen an article in the January No. of Blackwood[1]—alleging a charge of gross and unacknowledged plagiary against my father. As I do not possess the works of Schelling (and wish they had been in the red sea and Dante's Giu Decca before ὁ μακαρίτης had ever seen them) it is out of my power to confute this. I would spend the last hour of my life to do it—if it were possible.

You will have seen with pleasure the account of the foundation of a new church in the neighbourhood of Ottery. I wish the Bishop would give Derwent a good living.

My best respects to Lady Coleridge—and love to all your little ones—more particularly to her of beauteous locks, that did not put forth an angry hand against the kiss of a grey headed man and a Cousin. You cannot conceive how grateful I am for these things—even from a child.

If I resented injuries as violently as I remember kindnesses— But when or by whom was I injured?

> Dear John,
> Believe me, Your affectionate Coz.
> H. COLERIDGE.

Sometime during the spring of 1840, Hartley and his hosts, the Richardsons, moved from Grasmere to a cottage on the Keswick road. Behind the cottage rises Nab Scar, from which it derives its name (Hartley often choosing to spell it 'Knabb' or 'Knabbe'); just in front lies Rydal Water. Here Hartley remained until his

---

[1] Hartley wrote 'January' but obviously meant the March number of *Blackwood's*, where the article appears.

death, and it is with Nab Cottage that he is most often associated. The Nab is about a half-mile from Rydal Mount, so that Hartley was now settled almost at the feet of Wordsworth.

Certain changes have been made in Nab Cottage, but when one looks into Hartley's room something of the romantic flavour seems to remain. Fortunately a good description of the cottage and Hartley's room has been preserved.

'The cottage, is close upon the road which winds right under the scar and by the Lake, very low, and somewhat darkened by the mass of ivy which has got a footing on the old bird-nest chimney. Most days the window-blind was down, so that when you were in the room you had "a light much like a shade." Hartley was seldom in in summer or fine weather, it was only on dull cold days or in the evenings that he was at home and the fire was lit. Then the little chamber looked snug and cosy— one side was occupied by something which resembled rather a pigeon-box than a book-case. Then there was a door covered with red baize that looked like the entrance to a closet, but which you found to be the receptacle for a little white-curtained bed. The fire-place had large hobs, and what schoolboys would call "caves" where pipes rested. Over the mantlepiece hung a cocked Hat and feather and a sword, I believe his father's, and a print of one of his earliest friends —within arm's length of an old cushioned chair with dark grotesque arms was the book he most used, Anderson's British Poets. Floor and table and window-seat were piled up with dusty papers. When a visitor came the landlady brought an extra candle, and on special occasions bannock cakes.'

LETTER 71

To HENRY NELSON COLERIDGE, *No. 10 Chester Place, Regent's Park.*

The Nab, July 10, [Postmark 1840.]

Dear Henry

Your request deeply affected me, so deeply indeed, that notwithstanding your urgency, for an immediate answer, I have not been able till now to girdle up the loins of my resolution to a definite reply. As I have already no less than five God-children, in none of whom I have the same interest of blood as in your expected—I can of course plead no scruple of conscience. It will not—I trust—fall to my lot to train up the child in the way it should go. The Church could never mean to exonerate Christian parents from their most sacred and peculiar duty. How or in what cases, Sponsors should be allowed or call'd on to interfere or assist, is a question of considerable difficulty. I confess, I should have liked a more serious exposition of your views on that subject than your brief note contains. I do not see how one sinner can, in a spiritual sense, be bound for another; the best of us have no holiness of our own: our righteousness can neither remove our original sin, nor expiate our actual guilt. Seldom, alas, can we fully atone for the earthly consequences of our misdoings—still less can we remedy the injuries done to our own souls; and were it otherwise, I am no substantial bail— I am afraid—in the spirit of your rather professional metaphor. Most Godfathers are too like those men of straw, who used to offer their disinterested services with so much importunity at the gate of Sergeants Inn—But this is irreverent talk. Perhaps, I cannot more briefly communicate my views of the office of a Godfather and of the Christian initiation itself, than by transcribing a sonnet addressed to my dear little God daughter, Caroline Green—who promises to be as queer a mortal as her spiritual sire.

> I stood beside thee in the holy place
> And saw the holy sprinkling on thy brow
> And was both bond and witness to the vow
> Which own'd thy need, confirm'd the claim of grace,
> That sacred sign which time shall not efface
> Declared thee His—to whom all angels bow
> Who bad the Herald Saint the rite allow
> To the sole sinless of all Adam's race.
> It was indeed an awful sign to see
> And oft I fear for what my love hath done
> As vouched for thy sweet communion
> In thy sweet *Saviour*'s blessed mystery,
> Would I might give thee back my little one
> But half the good which I derive from thee.[1]

In fine—since you and Sara think me not unworthy, I will gladly, though not without fear, establish a new link of Christian affection between your dear family, and one who though a barren is not yet—I hope—altogether a severed branch. I shall be most anxious to hear that all is well over— Perhaps it will be—ere this reaches you. I would not willingly know the precise hours of trial—till it is past. Would that I were one of those whose effectual prayer availeth much. I am glad you have no thoughts of calling

---

[1] Cf. *Poems*, 179.

the stranger after me—I am superstitious—and in some moods at least—fancy that ill-luck attends every thing about me—even to my very name. Is it in compliment to the king of Hanover that you design the name Ernest? There are none of your kindred of that name. Whatever be your intent, there are those, who will think that you wish a change in the line of succession. Not I, however, for one.

I am happy to hear that S.T.C.'s works are making way, but I am much more surprized that they succeed in America, than in Oxford; but all the better, for I think there is both room and need for them across the Atlantic. I see the influence of the Aids—and the Church and State in various quarters. An article in the Quarterly—nominally upon the Universities—but really on the grounds of civil and ecclesiastical polity, had availed itself of the latter remorselessly—and without acknowledgement. It evidently emanated from Oxford. Did you see an article in the January number of *Blackwood*—'On the Plagiarisms of S.T.C.'? It not only reiterates the charges of De Quincy—(without however any hypocritical pretences of friendship or reluctance) but asserts that the metaphysical portion of the *Biographia Literaria* is with the exception of a few insignificant interpolations and variations seldom for the better translated verbatim from Schelling, and that the partial acknowledgements are calculated, if not intended, to mislead the reader as to the extent of obligation. It denies that S.T.C. had one idea of the transcendental philosophy which he did [not owe] to the German, and supports the charges with a formidable array of references (alleging that the limits of the Magazine admit not of quotation). Now as there are probably not fifty copies of Schelling in the three kingdoms, nor many more individuals who would or could refer to them to any purpose, the attack may be carried into many, many quarters where it has no chance of fair examination. But the question is—is it true or is it not? Even if I possessed the books asserted to have been rifled, I doubt whether I should be capable of an efficient reply. Yet something should be done before the Biographia is reprinted. The article was written, as I am informed, by James Frazer [Ferrier?], a son-in-law of Professor Wilson, whom I formerly knew. As he is neither Liberal, nor Dissenter, nor ever received advice or admonition from ὁ Μακαρίτης I can conceive no motive of personal dislike which could induce him to fill nearly a sheet of Maga with matter which

to 95 out of 100 of her readers must be fact. Yet I do not,
I will not, believe that he whose abhorrence of plagiary was
so vehement and whose admiration of German Philosophers
so excessive, wilfully and knowingly appropriated the labours
of another and a foreigner—and that in a case, where any
popular effect, or rapid sale was not to be expected. The facts
I take to be: first that Frazer [Ferrier] has greatly exaggerated the identity of thought and expressions in the two
authors; and secondly, that when writing the Biographia,
my Father copied not from Schlegel[1]—but from his own
memorandum-books—and had literally forgotten what was
his own, and what was translation. I well remember how
that book was composed—under what circumstances of
bodily pain, and mental anxiety, and constant solicitation
from friends and booksellers to get done. You cannot be
ignorant that his verbal memory was as fallacious as his
ratiocinative powers were trusty, and his reproductive faculty
was prolific. He was never accurate in matter of reference.
I never knew [him] relate an anecdote or a conversation
twice alike. The infirmity of his memory was, I fear, increased at Calne from a cause to which it is painful to allude.
I do not think he had the works of Schelling by him. But I
would write to Mr. Green on the subject, if I knew his direction. It perplexes and pains me greatly. I cannot well finish
my essay till something is done about it. I had rather that
said essay were prefixed to the Poems than the Biographia,
as I cannot say aught on the Metaphysical portion, and there
is much respecting W. W. that I wish out.

I have prosed away unmercifully and left no room for 50
things. I thank you for your favourable opinion of my introduction to Ford, etc. I quite agree with you that the notes
are superabundant and the digressions too frequent. Moxon
wishes me to add the comparative estimate still. I know not
how it can be inserted; but, however, I will send it. It may
be put to use in some way.[2] Spenser will be a tough job[3]—
such an immensity to read. Are not some letters of his in

---

[1] Hartley must have meant to refer to Schelling and not Schlegel, as the entire
article in *Blackwood's* is devoted to Coleridge's indebtedness to Schelling.
[2] Writing to his mother on March 13, 1840, Hartley says: 'I meant to have
enter'd at length into the comparative merits of the two dramatists, and have
collected a mass of observations on the subject; but found that I had outrun
my limits, and thought it better to stop where I did, than to give a scanty
abstract of what I may elsewhere make use of.'
[3] Spenser's *Works* were eventually edited by H. J. Todd in 1850.

print? Moxon spoke of some in MS. which he thought might be made available if the possessor were willing; but of course they must be transcribed wholly or in part by someone in town. It would never do to send them down here. Dear Hal —your time is so fully engaged—and you have done and are doing so much for us all—that I ought not to give you any additional labour: or I might perhaps send you some questions from time to time respecting Spenser, as you have knowledge that I have not and access to books which I cannot command, though Moxon is very liberal, and Mr. Wordsworth, and indeed all my friends, are very kind. I am sorry that Moxon has got himself into hot water about Shelley.[1] Mr. W. warn'd him, but——The Rydal Mount family are all pretty well—Dora at least in her better way. I dined there on Sunday last. Bertha is gone to Keswick with her good man and babe, which is a sweet creature. The Pupils are nice gentlemanly Lads. Glad to hear that Derwent and Mary are recreating on the Continent. Miss Trevennen must be a kind friend.

Best love to Mother and Sara. How I long to see you! But now of course is no time.

Let me know—at all early convenience—when all is over. I will write a continuation of this in reply.

Meantime believe me—

Your's very truly
H. COLERIDGE.

LETTER 72

To MARY CLAUDE

[1840.]

Dear Mary

But yesterday I dined in the dear old house, in the very dear old room, with very good people, to wit, John Crossfield and his Brother, with their respective spouses, and A. Rev. —Anderson, now officiating for Mr. Boutflower. All was very kind, very good, but very unlike old times—and very unquakerly. Plate-glass to the floor, not much but rather costly looking furniture, books, either hymn-books, etc., or expensive books of prints. Plenty, however, to eat and drink —all there in the good old Quaker style. In fact, I have seldom been better pleased with a first visit to any family than with my introduction to John Crossfield's, and I knew,

---

[1] In 1840, Moxon having issued Shelley's Works was tried for blasphemous libel and was found guilty, but no sentence was passed.

it was not *his* fault that all was not as in times of yore. Still I could not but deduce from the floating, departing, and recurring presentations of my thoughts, that it is very well, that when we die, and the self—the I—of each of us is taken from its abode, the old house becomes untenantable. Would it not be a fearful thing to see the body of an old friend walking about with a new soul, a new I in it? —Flowers have been noted for ingratitude and insensibility. You will not wonder, therefore, that yours appear to flourish still, unconscious that you are not there to watch their progress or decay.

I was delighted, my dear Mary, with your mother's telling me of the impression the Nightingale's song made on you, but still more, should I have been delighted, had my Father been alive, in as much as he was the first modern Poet, to explode and defy the old fancy, of the Nightingale's *Melancholy song*, and to call her (or, gallantry apart, it should be—him, for I believe only Male *Birds* sing)

> The merry Nightingale
> That crowds, and hurries, and precipitates
> With fast thick warble his delicious notes
> As he were fearful that an April night
> Would be too short for him to utter forth
> His love chant.

I know you never read these lines of my Father's, but perhaps it may not be unpleasing to you, to know that your feeling on a poetical subject coincides without communication with that of a departed Poet.

> A mighty bard there was, in joy of youth
>   That wont to rove the vernal groves among,
> When the green oak puts forth its scallop'd tooth
>   And daisies thick, the darkening fallows throng:
> He listened oft whene'er he sought to soothe
>   A fancied sorrow with a fancied song,
> For Philomela ancient tale of ruth,
>   And never heard it, all the long night long.
> But heard instead—so glad a strain of sound—
>   So many changes of continuous glee—
> From lowest twitter shot a quick rebound
>   To billowy height of troubled ecstasy:
> Rejoice, he said, for joyfully had he found
>   That mighty Poets may mistaken be.[1]

---

[1] Composed by Hartley on Sunday, September 27, 1840. See *Poems*, 158.

There, Molly. It's getting late. This is not an apology for a letter to your dear Mother—which shall come in proper time, but only a brief remembrancer

From your
HARTLEY COLERIDGE.

LETTER 73

To MRS. GILLMAN, *Highgate, near London.*

Dear Mrs. Gillman　　　Knabbe near Ambleside, Dec. 9, 1840.

Do not be surprized—the hand was once familiar to you— you have look'd on it, I flattered myself, with pleasure, ere now, and though it can never again be look'd on with the same hope and happiness, as heretofore; yet, I trust, you will not turn away from it, when it assures you, that you and yours have not been forgotten, though my gratitude has been silent for so many years. Our first meeting was joyous— many days have we spent happily—you were, I believe, the last to despair of myself or my fortunes, but ere we parted, a dark cloud settled upon me, which ever since, I have been struggling though—with occasional glimpses of light, ever and anon baffled by sad returns of utter darkness. Yet neither in light nor in gloom, have I forgotten you, your manifold kindness great to myself, but far more worthily bestowed on him that is no more, who owed to you and to Mr. Gillman the peace of his latter days. My Father's departure had indeed been signified to me long before it took place, but your dear Husband's was sudden, very sudden to me—Would to God, I might have seen them, but once, and been reconciled, for I have been a heavy offender against both.

I have little to tell you of myself. What I have put forth, you may have seen. I have much on hand which will shortly see the light. But I feel myself so utterly unable to produce any thing, I will not say worthy of my Father's son, but in any way answering to your hopes of me, that you are the last person to whom I would speak of my literary doings, knowing, as I do, Mr. Gillman's disappointment, and low estimation of my writings. Do not think that I am less grateful or affectionate to his memory therefore. He could not think more lowly of aught I have done than I do myself. I wish he could have known how deeply I feel for his zeal and ardour in my father's cause. Alas, I never thank'd him for the Book.

I am much distressed about my dear Mother. She seldom speaks of herself, much more frequently of you, and always with a deep feeling of what *you* and *He* have done and suffered for us all; but her last letters have told too much of her increasing infirmities. As if she had not enough of trouble, Derwent's affairs come at the eleventh hour. I always thought he was prospering at Helston,[1] and this reverse has almost drawn tears from an eye unused to flow. I feel an accumulation of self-reproach when I reflect that with a little prudence and a healthy energy I might have been of material pecuniary assistance. For any thing like advice or suggestion I never could have been available. Besides, my whole experience has convinced me that advice does more harm than good in the world. I believe I should myself have been a better and a happier man, had I been let alone—Laissez faire. My old friend James is now a Rev'd and a Husband, I hope a blessing to you. I dare not ask after other old friends, for some may be dead, and others, friends no more. You probably have often seen my little Niece and nephew. I think I should doat upon the girl. With Boys I should have nothing to do but at lesson time. Twice have I been an assistant at Sedbergh school, and in both instances, though I say that should not say it, I acquitted myself to the satisfaction of Master and Pupils. I should much like to have a permanent situation of the kind, provided I was only required to teach, and not to manage or be managed further than the regular discharge of my contract involved. I can instruct, but I have no skill to educate. I shall ever repent my imprudent undertaking to manage two or three great boys. I was foil'd in the attempt, and worse than that, roll'd down the hill when I was beginning to see the top. I am now, I hope, climbing upwards. Any assurance of your forgiveness and remembrance would give me a shove.

Kind loves and remembrances to all who remember me. I hope to see Highgate again ere either of us die. How is my old Pupil Henry?

I am, Dear Mrs. Gillman

Most gratefully yours

HARTLEY COLERIDGE.

---

[1] 'There must have been some obscurity in the way which this movement of his brother's was communicated to Hartley. Derwent came to London from Cornwall to better his fortunes.' Note by E. H. Coleridge.

LETTER 74

To MRS. CLAUDE

Surgery, Ambleside, March 21, 1841.
The product of *six* pipes—Smale—False—I only
smok'd one pipe and a precious black one.

Dear Mrs. Claude
Fell says, an undoubted and lamentable truth, that I'm
a great sinner, adding as a corollary thereto that I have not
written to you. Here we have general—original—sin, as the
major term, and an actual sin (of omission) as the minor—
the conclusion you will draw yourself. I wish it were equally
easy to remove it by confession and amendment. But sins are
like wounds, which however well healed leave an unsightly
cicatrice. The Man who promised that he would so unite a
broken bone that the fracture should be stronger than the never-
broken parts, was a Quack. But perhaps the heaviest part of
my offense is, that I have not acknowledged Mrs. R. [H. M.]
Rathbone's book. Now you know an establish'd mode of
rebutting, is recrimination. I have nothing, indeed, to recri-
minate upon you; but in publishing the Sonnets written in
Jane's and Louisa's Albums I must say, the Lady has somewhat exceeded her instructions.[1] They were not intended for
publication: and the former is so irregular in its measure and
faulty in diction, that I should never—myself—have put it
forth without considerable corrections. The latter is, in its
way, nearly as good as I could make it, but I do not like
to print things expressive of my personal feelings towards
individuals, albeit those feelings may have been among the
happiest and least censurable of my life. However, no great
harm is done. It is only the attachment of an elderly man to
a child, and I would not have you say any thing to Mrs.
Rathbone about it. I wish I had appended a short note to
the verses on Katey Jones, simply to say, that she is the darling of a blind grandfather, without which the drift must be
obscure to those who are unacquainted with the fact. Some
of her own and daughter's productions I like much. One I
presume to be from the pen of her husband, which is very
affecting. The selection in general is good. I could, perhaps,
have given her a few extracts from Greek and Roman

---

[1] Hartley's contributions to Mrs. H. M. Rathbone's *Childhood* (1841) were:
'The Sabbath Day's Child', 'The First Birthday', 'Primitiae', and 'To K.H.J.'

writers which might have shewn how the ancients regarded childhood, and perhaps, a few from older English; but it is remarkable, how abundant the authors, male and female, of the last half century, have been in baby poetry, compared to their predecessors. You seldom find an independent verse in the olden time, addressed to, or suggested by, a child, though there are incidental passages, both in the Dramatists and the Divines, which shew how well they felt the sweetness of childhood, and how deeply some of them meditated on its mystery. But it is easily enough explained. Mamas were not, in the 16th and 17th centuries, readers of poetry. Babes are not yet generally addicted to this vice. There is a *jeu-d'esprit* of Prior addressed to a little Lady Somebody, which is witty— and Ambrose Philips (of whom you perhaps never heard— and no harm if you've not) has several copies of rhime, in which the same flat compliments (to wit—that Miss did not know what execution her eyes were to do, etc.) is repeated again and again. I know not that any English poet before Watts ever wrote serious poetry for children, and some of his hymns, where the Calvinist did not predominate over the Poet and the Christian, are really beautiful. In Mr. Faber's volume[1] there are some lines addressed to his 'only Sister' which I think exquisite. By the way, I must undeceive Mary about that. The Copy sent was Faber's present not mine. He heard I had been enquiring in vain for the work at Troughton's for a Lady, and sent it to Thomas with true delicacy. I should like to know what you and what Mary think of the poems in general, or rather in particular, for my own judgement is very diverse on different parts. I think on the whole they indicate much genius, but those pieces, which, as indicative of his peculiar cast of devotion, may probably attract most public attention, are by no means the best.[2] I understand he is now on his way to Jerusalem with his pupil. It was not an original thought to baptize our little Princess with water from Jordan. Chateaubriand brought a bottle of the same sacred element to regenerate the King of Rome. I should conjecture that devout persons would not greatly approve of such sentimentality in connection with a holy rite, which, applied to a French or English child, has

[1] See Faber's *Cherwell Water Lily and other Poems*, 1840.
[2] Writing about the same time to Mary Claude, Hartley remarks concerning Faber's poems: 'Seriously, I do think that they shew more genius, than I find in any of the young Poets, Alfred Tennyson excepted; but genius as yet undisciplined, and not very well supplied with material to work on.'

hardly sentimental propriety. For a converted Jew, there might be some meaning—at least some feeling in it. I have heard that some pious Israelites have purchased earth from Palestine to line their graves, and I am not disposed to laugh, far less to scoff at the fancy. But to us, the seed of the Gentiles, who have no national claim to the Holy Land, I cannot see that the Earth or Water of Syria is holier than any other Earth or Water which was created through the Eternal Word. But good English Christians differ with me on this point.

I suppose there is little hope of Mr. Brancker's rescinding his resolution, so I can only wish him a good purchaser. But I am not the only one by hundreds that regret his absence. Does he not talk of going abroad?

Glad to hear that Louis takes well to his new employ—No doubt he, as well as all other good souls (myself ecstatically in the number) rejoiced to hear that H. White was yet in the land of the living, and likely to be soon on 'the immaculate island of the great and free'. I never gave much credit to the report of his having fall'n at Guznee, as several persons, well acquainted with Indian affairs, held it utterly unlikely he should be there, but it is pleasant to be sure. Louis's friend, Jones Greenwood, is at home, but doubtless they correspond. You would be glad to hear of the safe arrival of the Adolphs at Valparaiso. The journal was delightful. I heard a good deal of Mrs. Fell's translation, and much admired the perfect and vernacular command of the English language she displays. They seem to have had a favourable passage on the whole, though never to set foot on dry ground all the way must have been tantalizing. There was no want of Grubb at all events. Janetta is quite a little woman, and probably her removal to a foreign clime, where she may have few companions of like age, will rather confirm than abate her precocious gravity. I wish Mary, who is as great a noddy about Babies as myself, could see my little Cousin, Katey Hill. It is such a sweet Love! I have written some lines upon her, which I think about the best I ever produced.[1] You shall see them before long. I also made some to the Queen in her character of wife and mother, which Miss Spring Rice (now Mrs J. G. Marshall) presented to her Majesty.[2] I have a great many irons in the fire—I cannot say which will come out first.

---

[1] See *Poems*, 191–2.
[2] See 'A wanton bard in heathen time,' *Poems*, 259–60.

Dear love to Jane and Louisa. My next shall be to my once little, now tall and stately favourite.

Believe me—

Yours affectionately,

H.C.

LETTER 75

To EDWARD MOXON.

Aug. 12, 1841.

Dear Sir,

After so long an interval, you will perhaps be disposed to view my autograph with something of that unwelcoming would-be incredulity wherewith Poll of Wapping beholds her husband returned from transportation, when she has got another. Yet, sir, I assure you, I have not forgot our engagements; and if you persevere in your intention of publishing Spenser, shall be glad to prefix a Commentary on his Pastorals and Faery Queen, with some observations on his personal history, as indicated in his writings. I have no doubt that many particulars of his life, not uninteresting or unconnected with the public history of his time, might be gleaned from divers sources. Had I access to the many collections of papers in private hands, I would willingly perform the task; but in my present Patmos this is impossible. But however little I may have to say about Spenser that is dead, I think I can say much of the Spenser that lives, and will live for ever.

Did you see the abuse of me in the 'Atlas'?[1] I am glad of it; I find I can stand fire. I am like a soldier who has been in battle. I should like, though, to know who it is.

What I should have said, and have written on Massinger and Ford, will find a place in an Essay on the Age of Shakespeare, in which I purpose to set forth what in each author was catholic in relation to that age and phase of human existence, and what was each author's own.

But my more immediate intent in addressing you at present respects my poems, which are very nearly, if not quite out of print. In three weeks time I could, if you were disposed to publish, produce a volume, as large as the last, of sonnets or miscellanies; and before Christmas, 'Prometheus,' whom I think we shall do better to introduce to the public alone, and

---

[1] Only an 1829 number of the *Atlas* is to be found in the British Museum.

in a more convenient form. I have a considerable number of sonnets, and other short poems on scriptural subjects, which I sometimes have thought of publishing separately, as a Christmas present. But then they are so purely Catholic, neither high church nor low church, orthodox nor dissenting —have so little of Newman of M'Neil in them, and my own reputation has so little of the odour of sanctity, that I am half-afraid. By the way, the Chartists have been revenging their imagined wrongs on you, which is annoying enough; a good way of advertising a book, if mere publication of opinion were the thing desired, but not very agreeable to author or publisher. With my next I may perhaps send a portion of a small work to be entitled 'Church Sectarianism', for your consideration.

Believe me, yours truly,

H. COLERIDGE.

LETTER 76

To MRS. CLAUDE, *No. 36 Faulknor Street, Liverpool.*

Ambleside. Oct. 11th, 1841.[1]

without a pipe in his mouth.

Dear Mrs Claude

'Into the heart of mountain Solitudes'
Where one low dwelling, with its neighbour trees
Gives a meek sense of human life recluse,
Fit mansion for a hermit family—
(So may I speak a seeming Paradox
Yet only seeming), meet companion to the Tarn
Whose dark grey waters neither smile nor frown,
So far from that great mart of trade and trickery,
Thy present Patmos, would the graver's art
Displayed above in scanty space, convey thee,
And all thy brood that love the Hills so well.
But I would bring thee to the troug[h] or vale,
Or to the genial warmth of fire side—

Which indeed is the most, if not the only comfortable spot in the vale at present; for, as usual, it pours—Cats and Dogs—

---

[1] 'This letter is written on a great sheet of note-paper illustrated by an engraving of Blea Tarn, drawn by W. Banks. The sketch depicts the tarn at the foot of Ghimmer Crag, and the one above, [. . . ? . . .] of the *Excursion*, in the foreground.' Note by E. H. Coleridge.

a true English phrase, Mrs Fell's use of which, some minutes past, evinces her growing familiarity with our vernacular tongue. How people live in such weather at Blea-Tarn, which is Blea and bleak enough at all times, I cannot conceive, but I suppose, like the Eels, they get used to it.—Else might the vicinity of the iron pool - - - [*sic*] I never myself took any fancy to these closets in the hills, as places of permanent residence, since I was fifteen. I once thought, indeed, Robinson Crusoe the happiest of men. But even he was in a green sunny Isle of the West, with Parrots in the woods, and goats frisking about him, and grapes, and limes; and it is only the strong fancy and inexhausted spirit of childhood, that can so much as imagine entire solitude delightful. There may be a reach of melancholy, or spleen, or despondency, which seeks solitude as something less intolerable than society with whose cheerfulness it cannot sympathize, and whose sadness adds a burden to its own, but Heaven be praised I am not come to that yet, though sulky and misanthropic enough at times, when the rain pours sullenly and perseveringly, and the ground looks sodden, the lakes crop-full, the field sploshy, women with wretched babies at their backs, one scarce able to walk, clinging to its Mammie's ragged pettycoat; and two, three, four others, the eldest not six years old, trailing after; a bespattered chaise with all the glasses up, horses like drown'd rats, and driver like the weather itself; a howl of wind that shakes the black-spotted elm-leaves from their stalks, and drops them on the earth like blotting paper; within doors— a fire that will smoke and will not burn, the wet bubbling through the ill-set casement, a room dark at best, now dim with triple gloom, children squalling, mother scolding in a voice intermittingly furious and lugubrious; the day Sunday— time three in the afternoon; one wretched tinkling bell ding-dinging, (Parson alone at the desk, as dismal as myself) table covered with unanswered letters, unpaid bills, unfinished articles—

> Oh solitude where are the charms
> That sages have seen in thy face?

This to be sure, is a gloomy picture, and I will not say, that it is exactly daguerreotyped from my own case yesterday, but certainly I do at times find my abode at the Knabbe rather too retired, albeit [it] is on the Queen's highway. Now this comes of writing upon this new-fangled landscape paper, not a single word to the purpose, nor to any possible purpose. And yet what have I to tell you? Nothing, positively nothing, but my great joy to hear of Louisa's better prospects, which may God make perfect. I am glad to hear that Mr. Brancker has seen you frequently. I hope he was satisfied with Louis, as indeed, he needs must be. I shall write to him. I am rather in a state of uncertainty respecting my publications. My muse, however, has been productive of late, but I cannot produce either prose or verse to please myself completely, and some times when I read the trash that is so liberally set forth, I am tormented with the suspicion, that my own is no better; for no doubt A. and B. and so on to Z. had friends whose *sincere* opinion they desired, which sincere opinion responded—admirable! Beautiful!!! Too good I'm afraid, for the public taste!!!! But why should I trouble you with an author's perplexities? Faber is returned with his Pupil, but I have not seen either to speak to. Religious animosities run as high as ever. Mr. Combe's Synagogue opens (*on dit*) on the 15th. Sir Wilfred Lawson of Bray- nore hall, according to report, is to be present. I care nothing about the matter myself, but for the heart-burn- ings it will occasion. For curiosity will lead school- children, and servants and labourers and pensioners to the show, in despite of the interdict of the Church, and its secular champions, and there will be scoldings and recrimina- tions, ill-blood, and alleged ingratitude, to say nothing of falsehood and evasion—I cannot say in what quantity. A man should be *very* sure that his preaching is not only true, but essential, before he lets loose so much mischief. But High Church and Dissenter agree in this, that it is sinful to doubt, either the irrefragable certainty of their tenets, or their own effectual vocation to enforce them where, how, and when their own discretion inspires. Janetta has just got up and thaw'd the silence of the last hour. She is wonder- fully improved, and really grows quite a love, the sweetest temper. I have got another cousin, a little Herbert Southey Hill.

With my very best love to Mary, Jane, and Louisa, for whose returning health I wish I were good enough to make my prayers avail.

Believe me, dear Lady,

Yours truly,
H.C.

LETTER 77

To MRS. SAMUEL TAYLOR COLERIDGE, *No. 10 Chester Place,*
Regent's Park, London.

May 7, 1842.

My dear Mother

I was much relieved by the steady hand and cheerful tone
of your letter—its bad news, I knew before—its better prospects were welcome, because new. I shall send Moxon a
large parcel of essays soon, and then await his ultimatum.
If the trowzers would not burden Mrs. Wordsworth, I should
be thankful for them. Too few Trowzers don't become a
Gentleman. With respect to the washing bill, and others, I
confess a sin of omission. I ought to spare dear Mrs. W. all
the trouble I can. I wish, my dear Mother, I could confidently promise that those should [be] the last bills of mine
you should ever see, but I dare not promise this; all I can do,
is, by self-denial and industry to diminish them as much as I
can. I am afraid you may justly reproach me with not making hay when the sun-shined, but you are too much a Christian to reproach me with the irrevocable past.

I greatly love and admire Derwent's promptitude in
H.N.C.; he acted as he ought to and I *think*, under the circumstances, I should have done the same. You do not, my
dear Mother, tell me in your letter, how Derwent Jun.['s]
fracture happened, nor whether a dangerous one. Fell says
that at his age the bones knit easily. I hope it will produce
no lasting lameness or deformity.

My dear Mother, you will perhaps not blame me, because
in all the complication of affliction, I have thought more of
you than of the actual sufferers. For them, I had, and have
hope. They naturally look forward. It was ever my disposition to look back, and now I must look back—even for the
hope wherein I am to walk in the narrow path towards
Eternity.

That for a time I forgot you, at least that your image was
at one time no very welcome visitor in my memory's chambers, is most true. But think not it is so now. Grey hairs have
brought me, if not wisdom, and reflection, at least retrospec-
tion. I think of you daily, hourly, above all nightly, for I
dream of you or Derwent almost every night. I regret the
space that parts us. I think I could make any possible
exertion, or endure any possible privation, for any given

time, that would enable me to see you—once—before I die.

Bertha and Herbert are as well as can be expected. Their Chicks!—Oh, that you could see the Darlings. It would rejoice your old heart; for I believe you to be a woman not ashamed of being old—nor am I a man to love a woman the less for being old.

Your truly affectionate Son
HARTLEY.

LETTER 78

To DERWENT COLERIDGE, *Herbert White, Stanley Grove, Chelsea, near London.*

[Postmark August 22, 1842.]

My dear Derwent

I ought, long ere this, to have thank'd you for your pamphlet; but wish'd to give a more intelligent praise than it is yet in my power to do. I can only say, at present, that I admire your clearness of statement, your plain English, matter of fact style (at which I am a very bad hand) and wish your establishment all success, for your sake, and for the noble purposes to which it is devoted.[1] It is sad, my dear brother, that our conversation is so intermittent. You I know, have little time for letter-writing; but I can plead no such preoccupation. Yet I would not have you think that mere laziness is the fault; far less could I endure you to suspect, that I have forgotten you. No, Derwent, you are in my daily thoughts—my nightly dreams. But in truth, I fear to address, as I should fear to meet you. I should tremble in your presence, and yet more in your wife's, not only because, for manifold derelictions I am unworthy to be call'd your brother; but because, even in my best of hours, in my wishes, hopes, and prayers, I am not as you are. I feel that there are possible cases in which I should think it my duty to oppose you.

I do not now recollect what I said in my last scrawl, but I believe I spoke with less respect than I ought to have done of itinerant societarian oratory—not, I hope, of your friend. May I, for three days' acquaintance call him my friend[2]—the dear deceased Macaulay—best of the name? I know that he himself felt keenly, that he was advocating a good cause, in a

---

[1] Derwent was principal of St. Mark's College, Chelsea from 1841 to 1864.
[2] Hartley refers to Zachary Macaulay, who died in 1838.

way little to his taste; and for which I suspect he had as little talent as inclination—for tho' I did not hear him speak, all who did hear, pronounced him a very heavy and tiresome speaker. Little things are best done by little men. When noble minds, with the noblest intent, task themselves with unworthy work, they cannot escape a consciousness of self-degradation, which may provoke a lively mind to something not far removed from buffoonery, and freeze up the faculties of a graver nature to a sensible solemnity, more offensive to self than to any one else. In any case, it will beget a wish to be as unlike the habitual self as possible. To Societies I am a friend, whether their object be the increase of knowledge, by the concentration of individual discoveries, and observations (as in the Royal, Antiquarian, Zoological, etc.) or the diffusion of knowledge, by mutual communication, or the relief of poverty, or ignorance, by accumulated capital, or the extension of the Gospel in our own or foreign lands. In none of these respects do I see that they contravene or usurp the just prerogatives of the Church, even in the hypothesis that the clergy, for the time being, are the sole legitimate will and mind, the thinking and originating power, the heart and brain of the church; while the laity are no more than bowels, bones, and sinews, fingers and toes, which can have no independent life; save the morbid striving after life that appears in semi organized excrescences and hydatids.

But when religion, or even charity, is in question, I do mortally dislike all trick and exhibition, all peptic persuaders of the purse—Fancy balls, and Fancy bazaars—a step in immodesty beyond Heath's book of Beauty. I believe we feel alike—you judge perhaps more wisely, and more experimentally.

To the absolute, parliamentary control of the whole beneficence of the Community which you claim for your order, I demur. As for the laws of Mortmain, I wish they were done away with. The period of their usefulness is past. I wish the Church were far richer than it is, and that every wealthy man would devote such portion of his wealth as is not *morally* entail'd to the service of God in the mode whereby alone wealth can serve God—by enlarging the spiritual and intellectual in man. The Clergy may be the best advisers as to the direction of such bequests, for they have most opportunity of learning where the greater need exists. But it is not in the sick room, nor under the terror of approaching death, that the advice should be urged—nor should the offices of the Church, and the promises of pardon be bartered for money bestowed on pious purposes. This was the most crying sin of popery, and it was in this sense alone that the true Reformers preach'd against the efficacy of good works—not, as some slanderers assert, to the disparagement of active duties. But, after so long silence, why do I begin with controversy? Sink the Parson and let us talk a while on Hartley and Derwent. Oh, How I wish you could be here now—We have a glorious summer. I never saw the country lovelier. Westmorland is a very land of Goshen. Neither thunderstorms nor poverty have yet reach'd us—(though the multitude of tramps tells us enough about the latter). The Steam engine has preserved our streams from the mercantile contamination which Wordsworth deprecated in 'The Excursion', and if the building gentry do not always improve the prospect, they keep the people regularly employ'd. Your old friend, Herbert White, now a Captain in the India Service, (retired) is here, with a most amiable wife, and five children. He is the last of his family. Fanny, Sophy, and Howard are all dead! He is a noble fellow, and by no means the *wreck* you once thought him. Indeed there are few men who appear to me to have a clearer moral sense, or who express juster thoughts in purer language. I never knew a more complete gentleman. All that is good in the military character he interpenetrated with his individuality, while he has nothing of that professional constraint which is ungentlemanly in all professions but your own. He never thinks it necessary to say or think thus or thus because he has worn uniform. He has atoned as far as may be for his juvenile incontinence by educating his natural Son respectably as a medical man (he has just past his examination). He never boasts of his early irregularities, nor makes a parade of reformation. You will not, of course, expect an India officer to be as strict in theory, as a youth of your own training. His wife is not pretty, but very ladylike, and a sweet singer. I have heard her sing the song from Phantasmion, and I think it is prettily set. I should much like the music of your Sea-song. The words are musical. I have myself written words to 'My lodging is on the Cold Ground', 'Rousseau's Dream', 'Poor Mary Anne', and 'Robin Adair'. Also to 'God Save the King'—the most difficult I ever attempted. I suppose you have little time for verse making now. It is a pity your exquisite power of versification, and beautifully tender fancy should be lost. I know not whether you possess my little volume. Few of the pieces in it would satisfy your ear. I think myself the Sonnet 'What sound awakened first the untried ear?'[1] the best. I rather think that the couplet and the elegiac quatrain are the metres I manage best. In blank verse I cannot satisfy myself at all. Mr. Wordsworth thinks my prose stiff and elaborate. Elaborated it certainly is when I have time before me. Much of the life of Massinger was written four times over. Lazy folks take the most pains, is true in more senses than one. Indeed it would be impossible for any man who laboured after perfection—like our dear Father—to produce the quantity of Southey or Scott, who were content to let well alone. Moreover, correcting does not always produce correctness. I think Wordsworth's alterations almost always for the worse. What do you think of his last volume?[2] Is Sonnet a very good vehicle wherein to exhibit the Gallows? Yet those sonnets are more powerful than any thing else that his later years have produced. 'The Borderers', I confess, disappointed me. I didn't expect a good play, but I expected a profounder poem. The impossibility of the Story is comfortable, for it is a worse libel on Providence than that 'sorry legend' which excited the indignation of the Pedlar. To be more serious. A great revolution must have taken place in his mind in the interval between the production of the 'Borderers', 'Guilt and Sorrow' and perhaps the 'Mad Mother', and the writing of the first Preface. The author of those horrors could hardly say with more than *poetic* veracity:

> The roving accident is not my trade,
> To freeze your blood I have no ready wits.

Perhaps a tendency to be horrible is natural to the youth of Genius; when power is delightful in its own ἐνέργεια and ἐνεργεῖ apart from moral or sensuous beauty. I can almost believe that Shakespeare had at least a hand in Titus Andronicus. At all events, King Lear was the earliest of his great

---

[1] See *Poems*, 5.

[2] Cf. *Poems, chiefly of early and late years; including The Borderers*, 1842. Elsewhere Hartley says: 'Mr. Wordsworth is bringing forth a volume. It will doubtless create a sensation. He is the last of the Poets, I mean, the last of the men who were Poets when I was born, for Rogers does not write now. One by one, our lights go out. Byron burn'd dim soon and went out early; Scott went out at last; Southey is a Poet no more; Wordsworth and Campbell are the sole survivors of the Poets of my youth. They are not likely to have any successors. We have now plenty of clever men, but no great man, and no promise of greatness. But this is croaking.'

Dramas. I do not think an old man could or would have written it. But it's some sma' hours agit the twale, and I must adjourn.

Dear Derwent, I am almost ashamed to confess that more than a week has elapsed since I wrote the above, to which I have not a great deal to add; tho' I could write a magazine sheet. I believe I have not mentioned Derwent Junior. His accident was awkward and distressing; but will not, I trust, leave any permanent lameness. His Master, Kennedy, was an unsuccessful Candidate for Rugby. Since our own father was taken from us, I do not think England, her Church, or the world have had so great a loss as in Arnold.[1] I *never* knew any man—no not one—to whom I would so readily have surrendered my private judgement, because, though I have known men who possessed certain faculties in much higher perfection, I never knew a mind all whose faculties were so equally developed; a reason so perfectly in harmony with a pure Christian faith, interpenetrating and informing, so acute an understanding, commanding and enlivening an equally energetic will. Men as honest in regard to the world, I may have known; perhaps of equal integrity, objectively and relatively under yet more trying circumstances; but I never knew a man of like compass of thought and logical expertness who dealt so fairly and sincerely with his own intellect, thinking, as he spoke and acted 'as ever in his great task master's eye'.

Here I will pause for the present. Perhaps in a day or two I may send a supplement to this already two penny epistle.
With kind regards to Mary,

I am Dear Derwent,

[Signature cut away.]

LETTER 79

To MRS. SAMUEL TAYLOR COLERIDGE, *No. 10 Chester Place, Regent's Park, London.*

Knabbe, Jan. 28, [Postmark 1843.]

My dear Mother

A brief note from James inform'd me this day of the sad event, which Mary's letter of the preceding day had told me to expect.[2] Yet I could not give up all hope till I saw the

---

[1] Thomas Arnold of Rugby died in 1842.
[2] Henry Nelson Coleridge, after a lingering illness, died on January 26, 1843.

postman this day, and then at once I knew how it was, even before I saw the black-edged paper.

It is long since I have written, and at present I cannot write, nor will you be disposed to read much.

Consolation, either to you or to Sara, I will not offer. What ever the case admits, you both know where to seek and have kindred who will not be slow to administer far better than I know how. What I can do to supply the loss, I will with the aid of Heaven—but, alas, had I been wiser and better, I might have done much more. Never did I feel so sharp remorse for my many sins, more especially those [of] omission and procrastination, out of which the more positive delinquencies have chiefly arisen. But remorse is not repentance. That, God alone can bestow.

I have seen your note to Mrs. Wordsworth. Your own sufferings have been not little. Yours must indeed have been a home of mourning. I am glad that Sara is *tearful but calm*, those were good James' words. Tears are a great relief. She has been wonderfully supported—I do not fear, that she will bear up for a while, for recent affliction has a sort of excitement. I only fear for the ebb of her spirit which may take place some months, or perhaps a year hence. But she has her children, God bless them, and though they must needs increase her anxiety, they will prevent her sinking into herself in moody retrospect—making her duty to look forward.

> For who hath aught to love and love aright
> Shall never in the darkest strait despair.
> For out of love, exhales a living light
> A light that speaks in promise and in prayer.[1]

Excuse my quoting some unpublished, I believe never to be published, lines of my own. They were addressed to little Edward Green, on his birthday, four years old, and allude to the loss of his mother. You will perhaps like to be told that Mrs. Green is better. I had a letter from her, not long ago. Isaac was here last week, and well.

To have contributed in some measure to his recovery by assisting him in the school is one of the few acts of my life to which I look back with satisfaction.

I hope Herbert will not have to be removed from Eton, now that he has got the fagging over. I think our loss is worst of all for him. It is bad enough to be separated from a living

---

[1] Cf. 'The Fourth Birthday', ll. 9–12, *Poems*, 189.

father at the turn and crisis of life, when the boy is merging in the youth. It was bad enough for me—though I had a father. Was the dear boy aware of Henry's danger? How does Edith take it?

It is good that Miss Trevennen is so deeply interested in young Derwent, though I do not think public schools so essential either to this world's welfare or the next as some people do. I know nothing about the Charter-house now. It had a great run of prizes etc. at one time. But it is in London, and the youths who came thence to Oxford were not conspicuous for regularity, and told stories of scrapes and adventures in which I had rather my nephew had no share. But Derwent [is a] better judge than I. I am not glad that his dear Mary *is in the way*, as I perceive from your note she is. She has such bad times. I am sorry Derwent is bilious. May the Lord spare and preserve him. He is almost the only remnant of my childhood's company. My health has been mercifully spared. I was not very well a fortnight ago—oppression on the chest; but I am quite better now—and in a working mood—though anxiety has rather unsettled me.

God aid you all. Love to dear Edith.

Your truly affectionate Son
H.C.

N.B. I shall not need to get any thing now for mourning, except a crape round my hat. The poor old woman for whom you were so kind to send the shawl is dead and gone to Heaven. She was a pattern of patience and simple piety. I gave the shawl to a little girl, who though Mrs. Richardson's sister, officiates as Servant. Her husband is unfortunately out of employ—by no fault of his own, I am sure. He is a very industrious man, when he has work, and the most absolutely sober I ever saw in his class. The Hills go on Thursday next. Their little Herby, a lovely Babe, is poorly, and Kate not well. Bertha looks fagged. H. Hill has been at Keswick to take leave. Kate is not the thing. Aunt Lovell in low spirits— no [.. ? ..] alteration that I hear.

I have seen Cuthbert's wife and like her much. Though not beautiful she is attractive, but hardly the stately lady I should have thought C.'s aristocratic taste would have selected. It is a dreadful night and very late, so I must once more commend to Heaven. I anticipate uneasy doze and painful dreams.

LETTER 80

To MRS. HENRY NELSON COLERIDGE, *No. 10 Chester Place, Regent's Park, London.*

Rydal, March 21, [Postmark 1843.]

My dear injured Sister

I feel myself too utterly unworthy to have been consulted at all in the case, to deliver any opinion with regard to the trusteeship,[1] even were I, under any circumstances capable of giving one of weight.

Of course the Justice is the fittest person, but besides the delicacy of asking one so deeply engaged in important business, his necessary absences during Circuit might perhaps occasion inconvenience. Allsop, of course you would not condescend to ask, after his imprudent—to say the very least —imprudent exposure of our dear Father's somewhat hasty confidence. Mr. Montagu is perhaps as heavily task'd, as at his advanced period of life he can bear. Mr. Frere, I have not heard of lately. I know not, indeed, if he is living. He is probably the person my father would have preferred. His easy fortune would make the trouble comparatively less, but this I am afraid is out of the question. We must be beholden to the Judge.

I fear I am at present under such a cloud, I have shown myself so little worthy of reliance, that it is vain to make any offer of personal services in the only way in which I could be of use—that is to say, in regard to the care of the Works. Still I will finish the Essay on my Father's literary character, which he [Henry Nelson Coleridge] intended to prefix to the *Biographia*, though I confess I would rather it appeared in connection with the Poems, or almost any other of the works; for admirable as much of the matter of the *Biographia* unquestionably is, it is more fragmentary and worse put together than any of them: and I do think, there are some things relative to W. W. he would not have written in a calmer state of mind. That, under the circumstances, he could compose any thing at all, displays a vigour of mind almost unparalleled.

Would to Heaven, I could myself supply the place so well filled up by him that is gone—but to say nothing of worse disqualifications—I am shockingly ignorant of business. I

---

[1] 'The literary and other property bequeathed by S. T. Coleridge.'   Note by E. H. Coleridge.

hope your Herbert will not grow up in like ignorance—a sad cause of irregularity. I will indeed do my best to acquire some knowledge of affairs.

This will be but a short epistle. It was not without an effort of resolution that I dared to write it. I am now somewhat calmer and stronger, and feel rather more hope in myself than I did at the commencement. In the next, I shall be able to say one thing more comfortable than I can at present. Perhaps I may have to announce another departure from this vale of sorrow. The soul of Southey may be restored to more than its original brightness. I saw a short note from Kate announcing that he has been seized with Typhus—from which there is small chance of his recovering.[1] Hope would hardly be the appropriate word.

I will write to Derwent ere next post. I can lay myself open to him. I have a proposition to make on which he will be our best counsellor.

I fear neither you nor poor Mama are much better. I am better than I deserve. Most here as usual. No doubt you have heard of William Junior's approaching nuptials. But I cannot speak of cheerful things. Can I ever obtain, I will [not] say your forgiveness, but your esteem and confidence? I am sadly shorn of my own.

I remain

Your too little worthy Brother
H. COLERIDGE.

N.B. Some intellectual exertion will, I trust, restore me to a sounder feeling of self-command. I must not permit myself to despair.

LETTER 81

To MRS. SAMUEL TAYLOR COLERIDGE, *No. 10 Chester Place, Regent's Park, London.*

Knabbe, May 15, [Postmark 1843.]
Going to rain.

My dear Mother

One should never be ashamed of doing one's duty, but I am half ashamed to address you after my long and I fear apparently unkind silence, and the undeserved kindness of your two last letters. I will make the best amends I can, by

---

[1] Southey died on March 21, 1843, his mind having been impaired for several years.

answering those letters, as minutely as I can, for you sometimes justly complain of the irresponsive quality of my communications. First as to the wardrobe. I am perfectly well
provided with all sorts of under garments, having 17 day and
3 night shirts, wanting no repairs but what can easily be done
here, an old *junk* (one of your own lingo grandi words) may
be cut up to mend with, if necessary. I have a good suit for
Sundays. A good hat, (Mrs. W. objected to the price, but
good things are always cheapest in the end) two decent black
inexpressibles   white trowzers for hot weather (which I am
sorry to say, are rather expensive in washing, for I have not
the knack of keeping 'em clean a week) gloves and other
appurtenances. The Frock and white waistcoat will be acceptable, if they can be sent without much expense, but there is
no hurry. Give yourself no trouble, tho' I am anxious for the
books. I long to see the dear little creature's essay—Lord
love it. But I forget that I am speaking of a widow. I am
afraid you think that I am sparing of praise to friends and
relations' works, but she cannot justly complain on that score.
I have been a little mortified at the dulness of some folks with
regard to Phantasmion, which I think, sets her above all
female writers of the age—except Joanna Baillie. I had a
very pleasant stay at Keswick. It was very kind of the
Dentons to ask me. By a mistake (not of my own) I was too
late for the funeral. I know not whether to regret this or not.
It would have been painful to see persons by the grave side
equally related and equally dear to the departed, who would
not so much as speak to each other.[1] I was in hopes that all
would be heal'd now, but I will not pursue the painful subject. Aunt Lovell was marvellously well, but poor Kate
look'd sadly jaded: she smiled indeed, but it was more in
sorrow than in mirth. If she does not obtain heart's ease
soon, I fear it will go hard with her. She is going to give up
the house in Harrinan field (which is cruelly over rented)
and will reside for some time with Cuthbert, [whose wife] is
in a very prómising and prominent situation, and, perhaps,
has *faln seek* before now. I like her very much. She is very
pretty, tho' not critically beautiful, and has something of the
winning softness of Mrs. Gillman, quite a lady, yet not over
educated. I do not think very much literary attainment
improves women, unless there is a firm ground of natural

---

[1] Hartley refers to the dissension in the Southey household after Southey's
second marriage.

talent. It is a great mistake to suppose that education is to supply the place of natural gifts, or that natural gifts could dispense with education. The more fertile the soil, the more culture it requires, but I would have no intellectual corn laws to pay the expenses of forcing inferior land. After all they grow nothing wholesome or nutritious.

You never tell me half enough about Edith. She, I know, is to be learned, of which I ought to have no objection. Certainly in her probable station, it is better to be over-learned than over accomplished, and Latin is better than French.

I am glad Mrs. Joshua was pleased with my conversation. She looks well, and is as amiable as ever. She has her mother's heart and her father's sense, and I believe few men possess stronger natural sense than did Mr. Calvert. It was his misfortune to be under educated and too soon his own master. Alas Mary is the last of the family.

I have seldom heard a stronger instance of fortitude than William displayed in making his will and putting 'his house in order', with a certain prospect of Hydrophobia. Many men, with the means he, as a surgeon, must have had at hand, would have thought themselves justified in procuring an easier departure.

Mr. Thomas Spedding resides at Greta Bank, but not a room of the old house remains. Indeed Keswick can hardly be called 'the old familiar place'. Almost every thing that can change—is changed—and sadness overshadows some places that used to be the mansions of virtuous happiness. Few of the old familiar faces remain. Among them, Jonathan is conspicuous, a hale octogenarian, more and more like the sign of the Marquis of Granby. Miss Dinglinson—my guardian flame—has not got rid of her ugly name. By the way, had I been 25 years younger I am afraid I should have been half smitten—with the youngest Miss Lynn whom nobody else seems to like, though she is plain and wears spectacles. But she always laugh'd when I intended to be humourous and look'd grave when I meant to be sentimental. I was invited to dine at Mr. Lynn's, but thought it better to decline, as I had tax'd the Dentons' hospitality long enough (not that they gave any hints to the purpose) and William Denton, I knew, would not have gone, as for sufficient reason, he is not very partial to the Rev. Gent. I rather think he is settled at Keswick; he is a comfort to his sisters, neither of whom are strong, and the younger, Sarah, a confirm'd invalid, faded, but still pretty. Margaret Muckle is as nice as ever, and her brother a fine hearty Englishman, polish'd enough for me, though neither he, nor indeed any of the Keswick aristocracy that I am acquainted with, are finished up to your demands, with the exception of the elder Mr. Spedding, one of the finest old men I know. I am told, he misses his wife sorely, though his son and daughters in law are most attentive, and his niece most amiable, and not a bit of an heiress. I dined at Mire house, and had a pleasant evening, also at Mr. Stanger's, an excellent though not perhaps, very brilliant man. But I must abridge, or I shall lose the post. It has struck eleven.

I am sorry about the Consecration and don't well understand the difficulty. You I dare say, do not much regret the prohibition of bathing. Wish tho' the boys could meet oftener. Wish I could see them; will if possible before long, but Edith will be the Darling. You will be glad to hear that Mrs. Isaac Green is better, but I am afraid not to be depended on; I saw her malady before her husband was fully convinced of it. I said nothing, but, I believe, in such cases, truth is best and least painful in the end. People under that unhappy affliction always do and say things, which it is a comfort to know are not the issue of their proper selves. God grant that Mrs. J. Wordsworth may be saved. It will be a heartbreaking to John if he loses her, and he is a man that deserves happiness. Mr. Wordsworth is well, and feels great comfort in the society of the excellent Miss Fenwick, he bearing his laureate honours meekly. I plead guilty to not calling on Dora, but I will do it this very day.

I knew not Frederick, but am not less sorry for his parents' bereavement; for himself, I think an early death, if not hastened by sin or folly, a mark of divine favour. Would that I had died—innocent.

I will write to Derwent soon but must conclude for the present.

With love to Sara and Edith, the Judge, if you see him, etc.

I am your plague.

N.B. The quarter is paid. I have said enough about the washing bill not being sent in time, and so has Mrs. Richardson.

In the autumn of 1843 Derwent paid Hartley a visit, marking the first reunion since 1822. For neither of the brothers was the visit wholly satisfactory. A few weeks might have brought them into communion; as it was, Derwent left before any complete understanding occurred, not to return until Hartley lay on his death-bed. On the occasion of this visit, Hartley penned the following lines:

'We grappled like two wrestlers, long and hard,
With many a strain and many a wily turn;
The deep divine, the quaint fantastic bard,
From night to night we did the strife adjourn.

The one was stiff as any bending reed
Is stiff with ice, with frosty mail emboss'd,
By nature flaccid as the lank seaweed,
But seeming stanch, by might of brittle frost.

The other, like a pine, was like to yield,
But upward sprang, and heavenward pointed still;
The reed and pine to every blast reveal'd
How weak is wilfulness, how strong is will.

Thou wert the pine, and I, with woeful ruth,
Confess myself the reed: ah! woe is me,
If such be all the banded hosts of Truth,
Of Justice, Freedom and Humanity.'

LETTER 82

To MRS. SAMUEL TAYLOR COLERIDGE, *No. 10 Chester Place, Regent's Park, London.*

Nab. Feast of Crispian, October 25, 1843.

My dear Mother

Mrs. Richardson received yours yesterday (24th), but there was no sovereign enclosed. I hope it has not been extracted by the way—perhaps you meant, enclosed in the parcel, which I shall acknowledge as soon as it arrives. If we hear nothing, we shall conclude all is right. The letter has no appearance of ever having contain'd coin.

Dear Sara's treatise on Rationalism is a wonder.[1] I say not a wonder of a woman's work—where lives the man that could have written it? None in Great Britain since our Father died. Poor Henry was perfectly right in saying that she inherited more of her father, than either of us; and that not only in the amount but in the quality of her powers.

---

[1] The 'Essay on Rationalism' formed Appendix C to the second volume of the later editions of the *Aids to Reflection*.

Particular criticisms I shall reserve for herself, and perhaps delay, till repeated reperusal and thought as deep as I can bear have convinced me that I justly appreciate it. She must be aware, that it will not please all—too high-church for liberal-latitudinarian or evangelical; while to a large portion both of the high and low church the very word Reason is so terribly odious, that I verily suspect they think it was invented by Tom Paine. I am glad that she and dear Edith are well enough to go to Eton. Masters of the *old* school were averse to visits from Mama—mais nous avons changé tout cela. Derwent thinks Herbert's abilities, at least, his faculty of acquirement and retention, superior to those of Dervy Junior. I have no doubt he speaks sincerely, for he is not a man to depreciate himself or aught that is his for the sake of being contradicted; but I can't help fancying, that he is rather resign'd about his son's proficiency, when I can see nothing to be resign'd for. The poor boy has doubtless lost some time, and every Coleridge cannot be an S.T.C. or even a John or—alas a Henry. For my part I think distinguish'd intellect no more to be desired than distinguish'd beauty. They who possess either should be thankful and beware. By the way, I think Derwent is a wee bit proud of his wife's beauty, which, I doubt not, is still a beautiful autumn. I do not wonder at it. How I should like to see Christabel Rosa, though I don't like the names. I told him so. I should have voted for *Fanny*, after poor Lady Patteson. Derwent himself is as little altered, as could be expected in the time; yet I am not sure, I should immediately have recognized him, had I met him unawares. I see little likeness to Papa, except in the metaphysical turn of his mind, which is differenced by, a professional, or at least practical purpose ever present. The quantity of French phrases wherewith he tambours his conversation would have made Papa blaspheme outright without reverence to the cloth. He is the happiest mixture of Divine, Philosopher, Poet, Man of Business, and fine Gentleman (I had almost said *Courtier*) that I ever saw, and would be an ornament to the Bench. But I fear he is too definite and uncomplying in his opinions to reach a Mitre—as he might have a fair chance of doing, if he went the right way about it. His reading in the desk and at the Communion Table are the best I ever heard, with the exception, perhaps, of Bowles the Poet, and he owed something, in my eyes at least, to being an old and bald headed man. Derwent was exorbitantly admired by high and low; though except Mr. Dawes, Mr. Narsden, the Rydal family, Mrs. B. Harrison, and Herbert White, he had few remaining recollections of persons. I wish he could have staid longer. He was so much sought after, that we had very little quiet time together, and besides, the meeting after so long an interval, in which so much to regret, and on my part, so much to blame had taken place, produced a degree of nervous feverishness, which was only just subsiding, when his leave of absence expired. I own, the irritability was, chiefly, on my side—he has great command of temper, and if he be moved to wrath, anger makes him eloquent, while it renders me a pitiful stammerer. I am nothing without the pen, and but little, I fear, with it. You are aware I sent a pacquet by Derwent, which he gave to Moxon. As I have not heard, I suppose he wants more to make up a volume. It shall be sent forthwith. As to the wardrobe, I will speak at length when the parcel arrives. Some of the shirts are going, but I am not ill off. Perhaps Mrs. R. will write herself, some day soon. When the book comes out, I must have a new hat—for the rest, I must do over winter. I wish I could get out a Vol. of Sonnets, etc. before the New Year. As many of my pieces are about pictures, I think a few outline illustrations would help the sale, and amply pay for themselves; but I must consult Moxon, Derwent, and Mr. Wordsworth. I am composing something to the Memory of Uncle Southey, but know not how or where I shall publish it, or whether at all. I would not set his name to any thing I did not think good. Miss S. Briggs, my good little amanuensis, is transcribing Sonnets for me, and I have some in the hand of Juliet Fox, who is a sweet girl, like her Mother, tho' not so pretty. I spent some delightful hours with Sarah Fox at Grasmere. She is as kind, as lively, and as lovely as ever. We never quarrel about religion, or politics. Mrs. Richardson's respects and thanks. Sorry your breath is not better. The weather after unusually protracted fineness has grown cold and stormy, but to day is fine. You would be sorry to hear of poor Joanna's departure, and the old faithful servant is a loss to Mrs. W.

Believe me, dear Mother—

Your etc.

Mr. and Mrs. J. Wordsworth gone off this cold morning for Listian.

LETTER 83

To MRS. SAMUEL TAYLOR COLERIDGE.

Rydal, January 14 or perhaps rather the 15th, 1844.
My dear Mother
Dear little Edith's drawing, if nothing else, ought to have
had thanks and answer. Did you in remembrance of those
feline attachments of mine, which so often put you into a rage,
suggest the subject? She must have a decided turn for drawing, for the Cat is a very difficult subject and seldom well
executed. Perhaps she never heard of the Swiss Artist—Mind
—who was called the Raffaelle of Cats. There was a print from
one of his pictures—some time ago—in the Penny Magazine.
But this is hardly a proper mode to begin my letter—after so
long delinquency, for which I will offer no excuse as I have
not been either ill, or much from home, no wandering, and
very little gayety. We have a sad sick neighbourhood, but
those in whom you are most interested are pretty well.
I thought I had mentioned the book in my short epistle to
Mary. I have acknowledged it—indeed I did so, I believe
the day after it arrived. My letter was to Mrs. Warter. I
felt some awkwardness in writing to her, but of course made
no allusions, and acquitted myself pretty well. The book is,
I doubt not, a valuable one from its age and rarity. I do not
remember to have heard of it or seen it quoted. It seems to
belong to the first age of printing, in black letter, closely
resembling the Religious MSS. Missals, etc. The initials
illuminated by the hand—No date, place, or printer's name
that I can discover. What is worse, it has not Uncle's
Autograph. But Edith has inserted with her own hand—
'Purchased at the sale of my Father's Library for Hartley
Coleridge, with the affectionate love of his Cousin, Edith
May Warter'. (That does not sound so well as Edith May
Southey. She has not improved her name by marriage as
as much as her Mother and Aunts, but they indeed could
hardly change for the harsher.) Mrs. Warter has added 'I
selected this book as it was frequently in Southey's hands and
one which he used to point out to me with much satisfaction
for the clearness of the black letter and the antique knobs,
clasps, and old oaken boards'.[1] Its title—'Clarissimi viri, juris

---

[1] 'The "book" is now in my possession, the fly-leaf containing the signatures
recorded in the text of this letter. A third inscription was added by Mrs. H. N.
Coleridge: "My dear Herbert, I give this book to you with my dear love both

utriusque Doctoris Felicis Hemmerlini Cantoris quondam Thuriceñ varie oblectationis opuscula et Tractatus.' Sara will construe it for you. I am thankful for the kindness of the remembrance. I think it will please you, but it is not exactly the book I should have chosen, for I care little about clasps and knobbs—and being written in Monkish Latin, and crowded with Contractions, I cannot read it without considerable difficulty and straining of eyes. But I dare say it will repay perusal. Hemmerlin seems a name I should know something about, but I have forgotten him. When I am better acquainted with the book, I will give further account of it to Sara. The black Collar fits well, and looks respectable —but I am indebted to Mrs. Richardson for fastening it, which my clumsy fingers cannot effect. The shirts are perfection. I thank you for the Almanack and other useful things. I am sorry you thought Garnet's bill so unreasonable. The swansdown was for a waistcoat, a useful and needful one it is. The trowzers are stout and indispensable. The hat was very dear, as things go now, but I never got a good one for less. I have however, now got a handsome one, much lower, which may reconcile you to the fact that the hatter is a Papist. Fell says he pays but 10s. for silk hats, but that they last no time. He is, to be sure, out in all weathers, and cannot carry an Umbrella on horseback. He is almost work'd to death in this sickly time. Mr. Greenwood is very dangerously ill of Erysipelas. His daughter has also suffer'd severely in the same complaint, of which her aunt died not long ago, and was followed within a week by her daughter in law, but the cause of her death was fever. There can be little doubt that Erysipelas is infectious, for Miss Greenwood was with her aunt during her illness, and has communicated it to her father. But why should I oppress you with the suffering of people you know not, any farther than as you may have heard that they have been kind to me? You have sickness enough at hand. I wish I could believe Miss Martineau's tale of Mesmerism, as I have no doubt she believes herself, and as far as her own case is concerned, I see no impossibility—but the miraculous revelations of J. dumbfounder me. Would that our dear Sara could be mesmerised to health. Father,

in remembrance of my deeply lamented brother Hartley, whom unhappily you never saw, and of my revered Uncle, Robert Southey, your God father, whom you once beheld with your eyes of dawning intelligence, at two months of age, when he attended your Christening, Dec. 4th, 1830.
Feby. 27th, 1849." ' Note by E. H. Coleridge.

you know, was more than half a believer, and made poor Mr. Gillman swear horribly. It is long since I have heard any thing of Mrs. Gillman. I would write to her if I knew where to direct. Pray give my kindest love to dear Miss Brent. She is an excellent creature and has been sorely tried. You once sent a card, saying it pertain'd to Miss Brice of Asholt where I was so happy in childhood—I could not understand it. It must have been her daughter's, for the name was not Brice nor Penelope.

Mr. Dawes is better, but evidently much taken. His age, which must be above eighty, has overtaken him rapidly. Five years ago he walked like a man of forty—Now he can but just get to Ambleside and I hope will never again attempt the Church service—for which indeed he was never very highly appointed and always disliked the Profession into which he entered unwillingly. He is still cheerful and kind as ever—a stout Whig and hearty abuser of Bishops and Pusey-ism, of which you may suppose he knows very little. For my own part, I honour the men, while I widely differ from their opinions—thinking they tend to promote the schism they abhor. But my opinions are Arnold's. I know no book that of late years has done me so much good as his life and letters.[1] Highly as I always thought of him, I think much more highly of him now. My lines of which Mrs. Fletcher has given Mrs. Arnold a copy, refer chiefly to his merits as a teacher and moral disciplinarian, without reference to the disputed points of his doctrine.[2] I sent you the Newspaper containing my defence of Mr. Wordsworth,[3] but I suppose you have not got it. I wish the railway could be let alone during his life at least, and that I hope will be some good years. You have doubtless heard that three Monuments are proposed to be erected to Southey, in the Abbey, at Bristol, and at Keswick. It is a sort of Commemoration he never valued. He never would subscribe to Monuments. A para-graph is going the round of the papers, stating that a brother of the Laureate—a *Gentleman* and Scholar, is in London in a state bordering on starvation. Now this is one of those facts which are meant to do the work of lies. It probably originated with Edward himself. I have taken some pains to set people right about it.

[No conclusion or signature.]

---

[1] A. P. Stanley's *Life of Dr. Arnold* was published in 1844.
[2] Cf. *Poems*, 235–8.   [3] This essay has not been identified.

LETTER 84

To MRS. SAMUEL TAYLOR COLERIDGE.

Nab. Feb. 7, 1844.

My dear Mother

A few lines to day will be better than a great many to-morrow. I am very angry with myself for giving you cause to suspect me of indifference to you and your concerns, and the undeserved mildness of your rebuke makes my self-reproach the sharper. Poor dear Sara! I suppose the Psoriasis is something different from the nettle rash which tormented her childhood—but she was always prone to cutaneous irritation. I trust this will find her better, though perhaps her perfect recovery may be delay'd till the weather is improved.

Your account of the young ones is agreeable. Herby's fault is a good one, but letter writing is a juvenile propensity, and sometimes decays with age—when folks have more painful things to tell. Derwent is an excellent correspondent, at least as far as his wife is concerned. Indeed, he is most exemplary in all relations, and has no fault but a certain measure of, I will not call it presumption but assumption, probably owing in part to his habits of command and a little to the worship universally paid him—which is greater than either his father, or W. or S. obtained at his age. A man must be weak indeed if after twenty he is elated by praise of his talents, his genius, or even his poetry; but to be at once loved and admired, to be look'd up to as an oracle by his equals, and set forth as an example by his superiors, is a severe trial for any human humility. Of course, you have read Moultrie's address to him.[1] I confess I should not like to be so praised in print, but alas! I know that I deserve it not. It is not, however, good policy to overpraise a man in public. It not only embitters enmity if any exist, but it irritates friends who cannot themselves go quite so far. Derwent, however, can bear it, for he has few faults for any to discover. If he had, his freedom of rebuke and fearless assertion of his opinions, which are not those, not precisely those, of any sect, party, or denomination in Church or State would provoke some people to expose them with little mercy. I am glad that Herby takes an interest in his sister's studies. My coldness—and I am

---

[1] Book III of Moultrie's *The Dream of Life*, 1843, is inscribed to Derwent, along with a quotation from Wordsworth's 'Immortality Ode'.

afraid perhaps at times a little touch of satire with regard to Sara's classicalities were, I believe, the principal cause of that undisguised preference of Derwent, which I confess made me foolishly uncomfortable. Sara, I doubt not, judges well for her daughter. Learning has not injured her, or made her less lovable or lovely. It must be a great resource to her mind. Women with nothing in their heads but their family concerns are apt to be miserable and repining if those concerns go wrong. It is true—I am not and never was liable to be smitten with learned young Ladies. So very bad my taste, that I preferred Jane Bullar to the then Miss Poole, who—I see as Mrs. John Sandford[1] is a mighty authoress. I have not read many of her things, and can't say I greatly admire what I have read. Her sentiments are good enough, but her style is inflated and American. . . .[2]

I don't wonder at Mary's being pleased with her own good looks—her husband is proud enough of them. I am sorry her lameness continues. It must indeed have been trying to Sara to see Derwent in poor Henry's place, but better a brother than a stranger. I never saw Derwent do the honours of a large table. I should suppose he would excel as an Amphitryon. It is wonderful how much more he has acquired. This he must have inherited from you, for his father tho' eminently gentlemanly, had no marks of the high society he had occasionally met, and could no more have been tonish than vulgar. I may hint, however, that the manner is acquired, and not like Sir George Beaumont's hereditary. I don't know whether he thinks of it himself, but he makes others think of it, and feel their own ungainliness painfully. I do not like to eat fish, or take soup in his presence, because I cannot handle my fork and spoon as he does.[3] But *n'importe*. I am afraid I should squeeze the 'lovely lady' too much, though I certainly find that babies and little lassies somewhat nearer their teens like me much better since I was grey-headed. Perhaps I am less unlike other men, in my exterior at least, than I was unlike other boys, and little Misses have a respect for manhood. Babies I think are generally fond of aged persons. I am writing past post time but must go on a little more now I have begun. It is beginning that is the difficulty. You will

---

[1] Mrs. John Sandford was the author of *Woman in her Social and Domestic Character*, 1831, and *On Female Improvement*, 1836.   [2] MS. unintelligible.
[3] A friend records Hartley's remarks anent his brother's table manners: 'Do you know I never understood the gladiator's excellence till the other day? The way in which my brother eats fish with a silver fork made the thing quite clear.'

smile, if you can smile at any thing—to hear that I had my bust taken.[1] It was at the request of Cornelius Nicholson, a self-educated and prosperous man who has shewn me many little kindnesses, particularly in printing the lines on Owen Lloyd—without expense. He is the father of the little Cornelia to whom I wrote those lines. You have seen them, have you not, in which I took occasion to speak of Henry, of whose decease I had just heard. Of course I am to be nothing out. You may have a cast if you like it. I do not myself perceive the likeness; but Mrs. Richardson did, and for perception of likenesses the most unintellectual people are the best judges. I believe few persons have a correct image of themselves in their imagination. Thus I am told I am very like my father, which I cannot see at all. The form of the head is certainly different. My forehead is not so high and much more lined than I ever saw his. I am many shades darker—as hairy as he was smooth. My eyes are of a different colour—and my expression is far less benign and placid. I never, indeed, saw my father look angry—when out of sorts he look'd miserable and a bit cross, but never furious. I have, however, seen him look contemptuous. Contempt was his besetting sin— but I doubt not that Christianity subdued it. Derwent is undoubtedly a handsome likeness of his papa. Sara is the inheritrix of his mind and of his genius, Neither Derwent nor I have much more than the family cleverness, which with hardly an exception accompanies the name of Coleridge. If I might judge myself, I should say my sort of talent had more of Southey than of S. T. Coleridge. I have the sure fondness for historical research, and antiquities and pantagruelist oddities, and some thing perhaps of the same matter-of-fact invention, but I cannot follow S. T. Coleridge— either to the height of his imagination—or the depth of his philosophy. But this is egotism, and you would rather see me exert the talents I do possess, be they what they may, than define them. I have not given up the Vol. I will not fix the day, but it will not be distant. My good little amanuensis, Sara Briggs, has been transcribing poems for me. One Sonnet I inclose in her hand—does she not write nicely? My principal purpose in this letter I have not yet touch'd upon. Could not I correct the sheets for the Selections?[2] I can do it

---

[1] No record of this bust has come to light.

[2] The Selections referred to must have been Sara Coleridge's edition of Coleridge's *Notes and Lectures upon Shakespeare* in 1849.

very well—would do it punctually and could spare dear
Sara's eyes. My sight, which some time ago I was afraid was
going, is perfectly recovered, at least for reading. I never
could see distant objects distinctly and am apt to mistake
people on the road—make as if I was going to speak to folk,
whom I find I don't know—which is awkward. I have a
good pair of spectacles given me by Miss Fell, but I seldom
use them—they are rather too powerful and make my head
ache, which it does now, a rare occurrence. I think it is
the snow. I am on the whole well. Influenza is rife. One
of the children very ill with it—which is uncomfortable. I
had a very slight attack last week, but it might be nothing but
cold. I was shivery and sleepy, but not feverish, nor were
the internal organs affected. Quite better now. Of all Sara's
maladies I am most concerned for her sleeplessness. It is so
very wearing to the mind, and the use of Morphia, though I
believe it to be less injurious than any other form of opium,
is an evil. But sleep must be had if possible. I wish it would
please God to relieve poor Betty—her prolonged suffering
must be painful to herself and surely wearing to Kate. I am
glad she is coming to Rydal. Change of scene and the company of her best and wisest friends will relieve her much.
Her trials are indeed severe. God support her through
them—

What a lot I've written and began with talking of a few
lines. I've spoil'd my only steel pen—and it was a beauty.
I ought to have saved it for the public service. The great
coat does well—looks respectable. Mr. W. is very well, but
Mrs. W. looks harassed and very old. She is not, however,
afflicted with great maladies. Would I could relieve them—
or your heart either. Dora is very thin but seems happy and
cheerful. That, however, she always manages to do. I have
seen her all smiles and sweetness when her eyes were red
as fire with weeping. God bless her. I like Mr. Quillinan
hugely—he is the most liberal conservative I know. I must
walk out and see if I can get rid of this headache—and then to
work.

Kindest love to the dear ones all. Why did they call little
Dora Hill—Georgina? A name I abominate—but people
will name their babies without consulting

Your affectionate

H. COLERIDGE.

Can't get the Sonnet into the envelope—send it another time.

LETTER 85

To MARY CLAUDE.

Dear Mary   [1844.]

When thoughts too mighty crowd upon the brain
For usual phrase to utter or retain,
Then—the quaint art of verse—the neat disguise
Of many fancy-breeding similes—
Helps to unload a mind too sorely prest;
For motion sometimes eases more than rest.
Of birth, and death, of hope begun and ended,
Of two good Spirits to their home ascended,
Of one dear soul, with tiny body blent
Mere life as yet, a breathing innocent,
Are all the tidings that I have to tell—
What can I say, but that they all—are well?

She, long a pain-expecting sufferer,
Is now released—our loss is gain to her.
Kind Death unknit the sad perplexity
Of his worse sorrows' awful mystery.
Doubt not she hath a spiritual frame of light
That bears no symbol of the scars, which Eve
Bequeath'd to all her offspring, sore or slight;
But all must bear the portion they receive—
And surely he hath now his mind again.
No frail dependent upon nerve or brain,
But a pure reason, face to face to see
The truths he once believed in pure humility.[1]

Very bad, but they hint at my meaning—I will write more
in a day or two.

                     Believe me, with best love to all,
                            Yours affectionately
                                 H. COLERIDGE.

LETTER 86

To DERWENT COLERIDGE, *St. Mark's College, Chelsea, London.*

                     Ambleside, April 12, [Postmark 1845.]

Dear Derwent
    If not corresponsive you will at least admit that I am on
this occasion—responsive. May you and your good lady have

    'Unpublished—The references are, I guess, to old Betty, the Southeys'
servant, and to Southey himself. The "one dear soul, with tiny body blent"—
must be Christabel Rose Coleridge, born May 25, 1843.' Note by E. H. Coleridge.

cause to rejoice that a man-child is born into the world. It perhaps shews the infrequency of communication between us, that I was not aware of the probability of such an event. I appreciate the compliment implied in your conjunction of Rydalian praenomina—but having a Shandean Superstition respecting Christian names, and never having known that of Hartley (which as a prefix is by no means confined to myself) attended by fortune or the virtues that adorn prosperity, I would advise you to pause before you make your youngest hope in aught to resemble his heterodox Uncle. I have not tried the names anagrammatically, which I think of much importance, as *Honor est a Nilo* evinces. I wonder what the little chap is like and whether he is a Coleridge, or a Pridham, or a Fricker? N.B. Don't call him Fricker. It is a Dutch name, and may render him less averse to presbytery and republicanism, if not more addicted to red-herrings and Schiedam than you would desire.

I believe I should squeeze Christabel till she hated me. Babies and Kittens suffer more from love than from hatred. My present baby idol—I cannot do without one—is little Elleanour Fell, who, tho' no great shakes of a beauty, is the sweetest-tempered, happiest, lovingest creature: cannot quite walk, nor talk at all, but makes laudable attempts at both. She is in danger, if I may judge from her Mama's appearance, of being shortly deposed from her dignity of Babyhood.

You would be pleased to hear that a son of our judicial Kinsman has obtained a fellowship at Oriel. May he obliterate the blots which another left there on the name of Coleridge. Matthew Arnold is his fellow-probationer. Their Fathers obtained fellowships in the same term, tho' not in the same College—30 years ago.

I must conclude abruptly—for the post is nigh. With my next, I will send you many things (among others some verses on Wordsworth's 75th birthday,[1] and lines on the death of Arnold). Meanwhile—can only now congratulate Mary on her safety and remain—

Yours truly—
H. COLERIDGE.

I hope Snouderumpater and Sara are in their better way. Poor Dora Quillinan is woefully ill. Her husband thought of taking her with him to Portugal for the benefit of change of

---

[1] Cf. *Poems*, 206.

air, but Mrs. W. cannot bear the thoughts of it, and the purpose is given up. Better accounts of Mrs. John. The Bard is
wonderful, notwithstanding his rail-way afflictions, but Mrs.
Wordsworth ages fast. What do you think of Mr. Ward—and
the troubles at Helston?

LETTER 87

To MRS. SAMUEL TAYLOR COLERIDGE.

May 15, [1845.]

My dear Mother

You rebuke my negligence more severely by complaining
of it to my hostess than if you had told me of it in your few
lines which, however, shall not be useless, if a few lines in
return can be of any use. I ought certainly to have complied
with your request to write soon, but I was not aware that
the questions were of any pressing moment. However, I
know how nervously anxious you are, and should give you
no pain which any exertion of my own could spare. The
Shirt by Miss Fenwick arrived safe. The silver fork is very
acceptable. I am sorry there has been any trouble about
Robinson's bill, but do not see that either Mrs. Richardson or
I are to blame about it. The error must lie with Robinson's
Bookkeeper, for the old man himself—a compound of Falstaff's Belly and Bardolf's Nose—is no *Scholar*. It will be
righted in the course of the day, and you shall hear the result.
I ought to look more closely to my own affairs and will do so
in future. I do not exactly know how the bills come to be
presented at different times within the Quarter, but you are
probably aware that the Westmorland Tradesmen (Tailor,
Shoemaker etc.) bring in their annual accounts at Candlemas, an inconvenient custom which there has been some
talk of exchanging for two annual settlements. If I can
hinder, Mrs. Wordsworth shall have [no] unnecessary
trouble in future. She is very kind to take upon her a task
of no easy nature. I will send you the verses on Dr. Arnold's
death,[1] and hope you will like them. I confess I succeeded
better in pleasing myself than I can often do at present. I
was thoroughly in earnest. Arnold was a man whose high
merits in many ways none deny, but I confess I approve of
much in his writings which some censure. Of his life there
can be but one opinion. The Biography is admirably

---

[1] Cf. *Poems*, 235–8.

executed, and has just entered upon another edition. Mrs. Arnold, since her loss, has had many comforts—her eldest Son has obtained a fellowship—at the same election and college as the Judge's Son—her second has just taken a first class. I believe her daughters are excellent girls. I call occasionally. Mrs. A. has a copy of the verses which I would send herewith, but there is not time to transcribe them before post, for they are pretty long. They allude almost solely to his merits as a schoolmaster. Of his character as an historian, theologian, and philosopher, I may write hereafter. The present copy is complete in itself.

My friend Greenwood is no more. He expired after a long and painful illness, on Friday, May 2nd, and was buried Thursday 8th. I was present at the funeral. He was a very popular man in the vale, and will be much missed; for he had great knowledge and influence in local matters, and was, in a smaller way a sort of Tom Poole. Though his education had been merely mercantile, he was well read in English History and antiquities, had much taste in architecture, drew well, and understood church music. Latterly he read much on religious subjects, confining himself, however, to the Bible and to practical Divinity, and kept quite aloof from the questions which distract the Church. He has left a widow, a son, and a daughter—the latter about 17, a fine girl, and a great favourite of mine, tho' rather too big to pet. The son promises to be a stay to his mother and sister. They are left in good circumstances.

A more afflicting bereavement has taken place in the family of my excellent, aged friend Dr. Briggs, whose youngest, but only married daughter, has died in a state approaching to mental alienation, occasioned by the condition of her husband, the derangement of whose affairs, operating on an irritable constitution and haughty temper, has produced derangement of intellect—perhaps only the development of congenital insanity. He is a Clergyman of the utmost altitude of High-Church-man-ship and ultra-toryism, which made him somewhat obnoxious to his good father in law, who is a Whig and some thing more, but all is forgiven now. There are six children, motherless and worse than fatherless. When we add that the Dr. is a prisoner in his chair, and Mrs. Briggs all but bedridden, you may justly appreciate their energy, in the great exertions and sacrifices (for they are far from affluent) they make and have made for the unfortunate family. The youngest, a baby of five months, is just arrived with its Aunt Mary Jane, at what must henceforth be its home. But perhaps I do amiss to afflict you with the tale of distresses of sufferers, whom you know not, and can not relieve or assist but with prayer.

To take a more cheerful subject, I was pleased with your account of the christening of the Thampet. Hope D. and M. did not take my but half serious declining of the honour offered as any slight or sign of indifference. Mr. Wordsworth says that D. is harassed with his duties, and does not find support or even acquiescence in quarters where he thinks it due. I honour his perseverance and firmness of principle—More, I cannot say. I never heard of the pencil sketch, and certainly never saw it. Cannot promise to procure a copy. Mr. Fox will be in town at the May Meeting of Friends, but not accompanied by his wife or daughter. He will probably call upon Derwent at Chelsea.

My essays in *Janus* are ' Antiquity Pins', and a ' Preface—which may serve' etc. I hope Mr. Aubrey de Vere (whom I like better than his Poems, which are too Young-England for me) will see them, with some handsomer brethren ere long.

I must conclude hastily or shall miss post. Will write again in course of week. Well—but plagued with Corns. Sorry for your growing infirmities and confinement. Love to Sara and Edith.

And remain, Dear Mother
Your affectionate Son

H. COLERIDGE.

N.B. If Herbert can wait a little while, he will get the Lexicon for half the present charge. I am glad he is only extravagant in books, and not at the Confectioners, which often leads to worse places.

LETTER 88

To MRS. SAMUEL TAYLOR COLERIDGE.

This is the last letter from Hartley to his mother which has been preserved.

[Summer, 1845.]

My dear Mother

The Bills I hope you have received, and hope also that you will not find any objectionable items therein. You are probably aware that Shoemakers, Tailors etc., do not present their bills in this country till Candlemas—i.e. about the middle of February. This arrangement may be troublesome to you or to Mrs. Wordsworth. If so, I could easily get it altered. You have probably seen my daguerreotyped likeness—and started with horror to conceive yourself the Mother of such a hideous old Man.[1] I can only tell you that all I have seen in the same style, do look very old—a girl of sixteen looks like an old maid of fifty.

I am much obliged to you for the News of the World. Its politics go a little too far even for me, but it contains a great deal for the money, and the paper is valuable. I should not know how to do without it.

I shall be very happy to meet Mr. Aubrey de Vere.[2] I do not know any thing I should trouble him to bring.

Derwent has probably informed you of the death of Mr. Dawes.[3] He has left no will, and his little estate may be a bone of contention between sundry distant relations. He made Mrs. Claude's only Son a present of £500 before he died. Of course, I was present at his funeral. It was largely attended. In fact, I never saw so many self invited attendants at any funeral except Owen Lloyd's. He was much beloved. But his release is not to be regretted—for he was sadly fallen from his former self in body, and not quite himself in mind latterly.

You seem to assume in your last that I was cognizant of the death of my little Nephew. This, however, was not the case. On the other hand, your last letter but one gave hopes. I have had a few lines from Derwent.

The W.'s receive good accounts from Portugal. Not so good from Italy. There is a great party to night to celebrate the majority of Mr. M. B. Harrison, eldest son of my some time flame, *Chucky Doro.* Mr. Wordsworth and Miss Martineau are to be there—and it is time for me to dress. I will give Sara a full account and send the verses on Dr. Arnold.

Meantime—
Must remain, Your truly affec. Son,
H.C.

---

[1] This daguerreotype has been preserved and presents an old man, not of 50, but of 80.

[2] Aubrey de Vere, the friend of Sara Coleridge, has left a delightful sketch of Hartley in his *Recollections*, 1897, 133. Hartley apparently knew Aubrey de Vere. See p. 281.

[3] The Rev. John Dawes died in August 1845.

Hartley's mother died suddenly on September 24, 1845. While he had not seen her since 1831, he had been in constant correspondence with her, and she had watched over him as though he had remained a child. A sonnet written on this occasion is pathetically sincere.

'Oh! my dear mother, art thou still awake?
Or art thou sleeping on thy Maker's arm,—
Waiting in slumber for the shrill alarm
Ordain'd to give the world its final shake?
Art thou with "interlunar night" opaque
Clad like a worm while waiting for its wings;
Or doth the shadow of departed things
Dwell on thy soul as on a breezeless lake!
Oh! would that I could see thee in thy heaven
For one brief hour, and know I was forgiven
For all the pain and doubt and rankling shame
Which I have caused to make thee weep or sigh.
Bootless the wish! for where thou art on high,
Sin casts no shadow, sorrow hath no name.'

LETTER 89

To MRS. HENRY NELSON COLERIDGE, *No. 10 Chester Place, Regent's Park, London.*

Nab. Oct. 11, 1845.

My dear Sister-Orphan

Utterly unable as I am, either to console you under our common loss, or to lead you to one profitable reflection, which it has not, by God's grace, already suggested to your own heart, I fear you have thought me negligent of your sorrow, to have suffered nearly three weeks [to] elapse, without a line to signify that I knew myself Motherless. Day after day have I purposed, but words fail'd me, not from severity of grief—Alas—my heart is not capable of a grief equal to the hundredth part of her due, and I cannot shed above a few unsatisfactory tears, rather at the recollection of past days and tendernesses, and funny things—memories new dressed in mourning, than from a competent feeling of the great bereavement, and a humble yielding to the awful blow. But unprepared as I was for the announcement, at first hardly understanding that it really was my own Mother who had departed, I was at first more stunned and stupefied than afflicted. I could not think of her as dead. So long indeed, has she been to me, more a thing of the past than of the present, and, shame on me, I have been so careless or loath to realize her by frequent communication with herself or conversation with those who knew and loved her, that, wanting the witness of the senses, her death even now, is to me rather a fact which I am compelled to believe by stress of evidence, than a truth that makes itself known by its own power and presence. But I am now recovered from my first bewilderment. Thanks to the All Merciful, I am no longer, as I was, tempted to cry out—Pray I cannot; and as every garment I put on is a relic or a memorial of her hand and carefulness, a more affectionate regret begins to take place of that sense of destitution which beset me, when I awoke from the stupor, and to turn the angry bitterness of my self reproach and self-contempt into something, I trust, like wholesome contrition. I fear there is a selfishness, even in my penitence, not that it arises merely from the consciousness of a loss or the fear of punishment, but because it makes me think more of myself, than of her, more of my unworthiness than of her worth, more of my want of Grace, than of her over abounding kindness. Yet for none of my offenses, not even for those which added shame to her sorrow, and made her almost despise while she pitied me, am I so sharply self-reproached as for this, that I have loved her too little. Had I loved either her or our other blessed parent as I ought to have done, my powers had not rusted in disuse (for of my intellectual powers I cannot accuse myself of any serious misuse), and they had not both died without blessing me, when, at a day's distance I was to them as one banish'd and estrang'd—their last recollections of me would not have been as of a prodigal unreturned—they would have died hoping for me, as well as forgiving me. I did indeed hope that she would not have gone till I had given her some earnest of amendment, till she might have been comforted with the good report of my labours, till she might have look'd on my face with cheerfulness as in my days of childhood, but, *meâ culpâ*, it has [not] been so. And I could not even see her remains committed to the earth. With her I have lost one great argument for exertion and self-correction, one auxiliary against my deadly foe despondency. May God preserve me from indolent despair and enable me to feel and to bear the chastening pain—

Somewhat too much of this—most of which you know already. Miss Fenwick kindly imparted to me a letter from Edward [Coleridge], by which I learn that he officiated at the funeral, that the holy remains were interred at Highgate, doubtless next those of ὁ μακαρίτης—that Derwent, the Bishop, Judge and other relatives and connections were present, and that your feeling, yet calm demeanour beside the grave, and pious composure afterwards—were most comfortable and edifying. For all these things I am thankful. The removal to Highgate must have been attended with some additional trouble and expense, but it gives a sort of acknowledgement of the perfect reconciliation which your marriage was ordained to effect. In the manner of her passing away, there is much to rejoice at. She has been spared, what she most apprehended, a protracted bedrid confinement and dependency. Had I known, but a week, that she was in danger, I would *per fas et nefas* have seen her, but perhaps it is as well as it is. I know not whether your absence was to be regretted or not. The shock would in either case have been equal. It might have been a satisfaction to *you* and to *Derwent*, could she have partaken of the Offices of the Church, but you have the satisfaction of knowing that she did not wilfully reject or neglect them, or receive them in a state where their fitness might be dubious, and that Christ is able to supply all deficiencies. Happy are you both, for whatever vexation you have caused to your parents, you have atoned by your attention, your affection, your virtue and your good name—an ointment most precious to the departed.

Your children will retain a kind and reverend, and when their first grief is subdued, a happy remembrance of their Grandmother. They cannot I suppose, remember much of their Grandfather. I never had a Grandfather, living. Of one of my Grandmothers, tho' I must have seen her, I have no recollection, and, from reports of her sternness and formality, rather a repulsive imagination, which a personal knowledge of her goodness would probably have annull'd. The other I only remember as a sufferer.[1] Do you know C. Lamb's and C. Lloyd's verses to their Grandmothers which the anti-jacobin brutes had the no heart to ridicule? I don't clearly remember Lloyd's, but Lamb's are exquisite. I could not write in that strain.

Rydal Mount is vacant, except of poor Miss Wordsworth

---

[1] 'Mrs. Coleridge, the widow of the Rev. John Coleridge, died in 1809, and Hartley was not quite three years old when he visited Ottery for the first time in 1799; Mrs. Fricker also died Nov. 4, 1809, and Hartley spent several weeks under her roof in the summer of 1807, when he was in his eleventh year.' Note by E. H. Coleridge.

and her attendants. Miss Fenwick says that she is aware of
our Mother's decease, and talks quite rationally about it.
Indeed, upon most subjects, her words are rational, sometimes acute, sometimes beautiful; but her manner is strange
and irregular, at times almost painful to those who are
unaccustomed to her. I have not had courage to see her
since the event. It was very distressing to find the Ws.
absent when I call'd with Mary's sad letter. I had no one to
speak to who knew aught of the departed except Mrs. Cookson, whom I did not immediately think of. She very kindly
call'd on me the next day. The Wordsworths are not expected home for some time, as Mr. J. Hutchinson is about to
break up his establishment, and live with one of his clerical
sons—they therefore prolong their visit, as they may not be so
conveniently received hereafter. J. Wordsworth is return'd
from Italy. He left his wife somewhat better, but I fear,
with little prospect of permanent amendment. Excellent
accounts from Dora.

Mr. and Mrs. Wordsworth, and our three aged aunts are
now, I believe, the last survivors of that generation that can
remember our infancy, the latest standers of the forest in
which we were saplings. Mr. Dawes died some two months
ago, in his 80th year. His death was something melancholy,
for he had outlived his great powers both of body and mind,
had lost the art of managing himself and was very hard for
others to manage, especially as he was a batchelor with no
near relations. He could not be prevail'd on to make a will,
and his property, which is considerable, is disputed between
several distant cousins, and will probably get into Chancery.
This suggests to me that I must look after my own affairs in
the world and exert myself to save you trouble you can ill
endure, but of these matters I will talk to D. and perhaps to
the Judge. Believe me, dear Sara,

Your affectionate brother,

HARTLEY COLERIDGE.

P.S. If I knew how to direct to Mrs. Gillman, I would gladly
write to her, also to Mr. J. H. Green. I suppose I may find
the Judge's address in the red book. Thank Mary for the
feeling manner in which she imparted the sorrow.

We have very bad weather here, and I have a terrible cold.
All friends have been kind in inquiries and condolence. I am
rather in an industrious vein—now that I have recovered the
use of the pen. Are your children yet with you?

LETTER 90
To JOHN TAYLOR COLERIDGE.

My dear Sir   Rydal, January 9, 1846.

It is hardly necessary to say, how thankfully I assent to the
arrangement you propose, which appears to me far best for
all of us; but were my own surmises different, I have that
reliance on your knowledge of business, and that consciousness of my own ignorance thereof, that I should surrender
unconditionally to your judgement. It will probably be
necessary that I should signify my assent to Mr. Green in
something like a formal instrument. On this head, I crave
further information. Fear no delay on my part.[1] Other
arrangements I must make with Sara to render the care of
my concerns less burdensome both to her, and to good Mrs.
Wordsworth than they have hitherto been to the latter and
my blessed Mother.

I hope, almost I promise, that you will see me in the press
ere long. Tho' shockingly dilatory in putting forth, I assure
[you] I have not been altogether idle, tho' much less doggedly
diligent than with His aid I propose to be. Would that I could
take from Sara the toil of preparing the *Biographia*—which
must needs be great and harassing.

I have not forgotten my promise with regard to the
introduction, which I am still ready to supply, only with the
proviso that I am to speak in general of the characteristics of
the intellect of S. T. C. with a more particular examination
of what he has attained and what he might have attained as
a Poet. I do not feel competent to speak of him as Politician,
Philosopher, or Theologian, tho' I shall certainly speak of
him as a Christian-Man.

All whom you know and love in this neighbourhood are, I
believe, in health, but Mr. and Mrs. Wordsworth are afflicted
at the death of a little grandchild, the youngest Son of the
Revd. John, who has died in Italy, where his Mother has long
been with little hope of recovery. The last year has been one
of much mortality among my friends. May the next be
happier and better.

---

[1] This probably refers to the settlement of Hartley's mother's estate, which
consisted mainly of the proceeds from the insurance policy (about £2,500) left
by Coleridge. In the codicil added to his will Coleridge had especially provided
for Hartley, appointing executors to disburse the money for Hartley after Mrs.
Coleridge's death. John Taylor Coleridge (on the death of H. N. Coleridge)
and Joseph Henry Green seem to have administered the estate.

With kind remembrances to Lady Coleridge, and good
wishes of the Season to all your family.

I am, dear Sir,

Your much obliged Poor Relation

HARTLEY COLERIDGE.

LETTER 91

To MRS. HENRY NELSON COLERIDGE.

Nab. April 10th, 1847.

Dear Sara

This is not the *long* letter which I have been so long engaged upon, but it may serve to explain why that epistle is
not forthcoming according to promise.

You have probably been informed that I deliver'd a lecture in the Museum of the Natural History Society of Kendal
on the final Cause of Poetry,[1] which went off pretty well on
the whole, tho' some complained that it was too abstruse,
and the term, final Cause, was objected to by a Scotch
Doctor as pedantic and obsolete. However, I gave such satisfaction to as large an audience as a room pretty well cramm'd
with cases of minerals and stuff'd animals could accommodate, as to be requested to give readings of the English Poets,
with observations interspersed—which came off on the 8th
and 9th ult. I am now engaged to continue those readings
taking Dryden, Pope, and their followers and compeers for
the subjects. (Compeers in fact they have none, and I
believe that their indisputable pre-eminence in their own
ways, for a time exalted them to a higher place among Poets
in general than they actually deserved.) This is fixt for
Monday 12th inst. When over, I will finish and despatch the
pacquet which will respond to all your epistles, for I fear to
say how long. As the funds of the Society are not very ample,
I could not expect to be very largely remunerated. However,
I have received £4. and been at no expense, being kindly
convey'd, in the first instance with Mrs. Claude, in the
2nd in the carriage of Mrs. George Crawdson. A gig will
be sent for me on Monday. I have been always entertain'd,
and kindly entertained, at private houses. My last host is the
son of John Gough, the famous blind naturalist and Mathematician—of whom ὁ μακαρίτης (as I always designate our

---

[1] Among Hartley's remains is a transcript of a lecture entitled 'On the
Objects and Tendencies of Poetry'.

revered father in my adversaria) declared in the *Omniana* [1812] that his face was all eye over, and that he was a Quaker in all their blest negatives without any of their silly and factious positives.[1] His son, however, (an able medical practitioner and a good naturalist) is, I believe, of your Church—certainly not a Quaker, either in negatives or positives.

I inadvertently misinform'd you with respect to Miss M. Arnold's marriage. The ceremony was not perform'd by the Archbishop, tho' the Miss Whateleys were Bridesmaids, but I believe, by the Rev. Mr. Penrose, Mrs. Arnold's Brother. The Arch bishop, abhorred of Derx. and the Dublin University Magazine, has not been in Westmorland at all, tho' the recess of parliament might have given him leisure for a trip had he been so inclined. But what right has a Malthusian like him either to be married himself, or to marry other people? I was not present at, nor invited to the wedding. It was a cruel cold day—The happy couple set off southward after breakfast.

Mrs. Claude, who has been for some time residing at Broadlands, erewhile the school and dwelling house of good Mr. Dawes, whom I miss sadly, is now at Dulwich, with Mrs. Withington, the widow of a deceased friend of mine, who was a Falstaff in dimensions and the most sensible conservative I ever knew. I allude, of course, to political sense merely. Mrs. C.'s youngest daughter Louisa, once a little pet of mine, but now a tall and stately young matron, was married in February to a young Physician on the medical staff of the East India Company. They are now on their voyage to Bengal. Mrs. C. has still two unmarried daughters (her eldest died some years ago). Mary, the eldest surviving is beautiful—still beautiful in face and person, though her bloom has been prematurely paled by pain and pensiveness —in mind she is *beautiful exceedingly*. She translates from the German (you are aware that Mrs. Claude, like her deceased Husband is a native of Berlin) and has rendered several pieces of verse and stories in prose very sweetly, and I believe accurately, without any of that un-English air, which the very un-English construction of German prose, and particularly the cumbrous length and stiff convolution of German sentences (which remind me of petrified snakes) frequently impose not only on translations from the Teuton, but on the original Compositions of folks who read more

---

[1] Cf. Coleridge's brief essay, *The Soul and its Organ of Sense*, in which high tribute is paid to John Gough.

German than English—so different from the pliant intertexture of Greek and Latin. She has also in concert with her sister Jane, published a little book, entitled Verses for a child of six years old, in which she appears to me to have attain'd simplicity without silliness, and to have interfused exactly the kind and degree of religion calculated to nurture true Christianity in a child's heart. I will send it to you, when I can get a copy. The compositions of the two sisters are distinguish'd by their initials. Jane is not to me, quite so interesting or attractive as Mary, but her better health enables her to be more active in good works. She is indefatigable in well doing, not only attending schools, but teaching several children at her own home. It was wonderful what an improvement she made in the little Fells, not only in their learning, but in their manners, which truth to tell, were rather uncouth—yet they are very sweet creatures. Jane has nothing—with all her diligent charity—of the regular philanthropic Miss—a character which you know Papa could not bear. She never interferes with the Parson's business. But I perhaps tire you about people you don't know. You may be more interested to know that Mary has transcribed a number of my poems and sonnets—which D.V. shall not remain much longer in MSS., tho' I am afraid the times are not very favourable for publication. Strickland Cookson promised to call on you, and give you my ballad printed for the relief of the distressed Irish, which has sold very well. Miss Trevennen has sent for ten shillings' worth of them. You will think it no great shakes, but the end must apologize for the means.

I long to see Edith and little Christy, though I'm afraid I should bore the one and spoil the other. To my Nephews, I am not indifferent, but, except as a teacher of the dead languages, I can do nothing for boys as an elder ought to do it. But more of this in the long letter. I hope young Derwent is better. Is he not at Oxford? I see that Baby is called Ernest Hartley,[1] after I suppose, the King of Hanover and his poor ne'er-do-weel uncle—I hope he will take after neither. I am ashamed of myself for not having answered Mary's very kind letter—and am deeply in debt to Derwent, but they will wait a few days.

I am sorry that I cannot give a good account of Dora—but the weather, which in March, was precociously warm,

---

[1] Ernest Hartley Coleridge was born December 8, 1846.

has been awful for the last week. To day is bright, but I believe cold. I have not been out yet—but must be going—if this is to save post. I am you know 2 miles from Ambleside. There is a regular foot post to Grasmere who always brings the letters—and would carry them in the morning—if they were ready—but does not call as he goes, unless directed so to do—an alteration in the arrival of the mails gives time to answer letters same day. But the rail-road, which as yet stops at Birthwaite, some 6 miles from Ambleside, will open shortly—then the mails will be taken off, and a cart substituted. I know not how this will affect time. I hope the papers were right. I did expect—but I am a pretty fellow to be expecting—that I should have heard of their safe arrival. I sent them on the 7th. This is the 10th, and I'm too late for post after all. I enclose a sonnet written for friends only—and hope it will please you. Nurse's letter is too great a curiosity to be either burn'd or return'd.

With kind love to Edith and Herbert
I remain Dear Sara
Your affectionate Brother.

N.B. Tell Mr. Wordsworth there are hardly any Celandines out this year. He should write a sonnet about it. William Green has burn'd a hole in his breeches.

LETTER 92

To THOMAS BLACKBURNE.

[1847.]

Dear Blackburne
Your reproof of my long silence was both witty and just. I have been long intending to write to you; but procrastination borrows of Time at Compound Interest and at last can only compound at about a farthing in the pound. Yet I was not frozen by your threatened Tee totalism (of which I should rather approve), nor am I quite so etherealized as to hang like a dew drop on one horn of the Moon—but—but—in fact, I delayed writing till I was uncertain whether my letter would reach you or not. I am sorry that you are going to leave your present situation. It seems to suit you well. I do not suppose aught I could say would alter your determination, but I cannot help thinking your scruple more scrupulous, or truth to say, more nervous than conscientious. Suppose your Pupil is not very quick at Latin. I was myself

a Dunce at Arithmetic and not a bit better now. But if he be, as you say, of an affectionate heart and a capable intellect, if you cannot teach him Latin, you may teach him something quite as valuable, and he cannot be in the atmosphere and effluvia of a man to whom the Beautiful, the Good, and the True are beloved realities without being the better for it. For it were sad to think that nothing but Fevers were infectious—nothing but the Itch and the ἱερὰ νόσος (vide Herodot.) contagious, if there were no capacity in man to receive good from the contiguity of goodness.

I wish I could see that blessed spot within the wood where there are so many primroses and anemonies. It must be a place for meditative silence, where perhaps you might have had occasion to tell me to 'hold my bother'. I admire both your poems exceedingly. The Sonnet is very fine, but verses on pictures are seldom quite intelligible to those who have not seen the pictures which suggested them. Your sonnet enables me to present a picture to myself—were I capable of Painting I, perhaps, could paint a picture from it. But I dare say the Picture in my mind's eye is very different from the Picture which inspired you. The Rich Man and the Poor is beautiful. Fell has copied it. The Stanza

> Thou will be among the Dead
> Carefully coffined up in Lead
> With Marble blazon over head—
> With me shall worms and weeds be fed
> > Stingily—

is one of the finest I ever saw. The 'stingily' is capital. In regard to the Sonnet, is there any such word as 'sembled' or *can* such a word be legitimately, i.e. analogically coined?—I merely propose this as a question.

Winter has made us a long visit. Dr. Johnson in his Life of Savage [1744] (the best thing he ever wrote) excuses Savage's habit of keeping people up on the plea that he had no Lodging but the Street to go to. I suppose Winter to be in something the same condition, for certainly like Prior's Robber

> 'He often took leave but seemed loth to depart'—

And I'm afraid that even yet he may have left his Great Coat or Umbrella behind—may come again to fetch it. We must contrive to lend him a trifle and then according to the Vicar of Wakefield we shall see no more of him. The Primroses in

Rydal Woods were a month behind time. I was almost afraid that there was a Primrose disease as well as a Potato disease. The Cuckoo cuckooed as dis-satisfactorily as a London Star singing in a Provincial Theatre to Empty benches—and the Swallows were like guests by some perversity of Clocks arrived an hour and a half too soon—while the receiving room curtains and the Young Ladies ringlets were still in paper and the Mistress of the Feast instead of 'urbanity and turbanity' was nothing but 'mobocracy and termagant.' Now we have Spring to the eye, hues and sounds and flowers very pleasant to talk about by the Fireside of an evening; but if any thing could reconcile me to the running of cold iron through the bowels of this beautiful country it would be not the aesthetic advancement of the Manchester Operatives—but—Cheap Coals. Have you read Wordsworth's anti-railroad Sonnets?[1] As Petrarch with all his Sonnets could never prevail on Laura to more than admire him, and I believe no man by Poetry ever won any woman that would not have run away with a Strolling Player, how could the Bard imagine or fancy that 14 lines, though each line were instinct with living fire like an Electric Telegraph, would mollify the philanthropic no-heart of a Railway Company? But of Wordsworth—this is not the way I should have spoken at this time, for it is wrong to make a joke on any good man which he could not laugh at himself; and he is in no mood for laughing now, for his dear and only Daughter is passing away and will be we know not how soon in heaven.[2] You never knew her—perhaps never saw her. I have known her from her infancy. But if you had seen her as I have seen her and seen how a beautiful Soul can make a face not beautiful most beautiful, if you had seen how by the mere strength of affection she entered into the recesses of her Father's Mind and drew him out to gambol with her in the childishness that always hung upon her womanhood, you would feel, as we do, what earth is about to lose and Heaven to gain. May God support her Father and Mother under the loss and to that end join your prayers to mine,

And believe me,

My dear Fellow, Ever Yours

H.C.

---

[1] Cf. 'On the Projected Kendal and Windermere Railway' and 'Proud were ye, Mountains, when, in times of old'.

[2] Dora Wordsworth Quillinan died on July 9, 1847.

LETTER 93

To MRS. HENRY NELSON COLERIDGE, *No. 10 Chester Place, Regent's Park, London.*

Nab. May 18th, 1847.

Dear Sara

Excuse me, I am the last man in the world that ought to be fidgety about not receiving of letters, and I am justly enough punished for my own frequent delinquencies in that line, but I really am uneasy about my last containing the papers about the income Tax. That you have received it, I know from Mrs. Richardson's letter. Perhaps there is some trouble or delay, I did not anticipate—I hope you are not ill. If it is not right, you would have informed me before now.

I have nothing more hopeful to relate of Dora. She is sometimes easy, and sometimes in considerable pain— suffers most at night. She has been at her own request, fully informed of her state, and is not only resign'd but happy. Her parents bear up like Christians, but are quite absorb'd by their sorrow. I have not seen them—(excepting Mr. Wordsworth on the road, as I told you before). I would gladly go, if I could be of any use or comfort, but the Doctor advises me not. They wish to see no one. If they should wish to speak to me, they will probably send for me. Poor William was over from Carlisle a day or two ago, to take leave. John was at Rydal lately and administered the sacrament to his sister, a trying duty which he well supported. From what I gather, I anticipate it will not be long be very long. God's will be done—

　　　With love to Edith, I remain Dear Sister

　　　　　　In hope of a line

　　　　　　　　Your truly affectionate,

　　　　　　　　　　　H.C.

N.B. Mrs. Claude is returned, which is a great comfort to me.

LETTER 94

To MRS. HENRY NELSON COLERIDGE.

[1847.]

Dear Sara

Knowing that I deserved, and fully expected a sound rating for not answering your last about 'the Doctor', it will be some satisfaction, however, to you, that I did answer Mr.

Warter's letter, inquiring whether I had received the book.[1] Of course I thank'd him for the gift, and suggested that you might be waiting for an opportunity to transmit it by private hand. I shall be very glad when it arrives, but *of course* there is no hurry, tho' I have not yet read the last posthumous volume (except Cats Eden which I had seen at Keswick. I hope Edith is fond of Cats) but I can get it when it has gone the round of the Ambleside Book Society. What think you, Sara, of 'The Doctor' as a whole? Unquestionably it is a delightful book to take up and put down—a wonderful Museum of odd fancies, strange facts—Taylor's Gehenna of shreds and remnants—old things and new, cloths of gold, and scarlet, and beggars' velvet (you are aware that the Costumier's secret treasury of cabbage is call'd after the place that rhimes with Christabel) as multifarious as the handful of marble dust and comminuted porphyry of which Poussin said Questa è Roma antica—Material for a hundred workers in mosaic—but I cannot [see] that it is a skilful piece of Mosaic itself. Even Tristram Shandy derives a sort of continuity if not unity from assumption that Tristram is always the speaker, alike in the narrative and dramatic parts, and in the digressions of *course*. I do not put Southey on a level with Sterne, who can hardly be acquitted of dishonest plagiary—(tho' he could hardly expect to steal undetected from so common a book as Burton's Anatomy of Melancholy—and the very humour, and originality of Walter Shandy is to talk out of books) but in managing the mixture of monodram and story polylogue, in passing by chromatic slides and graduated toning from the purely humourous to the humourous pathetic—(not jerking, like Byron, from morbid woe—to mirthless laughter) I cannot help thinking the libertine parson greatly superior to the virtuous layman. Both are sometimes too merely nonsensical for print, but S.'s nonsense is never worse than nonsense, which cannot be truly said of Sterne's. Still, it is doubtful whether any nonsense, any thing 'redolent of joy' or light-heartedness, can consort well with the joy-killing, hope-forbidding, love-torturing dogmata enforced in certain parts of the 'Doctor.' I do not think our Uncle excelled in his delineations of character; at least it seems to me that the elder Daniel is the only approximation to a character in the book, and he is a character of reading and circumstance. William Dove I

---

[1] Hartley probably refers to volume six of Southey's *Doctor*, published by J. W. Warter in 1847. Volume seven appeared in the same year.

think a failure, tho' said to be suggested by a real Innocent. But I am sure you will allow that every poetic personage (taking ποίησις in its widest extent ἀπὸ τοῦ ποιεῖν) should testify its own truth, without reference to an original which few can ever have seen, none can longer see. This it is, that divides true imitative Art from mechanical Imitation. The truest characters, the most vivid landscapes in the world of Art, have probably been evoked by actual flesh and blood, actual land, wood, rock, and water. Wordsworth denies not, but rather glories, that every man, woman, scene, and incident in his poems has had its prototype in reality. He has given, or promised to give, to Miss Fenwick an authentic statement of the facts out of which his imaginations have grown—a precious commentary it will be; tho' not perhaps in all parts fit for publication.[1] The characters of Fielding, Sterne, Smollett, Addison—Parson Adams, Uncle Toby, Strap, Sir Roger, and Will Honeycomb—are known to have been sketched from the life. Sir Walter made no secret that all his good characters were recollections more or less idealized (his inventions are either nobodies, like most part of his Maritandi and nubendae, or monsters like Rashleigh Osbaldistone and Varney). Dickens should never draw without a model. It is the same with the Painters with pencil or brush. Hogarth studied incessantly in the streets, in the taverns, in the cock-pit, and all 'the wide darkness of London'. It is ascertained that there is much individual portrait in the historical (a vile word by the way) pictures of Raffaello, Michel, and Titian.

[No conclusion or signature.]

LETTER 95

To MRS. HENRY NELSON COLERIDGE, *No. 10 Chester Place, Regent's Park, London.*

Mrs. Claude's, Nov. 16, [Postmark 1847] of
course you know the anno Domini.

Dear Sara

After so long a suspension of animation, you will think this a very insufficient proof of restored vitality, but but—the post is fluttering to depart, and till this plague is over I can't write any thing worth reading.

---

[1] Referring to the Fenwick notes, which were first included in the 1857 edition of his poems.

Briefly. Mr. Benson Harrison being absent, I applied to the Rev. F. Fleming, incum—not brance—what is it! of Rydal, who signified the fact of my existence in the flesh, but confessed that he had never given a certificate of the kind before, and was apprehensive of insufficiency or informality. I despatched said paper to Mr. Green, who inform'd me that it was informal and sent the proper printed forms, to be kept for a model for the future. I find that it is necessary I should certify the precise day when the annuity or rather the moiety thereof became due, and also the precise amount of the annuity, even to a shilling—neither of which I can do, without further information, which I must request you to send by the earliest opportunity, for I am ashamed to trouble Mr. Green, and expose my own forgetfulness. When furnish'd with the necessary knowledge I will get a regular certificate from Mr. H. who is now returned to Ambleside, and all will be well, as I am at present. I am writing a long letter, but shall not perhaps finish it this week for I've a heavy job on hand. Therefore, no more at present but love to Edith.

You know all that—but I must tell you that I saw Mr. and Mrs. W. at Chapel on Sunday, pretty well. Dr. Christopher Wordsworth preach'd ! ! ! ! ! ! ! ! Alas too.

[No signature.]

LETTER 96

To EDWARD MOXON.

[January 1, 1848.]

Dear Sir

It is not without some degree of shame and misgiving that I venture to address you, after so long an interruption of our correspondence,—*meâ culpâ, meâ culpâ*—as the Papists say; (*à-propos de bottes*, you are not, I presume the Bibliopole that has joined the Church of Rome,) and after leaving an incomplete work so long on your hands; I am somewhat emboldened, however, by your confidence, in trusting the introduction into my hands for revision.[1] Our excellent friend, Mr. Robinson, shall have no trouble about it. With your leave I will omit some of that irrelevant matter, for which I was soundly castigated by Mr. Howitt's 'honest editor of the Atlas,' and supply the place with stuff more pertinent. I am

---

[1] The second edition of *Massinger and Ford* appeared in 1848 with slight revisions.

not angry with my critics. Rather, I am glad of the experience they have afforded me. I feel like a soldier that has smelt gunpowder, and found that he can stand fire. I will never be snuffed out with an article, I assure you. I know not whether it be worth while to reply to a more insidious attack in an obscure, and, I believe, defunct journal, the 'Metropolitan Conservative,' which, after some sham commendation, and an insinuation that I availed myself, without acknowledgment, of my father's sayings, accused me of using the word 'Catholic' as synonymous with Papist, which I have carefully guarded against, more perhaps in compliance with my father's scruples than with my own. I certainly refuse to all visible churches their claim of Catholicity. 'This jargon,' said my orthodox reviewer, 'might be excused in an alderman of London, but not in a Fellow elect of Oriel,' or something to the same purpose, evidently designing to recall to memory the most painful passage of a life not over happy. But perhaps it is as well to let it alone. The writer might be some one in whom my kindred are interested; for I am as much alone in my revolt as Abdiel in his constancy. Would it suit your purpose to insert a short dissertation on the character of Ford and Massinger, as dramatists? Much of it is ready. Concerning essays and poems, I will write when my performance of the work in hand has secured your confidence. I must and will rouse and exert myself while it is yet day—'for the night cometh.' I am fifty-one, and it's 1848—a snowy, murky, disagreeable New Year's day. Wishing you, and every one else, a better year than the last, I remain

> Yours gratefully,
>
> H. COLERIDGE.

On December 26, 1848, the Wordsworths watchful now as ever, sent word to Derwent that Hartley was dangerously ill. Derwent hastened northward and found his brother ably attended by three local physicians and Hartley's beloved friend, William Fell. A partial recovery occurred, but slowly Hartley's strength ebbed away, and he died on January 6, 1849. Like his father, who said 'he wished to evince in the manner of his death the depth and sincerity of his faith in Christ', Hartley spent his last hours 'in the most searching self-communion', that he might meet death fully prepared, and he twice received the Sacrament.

His death was deplored by every one, from the simple-hearted peasantry to the family at Rydal Mount. Wordsworth himself went with Derwent to select the spot for the grave in the Grasmere churchyard. Marking out a spot next to the place where his daughter Dora had only recently been laid, he said to the sexton: 'When I lifted up my eyes from my daughter's grave, he was standing there! Keep the ground for us—we are old people, and it cannot be for long.'

Before the funeral the Wordsworths called at Nab Cottage; Mrs. Wordsworth kissed Hartley's cold face three times and decked the body with flowers, but Wordsworth was too over-wrought to enter the room.

'It was a winter's day,' Derwent remarks, 'when my brother was carried to his last earthly home, cold, but fine, as I noted at the time, with a few slight scuds of sleet and gleams of sunshine, one of which greeted us as we entered Grasmere, and another smiled brightly through the church window. May it rest upon his memory!'

APPENDIX

A

Letter from DR. L. R. PHELPS *to* E. L. GRIGGS.

24 Norham Road, Oxford, 16 Oct., 1931.

Dear Sir

I have been lately reading, I need not say, with much interest your book on Hartley Coleridge, and I think that you may like to have a few lines on the subject of his connexion with Oriel, a college of which I have been a member since 1872 and of which I was lately Provost. Do not think that I intend in any way to impugn your account of his expulsion, it is very fair and Derwent's criticism that the sentence on H.C. was severe but not unjust is a judicious summing up of the incident. I will only add that my information in the main is at second-hand, derived from the Edward Hawkins who was then a Fellow and afterwards Provost.

It must be allowed at once that to be admitted to the society of the Fellows in the Oriel Common Room was a terrifying experience. Both Arnold and Keble found it uncongenial after the 'give and take' of the undergraduate society at Corpus Christi College. It was so for two reasons.

1. Oriel no doubt demanded a far higher standard of loyalty than other colleges. The Fellows were the picked men of the University and were encouraged by the Provost to set to other colleges a pattern in even the details of life. At a time e.g. when Common Rooms 'reeked' of port wine—the Oriel 'teapot' was a common source of chaff against its members. *Spartam nactus es hanc orna* was, down to my time, made the motto of the Society. For pursuit of knowledge, for devotion to their pupils the Fellows of Oriel had a reputation which they were jealous in preserving.

2. The life of the Common Room and its conversation was of a critical type—insisting on clear definition of terms and logical sequence in argument. I remember a Sermon by one who was a member of it at a later date on the text 'Why callest thou Me good?' in which the preacher remarked how often in our younger days when we had gone rather farther in statement or argument than our knowledge or our premises justified, we were properly taken up by some older man and called upon to prove our point more conclusively or to define more accurately. It was a reminiscence, we felt, of the old Common Room. Such a society is more likely to be a good training-ground for the wits, than a scene of cordial relations!

Now on both these grounds H.C. was chilled and repelled rather than encouraged and stimulated by the atmosphere in which he found himself. It stood in sharp contrast to the 'give and take', the genial discussions, the irresponsible statements, the camaraderie

300

of undergraduate society at Merton, where he, no doubt, 'ruled the roost' intellectually.

On the other hand, the old Provost, Dr. Hawkins, was always careful to say that he much admired H.C.'s ability and good qualities, that he took him in hand and warned him, and did his very best to keep him in the straight path, but in vain. He was a born rebel against convention—and could not help showing it.

The final crisis came, he said, when the then Provost, Dr. Copleston, was one day in the College Lodge, a knock was heard at the door, the Porter opened it, and poor H.C. fell prostrate through it. You will, I am sure, see how difficult it would be to keep in a college a don who set so deplorable an example to the undergraduates.

I doubt very much the reality of H.C.'s suspicions of eaves-dropping etc., as influencing the College.

Suffice it that H.C.'s portrait is in the Common Room to-day. We have forgotten his shortcomings and remember only the brilliance of his gifts and the pathos of his life.

Many thanks for your book.

Yours truly

(Rev. Dr.) L. R. PHELPS.

B

Memorandum by E. COPLESTON, *Provost of Oriel—dated June 15, 1820— recapitulating the charges against Hartley Coleridge and intimating the determination of the Fellows not to admit him at the end of the probationary year, or to extend the period of probation.*

Memorandum { Oriel College,
June 15. 1820.

Mr. Whately the Dean having informed me that he had heard very disagreeable accounts lately of the conduct of Mr. Coleridge, Probationer Fellow, who has been keeping irregular hours, and had frequently come home late in a state of intoxication we agreed to assemble all the resident Fellows on the 30th of May and to confer upon this subject.

In the mean time accurate enquiries were made of the servants of the College and of his lodging-house—from whom it was learnt that the suspicions of the College were but too well founded— that he was often guilty of intemperance and came home in a state in which it was not safe to trust him with a candle.

His year of probation being nearly expired, it thus became a matter of serious consideration whether he ought to be ad-mitted Actual Fellow; and upon a careful review of his whole conduct from the commencement of his probationary year, it was the unanimous opinion of myself and of all the resident Fellows that he was not fit to be received permanently into the Society.

I had had frequent occasions myself to advise and to expostulate with him about his conduct, which was not likely to recommend him to the favour and esteem of the College. I told him early in his probationary year, that he was not to regard himself as finally approved—that he was an entire stranger to us when he was elected—and that the year of probation was the means afforded us of discovering the worth of his character. I exhorted him to court the society of the Fellows and of the other Probationers, and in all respects to conform to the established habits and discipline of the College.

Notwithstanding this, his attendance at Chapel was very irregular, and all accounts agreed in representing him as not associating with the members of the Common Room, as is usual, but as giving his society to others, they knew not whom, and living differently from the rest of the College.

I had also had more than one occasion to reprimand him severely for inattention to the duty of 'Declaiming'. Once in particular the whole College were assembled on the appointed day, when he neither appeared, nor had any excuse to offer for his failure. After seriously reproving him for this offence, and expressing how anxious I was that the Probationers should perform this duty well and set an example to the Undergraduates, I told him he had an opportunity of repairing the fault by taking additional pains about his exercise next week. On the contrary, his declamation in the following week was only half-finished, and only half the usual length. It was moreover so bad that I refused to receive it, and made him appear again on the following Thursday.

For some time I had hoped that these irregularities, and his frequent absence from morning chapel were owing to a little eccentricity of character, unmixed with any immoral habits: but from the investigation lately instituted no doubt remained that intemperance was a principal cause of these delinquencies—that he was fond of society very different from that of his own Common Room, and by no means respectable.

Upon mature consideration of the case we were all of opinion that he was not fit to be admitted an Actual Fellow—and that had we known a tenth part of what his Probationary year had brought to light, he never would have been elected at all. It was thought also the best and kindest way to intimate to him this resolution of the resident Members of the Society, before the long vacation: which was accordingly done by the Dean—and was received by him with a very humble and contrite acknowledgment of its justice—although he supplicated to have his probation extended another year. He was however given to understand that such a measure could not be adopted; and that it was inconsistent with the very notion of *probation*—which was intended not to form and discipline a Junior Fellow, but to enable us to find out his real character.

E. COPLESTON
Provost.

C

Excerpt from letter of JOHN KEBLE, *Fellow of Oriel, to* JOHN TAYLOR COLERIDGE.

June 19, 1820.

The fact is, My dear John, and I grieve to say it on your account as well as on his, that Hartley, as we have just discovered and ascertained upon unquestionable testimony, has been living in habits of such continual irregularity and frequent sottishness, with all the degrading accompaniments of low company, neglect of College duties etc., as to make it quite wrong and unfit for the College to admit him to his actual Fellowship, or to retain him on the foundation any longer. After repeated warnings (for though I have but just known of the matter, it was known it seems to Whately and a few others long ago) he has still gone back again to his old courses, promising amendment continually, with the deepest apparent humility and contrition, but without any practical good effect. In short I am convinced that he is as utterly deficient (I will not say in good principles but) in moral energy and self-control, as he is wanting in conversational tact and good sense, and though it is most painful to have to say it, I am *sure* we should not be doing our duty if we kept him. It would be making a mere mockery of the probationary year. You know most of us too well, my dear Coleridge, to suspect us of coming to such a determination as this upon motives of personal dislike or pique at his oddities, or upon any motives whatever, without great and serious consideration. I can truly say that as far as his manner in conversation goes, his oddities never were of a kind to disgust me, or to make me wish him out of the company. I was only amused by them. When he has been reading in chapel, or declaiming in hall, I have sometimes been annoyed by the thought of his being never likely to prove at all useful to the society in any official character, but never without completely satisfying myself with the thought of which I was verily persuaded, that his abilities (which are certainly very great and his character, which I fancied peculiarly blameless) were more than enough to counterbalance that defect. Do not think, because I write so coolly about this sad affair that I want feeling either for poor Hartley himself or for his Mother and Sister, and other relations to whom I fear this will be a great blow. He knows our purpose himself, and has known it for this week past, and fully acquiesces in the justice of our decision at the same time that he has in different ways attempted to get each of us individually to alter his own opinion. Some parts of his conduct in this kind of negotiation have, I confess to you (but never let it go further), given me occasionally a kind of suspicion of his not being perfectly sincere. At any rate when he is to outward appearance most deeply impressed with a sense of what he has done he has his wits most thoroughly about him to take advantage of any palliation or anything else in the argument which may suggest itself. In short he has a thousand and one ways, indescribable on paper, of diminishing the sorrow one should otherwise feel at so harsh a step being found necessary, and I am almost sure that as to the degradation to a lower rank of society he will not feel that at all, even if it should come upon him. I may just hint to you, I hope, that it is not proposed to leave him at once destitute, but pray let this go no further, as I do not know that I am justified in communicating it at all till the other part of the transaction is finally settled, and this cannot be till the middle of October at our statutable time of admission. How had this better be communicated to Southey? and when? and by whom? It struck me that it might be better for you to tell him as much of this letter as you think proper before he leaves London, as he might gradually prepare Mrs. Coleridge for it and perhaps begin to look out for some safer and better situation for the poor youth. Any service that I can be of to him, short of giving him a good character in the particular respects I have mentioned, would give me real pleasure, and I am determined never to despair of anyone, particularly one bearing the name of Coleridge. But if ever I was certain of any college duty, it is that of declining absolutely to make him full Fellow.

D

Letter from RICHARD WHATELY, *Fellow of Oriel, to* HARTLEY COLERIDGE *relative to non-admittance to Fellowship.*

[June, 1820.]

Dear Coleridge

Your letter, painful as was the subject, gave me some pleasure still interested as I am in your welfare, on account of the frame of mind described in it, whose sincerity I do not question, and whose permanence I earnestly wish for. With regard to the point in question, you seem not clearly to perceive the nature of the case, tho' I have before now endeavoured to explain it to you. There is no *punishment* contemplated, no *sentence*, no *condemnation*: the matter is not *judicial*, but purely *deliberative*: a man petitions to be allowed to place himself under our inspection for a year, that we may judge (not what he is likely to *become*, but) what he actually *was* at the time of election: at the end of that year we are called on to deliberate whether we were justified in that opinion of him with which we originally elected him: and if we decide in the negative, that does not imply that we judge him *incurably* bad, but that we

think he has not shewn himself to be *already* such a man as ought
to be admitted into the society. The probation in short is not
designed to *make* a man what he ought to be, but to shew what he
is. If the Statutes (which is not clear to me) admit of our extending the term in any case, it is plainly in one where *from* a man's
necessary absence, illness, or any other cause our minds are left
in *doubt* (not as to his *future*, but) as to his present character. Now
all that you promise is to become quite a *new man*; I am far from
being without hope that it will be so: but even the fullest confidence of that, in all our minds could only relate to the *future*,
and would not justify us in admitting into the society one whose
past conduct had not proved him worthy of it.

You understand, I believe, that no formal decision of the
College has taken place; but in Octr. we shall be called on to
pronounce our opinion as to the period which has now expired;
and it is hardly to be doubted that the non-residents will be
guided by our observation, which lays us that are resident under
a still heavier responsibility. At that meeting if I thought that a
probationer had shewn himself worthy of admission I should
vote for it: if my mind was in *doubt* as to the character he had displayed, and I felt that *from* any circumstances I had not had
sufficient opportunity of observing him, I should perhaps feel
justified in proposing an extension of the term: but if I felt no such
doubt as to the past, whatever might be my hopes as to the future,
I could not in conscience sanction anything but his rejection. I
have a duty to the College to perform which if my own brother
was the person concerned I trust I should not shrink from. Do not
therefore cherish any hopes of this nature; but endeavour, (as
you profess your intention) to derive moral profit *from* what has
befallen you: remember that your delinquencies are not merely
academical but moral also: and consider that you are still under
a more important probation at the termination of which there
will be no profit in lamenting the past, no room to amend the
future, and no hope of eluding the eye of an 'All-Seeing' Judge.

Believe me, Yours very sincerely
R. WHATELY.

E

Letter from EDWARD HAWKINS, *Fellow of Oriel, to* HARTLEY COLER-
IDGE, *June 11, 1820, informing him that his letter had been read to the
Provost and Fellows, but that there was no probability of an extension of
his probation.*

Oriel College, June 11, 1820.

Dear Sir

I have read, as you desired, your letter to the Dean, and I shall
have unfeigned satisfaction in learning hereafter that your resolutions of amendment take effect.

It is with the greatest pain, however, that I express my conviction of the extreme improbability there is, after the disclosures which have been made to us, that the College should accede to your request of a further term of probation, if indeed such an indulgence were at all consistent with the spirit of our Foundation.

It may be some consolation to you to be assured that all the Fellows will continue to feel the most lively interest in your future welfare.

With every wish for your virtue and happiness.

I am, yours truly,
EDWD. HAWKINS.

F

Letter from JOHN TAYLOR COLERIDGE *to* JAMES GILLMAN—*June 29, 1820—announcing to him and so to* S. T. COLERIDGE—*the decision of the Fellows of Oriel.*

2 Pump Court, June 29, 1820.

Dear Sir

I am not aware whether my Uncle may have received from any other quarter the distressing news which this note will bring; but in case he should not, as it has been in some measure officially communicated to me, I think I can not help informing him of it, and for a great many reasons it seems advisable to do so through you rather than directly to him.

I find that the Provost and Fellows of Oriel have come to a resolution not to admit Hartley to his fellowship on the expiration of his probationary year. I never remember a similar determination being taken, and I am assured that they have come to it with the greatest reluctance and not till after repeated warnings, and repeated promises of amendment made by Hartley and broken. The charges against him are very painful ones to repeat; but for the purposes of admonition and reproof it is fit that my Uncle should be in possession of the whole case—they are 'sottishness, a love of low company, and general inattention to college rules.' Coupled with this I am informed from other sources, that he has contracted an attachment for a young person, the daughter I think of an architect; I hear her well spoken of individually, but any such engagement at his time of life and under the circumstances is to be deplored, and peculiarly so in his case if it is to be considered as connected with the alleged love of company beneath his own station.

Altogether it is a case of a most afflicting nature; what to advise in it I really do not know, or how to render him any effectual service. The college have no desire to make any unnecessary exposure, and if any situation could be procured for him which would give him a pretext of resigning before October, he might still keep his place in the world, and if he might be depended on for a steady amendment, all that he has now lost might be regained. I confess, however, I dread the perverse ingenuity of his mind in self-justification

Will you be good enough in communicating this to my Uncle to say how truly I sympathise with him and Hartley in what they must both suffer in different ways—and that if any mode occurs to me or them in which I can be of service, I shall certainly gladly exert myself.

I am just starting for the Sessions and Circuit, a long campaign, which will keep me out from the 7th July to the end nearly of August—any letter after the 16th July will find me directed 'Western Circuit'. That I have not seen my Uncle for so long has not been my fault—we were absent in Devonshire for March and April, a few days only after my return it pleased God to bereave me of my child, and to visit my wife with a lingering illness—she is only now returning to health and tolerable spirits. We shall not be settled again till October.

Will you remember me very kindly to my Uncle, and Derwent, whom I should have been truly happy to have seen—and with my best compliments to Mrs. Gillman,

believe me,
very truly yours,
J. T. COLERIDGE.

G

Letter from W. JAMES, *Fellow of Oriel, July 15, 1820, to the* REV. SAMUEL MENCE—*Incumbent of Chapel at Highgate intimating that the decision of the Fellows arrived at in June was final and would merely be confirmed in October.*

College Green, Worcester. July 15, [1820.]

My dear Mence,

As I am sure your own kind-heartedness will make you feel anxious on the very unpleasant subject of your letter, and what I have to communicate is of a painful nature, I send an immediate answer that I may not keep you in suspense.

There has *not yet* been any meeting of *all* the Fellows of my College to consider Hartley Coleridge's case—therefore I should not say that any Resolution has yet been formally made by the Society—but when we meet in October, the question will, in the ordinary course of things, come before us, and there cannot be the smallest doubt but that the Resolution expressed in your letter will then be made—though the decision of the College may be considered as already fixed (for there is but one opinion amongst all with whom I have communicated on the subject) it may not be without use to observe the distinction I have made above—for what we have yet done, will not be *publicly known*, which must be the case, if he is formally rejected by the Society: this he may yet avoid, by not offering himself, where he must be sure that he will not be admitted. Repeated instances of intoxication, one at least of which seemed strongly to show a love of drinking (for his companion was till that day a stranger to him, a man of no talent, who had nothing particularly to recommend him except to one who could find it in getting drunk with him)—at other times keeping late hours, which with other circumstances afforded the strongest presumption that he had been drinking, though it was not then so evident—this too, in the year of his probation, and notwithstanding that he had been warned again and again of the consequences of irregularity, marks him as unfit to be admitted into a society established 'ad augendum Clerum'.

At the same time I trust that he is not a sot in the strong sense which you attach to that word. Habits exist in different degrees, are more or less completely formed—and I cannot consider one so young and I will add, so ready to receive advice, as 'irreclaimable' —but he has a great deficiency of that common sense, which would make the advice given really useful to him. Still, he is a young man of talent and there are many situations in which he might distinguish himself—I know, it has been suggested to him to go to Canada—to engage in any literary work there, where talent one might expect would be more rare and therefore more valuable, would perhaps be an employment profitable, and well suited to him—so great a change in the plan of his life, the design of residing abroad for a term of years would give to the world some reason for his apparently resigning his fellowship—which to himself the real loss of it, if it acted as a warning strong enough to break off what otherwise I could not but consider as a growing habit of drunkenness, or at least should be apprehensive it might be so, will eventually turn out for his good.

I wish I could have sent you more acceptable intelligence. It is a subject very painful to reflect on—I never speak of it to any but members of our Society—and I am sure you will not to any but those whom it immediately concerns.

My mother desires her compliments to yourself and Mrs. S. Mence, to which I beg to add my own.

I am, dear Mence,
Yours very truly,
WM. JAMES.

H

Letter of the REV. S. MENCE *to* S. T. COLERIDGE, *enclosing the preceding letter from Wm. James.*

Friday, July 21, 1820.

My dear Sir,

I enclose you James's letter. I wish it were in my power to suggest any thing useful in a case so full of difficulty and embarrassment. In any use you may deem it expedient to make of the letter, I am sure you will recollect that it is a private communication from James to me, and to be shewn as such. I mention this, because should your son decline to follow the advice therein contained, that he should resign his Fellowship previous to the day of re-election, there is room for subsequent misunderstanding upon the subject, and I may possibly find myself charged with what I have certainly no intention to commit, a breach of confidence.

I am always,

My dear Sir, Very truly yours,

SAM MENCE.

I

The following fragments, in the handwriting of SAMUEL TAYLOR COLERIDGE, *are all that have come to light of the letter which Coleridge addressed to the* PROVOST OF ORIEL, *pleading for reconsideration of the refusal to confirm Hartley Coleridge's Fellowship. These fragments were written in early October, before Coleridge went to Oxford on October 15, 1820.*[1]

FRAGMENT I

[Early October, 1820.]

As the more serious articles of the Charge are grounded on *presumptions*; and as appearances and even admitted facts may excite, and be thought to warrant, a strong presumption against an Individual in the minds of those who are ignorant of his particular character, which would make no such impression and lead to no such inferences with those who had known the man intimately and understand his peculiarities; I have thought it right to lay before you what I myself know of Hartley Coleridge's Habits and Disposition, previous to his last Term at Oriel. To this, the sole Object of the present Letter, I propose to confine myself, without adverting—and as much as possible without alluding—to the recent Proceedings or the Provocations assigned for the same. And even here I have limited myself to such points of my Son's character as are equally well known and will be as cordially attested by men of the first respectability in rank, intellect and moral worth, as by myself—among whom I beg leave to name particularly and to *refer* to, Sir George and Lady Beaumont, Mr. Southey, and Mr. Wordsworth, who have all known and have had very frequent—the two latter Gentlemen almost constant—opportunities of observing my Son from his earliest childhood. And as few persons of his rank and age have been placed within

---

[1] Writing to Allsop on October 11, 1820, Coleridge says: 'It is my purpose, God willing! to leave this place on Friday, so as to take an afternoon coach, if any such there be, or the Oxford mail, . . . —and so to be in Oxford by Saturday morning, while my letter, which is unfortunately a very long one (and I could not make it otherwise), will reach Dr. Copplestone, if arrived, on Friday morning; thus giving him a day's preparation for the personal interview.'

a circle of equal eminence, so (let me be permitted to observe) scarcely any one perhaps been more esteemed and beloved, than He with all his defects and eccentricities has been even from his infancy—had been, at least, till his admission at Oriel.

[Breaks off thus.]

FRAGMENT 2

Honoured Sir

Heavily afflicted as I am, and stunned scarcely less by the suddenness of the Blow than by its weight, still if the purpose of this letter had been, in any degree or under any disguise, that of interference, whether to avert or to qualify your determination respecting my Son; or if its expressions could be interpreted as complaint or remonstrance; it might perhaps have been *written* in the first turbulence of grief, could I have been unwise enough to write at all at such a moment—but (I dare promise myself) it would have exposed my weakness to no eye but my own. The well-grounded Respect, which I formed and had publickly avowed from the proofs of your Powers and Principles, before I could have anticipated that I or any of mine would stand in any relation to you, as the Provost of Oriel, which nothing since then has or can have diminished, tho' I should have reason to blush for my own nature if the *feeling* had not been at least enlivened by your friendly kindness to my eldest, and your condescending and courteous [advice] to both my Sons, is of itself sufficient to secure you from any such impertinence. Dr. Copleston will not condemn me of Arrogance, if I add that I have myself claims to respect (from my *efforts* at least and the Ends and Objects to which they have been directed) which I would not forfeit by consciously obtruding on any man the language of mendicance or irritability. I can indeed find nothing that leaves room for the one or could furnish a pretext for the other in any part either of your conduct, Sir! singly and personally, or in the resolution formed by the Provost and resident Fellows of Oriel collectively and functionally. But if against the writer's will and purpose any words should escape, *susceptible* of a different interpretation, it will, I trust, be precluded by this distinct avowal. But I am not in any serious degree apprehensive, that I shall give you offence. Would, there were no greater likelihood of my wearying out your patience. In this point only I must be the Beggar, and in intreating your *patient* perusal of this letter—tho' I shall endeavor to express myself as concisely as possible—I feel that I am asking not a little; yet when I assure you that the Hope of its favorable reception acts as a relief to the wounded spirit of a Father, I dare promise myself that I shall not have asked in vain. O Sir! it was an unwise and as we say in Devonshire, a *cruel* kindness on the part of my friends, that kept the true state of things concealed from my knowledge, to burst upon me at once and irrevocably.[1] How often since I first read the anecdote (Southey's Life of Wesley, I. p. 39) Gravia passus sum; but whatever I am, my Hartley is Fellow of Oriel! It had so long been the prayer of my Heart to see my Sons in that profession, for which I was myself best fitted both by my studies and my inclinations, but from which I had been deterred in my 23rd year by insidious appeals to my unenlightened Conscience. I had so much reason to trust, that whatever doubts or difficulties might start for either in the course of their theological studies, he would have one man, and that man a Father, 'who with similar powers and feelings no less acute had entertained the same scruples; had acted upon them; and who by after research, and in less than two years had discovered himself to have quarrelled with received opinions only to embrace errors, to have left the direction tracked out for him on the high road of honorable distinction only to deviate into a labyrinth, where when he had wandered, till his head was giddy, his best good fortune was finally to have found his way out again, too late for prudence though not too late for conscience or for truth!' Biogr. Liter. I, 232. But I am transgressing on your time, and taking a liberty for which I can plead no adequate motive.

[Breaks off thus.]

FRAGMENT 3

. . . But as soon as this was used to give a colour to a darker charge, Hartley did not hesitate a moment; but gave up wine and every other liquor beyond table beer, as an ordinary practice, and even on what we call our company-days, days of rare occurrence, has strictly confined himself to one glass—during dinner, and a second after dinner, and this too at my recommendation, as I thought it at once bespoke more indifference to the pleasures of the table, and exercised more self-command than an entire rejection at all times, and was less calculated to attract notice. In this scheme he has not only persevere[d]; but in my inmost conscience I am convinced, that it never cost him a single effort. Let this fact be taken in combination with his Complexion, the condition of his digestive organs, his disposition to move after meals, etc.; and I dare appeal to any medical man, whether it does not afford more than a presumption against the cruel charge that he had formed a *habit* of intemperance.

[Breaks off thus.]

FRAGMENT 4

The more serious articles of the charge being grounded on Presumptions and Inferences; admitted that facts may excite

---

[1] The following sentence Coleridge inserted and later crossed out in MS.: 'like a Squall from a Fog-bank in which the secure Mariner had been fancying images of Shores and Coast land, all calm and with not a sail in reef.'

and appear to warrant a strong presumption against a man in the judgement of those who are ignorant or but imperfectly informed of his particular character, which would make no such impression on those, who know the man intimately, and understand his peculiarities—would lead to no such inference but on the contrary admit of a satisfactory solution by causes indifferent or venial and sometimes even creditable to the man's feelings;—you will not, I trust, regard it as an impertinent or useless interference, if I lay before you what I myself know of Hartley Coleridge's Habits and Dispositions, (I might say, of his Nature) previously to his last term at Oriel. This is the sole object of this letter, and to this I shall confine myself, without adverting and as much [as] possible without alluding to, the recent proceedings or the causes assigned for them. And even I shall limit my statement to those points of my Son's character, which are equally as well known and will be as cordially attested, by men of the first respectability in rank, intellect and moral worth, as by myself. Among many well meriting this description I beg leave to name and to refer you to, Sir George and Lady Beaumont, Mr. Southey, and Mr. Wordsworth, who have all known my Son from earliest childhood, and the two latter from his Birth.

The first point, which I must mention as it is the basis of all the rest, is the one that I have least hopes of communicating adequately and intelligibly—I mean the infrequent recurrence, amounting almost to the habitual absence, of the idea of Self in his Thoughts. I am not speaking of any virtue opposed to Selfishness; but of Self as contra-distinguished from *another*.—A gentleman of high philosophical celebrity

[Breaks off thus.]

FRAGMENT 5

There has not been the least intercourse with respect to this subject between myself, and either Sir G. B., Mr. Southey, Mr. Wordsworth, or Mr. Poole, but I could pledge my life, that each would at the first hearing of Hartley's artful ingenuity in putting the best construction on his errors, express with a livelier confidence their disbelief of the charge. From his earliest childhood he had an absence of any contra-distinguishing Self, any conscious 'I', that struck every one, the most unobserving, and which I never saw in the same *degree* in any other instance: and I have heard the same remark, and in far stronger terms, repeatedly from Mr. Southey, Mr. Wordsworth, Sir George and Lady Beaumont. It was either Mr. Rogers or Sir W. Scott (I am not certain which) who made the observation, that there was in this case no semblance produced by accident of language, or the more than usually prolonged habit of speaking in the third person, of himself and others indifferently, but a seemingly constitutional insensibility to the immediate impressions on the senses, and the necessity of having them generalized into *thoughts*, before they had an interest, or even a distinct place, in his consciousness. The remark was strictly just, and so much so, that this peculiarity not seldom made him appear deficient in affection and almost unimpressible, and never can I read De la Motte Fouqué's beautiful Faery Tale, founded on a tradition recorded in Luther's Table-Talk, of Undina, the Water Fay, before she had a Soul, beloved by all whether they would or no, and as indifferent to all, herself included, as a blossom whirling in a May-gale, without having Hartley recalled to me, as he appeared from infancy to his boyhood—never without reflecting on the prophecy, written by me long before I had either thought or prospect of settling in Canterbury, [sic] addressed to him then but a few months old in my Poem Entitled, Frost at Midnight,

> 'Dear Babe! that slumber'st cradled by my side,
> Whose gentle Breathings heard in this deep Calm
> Fill up the interspersèd vacancies
> And momentary intervals of Thought.
> My Babe so beautiful! it thrills my Heart
> With tender gladness thus to gaze on thee,
> And think, that thou shalt learn far other lore
> And in far other scenes. For I was rear'd
> In the great city pent and Cloisters dim
> And saw nought lovely but the Sky and Stars,
> But thou, my Babe, *shalt wander like a Breeze*
> By Lakes and sandy Shores, beneath the Crags
> Of ancient Mountains, and beneath the Clouds
> That image in their bulk both Lakes, and Shores,
> And Mountain Crags.'

To what degree this was fulfilled, is pourtrayed not less faithfully as fact than exquisitely as verse in Mr. Wordsworth's Lines, addressed to Hartley Coleridge, six years old and I did not wonder to hear, that Robert Southey burst into audible weeping when a few days after the first unexamined Tidings from Oriel his eye had happened to glance on the ¶ of that Poem beginning—

> I thought of Times when Pain might be thy guest,
> Lord of thy House of Hospitality!
> And Grief, uneasy Lover, never rest
> Save when she sate within the touch of thee.

To these men—and men of austerer morals and more enlightened minds where am I to find? I appeal—whether the charge of 'perverse ingenuity', '*artful* palliations' and the like had not the effect of inspiring hope that the whole Charge would be found exaggerated, from the utter contrariety of these portions to the whole nature and habits of the accused?—Except the *very* few who from experience of their own feelings, and thus by a sort of recognition not only understand but can attest the existence of the same in another, and I will venture to say, that they only who have long and intimately known my Son can conceive, to what a degree all *comparison* is absent from his mind in the Judgement which he passes on his own actions! how entirely he occupies the same relative Position, as that in which men like Herbert, Bish. Hall, Archbishop Leighton, present themselves in their confessions and words of humiliation. They were, confessedly, Men of clear and comprehensive intellects, Men intimately and extensively acquainted with the moral condition of the majority of mankind. For in the earlier periods of the Reformation the practice of *confession* was brought back indeed to its pure and primitive state but in this state enforced rather than discouraged by the wisest and most pious Protestant Divines: and this was, I doubt not, the cause of their intensive influence on the hearts of their contemporaries. If their superlatives are to be interpreted, not as intended to express the relation, in which they felt themselves standing in relation to the Alone Good, and to the absolute Command, Be perfect, even as your Father in Heaven is perfect! but as the result from a comparison of their own aims and actions with the average of men, who could acquit them of insincerity? of a Pharisaism that strives to unite the honors of humility and the gratification of Self-worship by chaunting its own praises in a palpable irony, in which every word was sure to be rendered by one of the contrary meaning?—an hypocrisy of no very rare occurrence if I may dare judge from scenes to which I have myself been present, in the dialogues of complimentary Contradictions between those Professors, whom Lord Bacon excellently pre-designated as Schismatics in *manners*, more effective in disunion than even the Dissentients in Doctrines or Ceremonies. But who will accuse, who will dare suspect, the men above named and their Compeers, of so loathsome a Trick, of so pitiful a self-delusion? Do I mean to identify my Son with these venerable men?—You will not suspect me of the absurdity. But I do affirm, that the same measuring of act and deed by the abstract rule of Right, without adverting to the frequency of still wider deviations in others of the same age, and under like circumstances, and without seeking a palliative from the fact of *comparative* Innocence —as was the result of religious Discipline, and profound meditation in *them*, is in him *nature*; for by what other word can I express a quality or character prominent from earliest childhood? the germ of which disclosed itself even in earliest Infancy. When he was not a year old, my Friend and at that time my Neighbor, Mr. Poole of Stowey now a justly distinguished Magistrate in the county of Somerset, used to remark, as a curious fact—that the little fellow never shewed any excitement at the *thing*, whatever it was, but afterwards, often when it had been removed, smiled or capered on the arm as at the *thought* of it. There is another and perhaps more justifying reason for calling this peculiarity his *Nature*, for like all other natural qualities or tendencies, not the result of Reason, Religion, or moral Habits, it has been 'a two-streaming Fount, Whence Good and Ill have flowed, Honey and Gall!'

And to this I intreat your attention with peculiar anxiety—A habit of being absent to the present, often indeed from the reverse extreme, and still oftener from eagerness of reasoning, and exclusive attention to mental acts or impressions, but not seldom from a mere absorption of the active powers, a seeming entire suspension of all distinct Consciousness. For it is of the last importance to the just appreciation both of what he is and has been, and of what he is likely to become, that it should be known that this habit so far from having been gradually contracted at School or at the university, and so far from growing on him, was strongest and most glaring from two years old to seven or eight, and for the last four years, my Son has been with me twice yearly, from three weeks to two months each time, and for the last three years I have been each visit congratulated by the sincere and enlightened friends whose hospitable roof and regard he shared with me, and at the last time but one, when he accompanied his Brother Derwent, was most warmly congratulated by all his and my friends in this neighborhood on his manifest improvement in this point. The worthy Clergyman of this place, late Fellow and Tutor of Trinity, Oxford, expressed his satisfaction in words to this purpose and to the best of my recollection in these very words:—'Hartley will never be the Man of the world, nor have the polish and conciliatory manners, which Experience and good Company will ensure to his Brother, Derwent; but he has won so much mastery over himself since I first knew him, is so evidently trying and learning to accomodate himself to the customs and regulations of society, that tho' he will not be more loved by those who love him, he will however give no just cause of Dislike to those who do not.' Let your heart plead in excuse for me, if I add his concluding words, that have since haunted my ear like a death-watch, in my own despite. 'But just or unjust, with such Talents, and such unsuspecting and unregarding openness, requiring more than negative manners to counterbalance, Enemies he will be sure to have; and it made me sigh when I heard him express his belief that he had not an Enemy in the world.' Indeed I cannot in truth and common justice press this point too strongly. When a little child, as soon as he [was] made to sit and had begun to take his food, he used to sink at once from a state of whirling activity into—it is painful to me even to recollect him—for he looked like a little statue of Ideotcy—and even up to the present year no one can have been intimate with him without having occasionally seen him, sometimes in abstraction, but of late more frequently in eagerness of conversation, eating fruit, or bread, or whatever else was before, utterly unconscious of what he was doing, or repeatedly filling his glass from the Water-bottle (for his friends were so well aware of this, that they either recalled his attention to what he was doing, or putting the Water by him silently, counted the times, in order to impress him afterwards with the unbecomingness and even danger, of these fits of

[Breaks off thus.]

J

Letter from DR. COPLESTON, *addressed to* S. T. COLERIDGE, *Cross Inn, Cornmarket, Oxford, enclosing a memorandum of the charges against Hartley and the action of the Oriel authorities.*

Oriel College, Oct. 15, 1820.

Sir

After the conversation of this morning it is almost needless for me to state how much I respect the feelings which you expressed during our interview and how anxious I am to lighten the load of this affliction which presses upon your mind, as far as I can consistently with the plain duties of my station. The enclosed *Memorandum* [cf. B] which I made for my private use (and in case of my inability to attend the College Meeting at Michaelmas for the use of the College) explains so particularly the grounds of our proceeding, that it is not necessary to enter upon the painful task of describing your Son's case. But as it seems that exaggerated and even false reports have been spread of the nature of his offences, I declare most solemnly that I never heard the charge of licentious conduct with women laid against him, nor the slightest suspicion of that kind expressed.

I also say that although frequent intemperance during his probationary year was alledged, and the College were satisfied of the truth of the charge, yet it never occurred to my mind, nor do I believe that any of the Fellows entertained the opinion that he was addicted to solitary drinking, which as you justly observe, is commonly included under the imputation of 'sottishness.'

I will not lose this opportunity of declaring that in my opinion he possesses very amiable qualities, and that his abilities and attainments promise fair to place him in most respectable and useful stations, provided his conduct in future should be correct, and his choice of companions prudent. He will always have my best wishes, and my endeavours to serve him, wherever it can be done without a compromise of duty.

I remain Sir with great respect
Your Most Obedt. Servant
E. COPLESTON

P.S. Mr. Whately being absent I do not send a copy of his *Memorandum* which I read to you to-day, but I beg leave to remind you that he states that besides advising your Son frequently how to conduct himself so as to gain the approbation of the College, he repeatedly explained to him the precarious holding he had, and set before him the danger of ultimate rejection.

K

Letter from DR. COPLESTON *to* S. T. COLERIDGE, *requesting an interview in London.*

[Postmark, Oct. 19, 1820.]

Dr. Copleston presents his compliments to Mr. Coleridge, and as he is passing two days in London, would with great pleasure meet him any where in town for the purpose of a few minutes conversation on the subject which he hinted to Mr. Coleridge at Oxford, namely some allowance from the College on his Son's leaving the University.

If Mr. Coleridge will mention any time and place on Friday Dr. C. will take care, if it is in his power, to meet him. A note directed to him at Murray's, Albemarle St. will be safely delivered.

Hatchet's Hotel—Wednesday evening.

L

This fragment, addressed to the WARDEN OF MERTON COLLEGE, *is in* HARTLEY's *handwriting, but with interlineations in the hand of* SAMUEL TAYLOR COLERIDGE, *who wished Hartley to write a defence of himself.*

[December, 1820.]

Reverend Sir.

The recent determination of the Provost and resident Fellows of Oriel, and the grounds assigned for the same by several Individuals of that body, have made it my duty to lay before you, a plain and to the best of my recollection a full and accurate—but at all events a strictly *conscientious*—statement of my conduct, from the time that I removed from under your protection and superintendence in consequence of my Election as Probationer of Oriel. As to my demeanour previously and during my terms at Merton, I trust that your Testimonials, are a sufficient proof, that it was not sullied by any such glaring or frequent aberrations from duty as to distinguish it to my disadvantage, from that of other Undergraduates, or of young men in general under the same or similar circumstances. I feel assured, that you, who were the proper judge, will answer for me, that my errors and defaults were not such as to exclude me from the regard and good hopes, of those who best knew me, whether the superiors of my College, or my equals. At all events, this point must be supposed to have been enquired into by my Electors, previous to my election, as one indispensable condition of my eligibility. For if the Probationer is to be subjected to an inquisition into his conduct, not merely from the time when his electors became his lawful censors, but extending indefinitely backward, (perhaps even to his schoolboy-days, comprizing all those years and circumstances, in which faults and errors, that imply no baseness, or defect or perversion of moral principle, are usually considered as having their sufficient and appropriate punishment provided by the discipline, the rules of which they transgress)—what man, with the slightest self-respect would, from any, the strongest prospect of contingent advantage expose himself to such a Risk? What degrees of comparative good behaviour could ensure the result of such a trial, if it were to be conducted by secret evidence, the items of which were concealed, and the Defendant (the term is not inappropriate) neither confronted with his accusers, or even questioned as to the truth of their allegations? Who, from any pecuniary motive would thus put it in the power of mistake or misrepresentation to deprive him at once of subsistence, of reputation, of the profession for which he had been educated, and of the esteem of those friends, upon whom he is again render'd dependent?

You will not condemn these remarks as vague or irrelevant, if you find that they are no mere comment or general reasoning on my case, but a necessary part of its statement. On no hypothesis indeed, on no possible extension of the inquiry, could many of the charges against me be substantiated—but it is not impossible that a pretext or likelihood for some of them might be derived from the earlier period of my academical life, which might serve to screen my accusers from the imputation of direct and willful falsehood, tho' not of gross exaggeration and strange misstatement. You will remember that I consider the Provost and Fellows not as my accusers, but as my judges, acting upon the reports of my accusers. Far be it from me, to suspect any *Gentleman*, not to say Clergyman, of forging the Calumnies I complain of.

You will understand therefore, that now I have to speak solely of the period intervening from my Election as Probationer of Oriel, to the time when the unalterable determination of the Provost and Resident Fellows was announced to me, with the advice to resign my Fellowship in order to prevent an *exposure*.

Tho' at the time of my Election, I was perfectly ignorant what, beyond general correctness and decorum, was required of me as Probationer, yet, I must gratefully allow, that care was taken to put me fully in possession of all points of my duty, and to make me acquainted with the conditional nature, of Probation. Not only in general terms, but by distinct, specific, advice, and warnings, I was apprized of what the College expected: that is to say: an exemplary attention to discipline, constant attendance at Chapel, especially in the morning, conformity in dress, manners, and mode of living to the habits of those with whom I was associated by my Election, and a regular and diligent performance of certain exercises: irreprehensible morals were, of course, taken for granted. I was also given to understand that a Fellow-elect was to consider the members of his Common-room, not in the light of strangers, to whom he had been just introduced, but as elder brothers, and friends, with whom he was to live, and by all means, to make himself, known and agreeable. That after receiving this warning, first, in the friendliest manner possible from Mr. Whately, and afterwards from the authority of the Provost, I did not follow it as was doubtless expected; nor make Oriel my home, but still continued in the same society, I had kept during my latter years at Merton, and with much the same habits, I freely confess—but I deny that either that society, or those habits, were in themselves criminal, or objectionable in any degree—if somewhat later hours than were advisable be excepted—a thing too common among studious men, who are apt to carry into company a habit acquired in solitude. My principal associates were Battiscombe, Wilson, Chester, Sandby, Neach, and Monro—all men, I can safely say, of excellent principles and literary pursuits, several of whom had behaved towards me with such kindness, while I was Academically their equal, that it would have been base ingratitude to have deserted them when I was advanced. You, Sir, know, or can easily ascertain, that these are not men whose acquaintance could disgrace anyone.

During the first term after my admission as Probationer, I was indeed so constantly engaged with my Pupil St. Aubyn, as to have little time for other society. Indeed here I may mention, that almost all the dealings, I had with any persons out of Oriel, Merton and Exeter (in which latter Colleges most of my Undergraduate acquaintance were comprized) began in literary assistance: which I was perhaps too ready to afford, when and wherever it was required. This brought me occasionally in contact with men, whom perhaps I should not otherwise have known, and of whom I knew little, except their need of a Tutor, who could content himself with saving them from absolute failure. But even among these I could not mention one, whose intimacy, in any degree, in which I partook of it, could be considered either as disreputable or dangerous. Still I admit, that my choice of Undergraduate society, bore in some degree the mark of preference, and that tho', my associates were all gentlemen and men of principle (at least to the best of my knowledge) yet few of them bore any *academic* rank, or were known to the Fellows of Oriel. I must also allow, that at first my attendance at Chapel was very irregular, and that my amendment after more than one admonition, was but partial—that in respect to Declamations, I was in one instance a great defaulter. For having procrastinated the composition till I was unable to complete it in time, I dared not face the College with a fair confession of the fact, but absented myself, to the considerable inconvenience and disorder of the assembled fellows; and this offence being overlook'd, on condition, of a better performance, my production was not such, either as to quantity or quality, as to give satisfaction.

I cannot deny moreover that in two or three instances, I drank somewhat too freely, so as to be visibly disorder'd on my return home—but not so as to produce any deprivation, either mental or bodily, of the power of directing my own words, and actions: two of these instances occur'd at passing parties of my own Pupils; the other, which has been much dwelt upon, arose from my thinking (perhaps erroneously) that I was bound in civility not absolutely to refuse a stranger, who had just taken his Master's degree. As I was not previously acquainted with this man, who, it seems, had not acquired the favour of his superiors while an Undergraduate, my remaining with him, and drinking more certainly than was prudent, has been adduced to prove a love of liquor, and predilection for improper Society. I can only reply, and that with heartfelt confidence, that it was nothing but a fear of seeming inhospitable that prevented me from declining the introduction of more wine after the other fellows had left the Common-room, and that whatever I drank myself—was solely from compliance with what I conceived to be politeness; in fact, my offence was, the not having fortitude enough even tacitly to reprove another. As to my inviting him to dine with me next day, it arose from a mere compliment on my part, which he understood so, as to lay me almost under a necessity of paying him that attention. Of his character I knew nothing—this doubtless made my behaviour towards him imprudent, but I leave you to judge how far the above-mentioned inference from it was fair or candid. In no instance did I continue drinking after I felt myself sensibly affected, nor did any of the cases I have spoken of occur till after I had that conversation with Mr. Whately, in which I denied intemperance to have been the cause of late hours, or College irregularities.

[Letter breaks off thus.]

M

This fragment of a letter in SAMUEL TAYLOR COLERIDGE's *handwriting, addressed to the* WARDEN OF MERTON COLLEGE, *was apparently drafted by Coleridge for Hartley's use in formulating the preceding letter.*

[December, 1820.]

. . . to put you in possession as fully as it is in my power to do, of the relation in which I stand at present to my Electors, and in the first place of all the facts connected with my own conduct that I am myself aware of, and can suppose in any degree calculated to influence their recent determination. These facts I shall communicate without attempting to define the degree of culpability which may be fairly attached to me in consequence, nakedly and with one single exception, without any comparative comment. To extenuate my Conscience forbids, and I have been taught by a sore experience henceforward not to take on myself the business of condemnation, unless I wish to be a wilful accomplice in the misconceptions to which, writing under the fear of appearing to extenuate, I might too probably furnish occasion by my own words.—I will then state in the same way the Charges, that have been *formally* alledged against me as the grounds of the hitherto unprecedented determination not to confirm my election —then those which, tho' not alledged or avowed by the Provost and Fellows of Oriel collectively, have yet been communicated to my Friends or Relations by the Provost or some one of the Fellows individually—and having solemnly and deliberately assured you of the falsehood (or gross exaggeration fully tantamount in its effects to falsehood) of all and each of these charges, except as far as they have been anticipated in my own statement, I will truly describe the nature and amount of the injury or at least detriment inflicted on me, not only or chiefly by the determination itself, or as the loss of the Fellowship is alone considered; but likewise and in a far higher degree, by the measures necessarily consequent on the determination, by the charges on which it is professedly grounded; and by the yet heavier private representations by which its justification has been attended—and then with perfect resignation submit it to your judgement, what proportion there has been between the demerit and the punishment, and what equity in depriving me at once of my fellow-ship and my good name on secret evidence which they refuse to name, and will not allow me to confront. But there is one point on which I cannot too soon enter a *disclaimer*, by a distinct declaration, that I do not put my veracity against the veracity of the Provost and resident Fellows of Oriel; but my disavowals against the assertions of their *Informers*, whose evidence I solemnly assert to be false.

As to my conduct during my Terms at Merton, I trust that your Testimonials are a sufficient proof, that it was not sullied by any such glaring or frequent aberrations from Duty as to distinguish it to my disadvantage from the average conduct of Undergraduates. Compared with the men in general of the same age and under the same or similar Circumstances, I hope and dare assure myself that my errors and defaults were not such as to deprive me of the regard or exclude me from the good hopes of those who had the best means of knowing me, both among the superiors of my

College and my equals. At all events, this point must be supposed to have been inquired into by my Electors, as one necessary condition of my eligibility, previous to my Election. Otherwise instead of a benefit it would rather be an injury, inasmuch as the advantages derivable from the *confirmation* of the Fellowship would not bear a comparison even with the risk of such Evils as must needs follow a rejection. Who indeed with any sense of self-respect would from a pecuniary motive expose himself to a secret inquisition of all his past conduct in all its minutiae to an indefinite period backward—perhaps even to his School-boy Days, but certainly comprizing all those years and circumstances, in which Faults and Errors, that imply no baseness, or deliberate perversion of principle, are usually considered as having their sufficient and appropriate punishment provided for them by the Discipline, the rules of which had been transgressed. We know, that among his sharpest grievances Job complained of those, who brought against him the follies of his Youth. But how much stronger would the objection be, if this inquisition was carried on by means of secret information? If the names of the informers were withheld from the accused, his intreaties to be confronted with them repelled, his pledges to prove the contrary as far as *a negative* can be proved set at nought, and his solemn assertions of *their* falsehood, tho' presumptively Servants and Dependents of his Inquisitors, and where assertions were the only things in his power, to be treated as falsehoods of his own? And if the *consequences* were, that he must begin life with a public Brand on his character, and by their denial of the usual credentials rendered necessary in order to preserve the consistency of his rejectors, not merely deprived of his immediate resources but precluded from the profession for which he had been educated?—May I not confidently appeal to you, honored Sir! whether the strongest probability of a Fellowship could be put by any honorable mind in competition with the chance of such evils; especially when he knows, that an unfavourable result would tend to compromise the names even of the revered Friends, to whose attestations in his favor he was indebted in part for his election in the first instance. You will not condemn these remarks as impertinent, if you find that they are no *comment*, no mere General Reasoning on my Case; but a necessary part of its statement. On no hypothesis indeed, and to whatever period of my past life I suppose the inquisition to have extended, can I conceive how some of the Charges alledged against me could be substantiated; but on this only can I imagine even a *pretext* for such accusations, or am able to acquit the unknown Informants of wilful Falsehood, tho' I cannot acquit them of gross exaggeration and the strangest misstatements—

Be this, however, as it may, my statement as far as it refers to my own conduct and actions, must be confined within the interval from my election as probationer of Oriel to the time when the unalterable determination of the Provost and Resident Fellows to exclude me from the Fellowship was formally communicated to me with the advice to resign before hand of my own accord, as the only means of preventing an *exposure*: that is, as I cannot but understand it, of going into life under *false colors*. At that time indeed and for some weeks afterward, I neither comprehended the extent of the charge, nor even conjectured the nature of the most serious articles; but now that I have the whole before me, I can confidently appeal to any honest and conscientious man, whether on the assumption of such charges having been satisfactorily proved, the *exposure* of the truth or at least the abstaining from all participation in any attempt to conceal it, would not have been their duty. With these impressions, and under such heavy afflictions, which grievous as they are on my own account are tenfold more so on account of my Father, and Mother, and the kind Friends who have assisted them in procuring for me the advantages of a learned and Academic Education, I earnestly intreat your perusal of the accompanying documents, corresponding to the purposes expressed in the beginning of this letter; and to which at my Father's instance I have added an extract from a letter addressed by him to Dr. Copleston previous to his first interview with the Provost. And permit me to assure you, which I do with heart-felt sincerity that it will be no slight alleviation of my misfortunes to know, that my errors have not been of such a nature as to deprive me wholly of that portion of esteem and regard, with which, reverend Sir, you had heretofore honored

Your obliged and grateful
Humble Servant,
HARTLEY COLERIDGE.

INDEX